Lecture Notes in Artificial Intelligence   1904

Subseries of Lecture Notes in Computer Science
Edited by J. G. Carbonell and J. Siekmann

Lecture Notes in Computer Science

Edited by G. Goos, J. Hartmanis and J. van Leeuwen

Springer
Berlin
Heidelberg
New York
Barcelona
Hong Kong
London
Milan
Paris
Singapore
Tokyo

Stefano A. Cerri   Danail Dochev (Eds.)

Artificial Intelligence: Methodology, Systems, and Applications

9th International Conference, AIMSA 2000
Varna, Bulgaria, September 20-23, 2000
Proceedings

Springer

Series Editors

Jaime G. Carbonell, Carnegie Mellon University, Pittsburgh, PA, USA
Jörg Siekmann, University of Saarland, Saarbrücken, Germany

Volume Editor

Stefano A. Cerri
Université de Montpellier II, Sciences et Techniques du Languedoc, LIRMM
161 Rue Ada, 34392 Montpellier Cedex 5, France
E-mail: cerri@lirmm.fr

Danail Dochev
Bulgarian Academy of Sciences, Institute of Information Technologies
Artificial Intelligence Department
Acad Bonchev Str., Building 29A, Sofia 1113, Bulgaria
E-mail: dochev@iinf.bas.bg

Cataloging-in-Publication Data applied for

Die Deutsche Bibliothek - CIP-Einheitsaufnahme

Artificial intelligence : methodology, systems, and applications ; 9th
international conference ; proceedings / AIMSA 2000, Varna, Bulgaria,
September 20 - 23, 2000 / Stefano A. Cerri ; Danail Dochev (ed.). -
Berlin ; Heidelberg ; New York ; Barcelona ; Hong Kong ; London ;
Milan ; Paris ; Singapore ; Tokyo : Springer, 2000
  (Lecture notes in computer science ; Vol. 1904 : Lecture notes in
  artificial intelligence) ISBN 3-540-41044-9

CR Subject Classification (1998): I.2, F.2.1

ISBN 3-540-41044-9 Springer-Verlag Berlin Heidelberg New York

Springer-Verlag Berlin Heidelberg New York
a member of BertelsmannSpringer Science+Business Media GmbH
© Springer-Verlag Berlin Heidelberg 2000
Printed in Germany

Typesetting: Camera-ready by author, data conversion by DA-TeX Gerd Blumenstein
Printed on acid-free paper   SPIN: 10722654   06/3142   5 4 3 2 1 0

Preface

Since 1984, the Artificial Intelligence: Methodology, Systems, and Applications (AIMSA) conference series has provided a biennial forum for the presentation of artificial intelligence research and development. The conference covers the full range of topics in AI and related disciplines and provides an ideal forum for international scientific exchange between central/eastern Europe and the rest of the world. The AIMSA conferences were previously chaired by Wolfgang Bibel, Tim O'Shea, Philippe Jorrand, Ben du Boulay, Allan Ramsay and Fausto Giunchiglia. AIMSA 2000 is sponsored by ECCAI, the European Coordinating Committee for Artificial Intelligence.

The AIMSA 2000 call for papers suggested that authors focus on Web processing: knowledge construction from the Web, agents and communication languages, Web-based documents and interfaces, distance learning and electronic commerce. The importance of the conference for AI, and computer science research in general, was reflected by the presence of 60 qualified papers, out of which 34 were selected for publication by the Program Committee. Each paper was submitted to at least two independent referees and, in order to be accepted, had to be accepted by at least two of them. The high percentage of the accepted papers reflects the autonomy of the Program Committee members, who judged that more than 50% of the contributions were worth publishing in the Proceedings. Most rejected papers were not considered of a low scientific quality, but the Program Committee members judged that the required revisions on the texts could not be completed in the time required to allow editing of the paper before the final presentation.

This LNAI volume includes the selected papers, sorted into topics respecting the sequence of presentations at the conference as much as possible. The reader can evaluate if and how the suggestions from the Committee concerning the focus were influential for the Authors.

AIMSA 2000 invited two internationally recognized scientists: Enrico Motta from the Knowledge Media Laboratory, The Open University, Milton Keynes, UK, for his work on ontologies and knowledge reuse, and Christian Queinnec from the Laboratoire d'Informatique de Paris VI (LIP6), France for his contributions to Web processing by reinterpreting functional language primitives in terms of navigation on the Web.

The Program and the Organizing Committees were very honored and satisfied with the success of the conference. AIMSA 2000 achieved the important goal of supporting advanced research activities, collaborations and joint endeavors between current and future leading scientists in artificial intelligence. In particular, AIMSA 2000 contributed to the peaceful and productive east–west European unification process, connecting countries from the North and the South of the world as well, around the common interest of collaborative scientific discovery and cultural development.

We are pleased to thank the authors for their significant efforts, both in improving the content and the form of their papers. We are grateful to the Program Committee members: all have been very collaborative and have taken great care in their evaluations. Authors and Program Committee members, as well as an extremely active Organizing Committee, have made it possible to believe that competence and skills in AI research are still considered very attractive activities in the year 2000, even when the explosive growth of business interests around information and telecommunication applications worldwide seems to call irresistibly our students and young colleagues directly from their early academic experience into business.

July 2000

Stefano A. Cerri
Danail Dochev

Programme Committee Chair

Stefano A. Cerri
Laboratoire d'Informatique, de Robotique et de Microelectronique de Montpellier LIRMM, Université de Montpellier II, Sciences et Techniques du Languedoc, France

Program Committee

Gennady Agre (Bulgaria)	agre@iinf.bas.bg
Galia Angelova (Bulgaria)	galja@lmlserver.bas.bg
Giuseppe Attardi (Italy)	attardi@di.unipi.it
Ivan Bratko (Slovenia)	bratko@fri.uni-lj.si
Joost Breuker (The Netherlands)	breuker@swi.psy.uva.nl
John Campbell (United Kingdom)	j.campbell@cs.ucl.ac.uk
Stefano A. Cerri (France)	cerri@lirmm.fr
Cristina Conati (Canada)	conati@cs.ubc.ca
Christo Dichev (Bulgaria)	dichev@ncat.edu
Danail Dochev (Bulgaria)	dochev@iinf.bas.bg
Claude Frasson (Canada)	frasson@iro.umontreal.ca
Guy Gouardères (France)	guy.gouarderes@larrun.univ-pau.fr
Daniele Herin (France)	dh@lirmm.fr
Philippe Jorrand (France)	philippe.jorrand@imag.fr
Vladimir Khoroshevsky (Russia)	khor@ccas.ru
Alfred Kobsa (Germany)	alfred.kobsa@gmd.de
Igor Kononenko (Slovenia)	igor.kononenko@fri.uni-lj.si
Irena Koprinska (New Zeland)	ikoprinska@infoscience.otago.ac.nz
Philippe Laublet (France)	philippe.laublet@lip6.fr
Vincenzo Loia (Italy)	loia@dia.unisa.it
Stefan Trausan Matu (Romania)	trausan@valhalla.racai.ro
Alessandro Micarelli (Italy)	micarel@dia.uniroma3.it
Marc Nanard (France)	mnanard@lirmm.fr
Pavol Navrat (Slovakia)	navrat@dcs.elf.stuba.sk
Tim O'Shea (United Kingdom)	master@bbk.ac.uk
Julian Padget (United Kingdom)	jap@maths.bath.ac.uk
Maria Teresa Pazienza (Italy)	pazienza@info.uniroma2.it
Rachel Pilkington (United Kingdom)	rachel@cbl.leeds.ac.uk
Allan Ramsay (United Kingdom)	allan@ccl.umist.ac.uk
Jean Sallantin (France)	js@lirmm.fr
Oliviero Stock (Italy)	stock@itc.it
Paolo Traverso (Italy)	leaf@irst.itc.it
Dimitar Vakarelov (Bulgaria)	dvak@fmi.uni-sofia.bg
Gerhard Weber (Germany)	webergeh@ph-freiburg.de

External Reviewers

S. Aguzzoli (Italy)
B. Apolloni (Italy)
C. Barbero (Italy)
P. Bonissone (USA)
A. Gertner (USA)
G. Gluhchev (Bulgaria)
F. Koriche (France)
B. Magnini (Italy)
A. A. Martino (Italy)

P. Mateev (Bulgaria)
E. Pianta (Italy)
P. Poncelet (France)
A. Sadikov (Slovenia)
L. Serafini (Italy)
C. Strapparava (Italy)
R. Tagliaferri (Italy)
V. St. Vassilev (Bulgaria)

Local Organising Committee

Danail Dochev (Chair)
Gennady Agre

Galia Angelova
Ognian Kalaydjiev

Acknowledgements

The Program and Organizing Committees also wish to thank Corine Zickler for her collaboration as secretary of the Program Committee and Adorjan Kiss for his technical help during the editing of the book.

Table of Contents

Best Paper Award

Actors, Agents

Web, Mining

Natural Language

Complexity and Optimization

Fuzzy, Neural

Learning

Invited Papers

Dynamic Knowledge Representation and Its Applications[*]

José Júlio Alferes[1], Luís Moniz Pereira[1], Halina Przymusinska[3]
Teodor C. Przymusinski[4], and Paulo Quaresma[1,2]

[1] Centro de Inteligência Artificial, Fac. Ciências e Tecnologia, Univ. Nova de Lisboa,
P-2825-114 Caparica, Portugal
{jja,lmp}@di.fct.unl.pt
[2] Dept. de Informática, Univ. Évora,
Rua Romão Ramalho, 59, P-7000 Évora, Portugal
pq@di.uevora.pt
[3] Department of Computer Science, California State Polytechnic University
Pomona, CA 91768, USA
halina@cs.ucr.edu
[4] Department of Computer Science and Engineering, University of California
Riverside, CA 92521, USA
teodor@cs.ucr.edu

Abstract. This paper has two main objectives. One is to show that
the dynamic knowledge representation paradigm introduced in [ALP+00]
and the associated language LUPS, defined in [APPP99], constitute *natural, powerful and expressive tools for representing dynamically changing
knowledge*. We do so by demonstrating the applicability of the dynamic
knowledge representation paradigm and the language LUPS to several
broad knowledge representation domains, for each of which we provide
an illustrative example.
Our second objective is to extend our approach to allow proper handling
of *conflicting updates*. So far, our research on knowledge updates was
restricted to a two-valued semantics, which, in the presence of conflicting updates, leads to an *inconsistent* update, even though the updated
knowledge base does not necessarily contain any *truly contradictory* information. By extending our approach to the *three-valued semantics* we
gain the added expressiveness allowing us to express *undefined* or *non-
committal* updates.

Keywords: Updates of Knowledge Bases, Dynamic Knowledge Representation, Generalized Logic Programs, Theory of Actions.

1 Introduction

One of the fundamental issues in *artificial intelligence* is the problem of *knowledge representation*. Intelligent machines must be provided with a precise defi-

---

[*] This work was partially supported by PRAXIS XXI project MENTAL, and a NATO
scholarship while L. M. Pereira was on leave at the Department of Computer Science,
University of California, Riverside. We thank João Leite for helpful discussions.

S. A. Cerri and D. Dochev (Eds.): AIMSA 2000, LNAI 1904, pp. 1–10, 2000.

nition of the knowledge that they possess, in a manner, which is independent of procedural considerations, context-free, and easy to manipulate, exchange and reason about.

Any comprehensive approach to knowledge representation has to take into account the *inherently dynamic* nature of knowledge. As new information is acquired, new pieces of knowledge need to be dynamically added to or removed from the knowledge base. Such *knowledge updates* often not only significantly modify but outright contradict the information stored in the original knowledge base. We must therefore be able to *dynamically update* the contents of a knowledge base KB and generate a new, *updated knowledge base* KB^* that should possess a *precise meaning* and be *efficiently computable*.

1.1   Dynamic Knowledge Representation

In [ALP$^+$00] we proposed a comprehensive solution to the problem of knowledge base updates. Given the *original* knowledge base KB, and a set of update rules represented by the *updating* knowledge base KB', we defined a new *updated* knowledge base $KB^* = KB \oplus KB'$ that constitutes the *update of the knowledge base KB by the knowledge base KB'*. In order to make the meaning of the updated knowledge base $KB \oplus KB'$ declaratively clear and easily verifiable, we provided a *complete semantic characterization* of the updated knowledge base $KB \oplus KB'$. It is defined by means of a simple, *linear-time* transformation of knowledge bases KB and KB' into a *normal logic program* written in a *meta-language*. As a result, not only the update transformation can be accomplished very efficiently, but also query answering in $KB \oplus KB'$ is reduced to query answering about *normal logic programs*. The *implementation* is available at: http://centria.di.fct.unl.pt/~jja/updates/.

Forthwith, we extended the notion of a *single* knowledge base update to updates of sequences of knowledge bases, defining *dynamic knowledge base updates*. The idea of dynamic updates is very simple and yet quite fundamental. Suppose we are given a set of knowledge bases KB_s. Each knowledge base KB_s constitutes a knowledge update that occurs at some state s. Different states s may represent different time periods or different sets of priorities or perhaps even different viewpoints. The individual knowledge bases KB_s may therefore contain mutually contradictory as well as overlapping information. The role of the dynamic update KB^* of all the knowledge bases $\{KB_s : s \in S\}$, denoted by $\bigoplus \{KB_s : s \in S\}$, is to use the mutual relationships existing between different knowledge bases (as specified by the ordering relation on $s \in S$) to precisely determine the *declarative* as well as the *procedural* semantics of the combined knowledge base, composed of all the knowledge bases $\{KB_s : s \in S\}$.

Consequently, the notion of a dynamic program update allows us to represent dynamically changing knowledge and thus introduces the important paradigm of *dynamic knowledge representation*.

1.2 Language for Dynamic Representation of Knowledge

Knowledge evolves from one *knowledge state* to another as a result of *knowledge updates*. Without loss of generality we can assume that the initial, *default* knowledge state, KS_0, is empty[1]. Given the *current knowledge state KS*, its *successor knowledge state* $KS' = KS[KB]$ is generated as a result of the occurrence of a non-empty set of simultaneous (parallel) *updates,* represented by the *updating* knowledge base KB. Consecutive knowledge states KS_n can be therefore represented as $KS_0[KB_1][KB_2]...[KB_n]$, where KS_0 is the default state and KB_i's represent consecutive *updating knowledge bases.* Using the previously introduced notation, the n-th knowledge state KS_n is denoted by $KB_1 \oplus KB_2 \oplus ... \oplus KB_n$.

Dynamic knowledge updates, as described above, did not provide any *language* for specifying (or programming) changes of knowledge states. Accordingly, in [APPP99] we introduced a fully declarative, *high-level language for knowledge updates* called *LUPS* (*"Language of UPdateS"*) that describes transitions between consecutive knowledge states KS_n. It consists of *update commands,* which specify what updates should be applied to any given knowledge state KS_n in order to obtain the next knowledge state KS_{n+1}. In this way, update commands allow us to *implicitly* determine the *updating* knowledge base KB_{n+1}. The language LUPS can therefore be viewed as a *language for dynamic knowledge representation.* Below we provide a brief description of LUPS that does not include all of the available update commands and omits some details. The reader is referred to [APPP99] for a detailed description.

The simplest update command consists of adding a rule to the current knowledge state and has the form: *assert* $(L \leftarrow L_1, \ldots, L_k)$. For example, when a law stating that abortion is illegal is adopted, the knowledge state might be updated via the command: *assert* (*illegal* $\leftarrow$ *abortion*).

In general, the addition of a rule to a knowledge state may depend upon some preconditions being true in the current state. To allow for that, the assert command in LUPS has a more general form:

$$assert \ (L \leftarrow L_1, \ldots, L_k) \ when \ (L_{k+1}, \ldots, L_m) \tag{1}$$

The meaning of this assert command is that if the preconditions $L_{k+1}, \ldots, L_m$ are true in the current knowledge state, then the rule $L \leftarrow L_1, \ldots, L_k$ should hold true in the successor knowledge state. Normally, the so added rules are *inertial,* i.e., they remain in force from then on by inertia, until possibly defeated by some future update or until retracted.

However, in some cases the persistence of rules by inertia should not be assumed. Take, for instance, the simple fact *alarm_ring*. This is likely to be a *one-time event* that should not persist by inertia after the successor state. Accordingly, the assert command allows for the keyword *event,* indicating that the added *rule* is *non-inertial.* Assert commands thus have the form (1) or[2]:

$$assert \ event \ (L \leftarrow L_1, \ldots, L_k) \ when \ (L_{k+1}, \ldots, L_m) \tag{2}$$

---

[1] And thus in KS_0 all predicates are *false* by default.

[2] In both cases, if the precondition is empty we just skip the whole *when* subclause.

Update commands themselves (rather than the rules they assert) may either be one-time, non-persistent update commands or they may remain in force until cancelled. In order to specify such *persistent update commands* (which we call *update laws*) we introduce the syntax:

$$\text{always } [event] \; (L \leftarrow L_1, \ldots, L_k) \text{ when } (L_{k+1}, \ldots, L_m) \qquad (3)$$

To cancel persistent update commands, we use:

$$\text{cancel } (L \leftarrow L_1, \ldots, L_k) \text{ when } (L_{k+1}, \ldots, L_m) \qquad (4)$$

To deal with rule deletion, we employ the *retraction* update command:

$$\text{retract } (L \leftarrow L_1, \ldots, L_k) \text{ when } (L_{k+1}, \ldots, L_m) \qquad (5)$$

meaning that, subject to precondition $L_{k+1}, \ldots, L_m$, the rule $L \leftarrow L_1, \ldots, L_k$ is retracted. Note that cancellation of a persistent update command is very different from retraction of a rule. Cancelling a persistent update means that the given update command will no longer continue to be applied, but it does not remove any inertial effects of the rules possibly asserted by its previous application(s).

2   Application Domains

In this section we discuss and illustrate by examples the applicability of the *dynamic knowledge representation* paradigm and the language LUPS to several broad knowledge representation domains.

2.1   Reasoning about Actions

An exceptionally successful effort has been made lately in the area of *reasoning about actions*. Beginning with the seminal paper by Gelfond and Lifschitz [GL93], introducing a declarative language for talking about effects of actions *(action language $\mathcal{A}$)*, through the more recent paper of Giunchiglia and Lifschitz [GL98b] setting forth an enhanced version of the language (the so called *language $\mathcal{C}$)*, a number of very interesting results have been obtained by several researchers significantly moving forward our understanding of actions, causality and effects of actions (see the survey paper [GL98a] for more details on action languages).

The theory of actions is very closely related to knowledge updates. An *action* taking place at a specific moment of time may cause an *effect* in the form of a change of the status of some *fluent*. The *effect* can therefore be viewed as a simple (atomic) *knowledge update* triggered by a given action. Similarly, a set of *parallel* actions can be viewed as triggering (causing) *parallel atomic updates*. The following *suitcase* example illustrates how LUPS can be used to handle parallel updates.

Example 1 (Suitcase). There is a suitcase with two latches which opens whenever both latches are up, and there is an action of toggling applicable to each latch [Lin95]. This situation is represented by the three persistent rules:

$$always \ (open \leftarrow up(l1), up(l2))$$
$$always \ (up(L)) \ when \ (not \ up(L), toggle(L))$$
$$always \ (not \ up(L)) \ when \ (up(L), toggle(L))$$

In the initial situation $l1$ is down, $l2$ is up, and the suitcase is closed:

$$KS_1 = \{assert \ (not \ up(l1)), assert \ (up(l2)), assert \ (not \ open)\}$$

Suppose there are now two simultaneous toggling actions:

$$KS_2 = \{assert \ event \ (toggle(l1)), assert \ event \ (toggle(l2))\}$$

and afterwards another $l2$ toggling action: $KS_3 = \{assert \ event \ (toggle(l2))\}$. In the knowledge state 2 we'll have $up(l1), not \ up(l2)$ and the suitcase is not open. Only after KS_3 will latch $l2$ be up and the suitcase open.

However, there are also *major differences* between dynamic updates of knowledge and theories of actions. While in our approach we want to be able to update one knowledge base by an arbitrary *set of rules* that constitutes the *updating knowledge base,* action languages deal only with updates of *propositional knowledge states*. At the *semantic level,* however, the situation is not so simple. The main motivation behind the introduction of the language $\mathcal{C}$ was to be able to express the notion of *causality*. This is a very different motivation from the motivation that we used when defining the semantics of updated knowledge bases.

In spite of these differences, the strong similarities between the two approaches clearly justify a serious effort to *investigate the exact nature of the close relationship between the two research areas* and between the respective families of languages, their syntax and semantics.

2.2   Legal Reasoning

Robert Kowalski and his collaborators did a truly outstanding research work on using logic programming as a *language for legal reasoning* (see e.g. [Kow92]). However logic programming itself lacks any mechanism for expressing *dynamic changes in the law* due to *revisions* of the law or due to *new legislation*. Dynamic knowledge representation allows us to handle such changes in a very natural way by augmenting the knowledge base only with the newly added or revised data, and *automatically* obtaining the updated information as a result. We illustrate this capability of LUPS on the following simple example. Another, slightly more ellaborate example, was given in [APPP99].

Example 2 (Conscientious objector). Consider the situation where someone is conscripted if he is draftable and healthy. Moreover a person is draftable when he attains a specific age. However, after some time, the law changes and a person is no longer conscripted if he is indeed a conscientious objector.

$$KS_1 : always \ (draftable(X)) \ when \ (of\_age(X))$$
$$assert \ (conscripted(X) \leftarrow draftable(X), healthy(X))$$
$$KS_2 : assert \ (healthy(a)). \ assert \ (healthy(b)). \ assert \ (of\_age(b)).$$
$$assert \ (consc\_objector(a)). \ assert \ (consc\_objector(b))$$
$$KS_3 : assert \ (not \ conscripted(X) \leftarrow consc\_objector(X))$$
$$KS_4 : assert \ (of\_age(a))$$

In state 3, b is subject to conscription but after the assertion his situation changes. On the other hand, a is never conscripted.

In addition to providing automatic updating, dynamic knowledge representation allows us to keep the entire *history* of past changes and to query the knowledge base *at any given time in the past.* The ability to keep track of all the *past* changes in the law is a feature of crucial importance in the domain of law. We expect, therefore, that by using LUPS as a language for representation and reasoning about legal knowledge we may be able to significantly improve upon the work based on standard logic programming.

2.3   Software Specifications

One of the most important problems in *software engineering* is the problem of choosing a suitable *software specification language.* It has been argued in several papers (see e.g. [LO97,EDD93,FD93]) that the language of *logic programming* is a good potential candidate for the language of software specifications. However logic programming lacks simple and natural ways of expressing conditions that change dynamically and the ability to handle inconsistencies stemming from specification revisions. Another problem is called *elaboration tolerance* and requires that small modifications of informal specifications result in *localized and simple modifications* of their formal counterparts. Dynamic knowledge representation based on generalized logic programs extends logic programming exactly with these two missing dynamic update features. Moreover, small informal specification revisions require equally small modifications of the formal specification, while all the remaining information is *preserved by inertia.* The following *banking example* illustrates the above claims.

Example 3 (Banking transactions). Consider a software specification for performing banking transactions. Account balances are modelled by the predicate *balance*(*AccountNo, Balance*). Predicates *deposit*(*AccountNo, Amount*)   and *withdrawal*(*AccountNo, Amount*) represent the actions of depositing and withdrawing money into and out of an account, respectively. A withdrawal can only be accomplished if the account has a sufficient balance. This simplified description can easily be modelled in LUPS by KS_1:

> *always* (*balance*($Ac, OB + Up$)) *when* (*updateBal*(Ac, Up), *balance*(Ac, OB))
> *always* (*not balance*(Ac, OB)) *when* (*updateBal*(Ac, NB), *balance*(Ac, OB))
> *assert* (*updateBal*($Ac, -X$) ← *withdrawal*(Ac, X), *balance*(Ac, OB), $OB > X$)
> *assert* (*updateBal*(Ac, X) ← *deposit*(Ac, X))

The first two rules state how to update the balance of an account, given any event of *updateBal*. Deposits and withdrawals are then effected, causing *updateBal*.

An initial situation can be imposed via *assert* commands. Deposits and withdrawals can be stipulated by asserting events of *deposit*/2 and *withdrawal*/2. E.g.:

> KS_2 : {*assert* (*balance*(1, 0)), *assert* (*balance*(2, 50))}
> KS_3 : {*assert event* (*deposit*(1, 40)), *assert event* (*withdrawal*(2, 10))}

causes the balance of both accounts 1 and 2 to be 40, after state 3.

Now consider the following sequence of informal specification revisions. Deposits under 50 are no longer allowed; VIP accounts may have a negative balance up to the limit specified for the account; account #1 is a VIP account with the overdraft limit of 200; deposits under 50 are allowed for accounts with negative balances. These can in turn be modelled by the sequence:

KS_4 : assert (not updateBal(Ac, X) ← deposit(Ac, X), X < 50)

KS_5 : assert (updateBal(Ac, −X) ← vip(Ac, L), withdrawal(Ac, X),
$$balance(Ac, B), B + L ≥ X)$$

KS_6 : assert (vip(1, 200))

KS_7 : assert (updateBal(Ac, X) ← deposit(Ac, X), balance(Ac, B), B < 0)

This shows dynamic knowledge representation constitutes a powerful tool for software specifications that will prove helpful in the difficult task of building reliable and provably correct software.

3   Representation of Conflicting Knowledge

Let us consider the following *contradictory advice* example, which models a situation where an agent receives *conflicting* advice from two reliable authorities. Since the agent's expected behaviour is *not* to do anything that he was advised not to do by a reliable authority, the agent should neither perform the given action nor refuse to do it. Instead, the agent should remain *non-committal* and the outcome of his decision process should therefore be *undefined*.

Example 4 (Conflicting Advice). An agent receives advice from two reliable sources: his father and his mother. The agent's expected behaviour is to perform an action recommended by a reliable authority unless it is in conflict with the advice received from another authority.

$$always\ (do(A) ← father\_advises(A), not\ dont(A))$$
$$always\ (dont(A) ← mother\_advises(noA), not\ do(A))$$
$$always\ (⊥ ← do(A), mother\_advises(noA))$$
$$always\ (⊥ ← dont(A), father\_advises(A))$$

Suppose the father advises buying stocks but the mother advises not to do so:

$KS_1 = \{assert\ event\ (father\_advises(buy)), assert\ event\ (mother\_advises(nobuy))\}$

In this situation, the agent is unable to choose either $do(buy)$ or $dont(buy)$ and, as a result, does not perform any action whatsoever.

The above illustrates the need for a *3-valued semantics* for knowledge updates. So far, in our research on knowledge updates, we were exclusively using a 2-valued semantics, namely, the *stable semantics* [GL88],suitably extended to the class of generalized logic programs [3]. Under the 2-valued semantics, the

---

[3] The class of generalized logic programs can be viewed as a special case of a yet broader class of programs introduced earlier in [LW92].

above situation results in an *inconsistent* update, because of integrity constraint violation. In this section we extend our approach to the (3-valued) *well-founded semantics* of generalized logic programs. This will enable us to model knowledge updates with *non-committal* or *undefined* outcome, as required.

Recall that both the dynamic updates and the LUPS semantics can be defined by means of linear-time transformations into generalized logic programs. The transformation encodes both the declarative meaning of the update and the inertia rules. To generalize both semantics to a 3-valued setting, one needs to extend the semantics of normal logic programs with default negation in the heads to a 3-valued setting. The resulting update program semantics is based on the well-founded semantics instead of the stable models. Accordingly, below we generalize the well-founded semantics of normal logic programs to generalized logic programs.

We start by presenting the definition of the stable model semantics of generalized logic programs[4].

Definition 1 (Generalized Logic Program). *A generalized logic program P in the language $\mathcal{L}$ is a set of rules of the form $L \leftarrow L_1, \dots, L_n$, where L and L_i are literals. A literal is either an atom A or its default negation $not\, A$. Literals of the form $not\, A$ are called default literals. If none of the literals appearing in heads of rules of P are default literals, then the logic program P is normal.*

In order to define the semantics of generalized programs, we start by eliminating all default literals in the heads of rules.

Definition 2. *Let $\overline{\mathcal{L}}$ be the language obtained from the language $\mathcal{L}$ of a generalized logic program P by adding, for each propositional symbol A, the new symbol $\overline{A}$. $\overline{P}$ is the normal program obtained from the generalized program P through replacing every negative head $not\, A$ by $\overline{A}$.*

The definition of the stable models of generalized programs can now be gotten from the stable models of the program $\overline{P}$. The idea is quite simple: since $\overline{P}$ is a normal program, its stable models can be identified via the usual definition by means of the Gelfond-Lifschitz operator Γ [GL88]; afterwards, all it remains to be done is to interpret the $\overline{A}$ atoms in the stable models of $\overline{P}$ as the default negation of A. Since atoms of the form $\overline{A}$ never appear in the body of rules of $\overline{P}$, this task is trivial: if $\overline{A}$ is true in a stable model then $not\, A$ must also be true in it (i.e. A cannot belong to the stable model); if $\overline{A}$ is false in a stable model, then no rule in P concludes $not\, A$, and so the valuation of A in the stable model is independent of the existence of rules for $\overline{A}$.

Definition 3 (Stable models of generalized programs). *Let P be a generalized logic program, and let I be a stable model of $\overline{P}$ (i.e. I be such that $I = \Gamma_{\overline{P}} I$) such that for no atom A both A and $\overline{A}$ belong to I. The model M, obtained from I by deleting from it all atoms of the form $\overline{A}$, is a stable model of P.*

---

[4] The definition below is different from the original one in [ALP+00], but their equivalence can easily be shown given the results in [DP96]

Now, a naïve extension of the well-founded semantics to generalized programs would simply consider the fixpoints of the compound operator Γ^2 for the transformed programs $\overline{P}$, and then remove all fixpoints where, for some atom, both A and $\overline{A}$ held. In fact, for normal programs, the least fixed-point of Γ^2 characterizes the well-founded semantics. However, this naïve definition does not engender intuitive results:

Example 5. Consider the generalized program $P = \{not\, a;\ a \leftarrow not\, b;\ b \leftarrow not\, a\}$. According to the naïve semantics, the well-founded model would be $\{not\, a\}$. In this case, since $not\, a$ is true, one would expect b to be true as well.

In the definition of stable models for generalized programs, whenever an atom $\overline{A}$ is true in some interpretation I (in the extended language $\overline{\mathcal{L}}$), and hence by definition $A \notin I$, it is guaranteed that after applying the Γ-operator once all occurrences of $not\, A$ are removed from rule bodies. In other words, whenever $\overline{A}$ is true, A is assumed false by default in rule bodies. In the well-founded semantics, one must ensure that, whenever $\overline{A}$ belongs to a fixed-point of Γ^2, all literals $not\, A$ in the bodies must be true. In other words, whenever $\overline{A}$ belongs to a fixed-point I of Γ^2, A must not belong to $\Gamma(I)$. This is achieved by resorting to the semi-normal version of the program:

Definition 4 (Semi-normal program). *The semi-normal version $\overline{P}s$ of a normal program $\overline{P}$ is obtained by adding to the body of each rule in $\overline{P}$ with head A (resp. $\overline{A}$) the literal $not\, \overline{A}$ (resp. $not\, A$).*

Definition 5 (Partial stable models of generalized programs). *Let I be a set of atoms in the language $\overline{\mathcal{L}}$ such that:*

$$(1)\ I = \Gamma_{\overline{P}}(\Gamma_{\overline{Ps}}(I)) \quad \text{and} \quad (2)\ I \subseteq \Gamma_{\overline{Ps}}(I)$$

The 3-valued model $M = T \cup not\, F$ is a partial stable model of the program P, where $not\, \{A_1, \ldots, A_n\}$ stands for $\{not\, A_1, \ldots, not\, A_n\}$, and T is obtained from I by deleting all atoms of the form $\overline{A}$ and F is the set of all atoms A that do not belong to $\Gamma_{\overline{Ps}}(I)$.

With this definition there is no need to explicitly discard interpretations comprising both A and $\overline{A}$ for some atom A. These are already filtered by condition (2). Indeed, if both A and $\overline{A}$ belong to I then, because in $\overline{P}s$ all rules with head A (respectively, $\overline{A}$) have $not\, \overline{A}$ (respectively, $not\, A$) in the body, neither A nor $\overline{A}$ belong to $\Gamma_{\overline{Ps}}(I)$, and thus condition (2) will fail to hold.

Definition 6 (Well-founded model of generalized programs). *The well founded model of a generalized program P is the set-inclusion least partial stable model of P, and is obtainable by iterating the (compound) operator $\Gamma_{\overline{P}}\Gamma_{\overline{Ps}}$ starting from $\{\}$, and constructing M from the so obtained least fixpoint.*

Example 6. The well-founded model of the program in example 5 is $\{b, not\, a\}$. In fact, $\Gamma_{\overline{Ps}}(\{\}) = \{a, b, \overline{a}\}$, $\Gamma_{\overline{P}}(\{a, b, \overline{a}\}) = \{\overline{a}\}$, $\Gamma_{\overline{Ps}}(\{\overline{a}\}) = \{b, \overline{a}\}$, $\Gamma_{\overline{P}}(\{b, \overline{a}\}) = \{b, \overline{a}\}$. Accordingly, its well-founded model is $\{b, not\, a\}$. Note, in the 3rd application of the operator, how the semi-normality of P is instrumental in guaranteeing truth of b.

4   Concluding Remarks

While LUPS constitutes an important step forward towards defining a powerful and yet intuitive and fully declarative language for dynamic knowledge representation, it is by far not a finished product. There are a number of update features that are not yet covered by its current syntax as well as a number of additional options that should be made available for the existing commands. Further improvement, extension and application of the LUPS language remains therefore one of our near-term objectives.

References

ALP⁺00. José J. Alferes, João A. Leite, Luís M. Pereira, Halina Przymusinska, and Teodor C. Przymusinski. Dynamic updates of non-monotonic knowledge bases. *Journal of Logic Programming*, page (to appear), 2000. Extended abstract appeared in *KR'98*, pages 98-111. Morgan Kaufmann, 1998. 1, 2, 8

APPP99. José J. Alferes, Luís M. Pereira, Halina Przymusinska, and Teodor C. Przymusinski. LUPS - a language for updating logic programs. In *LPNMR'99*, Lecture Notes in AI 1730, pages 162–176. Springer, 1999. 1, 3, 5

DP96. C. V. Damásio and Luís M. Pereira. Default negated conclusions: why not ? In R. Dyckhoff, H. Herre, and P. Schroeder-Heister, editors, *Int. Workshop on Extensions of Logic Programming (ELP'96)*, number 1050 in LNAI, pages 103–117, 1996. 8

EDD93. Abdel Ali Ed-Dbali and Pierre Deransart. Software formal specification by logic programming: The example of standard PROLOG. Research report, INRIA, Paris, France, 1993. 6

FD93. Gerard Ferrand and Pierre Deransart. Proof method of partial correctness and weak completeness for normal logic programs. Research report, INRIA, Paris, France, 1993. 6

GL88. M. Gelfond and V. Lifschitz. The stable model semantics for logic programming. In R. Kowalski and K. A. Bowen, editors, *ICLP'88*. MIT Press, 1988. 7, 8

GL93. Michael Gelfond and Vladimir Lifschitz. Representing Actions and Change by Logic Programs. *Journal of Logic Programming*, 17:301–322, 1993. 4

GL98a. M. Gelfond and V. Lifschitz. Action languages. *Linkoping Electronic Articles in Computer and Information Science*, 3(16), 1998. 4

GL98b. E. Giunchiglia and V. Lifschitz. An action language based on causal explanation: Preliminary report. In *Proceedings AAAI-98*, pages 623–630, 1998. 4

Kow92. R. Kowalski. Legislation as logic programs. In *Logic Programming in Action*, pages 203–230. Springer–Verlag, 1992. 5

Lin95. F. Lin. Embracing causality in specifying the indirect effects of actions. In *IJCAI'95*, pages 1985–1991. Morgan Kaufmann, 1995. 4

LO97. K. K. Lau and M. Ornaghi. The relationship between logic programs and specifications. *Journal of Logic Programming*, 30(3):239–257, 1997. 6

LW92. Lifschitz and Woo. Answer sets in general non-monotonic reasoning (preliminary report). In B. Nebel, C. Rich, and W. Swartout, editors, *KR'92*. Morgan-Kaufmann, 1992. 7

Using Consensus Methods for Determining the Representation of Expert Information in Distributed Systems

Ngoc Thanh Nguyen

Department of Information Systems, Wrocław University of Technology
Wyb. St. Wyspianskiego 27, 50-370 Wrocław, Poland
thanh@zsi.pwr.wroc.pl

Abstract. By the expert information we mean the information given by a man-expert of a field of science and technology, or by some intelligent program (for example intelligent agents) in solving of some task. We assume that in an intelligent distributed system for the same task the system sites may generate different solutions, and the problem is for the management system to determine a proper one solution for the task. In this paper we propose solving above problem by determining consensus of given solutions and treat it as the final solution. We present a general consensus problem, the postulates for consensus choice and their analysis. This analysis shows that the final solution being the consensus of given solutions should be the most credible solution in the uncertain situation.

1 Introduction

Distributed intelligent systems consist of autonomous sites and the autonomous feature is the resource of such kind of conflicts that the expert information generated by the sites on some matter is inconsistent. By the expert information we mean the information given by a man-expert of a field of science and technology, or by some intelligent program (for example intelligent agents) in solving of some task. We assume that in an intelligent distributed system for the same task the system sites may generate different solutions, and the problem is how to determine a proper one solution for the task. Generally, this kind of situations is related with preserving of data consistency. For non-distributed systems it seems that the problem is solved naturally by their integrity constraints, however in distributed systems (even with homogeneous databases) the data inconsistency problem is more complicated [3,4,19]. Below we present some examples.

As the first example, let us consider a distributed database system for a bank. Assume that a client of the bank takes credits in different branches, and he pays them progressively. Thus in these branches different opinions about the credibility of the

S. A. Cerri and D. Dochev (Eds.): AIMSA 2000, LNAI 1904, pp. 11-20, 2000.
© Springer-Verlag Berlin Heidelberg 2000

client may arise. If, in the future, this client will want to take another credit, then a univocal opinion should be useful for the bank to make a decision. The second example refers to time indeterminacy [10]. Let us consider a distributed system whose sites' tasks are based on monitoring meteorological situations in their regions, and forecasting, for example a period of rain. If the regions occupied by these sites overlap then it is possible that the sites can give different (even contradictory) forecasts for the common towns. Of course these data are still consistent from the point of view of database integrity constraints. However, when it is needed to make a forecast for the whole country, the management system must create a view of fragments generated by the sites, and in the view there may exist inconsistency of the data.

The above examples show that in intelligent distributed systems there may exist conflict situations in which for the same matter different versions of information are generated. In such cases the management system must determine such version of the information, which should be the proper one. In this paper we propose a tool for resolving this kind of conflicts. These conflicts refer to data semantics in distributed database systems. The tool proposed here consists of consensus methods for data analysis. The version of data, which is a consensus of given versions, should be the most credible one. Generally, consensus of given versions of data (some of which may be contradictory with each other) should be chosen only if these versions refer to the same subject and it is not possible to re-create the proper version on the basis of certain and exact information. The intention of the author is to present in this work a formal and general problem of consensus choice (section 3). In section 4 the postulates for consensus and their analysis are presented. This analysis shows how to choose the consensus satisfying fixed properties. A numerical example is also given in this work.

2   Related Works

Consensus theory has a root in choice theory. A choice from some set A of alternatives is based on a relation α called a preference relation. Owing to it the choice function may be defined as follows

$$C(A)=\{x\in A:(\forall y\in A)((x,y)\in \alpha)\}$$

Many works have dealt with the special case, where the preference relation is determined on the basis of a linear order on A. The most popular were the Condorcet choice functions. A choice function is called a Condorcet function if [12]:

$$x\in C(A)\Leftrightarrow(\forall y\in A)(x\in C(\{x,y\}))$$

In the consensus-based researches, however, it is assumed that the chosen alternatives do not have to be included in the set presented for choice, thus $C(A)$ need not be a subset of A. On the beginning of this research the authors have dealt only with simple structures of the set A (named *macrostructure*), such as linear or partial order. Later with the development of computing techniques the structure of each alternative (named *microstructure*) have been also investigated. Most often the authors assume that all the alternatives have the same microstructure. On the basis of the microstructure one can determine a macrostructure of the set A. Among others, following microstructures have been investigated: linear orders [1], ordered set partitions [6,7], non-ordered set partitions [9], n-trees [9], time intervals [17]. The following macrostructures have been considered: linear orders and distance (or similarity) functions. Consensus of the set A is most often determined on the basis of its macrostructure by some optimality rules. If the macrostructure is a distance (or similarity) function then the Kemeny's median [1] is very often used to choose the consensus. According to Kemeny's rule the consensus should be nearest to the elements of the set A.

Consensus as the tool for experts' classifications analysis has been investigated in works [5,14,15], in which the authors have dealt with such structures that ordered partitions, ordered coverings and non-ordered partitions of a set.

In the field of distributed systems, it seems that consensus is an efficient method for restoring inconsistency of replicated data [8] or for solving the conflicts among agents [11,16]. For faulty tolerance many works have used consensus methods for solving problems. Among others a consensus problem was formulated and solved for asynchronous systems where processors can crash and recover [13]. In [21] the authors propose a protocol, which enable tolerance faulty of links by determining consensus of different possibilities of failure. Solving consensus problem in a mobile environment is investigated by work [2]. An anatomy of conflicts is shown in work [20], which presents a formal model and the measurements for conflicts.

3   Structure of Consensus

3.1   Basis Notions

We assume that some real word is investigated by sites of a distributed system. This real word is represented by a set of objects that may be classified into more than one group (for example group of peoples, group of buildings etc). Subject of investigation of the sites is a set of features (relations), which can be possessed by the real world objects. The relationships between the features should be represented by some logic formulas (they can be interpreted likely as the integrity constraints for databases).

Thus by a structure of consensus we call an extended relation system

$Consensus\_Str = (X,F,R,Z)$

where
- X: finite set of consensus carriers
- F: finite set of functions
- R: finite set of relations on carriers
- Z: set of logic formulas which must be true in the model (X,F,R).

The idea of the formalism is relied on including all the information about the situation, which requires consensus choice and all circumstances needed for this process. The aim of building the structure is to include in a system all information needed for consensus choice and to enable defining a formal language, which should serve to the implementation of the choice. Following example should give more explanations of above notions.

Example. Let us take a multiagent system functioning in a distributed environment. The agents' tasks are based on analysis of meteorological data and making weather forecast for their regions for next day. If regions occupied by several agents overlap then the versions of the forecast for an overlapped sub-region may differ from each other. Thus we deal with the conflict in determining one version of forecast for the common region. Assume that the weather forecast refers to the degree and occurrence time of such phenomena as rain, snow, sun, temperature etc. We define above notions as follows:

- $X = \{ Agent, Region, Degree, Time, Temp \}$,

where

$Agent = \{a_1, a_2, a_3, a_4\}$,

$Region = \{r_1, r_2, ..., r_{10}\}$,

$Degree = [0,1]$,

$Time$ = set of time intervals represented by time chronons' identifiers (e.g. [2000-09-20:5AM –2000-09-20:11AM] or [5AM –11AM] if the day is known),

$Temp$ = set of intervals of whole numbers representing Celsius degrees, for example [3,6] or [-10,-1].

The names of carriers are also used as attributes name.

- $F = \{Credibility\}$

where $Credibility : Agent \rightarrow Degree$ is a function which assigns to each agent a degree of credibility, because for example in dependence from the modernity of devices the credibility degrees of agents may differ from each other.

- $R = \{Rain^+, Rain^-, Snow^+, Snow^-, Sun^+, Sun^-, Temperature^+, Temperature^-\}$

where

$Rain^+, Rain^- \subseteq Agent \times Region \times Time$

$Snow^+, Snow^- \subseteq Agent \times Region \times Time$

$Sun^+, Sun^- \subseteq Agent \times Region \times Time$

$Temperature^+, Temperature^- \subseteq Agent \times Region \times Temp$

In this example the relations $Rain$ and $Temperature$ are presented as follows:

Relation $Rain^+$

Agent	Region	Time
a_1	r_1	3AM–10AM
a_1	r_2	7AM–10AM
a_1	r_3	2PM–6PM
a_2	r_3	5AM–8AM
a_2	r_3	3AM–10AM
a_2	r_5	7AM–11AM
a_3	r_6	4AM–8AM
a_3	r_7	3AM–8AM
a_3	r_4	2PM–8PM
a_4	r_8	6AM–5PM
a_4	r_9	2AM–8AM
a_4	r_{10}	3AM–7AM

Relation $Rain^-$

Agent	Region	Time
a_1	r_1	3PM–8PM
a_1	r_2	11AM–3PM
a_1	r_3	5AM–11AM
a_2	r_3	3PM–8PM
a_2	r_4	10AM–3PM
a_2	r_5	12AM–2PM
a_3	r_6	10AM–12PM
a_3	r_7	1PM–3PM
a_3	r_8	10AM–12AM
a_4	r_8	6PM–11PM
a_4	r_9	12AM–5PM
a_4	r_{10}	8AM–3PM

Relation Temperature$^+$		
Agent	Region	Temp
a_1	r_1	3-6
a_1	r_2	4-8
a_1	r_3	2-5
a_2	r_3	2-6
a_2	r_4	3-8
a_2	r_5	4-10
a_3	r_6	2-7
a_3	r_7	(-1)-8
a_3	r_8	(-1)-5
a_4	r_8	2-4

Relation Temperature$^-$		
Agent	Region	Temp
a_1	r_1	>7
a_1	r_2	>10
a_1	r_3	>7
a_2	r_3	>8
a_2	r_4	<0
a_2	r_5	>7
a_3	r_6	>8
a_3	r_7	>9
a_3	r_8	>8
a_4	r_8	>7

We interpret a tuple (for example $<a_1,r_1,3AM-10AM>$) of relation $Rain^+$ as follows: according to forecasting of the agent a_1 in region r_1 rain will fall during 3AM and 10AM. A tuple $<a_1,r_1,15AM-20AM>$ of relation $Rain^-$ is interpreted as follows: according to forecasting of agent a_1 in region r_1 rain will not fall during 3PM and 8PM. It means that in the rest of next day time (viz. between 0AM and 3AM, 10AM and 3PM, 8PM and 12PM), agent a_1 does not have any basic to state if rain will fall in region r_1 or not. The interpretation of other relations is similar.

Logic formulas from set Z have to present the conditions which should be satisfied by relations from set P. In this case we have following formulas of first order logic

$$Z = \{Sun(a,r,t,d) \Rightarrow (z>6AM \wedge z<6PM), Rain(a,r,t,d) \Rightarrow \neg Sun(a',r,t,d')\}$$

The first formula represents a condition that if in region r at time t is sun then the time must be between 6AM and 6PM, this condition is, of course, dependent from given month. The second formula requires that if in region r at time t there is rain, then at the same time may not be sun.

3.2   Basis of Consensus

To the foundation of consensus choice we take the set P of relations on the carriers of the relation system. We firstly define a *consensus resource* Re as follows:

$$Re = \{P^+,P^\pm,P^-: P^+,P^- \in R \text{ and } P^\pm = Dom(P) \backslash (P^+ \cup P^-)\},$$

where $Dom(P)$ is the whole Cartesian product of the carriers on which relations P^+ and P^- are defined. For example $Dom(Rain) = Agent \times Region \times Time$. Next we define a *consensus domain* as a pair of two sets: set of relation names and set of consensus relationships between attributes, for example

$$<\{Rain^+,Rain^\pm,Rain^-\},\{Region-Time\}>, \text{ or}$$

$$<\{Rain^+\},\{Region-Time\}>.$$

The first component (a subset of consensus resource) of above tuples is called a *consensus basis*, and the second component is called a *consensus subject*. We interpret these components as follows: the consensus basis consists of all information which is needed for consensus choice, by a consensus subject *Region-Time* we means that for a given value of attribute *Region* there should be only one value for attribute

Time. Thus a consensus resource should include all information needed for different choices of consensus, a consensus domain presents a basis from what the consensus should be chosen and subject to which the consensus refers.

If consensus basis is of form $\{P^+,P^\pm,P^-\}$ then its elements are called:

- P^+: positive component
- $P^\pm$: uncertain component
- P^-: negative component

The interpretation of elements of relations P^+ and P^- is given above. Notice that set $P^\pm$ is also a relation on the same carriers as relation P^+ and P^-, and its elements should be interpreted as the uncertainty of the agents. For example if tuple $<a_1,r_1,0AM\text{-}3AM>$ belongs to relation $Rain^\pm$ then it means that the agent a_1 has no foundation to state if it will rain in region r_1 during 0AM and 3AM or not. The concept of interpretation of relations P^+, $P^\pm$ and P^- is adopted from the work [20]. Notice also that sets $P^+,P^\pm,P^-$ are dijoint from each other, and $P^+\cup P^\pm\cup P^-=Dom(P)$, thus set $\{P^+,P^\pm,P^-\}$ is a partition of $Dom(P)$.

3.3   States of a Consensus Domain

Let $P = \{P^+,P^\pm,P^-\}$ be a basis of consensus, notice that these relations consist of a number of tuples, each of which refers to one property of the real world. Following we define some states of a consensus domain. Herein we consider only the cases when the basis of consensus is of form $\{P^+,P^\pm,P^-\}$. In what follows by r_A we mean the value of attribute A in the tuple r belonging to some relation.

Definition 1. *Consensus domain* $<\{P^+,P^\pm,P^-\},\{A\to B\}>$ *is inconsistent if there exist 2 tuples r and r' from set P^+ (or P^-) such that $r_A=r'_A$, but $r_B\neq r'_B$.*   •

Definition 2. *Consensus domain* $<\{P^+,P^\pm,P^-\},\{A\to B\}>$ *is contradictory if there exist 2 tuples $r\in P^+$ and $r'\in P^-$ such that $r_A=r'_A$ and $r_B\cap r'_B\neq\varnothing$.*   •

Some commentary is needed for above definitions. According to definition 1, if in a consensus domain there exist 2 tuples which have the same value of attribute A (e.g. *Region*) but different value of attribute B (e.g. *Time*) then it is in inconsistent state, because for the same region there exist 2 different forecasts of rainfall. Definition 2, however, treats the inconsistency more sharply, a consensus domain is contradictory if for the same region there exist 2 forecasts one of which states that rain will fall at some time, and the second states that rain will not rain at the same time.

4   Consensus Definition and Its Postulates

Let A and B are attributes, by $Dom(P)_{\{A,B\}}$ we denote the set of all tuples belonging to $Dom(P)$ but restricted to these attributes.

Definition 3. *By a consensus of domain* $<\{P^+,P^\pm,P^-\},\{A\to B\}>$ *we call a relation* $C(P)\subseteq Dom(P)_{\{A,B\}}$ *which satisfies 1 or more of the following conditions*

a) For $r,r' \in C(P)$ if $r_A=r'_A$ then $r_B=r'_B$,
b) One or more of the following general postulates are satisfied

P1. $(\forall a \in A)(\exists\, c \in C(P))[(c_A=a) \Rightarrow (\bigcap_{\substack{r \in P^+ \\ r_A=a}} r_B \subseteq c_B)]$

P2. $(\forall a \in A)(\exists\, c \in C(P))[(c_A=a) \Rightarrow (\bigcap_{\substack{r \in P^- \\ r_A=a}} r_B \not\subseteq c_B)]$

P3. $(\forall a \in A)(\exists\, c \in C(P))[(c_A=a) \Rightarrow (\bigcap_{\substack{r \in P^\pm \\ r_A=a}} r_B \not\subseteq c_B)]$

P4. $(\forall a \in A)(\exists\, c \in C(P))[(c_A=a) \Rightarrow (c_B \subseteq \bigcup_{\substack{r \in P^+ \\ r_A=a}} r_B)]$

P5. $(C(P) \cap C(P') \neq \varnothing) \Rightarrow (C(P \cup P')=C(P) \cap C(P'))$

P6. $(\forall a \in A\ \forall b \in B)[(\forall r \in C(P)(r_A=a \Rightarrow b \not\subseteq r_B)) \Rightarrow$
$(\exists\, P' \exists\, r' \in C(P \cup P'))(r'_A=a \wedge b \subseteq r'_B)].$ •

The above postulates require some commentary. The first postulate states that if for some value a of attribute A all the voices in their positive components of consensus basis qualifies among others the same value b of attribute B, then this qualification should have also place in the consensus. Postulates P2 and P3 treat in the similar way the negative and uncertain components of consensus basis. According to postulate P4 if any of voices does not qualify a value b of attribute B to a value a of attribute A then there does not exists any such tuple in the consensus. Postulate P5 states that if for 2 bases their consensuses have not empty common part then this part should be the consensus of the sum of these bases. At last, postulate P6 states that for each tuple of attributes A and B there should exist a basis whose consensus contains the tuple.

Each of these postulates treated as a characteristic property of consensus choice function would specify in space C of all consensus choice functions a region denoted as $P1, P2,..., P6$ respectively. Notice that all regions $P1, P2,..., P6$ are independent, it means $Pi \not\subseteq Pj$ for all $i,j=1,...,6$ and $i \neq j$. Below we present some properties of these postulates.

Theorem 1. $P1 \cap P2 \cap ... \cap P6 \neq \varnothing$ •

Theorem 1 states a very important property of consensus postulates, namely there should exist at least one consensus function, which satisfies all these postulates.

Theorem 2. *If there is defined a metric δ between tuples of $\mathrm{Dom}(P)_{\{A,B\}}$, then for given domain $<\{P^+,P^\pm,P^-\},\{A \rightarrow B\}>$ the following consensus function*

$$C(P) = \{c \in \mathrm{Dom}(P): (c_A=a) \Rightarrow (\Sigma_{x \in P^+} \delta(c_B,x) = \min_{y \in Dom(P)} \Sigma_{x \in P^+} \delta(y,x))\}$$

satisfies dependency $C \in (P1 \cap P2 \cap ... \cap P6).$ •

The second theorem shows very practical property of the consensus postulates, viz. it determines a consensus function which satisfies all these postulates.

The proofs of these theorem are given in report [18].

For above example let $P=Rain$, $A=Region$, $B=Time$ and the metric δ between tuples $r,r' \in \mathrm{Dom}(Rain)_{\{Region, Time\}}$ defined   as   follows: $\delta(r,r')=d(r_{Time}, r'_{Time})$ where $d(r_{Time}, r'_{Time})=| r_{Time}{}^* - r'_{Time}{}^* | + | r'_{Time*} - r'_{Time*} |$ for time intervals $(r_{Time*}, r_{Time}{}^*)$ and

$(r'_{Time*}, r'_{Time}{}^*)$. Next we use the following algorithms for determining consensus of time intervals:

Given: Set J (with repetitions) of n time intervals, $J=\{i_j \mid i_j=(i_{j*}, i_j{}^*)$ for $j=1,2,...,n\}$

Result: Consensus $i=(i_*, i^*)$ satisfying condition $\displaystyle\sum_{j=1}^{n} d(i, i_j) = \min \sum_{i' \in I} d(i', i_j)$ where

I is the set of time intervals.

Procedure:

```
BEGIN
    if n=1 then set i=i₁ and go to END, else
      begin
          {Create sets with repetitions}
          X₁:=(i_{j*}| j=1,2,...,n)   {set of lower chronons}
          X₂:={i_{j}*| j=1,2,...,n}; {set of upper chronons}
      end;
    sort sets X₁ and X₂ in increasing order;
    for X₁ do
      begin
          k:=[(n+1)/2];   {where [x] is the greatest integer
                              not reater than x}
          k':=[n/2]+1;
      end;
    set integer i* such that i_{k'*}≥i*≥i_{k*};
    for X₂ do
      begin
          k:=[(n+1)/2]; k'=[n/2]+1;
      end;
    set integer i* such that i_{k'}*≥i*≥i_{k}*;
    i:=(i*,i*);
END.
```

Thus we should have the following consensus $C(Rain)$

Consensus C(Rain)

Region	Time
r_1	3AM–10AM
r_2	7AM–10AM
r_3	5AM–10AM
r_4	2AM–8AM
r_5	7AM–11AM
r_6	4AM–8AM
r_7	3AM–8AM
r_8	6AM–5PM
r_9	2AM–8AM
r_{10}	3AM–7AM

The algorithm for determining consensus for time intervals is given in work [17]. In dependence of the structure of the values of attribute B the algorithms for determining values of function C defined in Theorem 2 may be less or more complex. In work [8] the authors proposed some algorithms for the case when the values of attribute B are binary sequences, which represent data in computer memory. Earlier in [7] the ordered covering of a set was investigated and the algorithms were also proposed. It often happens that these computation problems are NP-hard, and it is necessary to work out heuristics or genetic algorithms.

5   Conclusion

From the results of postulates' analysis it is possible to determine a consensus for given conflict situation if the structure of versions are known. Future works should be concentrated on investigation when a consensus is good enough for given conflict. In other words, from Theorem 2 we can always determine consensus, but the question is if this consensus is sensible or given conflict situation is susceptibility to consensus? If it is possible, there should be defined a measure for given situation, which informs about the sensibility for consensus choice.

References

1. Arrow, K.J.: Social Choice and Individual Values. Wiley New York (1963).
2. Badache, N., Hurfin, M., Madeco, R.: Solving the Consensus Problem in a Mobile Environment. In: Proceedings of IEEE International Performance, Computing and Communications Conference. IEEE Piscataway NJ (1999) 29-35.
3. Ceri, S., Pelagatti, G.: Distributed Databases, Principle and Systems. McGraw-Hill (1984).
4. Coulouris, G, Dollimore, J., Kindberg, T.: Distributed Systems, Concepts and Design. 3rd edn. Addison-Wesley (1994).
5. Daniłowicz, C., Nguyen, N.T.: Determining of the Problem Solutions Representations. In: Plander I. (ed.): Artificial Intelligence and Information-Control Systems of Robots-87. North-Holland (1987) 187-192.
6. Daniłowicz, C., Nguyen, N.T.: Consensus-Based Partition in the Space of Ordered Partitions. Pattern Recognition **21** (1988) 269-273.
7. Daniłowicz, C., Nguyen, N.T.: Methods for Determining Representation of Experts' Opinions in Classification Tasks. In: Bubnicki, Z., Grzech, A. (eds.): Knowledge Engineering and Expert Systems. Wrocław University of Technology (1997) 279-287.
8. Daniłowicz, C., Nguyen, N.T.: Consensus-Based Methods for Restoring Consistency of Replicated Data. In: Kłopotek, M., Michalewicz, M., Wierzchoń, S.T. (eds.): Advances in Soft Computing. Physica-Verlag Heidedelberg New York (2000) 325-335.
9. Day, W.H.E.: Consensus Methods as Tools for Data Analysis. In: Bock, H.H. (ed.): Classification and Related Methods for Data Analysis. North-Holland (1988) 312-324.
10. Dyreson, C.E., Snodgrass, R.T.: Supporting valid-time indeterminacy. ACM Transaction on Database Systems **23** (1998) 1-57.
11. Ephrati, E., Rosenschein, J.S: Deriving Consensus in Multiagent Systems. Artificial Intelligence **87** (1998) 21-74.
12. Fishburn, P.C.: Condorset Social Choice Functions. SIAM J. App. Math. **33** (1977) 469-489.

13. Hurfin, M., Mostefaoui, A., Raynal, M.: Consensus in Asynchronous Systems where Processes Can Crash and Recover. In: Proceedings of Seventeenth IEEE Symposium on Reliable Distributed Systems. IEEE Comput. Soc. Los Alamitos CA (1998) 280-286.

14. Litvak, B.G.: Expert Information: Methods of Analysis and Gathering. Radio i Sviaz, Moscow (1982).

15. Nguyen, N.T.: The Axiom Approach to the Experts Opinions Representation Choice Problem. In: Bubnicki, Z. (ed.): Proceedings of the 13th International Conference on System Science. Wrocław University of Technology (1998) 224-229.

16. Nguyen, N.T.: A Computer-Based Multiagent System for Building and Updating Models of Dynamic Populations Located in Distributed Environments. In: Kącki E. (ed.): Proceeding of 5th International Conference on Computer in Medicine. Lódź University of Technology (1999) 133-138.

17. Nguyen, N.T.: Using Consensus Methods for Determining Timestamps in Distributed Temporal Databases. Reports of Department of Information Systems, series: SPR, No. 26, Wrocław University of Technology (2000).

18. Nguyen, N.T.: Consensus Methods for Resolving Conflict Situations in Distributed Information Systems. Reports of Department of Information Systems, series: SPR, No. 29, Wrocław University of Technology (2000).

19. Ozsu, T.M.: Principles of Distributed Database Systems. Prentice-Hall (1991).

20. Pawlak, Z.: An Inquiry into Anatomy of Conflicts. Journal of Information Sciences **108** (1998) 65-78.

21. Yan, K.Q., Wang, S.C., Chin, Y.H.: Consensus under Unreliable Transmission. Information Processing Letter **69** (1999) 243-248.

Drafting and Validating Regulations: The Inevitable Use of Intelligent Tools

Joost Breuker, Emil Petkov, and Radboud Winkels

Department of Computer Science and Law (LRI), University of Amsterdam
P.O. Box 1030, NL 1000 BA Amsterdam, the Netherlands
{breuker,petkov,winkels}@lri.jur.uva.nl

Abstract. In this paper we describe first the nature of laws and regulations, which are not-normal, fragmented pieces of text, that can only be understood by using some (implicit) model about the world to be regulated. Then we describe the process of drafting regulations, in particular the need to verify and validate their intended effects, i.e. deontic statements. We present an ontology, FOLaw, [13] and a prototype system, TRACS (Traffic Regulation Automation and Comparison System), which was created to test new traffic regulations [2]. Even a few runs of tests showed major deficiencies in this regulation. An extended version of TRACS also enables the generation of paraphrases of regulation, and even to some extent, from scratch. The implication of the use of these kind of tools are discussed; not only for checking consistency, but also for aligning ("harmonizing") regulations of different legal systems (nations).

1 What's in a Regulation?

"Can you develop a computer program that can check if the new traffic regulations are consistent and complete?" This apparently innocent question, posed by a government agency concerned with traffic safety, SWOV [1] triggered a decade of research at our institute, LRI.

The first and smallest step consisted of a close reading of the draft text of the regulation. It does not take much to notice that a legal text is not a normal text. It consists of individual statements (articles), many of which have a deontic nature. However, we understand these statements in various ways, as can be illustrated by the following two articles from this traffic regulation (draft-RVV-90)

Art 3 Vehicles should keep as much as possible to the right
Art 6 Two bicyclists may ride side by side.

We understand that Art 6 is an exception to Art 3, but we can only draw this conclusion after we have made some spatial model from which we can see that the left bicyclist of the two is not keeping fully to the right: the right hand

---

[1] Stichting Wetenschappelijk Onderzoek Verkeersveiligheid; Foundation for Research on Traffic Safety.

S. A. Cerri and D. Dochev (Eds.): AIMSA 2000, LNAI 1904, pp. 21–33, 2000.

bicyclist prevents this. If this were the point, normal texts would explain this, but regulation texts ("laws") assume that the reader has already a full understanding, i.e. a generic model, of the domain concerned, i.c. traffic. Moreover, *in principle* these statements only mark *what is undesirable behaviour* among all possible behaviours [1]: that is the reason many of these statements have a deontic meaning ('should', 'may').

In view of the request of checking consistency and completeness, drafting regulations can be compared to programming [7]. In software engineering a program is regarded as correct when it has no errors and is effective, i.e. has been verified and validated. The request of SWOV is a verification question. We will discuss the validation issues later, but it is already apparent that verification is problematic, as laws are riddled with exceptions and exceptions are logical inconsistencies. Moreover, the notion of completeness becomes very problematic for two reasons. First, the completeness is relative to the model of the world (domain) to be regulated and this model is implicit and largely based on common sense (see below). Second, it is hard to design a method to assess whether the regulation fully covers the intentions of the legislator, as these intentions are often expressed at a global level of desires from which the legal drafter has to infer undesirable situations and also has to take into account all kinds of implicit, undesirable side effects. Finally, as we will also show, undesirability of situations cannot directly be expressed, but only via the use of the famous three deontic operators: O(bliged), F(orbidden) and P(ermitted) for very pragmatic reasons. As we will show in the next section, these pragmatic reasons are also the cause of the many exceptions one finds in regulations. The completeness with respect to covering of the intended effects by a regulation is rather a question of validation than of verification.

2   FOLaw: A Functional Ontology for Reasoning with the Law

According to Valente ([12] see also [13]) reasoning in law can be summarized by a number of dependent functions, where each function refers to specific categories of knowledge with specific properties. Here we can only present the global picture of this core ontology (see Fig 1), and we will focus on world knowledge and normative knowledge.

The basic assumptions of this core-ontology are that there is a legal system that controls social behaviour in a reactive manner. Of course, the role of law is not only to 'correct' illegal behaviour, but also to instruct/prevent undesirable behaviour. These are crude, simplified assumptions, but for details see [13].

A reactive cycle starts with a case, i.e. a *real world situation*, which is interpreted in order to generate an abstract description of the case in the terms that the legal sources use. This abstract case description is called a *legal situation*, and the knowledge used to produce this step is the *world knowledge*, which forms the *legal abstract model*(LAM). Then, the legal situation is analyzed against the *normative knowledge* to verify whether it violates any norm, thus producing what

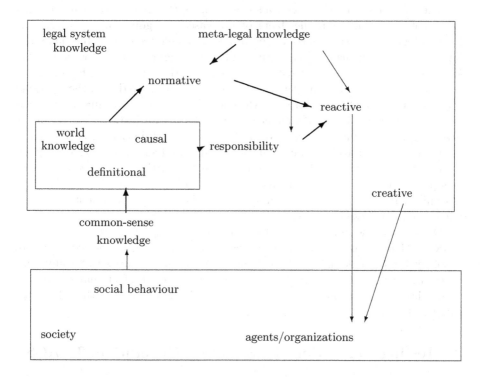

Fig. 1. FOLaw functional core-ontology distinguishing types of knowledge and dependencies

is called a *classified situation* (a situation classified as either 'allowed' or 'disallowed'). In another path, the situation is analyzed using again *world knowledge* (but here particularly its *causal* component) in order to find out which agents in the world (if any) have caused the situation. This information is then used as input to the *responsibility knowledge* which determines which agents (if any) are to be held responsible for the situation. The results obtained in these two paths (the classified situation and the responsible agents) are then used as inputs for a function that defines a possible *legal reaction* using *reactive knowledge*. Further, outside this cycle, the law may also create an abstract entity (part of the legal system) using *creative knowledge*; this entity is also added to the *legal abstract model*. Finally, *meta-legal knowledge* refers to all these entities.

Another way to see the interdependencies shown in Fig 1 is that they provide the connections between the (sub)functions from a reasoning point of view. That is, legal reasoning can be made modular, with each function corresponding to a module and the dependencies between the modules being provided by the dependencies between the functions. Such dependencies must of course be detailed.

The main path in Fig 1 can also be seen as the global structure of legal arguments: starting from the 'facts of the case' and going up to sentencing. Each category corresponds to a type of argument that has as antecedents the inputs and as conclusions the outputs of each function, and as warrants the knowledge belonging to that category. For normative knowledge, for instance, the conclusion is whether a situation is allowed or disallowed, and the warrants are normative knowledge. Moreover, the conclusions in a legal argument are concatenated as shown by the dependencies in the figure; for instance, an argument involving world knowledge (say, concluding that a certain person is considered a 'minor' according to a certain definition) being used as subsidiary for an argument involving normative knowledge (say, concluding that a situation in which this person was driving a car is disallowed according to a certain norm). Legal reasoning can be thus seen as the production and analysis of arguments involving one or more of these categories.

Ours is not the only core ontology for law (see e.g. [16] and [15]. Also, the work by McCarty on a "language for legal discourse" can be viewed as a core ontology for legal domains [9]. Although the ontologies are structurally very different, there is an important overlap of categories. The fact that competing ontologies have been proposed has lead to a reflective debate in the AI & Law community (e.g. [17]).

3   Testing Regulations by Situation Generation: TRACS

In regulations, one will hardly find statements about responsibility: responsibility, e.g. guilt, liability, is generally established using (common sense) causal reasoning [6]. In general, a regulation contains definitions about terms (world knowledge) and deontic statements (normative knowledge). This is also the case for the RVV90, the Dutch traffic regulation. In order to test this regulation, we constructed a KBS; TRACS (see Fig 2)

There are two knowledge bases (KB) corresponding to world, respectively normative knowledge distinction of FOLaw: one that contains a model of the domain of law (WORLD MODEL), and one that represents the regulations (LEGAL SOURCE). The WORLD MODEL model consists of the objects, agents and actions that can be used to generate or interpret situations in the world, i.e. cases. The *legal* world of traffic is very abstract and simplified compared to that of the physical/social one. Spatial reasoning is reduced to positions on parts of roads; time is of no importance, because the law does not look at the past, but only at a situation – e.g. being parked – or at a single action – e.g. crossing. The ontology consists of types of "traffic participants" (agents/vehicles), roads and parts of roads, and actions, which are represented naturally by a terminological classifier (LOOM). There are rules to compose or parse roads and crossings. Because of symmetry, and many other constraints the number of possible generic situations for this world is limited, but still combinatorial. This is of importance because we wanted to test the new traffic code (RVV-90) by generating all possible situations. The user in Fig 2 is replaced by a module that is a "situation

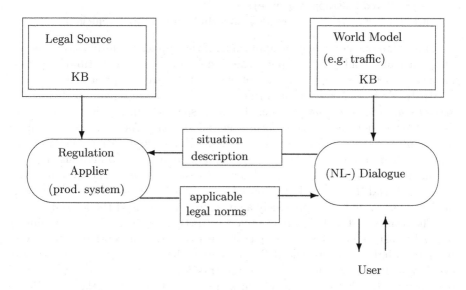

Fig. 2. Architecture of TRACS for testing regulations [den Haan, 1996]

generator". which produces all possible situations; legal or illegal. There is no user to feed the system – it runs in batch mode – and only the outputs are checked.

The legal reasoning starts when a SITUATION DESCRIPTION is fed into the REGULATION APPLIER. This component is a simple production system that matches the SITUATION DESCRIPTION to the representation of the regulation in the LEGAL SOURCE. A legal norms is represented as a generic situation description with functions that represent the deontic operators and yield "allowed/disallowed" as output when applied to a situation description. This formalism as described in [13] enables us to avoid the use of some deontic logic, which are known to have no tractable realizations, and need exotic extensions to handle 'paradoxes'.

A legal norm matches a SITUATION DESCRIPTION, if at least one *sort* of all conditions can be unified with the states of the SITUATION DESCRIPTION. This means that the legal norm is applicable. For instance:

SITUATION DESCRIPTION: (a',b',c',d'),
whereby c is-a-sort-of f, matches
LEGAL NORM: a,b → prohibited(f)
e.g. (place(my-volvo, crossing1), consists-of(crossing1, road1,road2),
is-parked(my-volvo), lights(my-volvo, on))
whereby, instance-of(my-volvo, car), sort-of(car, vehicle), and
sort-of(parking,stopping)

LEGAL NORM: (place(car, crossing), consists-of (crossing-x, road-x, road-y)
→ prohibited (is-stopped(vehicle))
(art. 15: "at a crossing of roads it is forbidden to stop a vehicle")

More than one norm may be applicable. If the applicable norms have overlapping parts and conflicting outputs, the norms are inconsistent. However, these inconsistencies may be due to 'exceptions'. If they are exceptions, they should be resolvable by the known meta-rules of the law, the most famous being *"lex specialis derogat legi generali"*, i.e. the more specific wins, which is similar to conflict resolution mechanisms in production systems. As TRACS was only a prototype, the first trials were made when an exhaustive situation generator was only specified on paper. However, these trials were already so illuminating that no further testing was required. Almost all cases that were specified by hand (about 40) lead to unexpected inconsistencies which wee not due to exceptions, or to outcomes that were obviously against the intentions of the legislator.

The results of TRACS were even very surprising in the sense that a number of really nasty contradictions – not of the permission/exception type – were brought to light in testing the RVV-91, the Dutch traffic code [3]. For instance, every situation containing a tram on the tramway was identified as a violation of an article that excepted a list of types of vehicles from taking the road (riding track). The tram is not in that list. However, adding the tram to this list has other nasty side effects. For instance, every situation containing a tram on the tramway was identified as a violation of an article that excepted a list of types of vehicles from taking driving lanes. The tram is not in that list, so that the tram is obliged to take such a lane. As the example shows, inconsistencies may easily arise in indirect ways. We also found that often there are no easy, straightforward repairs. For instance, adding the tram to this exception list would only mean that the tram should use the sidewalk. It turned out that most repairs required either 'structural' re-drafting, or ad-hoc articles. For instance, adding the article that trams should run on the tramway would be such a repair, but the legal drafters thought this was too stupid for words.

4   Generating Regulations

Legislative drafting can be semi-automatically supported in at least three different ways which are complementary. The first one is by providing information services that relate general legal information to the specific tasks of the legal drafters. An example is the LEDA system, that follows the officially recommended drafting procedures, directives and styles [18]. LEDA offers access to relevant legislation in hypertext format, and provides the initial normative structure formats. A second way is by providing tools that check the consequences of a regulation. ExpertiSZe [11] and TRACS [2] are examples. In this paper we also present a third kind of tool and approach which automates the construction of paraphrases of regulations on the basis of normative goals ((un)desired social behaviour) and a model of the domain (world knowledge) to be regulated.

The same normative goals can be expressed in different ways for different purposes (e.g. legal subjects concerned), like paraphrases of text that express the same underlying conceptualization [21]. In this paper we present procedures for generating paraphrases of norms.

4.1   An Outline and Rationale for Generating Normative Rules

The basic assumptions and steps in the process of generating regulations can be summarized as follows. As explained in Section 1 a legal domain refers to some social subsystem. A description of how such a world actually *works*, i.e. what behaviours can be exhibited by this world we have called legal abstract model (LAM, see Fig. 1). Behaviour at a particular moment is called a situation, consisting of some configuration (relations) of objects which are in a particular state. Situations can be instantaneous (actual), or generic (abstract). Norms are generic situations marked as being obliged, forbidden or permitted. [2]

The LAM should cover all possible situations in the domain. As these cannot be enumerated, a LAM is a generic abstraction similar to behavioural models in model based reasoning. In the current practice of legal drafting, no explicit modeling occurs. It is implicit in the understanding of the problems and the debates – political and technical – that are preliminary to and contingent upon the drafting activities proper. Making such a model explicit in a process of knowledge acquisition, as automation requires, may have the important side effect of clarifying more precisely and coherently what is at stake in a law. It may result in well defined terms, which may be an explicit part of a regulation as well. The disadvantage is also obvious: it takes a lot of effort – up to one or more personyear – which may be relatively large for small legal drafting projects (e.g. local repairs). A second step is going from an articulate and parsimonious world model into a version that consists of a list of all possible situations: this we call situation generation (see below, Sec. 4.2).

The partioning of a world model into two disjoint sets of illegal (undesired) and not illegal (not undesired) is called the Qualification Model (QM) [2]. Because in (political) practice normative goals (rather: intentions) are formulated in more global and vague terms than legislation requires, the process of turning these into the QM specification involves assessment.

The final step involves the construction of one or more regulation models (RM). An RM is not the same as the text of a regulation. It consists of a structure of norms, which can be expressed in various (ways in) natural languages. A norm has a simple structure as explained in the previous section, but the inter-norm structure may be rather complex, because it contains exceptions, which may be exceptions to exceptions etc. This structure is called the exception structure.

Figure 3 depicts the steps and their dependencies in this process. In the following section (4.2 we discuss situation generation and norm generation.

---

[2] In fact, these deontic operators are pragmatic, i.e. efficient expressions to translate the goals of the legislator, which are in principle in terms of legal/illegal. We present

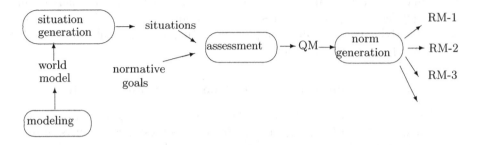

Fig. 3. Generating regulation models from world knowledge and normative goals

4.2   Generating Situations

A qualification model (QM) is a further qualification of the set of possible situations that models a specific domain. It is possible to generate such a set automatically, from the definitions of terms and by combining the possible states of objects.

First, we need an ontology that provides the definitions of terms [14, 13]. In legal domains, human agents play a pivotal role, so we will distinguish two types of entities: (human) agents and objects. Further, agents and objects can be related in dynamic and in static ways. The dynamic relations are actions or processes, while the terms relation will denote all other types of relations. As attributes are typical one place, relations, actions and processes have in general more arguments. For each type of action or process defined in the ontology we can generate in principle in a combinatorial way all types of arguments (objects, agents) that may fill these roles. Common sense ontologies may be used to obtain the semantics of these actions (e.g. Wordnet, CYC).

For instance, in a simplified combinatorial view an action like *give* has two agents (actor and recipient) and one object (for the object role). Now, if we distinguish in the domain three types of agents, and four types of objects, $3 * 3 * 4 = 36$ possible "giving"-situations are generated. [3] To illustrate what is involved, we may assume that situations consist of variables, agents (a), actions

---

here a rather narrow view of norms. Norms may contain rights and duties [8, 10], but we will not discuss here these complications (see also [12].

[3] This is not really correct. An action or process changes a situation into another situation. Therefore, one may assume that the give-action should be decomposed into an antecedent *situation1* in which an agent possesses an object, and a consequent *situation2* in which another agent possesses the object. Both situations are causally and intentionally related by the agent who is the actor of the change of possession (giving). This conceptualization is ontologically more correct, but does not really change the notion of combinatorics involved in situation generation. In this paper we treat actions as parts of situations; not as 'bridges' between situations. The latter view complicates, but does not really change the processes of situation and rule generation. It is part of current research.

(c), objects (o) and relations (r). Furthermore, there are not only elementary situations that consist of one action, but also complex situations in which more actions or relations are involved (N_{cr} per situation):

- Number of agents: a
- Number of objects: o
- Number of actions: c
- Number of relations: r
- Average arity of action and relation predicates: n
- Average number of actions and relations per situation:N_{cr}

Each predicate may be an action or a relation ($c + r$). Each argument is is either an agent (a) or an object (o). Each predicate has arity n, so there are $(a + o)^n$ possible combinations of the arguments per predicate. This yields the total of possible actions and relations, which is the multiple (.) of ($c + r$) and ($a + o$):

$$Tot_{pred} = (c + r).(a + o)^n$$

Suppose that a situation consists of an average of N_{cr} action or relation predicates, then the number of possible situations is:

$$Tot_{sit} = (Tot_{pred})^{N_{cr}} = ((c + r) * (a + o)^n))^{N_{cr}}\ [4]$$

Indeed a classical combinatorial explosion. However, this is a worst case analysis, because we have only blindly applied the terms and types from the ontology and used an almost unconstrained version of the action frame (only the types of role fillers are given).

There are various sources for limiting the number of possible (and meaningful) situations (see also [1])

- *Redundancy and tautology*
  There is a lot of redundancy when one does not carefully choose basic terms in representing knowledge. Many relations may have tautological family members. For instance, in the traffic domain there is a lot of symmetry and inversion.
- *Constraints*
  When the world knowledge contains descriptions of the physical limitations in the world, the physically and logically impossible situations are pruned. For instance, an object cannot be at different locations at the same time. Many of these are of a very general nature, like the roles in actions or physical principles, but there are often many domain specific ones as well. For instance, in the traffic domain, all actions are viewed as taking place in 'only' two dimensional space.
- *Abstraction or grain size level*
  As in all modeling, and particularly in AI, abstraction is what keeps the world manageable, even if it leads to sometimes incorrect identifications at lower levels of grain size.

---

[4] Filling the values of the traffic world into the equation above yields: $Tot = ((c + r).(a + o)^n)^{N_{cr}} = ((20 + 20).(15 + 20)^2)^2 = 2,401,000,000$.

– *(Legal) Relevance*
   In modeling worlds for legal (normative) control, worlds are only considered
   from the point of enforceable law. For instance, a traffic regulation is aimed
   at enhancing the safety of the participants.

Once the situations have been generated, they have to be distributed over two
sets to form the qualification model QM. We mention three possible approaches:

– Qualify each situation by hand according to the initial normative goals. An
   important source for qualification this way may be precedence law.
– Formulate a limited number of situations of a high abstraction level, and
   qualify these by hand according to the initial normative goals or intentions.
– Because legal drafting hardly ever occurs with a completely fresh start, one
   may qualify each situation using the older version of the regulation, using
   automated legal assessment. As in most political and technical debate the
   differences between the old and the new are emphasized, it is not difficult to
   use this method followed by the first one.

For the relatively small domains we are using as our testbeds, qualification
by hand is not yet a problem. Neither do we think that in practice one ever will
have to rely only on this by hand method, but rather on the last one.

4.3   From Qualification to Regulation

The input for the norm generation is the QM, which consists of the subset
Σ^- of the undesired situations, and Σ^+ of the not undesired situations. Σ is
the normative default chosen, i.e. in law this is in general Σ^-, reflecting the
principle that what is not forbidden is permitted in law. σ is a situation. RM is
the set of generated norms; ρ is a norm.

The overall algorithm for the generation of normative norms is defined as
follows:

$$
\begin{array}{|l|}
\hline
\textbf{while } \Sigma \neq \emptyset \\
\quad \textbf{select}(\sigma, \Sigma) \\
\quad \textbf{translate}(\sigma, \rho) \\
\quad \textbf{add}(\rho, RM) \\
\quad \textbf{adjust}(\rho, RM) \\
\hline
\end{array}
$$

Here we do not further elaborate the **select** and **add** procedures as they are
simple set operations. Below, we discuss the **translate** and **adjust** procedures.

The translation procedure is required, because norms in regulations are in
general not expressed as situations, as in the QM, but as *rules*, which means that
a particular action in a norm is selected as a forbidden, permitted or obliged
consequent, while the other situation descriptors are viewed as conditions, or
'grounds for application'. For instance, $O((agent - 1, age(> 18)) \wedge (agent - 1, voting))$ is expressed as *"if one is older than 18 years old, one is obliged to
vote"*. In a formal sense, these expressions are equivalent, in particular because

the *"if"* does not mean a real (material) implication, but rather a conjunction. This translation is required for communicative (pragmatic) reasons rather than for semantical reasons. Besides producing these expressions, the translation procedure also contains the algorithms to select the application grounds. The more abstract the application grounds, the simpler the rules become, but also the more exceptions the regulation will contain. The adjust algorithm takes care of the 'sign' of the deontic operator to create exceptions in an efficient manner, and feeds-back constraints to the **select** procedure. The algorithms are described in more detail in [2, 4, 5]. Thus far, these have been implemented as extensions to TRACS and tried out in experimentally in small, artificial domains.

5   Conclusions

We have described TRACS in supporting drafting regulations in two ways: one by testing regulations (TRACS proper) and the other way is by generating regulations (TRACS extended). TRACS is based upon the FOLaw ontology in which 'world' and 'normative' knowledge are distinguished. Pivotal for all legal reasoning is the world knowledge which models a particular legal domain, independent of its normative assignments. This world model, or LAM (Legal Abstract Model) allows the variety of functions of TRACS to support legal drafting. In fact, the LAM for a particular legal domain may be reused beyond the particular legal system for which it has been constructed. With the the globalization of human activities, harmonization and coordination of legalization becomes more and more urgent. In a very explicit manner this is the case in and around the European Community. The traffic regulations provide a good example, as the world of traffic is more or less the same all over the world, but the regulations differ enormously, and it is hard to assess by hand/eye/brain in which respects they are different. As we have seen in Section 3, it is for human legal drafters already difficult to trace the implications of an individual regulation, comparing and adjusting two or more regulations for the same domain becomes a factor more difficult. In fact, TRACS-test can easily put into a comparative mode, once a LAM has been constructed, as its systematic situation generator may be the input to more than one regulation knowledge base and TRACS records all differences in outcomes [5]. For instance, in this way we have compared (parts of) the old with the new Dutch traffic regulation. As we have also experienced, repairing and adjusting regulations is neither a task that is self-evident as it may bring new design errors. Therefore, we view TRACS-extended rather as a tool for adjustment, repair and communication in legal drafting than for full blown legal drafting from scratch.

TRACS has been thus far only an experimental testbed. Its basic philosophy and architecture is currently applied in an Esprit project, CLIME (http://www.bmtech.co.uk/-clime/index.html), aimed at information serving of huge regulation bases, based upon a LAM and similar assessment algorithms as in TRACS [19], [20]. However, we have identified at least two problem areas that may limit our approach.

- Situation generation is a combinatorial process. Although there are many sources to reduce complexity, many of which are classical in AI, they may not lift completely all barriers to scaled up applications. This is typical for model based approaches in AI. It should be noted that the same combinatorial problem is also one of the major reasons that human legal drafters – or for that matter, society – are not capable of tracing the implications of any non-trivial regulation. In fact, drafts of legislation are assessed in practice by evaluating a set of typical cases and having interest groups give comments. Even a 'case-based' input rather than full situation generation may improve quality as the test runs of TRACS have shown.
- Our account of the **translate** process has been somewhat over-optimistic. If we want to translate generic situation descriptions and we have to distribute these over application grounds and conclusions, we have to assume probably too much common sense knowledge about the world. For instance, TRACS may also decide that in the example about voting, the agent at voting should become over 18 years old. In other words, it should be able to distinguish about actions over which an agent can have control and those processes and actions he/she has not. Again the semantics of the actions may help, but the basic message is that we will hit here the same bottom as many KBS applications: the need to fall back on common sense reasoning about the world. Indeed, legal reasoning proceeds in close association with common sense reasoning.

References

[1] BREUKER, J., AND DEN HAAN, N. Separating regulation from world knowledge: where is the logic. In *Proceedings of the 4th International Conference on AI and Law* (New York, NJ, 1991), M. Sergot, Ed., ACM, pp. 41–51. 22, 29

[2] DEN HAAN, N. *Automated Legal Reasoning.* PhD thesis, University of Amsterdam, 1996. 21, 26, 27, 31

[3] DEN HAAN, N., AND BREUKER, J. TRACS: Een juridisch KBS voor het RVV90. In *Juridische toogdag 1992* (Amsterdam, 1992), VU, pp. 21 – 32. 26

[4] DEN HAAN, N., AND BREUKER, J. Constructing normative rules. In *Proceedings of JURIX-96* (1996), R. van Kralingen, Ed., pp. 41–56. 31

[5] DEN HAAN, N., BREUKER, J., AND WINKELS, R. Automated legislative drafting. In *Proceedings of the 8th Dutch Conference on Artificial Intelligence, NAIC* (1996), J. Meyer and L. van der Gaag, Eds., pp. 167–178. 31

[6] HART, H., AND HONORE, T. *Causation in the Law,* second edition ed. Oxford University Press, New York, 1985. 24

[7] KOWALSKI, R., AND SERGOT, M. Computer representation of the law. In *Proceedings of the ninth IJCAI* (1986), pp. 1269–1270. 22

[8] MALT, G. Methods for the solution of conflicts between rules in a system of positive law. In *Coherence and Conflict in Law* (Deventer/Boston, 1992), P. Brouwer, T. Hol, A. Soeteman, W. van der Velde, and A. de Wild, Eds., Kluwer, pp. 201–226. 28

[9] MCCARTY, L. A language for legal discourse i. basic structures. In *Proceedings of the 2nd International Conference on AI and Law* (Vancouver, 1989), ACM. 24

[10] Ross, A. Tu-tu. *Scandinavian Studies in Law* (1957), 139–153. 28

[11] Svensson, J., Kordelaar, P., Wassink, J., and van 't Eind, G. ExpertisZe, a Tool for Determining the Effects of Social Security Information. In *Proceedings of Legal Knowledge Based Systems: Information Technology and Law, JURIX–1992* (Lelystad, NL, December 1992), C. Grütters, J. Breuker, H. van den Herik, A. Schmidt, and C. de Vey Mestdagh, Eds., Koninklijke Vermande, pp. 51–61. 26

[12] Valente, A. *Legal knowledge engineering: A modelling approach.* IOS Press, Amsterdam, The Netherlands, 1995. 22, 28

[13] Valente, A., Breuker, J., and Brouwer, P. Legal modelling and automated reasoning with ON-LINE. *International Journal of Human Computer Studies 51* (1999), 1079–1126. 21, 22, 25, 28

[14] van Heijst, G., Schreiber, A. T., and Wielinga, B. Using explicit ontologies for kbs development. *International Journal of Human-Computer Studies 46, 2/3* (1997), 183–292. 28

[15] van Kralingen, R. W. *Frame-based Conceptual Models of Statute Law.* PhD thesis, University of Leiden, The Hague, The Netherlands, 1995. 24

[16] Visser, P. *Knowledge Specification for Multiple Legal Tasks; A Case Study of the Interaction Problem in the Legal Domain.* PhD thesis, University of Leiden, The Hague, The Netherlands, June 1995. 24

[17] Visser, P., and Winkels, R., Eds. *First International Workshop on Legal Ontologies* (Melbourne, Australia, 1997), University of Melbourne. 24

[18] Voermans, W., and Verharen, E. LEDA: a semi-intelligent legislative drafting-support system. In *Intelligent Tools for Drafting and Computer-Supported Comparison of Law – Sixth International Conference on Legal Knowledge-based Systems Legal Knowledge-Based Systems, JURIX–1993* (1993), Koninklijke Vermande, pp. 81–94. 26

[19] Winkels, R., Bosscher, D., Boer, A., and Breuker, J. Generating exception structures for legal information serving. In *Proceedings of the Seventh International Conference on Artificial Intelligence and Law (ICAIL-99)*, T. F. Gordon, Ed. ACM, New York, NJ, 1999, pp. 182–195. Also in Proceedings of the 11th Belgium-Netherlands Conference on Artificial Intelligence (Maastricht, November 3-4, 1999). 31

[20] Winkels, R., Breuker, J., Boer, A., and Bosscher, D. Intelligent information serving for the legal practitioner. In *Proceedings of the IASTED Conference on Law and Technology, LawTech-99* (1999), pp. 103–114. 31

[21] Winkels, R., and den Haan, N. Automated legislative drafting: Generating paraphrases of legislation. In *Proceedings of the Fifth International Conference on AI and Law* (College Park, Maryland, 1995), ICAIL-95, Ed., ACM, pp. 112–118. 27

Steps towards C+C: A Language for Interactions

Stefano A. Cerri, Jean Sallantin, Emmanuel Castro, and Daniele Maraschi

LIRMM, Rue Ada 161, 34392 MONTPELLIER CEDEX 5, France
{cerri,js,castro,maraschi}@lirmm.fr
http://www.lirmm.fr

Abstract. We present in this paper our reflections about the requirements of new architectures and languages for the Web, confronted with the ones emerging from qualified scientists such as Mc Carthy [1] and Wegner [2]. The contribution highlights if and how these reflections may be concretely realized by means of extensions of non standard models and tools that we have already experimented and that appeared in previous papers (the STROBE model and Phi Calculus). We conclude with the preliminary specifications of a new language for modeling and programming Interactions, called C+C, that represents constructively our approach, privileging the communicational aspects among Autonomous Agents, with respect to the more traditional algorithmic ones.

Keywords: Agent Communication Languages, Interaction Languages, Web Languages.

1   Introduction

Communication among intelligent Agents on the Web is one of the popular research issues at the moment. Enhancing the expressiveness of Web documents is another fashionable research area. They reflect the view that Computing consists of active elements, i.e. Programs – such as Agents [3]- and passive ones, i.e. Data – such as XML [4] (eXtensible Markup Language) Documents or ACL[5](Agent Communication Language) Messages -. Active and passive elements, perhaps structured as Objects, interact between them and with Human users in order to activate Processes in the modern context where the Computer has become a notion relative to any singular Agent: anything on the Web that may help in solving problems.

In this totally new scenario most of the efforts are focussed in extending traditional models, languages and systems in order to account for the Web. Even the less formalized streams of research in Computing – Agents and Markup Languages – seem to consist essentially of technical extensions of old paradigms. Agent's fundamental research approaches – and researchers in the area - look for an official, theoretically supported recognition of Agents as extension of Actor's or Object's

S. A. Cerri and D. Dochev (Eds.): AIMSA 2000, LNAI 1904, pp. 34-48, 2000.

paradigms. This seems quite odd, since even formal theories justifying Actors and Objects, when and if they have been developed, (see, e.g. [6]) are far from becoming a justification for the impressive expansion of usage of Objects in the real Computing scenario. Similarly, the emergence of XML-like standards and languages and, in parallel, of industrial interests around Agent Communication Languages based on Speech Acts and Ontologies stimulate endless debates about what is what, always in traditional Computing terms. These focus often on the old need to develop standards at the syntactic level, while trying to extend the standards at the semantic one. Both trends are justified. However, the first need is often contradictory with the second one, dependent on the application and therefore on the viewpoints of real users.

For instance, several times people ask simple questions such as: is an Agent different from a Program [7]? Is an XML document, different from a complex datum [8]? Is there a semantics associated to XML documents, or are DTDs just ways to express well-formed ness properties of tags and nothing more?

Wegner [2] has several arguments for supporting the view that there is an essential difference between algorithms and interactive systems. We did not really work out the same profound reflections, but our intuitions years ago do match well with his conclusions [9.10]. We agree with Wegner that computing on the Web has to be entirely revisited analyzing the interactive communicational phenomena that have no counterpart in traditional models, such as Turing Machines, Lambda Calculus or Von Neumann machines. These historical models are essentially founded on the closed world assumption.

Mc Carthy [1] did understand perfectly the way to follow when he wrote: *"A very large fraction of office work involves communicating with people and organizations outside the office and whose procedures are not controlled by the same authority. Getting the full productivity benefit from computers depends on computerizing this communication. This cannot be accomplished by approaches to distributed processing which assume that the communication processes are designed as a group."*

In the cited papers [9,10] we wrote: *"The paper reflects on the difference between knowledge systems and knowledge communication systems. Most real world situations are inherently open: there is a need for unforeseen interactions with external autonomous agents such as humans or programs. ... omissis... For these reasons, the theme of understanding the partner in dialogues becomes central. ... omissis... The example shows in a simple way that if a computational object models a situation that has a history, the course of which can not be foreseen in any possible way (such as the history of interactions between the bank account object and the requests for withdrawals issued by external agents) that object needs state variables to be able to model the history and therefore the "context". We must now ask, when is it the case that a situation is characterized by a history the evolution of which cannot be foreseen in any possible way? Is a flight control program such a situation? Is a chess program such a situation? Is an information system, a diagnostic system, a scheduler, an expert system in this situation? The question can be rephrased in terms of closed worlds. When is it the case that we are entitled to design models of a situation under the closed world assumption ? "*

We are not sure to be able, in this paper, to convince the reader that the two contradictory requirements indicated above – new theoretical foundations for

Interactive Systems and practical tools for Web processing - may coexist, and even be synergic in a promising joint effort. We present here, just a partial view of the results of a preliminary work in progress that testimonies the convergence of ideas emerged and documented by the senior authors (JS, SAC) in the course of the last years, currently at the ground of the research activities of the junior authors (EC,DM) in the future ones.

2   Rationality, Adequacy and Learning in Collaborative Theory Formation: Phi Calculus

This stream of work conducted mainly by Jean Sallantin and his group [11-16] starts from a view of Artificial Intelligence that is non standard, even if it is shared by an increasingly important number of scholars. The view is summarized hereafter.

In Artificial Intelligence, we look for machines able to amplify the capacity for the human to solve problems. At the core of these studies, we have two questions:

1. how to define the interactions between theory and practice in problem solving;
2. how to define the interactions between humans and machines or among humans through machines during the problem solving process.

Both core questions are centered around the notion of Interaction, i.e. mutual action resulting from dialogues among Human and/or Artificial Agents. More specifically, the main question is to study how a dialogue may lead to an agreement legally acceptable on actions eventually performed by the participants.

The application investigated and proposed by Castro et al. [13] does not assume the availability of a common "Ontology" between Agents, but instead wishes to look at the communicative phenomena emerging in order to build incrementally such a shared Ontology, in such a way that the shared Ontology expresses the conditions for the agreement. In other words, looks at the rationality of interacting Agents when they attempt to converge towards a shared view of a domain, represented by an Ontology.

According to these author's approach, it is not realistic to expect that Ontologies are standards that anyone has to accept and learn in order to solve problems collaboratively, a kind of "shared truth". This would imply eliminating negotiations, i.e. assuming to be in a completely known environment where methods of problem solving are known , mastered and have been previously applied with success.

On the contrary, the first step in solving problems collaboratively consists of building a shared Ontology with the partners (see also the same ideas expressed in the literature on cognition and language [17]). This need for separating the shared rationale in question answering – called: the search phase - from the access phase, typical of well formulated questions, was also behind the work of [18]: before the user may put a query (s)he has to know if and how the system may offer answers in the domain of the query.

While most work on Ontologies, attempts to study the first order logical well formed-ness of Ontologies (consistency and/or completeness with respect to deductible formulas), Sallantin et al., modestly and effectively, reduce Ontologies to hierarchies of Terms, Propositions about the terms and Constraints. Ambitiously, instead, they guide their Agents – human or artificial – to "learn" how to eliminate the paradoxes occurring during the dialogue engaged for constructing the Ontology.

The interactive, communication process is the object of study for them. The control process is just state of the art: trees of symbols, constraint propagation and standard machine learning are sufficient even for applications such as the one in [15] where negotiation allows the management of documents.

The communication process, observed from outside, seems quite obvious: it consists of clicking on a screen, entering a term, relaxing a constraint, validating an example, learning some constraints on the examples, keeping or eliminating or using examples for generalizing and the like. But the semantics and pragmatics associated to these – apparently simple – actions is much more complex, as it addresses notions such as abstraction, generalization, rationality (limited, deliberated, computed), adequacy (ontological, heuristic, epistemological), postulate, axiom, theorem, fact, hypothesis, lemma, justification, promise, exists, confirmed, the modals will, can, may, know, wish, etc. The analysis of how these notions are hidden behind interactions among generic Agents, leads to make systems that facilitates their explicit use. This is the goal of the research.

In general, these notions emerge historically mainly from Philosophy and therefore have been subjectively described by philosophers. Sallantin et al, by adopting at the kernel of their studies these philosophical notions, attempt to rigorously define a framework for theory formation by revisiting the process in terms of eliminating or circumscribing paradoxes in the collaborative construction of Ontologies by rational Agents. If it is acceptable to say that the first step in any collaborative problem solving process is the construction of a shared, adequate Ontology, then this construction becomes the main objective of formal as well as practical studies on the future of Computing and AI.

Their objective - called Phi Calculus (Philosophical Calculus) –, in order to be acceptable outside the community where it emerges, requires:

a.   a formal (mathematical) theory,
b.   a methodology for the development of software interactive applications – a language for interacting Agents - and
c.   a set of real world applications demonstrating the value added by the approach and the language for implementing the consequent solutions.

In other documents we present the current results of a. [14] and c. [16]. Hereafter we concentrate on b. because they have been reached jointly with the previous stream of work around the other senior author of this paper (SAC).

3   A Model and a Language for Generic Dialogues: STROBE

In a series of papers appeared both at Conferences or in Edited books about Artificial Intelligence and Education, Intelligent Tutoring Systems, Functional Programming, User Modeling, Agents and Soft Computing [19-22] and also in a number of unpublished master's thesis [23-26], the authors have presented a non standard model of Agent communication, called STROBE, and a few excerpts of experiments on implementations of the model using different technologies.

The novelty of the model may be summarized as in the following.

1. The model emerges from observations of the communicative behavior of Agents; not from their control behavior as it is frequently the case. Agents are considered firstly communicative entities, then control entities.

2. The model is not a formal - mathematical or logical - model, even if it has been used for implementing several prototypes. It is not an extension of lambda calculus, even if it uses Scheme as a description language for complex, newly revisited, communication and control phenomena. In spite of the fact that it is not a formal model, it is embodied in usable programs expressed by formal languages (mainly Scheme and Java).

3. The model does not pretend to solve all the problems envisaged, but allows to reduce the problems to a minimum set of simple linguistic and computational concepts. These are, in the essence, the notion of STReam (delayed evaluation) modeling the Communication among Agents;   that of OBject as a function-instance resulting from another function-class in a language where functions are first class, modeling the Control of Agents; that of Environment as a first class abstract data type in a dynamically typed language, modeling the Memory. The important consequence of this view, is that one may dedicate first-class Environments to Conversations within Agent pairs, as well as, for each Agent pair, to Ontologies. The explicitly labeled tree-structured knowledge repositories have been called Cognitive Environments. As a consequence, Cognitive Environments may be used for modeling in a straightforward way the supposed partner's beliefs, exactly when they are partially inconsistent with the Agent's belief. There have not been further studies on how exactly to cope with Cognitive Environments as Agent's memory models, but we are confident that these may inherit algorithms from currently available practices in non-homogeneous, federated Databases.

4. The model accounts poorly for the intrinsic asynchronous behavior of Agents. All what is said is that an Agent should have a dynamic scheduler that asynchronously processes incoming messages and produces outgoing messages. In every figure published, however, there is no mention of the fact that the clock – in Agent's conversations – is not a shared variable. Figures and tables seem to respect synchronization, thus they are not reflecting what the text says.

In the rest of the paper we will present an improvement of the model as the basis for our proposed language C+C. Improvements concern three aspects:

a. time will be explicitly considered proprietary for each Agent engaged in the transaction, and not necessarily shared by any pair of Agents. Synchronization of events is not ensured by the model. Eventually, synchronization is left to the application designer (cf. the discussion on Time at page 9 of [1]);

b. there is an intuitive, generic description of Agents in terms of a (functional) semantics. We may consider this as a preliminary specification of C+C;

c. there are guidelines for a constructive method for designing the communicative level, i.e. the primitive and the composite "Acts" that may be required in order to make Phi Calculus an effective methodology, thus in order to develop the corresponding applications;

d.   there are realistic guidelines for exploiting the notion of Stream and implementing non strictness in parameter passing (lazy control) and a distributed, asynchronous, lazy communication model accounting for a view of the Web as an extension of the local memory.

In order to reach that level of clarity in the description of our approach, let us consider first an important external contribution that may be supportive – and controversial – with respect to our own choices, that of McCarthy's Elephant 2000 paper[1].

4   Elephant 2000

In a paper dated 10 June 1989 (appeared much later on the Web site of the author), John McCarthy presents his view for a programming language for the years 2000 [1]. He called it Elephant 2000, as – he writes – *"an elephant never forgets!"*.

Hereafter a set of annotated statements from the cited paper.

Goal of the proposed language: Interaction

> *Elephant 2000 is a proposed programming language good for writing and verifying programs that interact with people (e.g. transaction processing) or interact with programs belonging to other organisations (e.g. electronic data interchange).*

It is important to recognize that there is no significant difference in interacting with people or with programs.

Writing and verifying are the two aspects. What "good" means is still an issue. Does he mean: expressive enough (for writing, for verifying …)? Or also: simple to use (in writing, in verifying …)?

Fundamental components of Interactions: Speech Acts

> *Communication inputs and outputs are in an I-O language whose sentences are meaningful speech acts identified in the language as questions, answers, offers, acceptances, declinations, requests, permissions and promises.*

A first list of Speech Acts is made explicit. The semantics should be formally defined. For instance, a question may have the intention to know the answer, when the querier is interested to know it and does not know it (see: Information Systems), or to test if the partner knows the answer and, in the positive case, if the partner's answer coincides with the querier's view of what the partner knows (as in Tutoring Systems, when the Tutor tests the Student's knowledge). A careful analysis of needs around Speech Acts in context [27] suggests that it would be rather utopistic to have "standard" Speech Acts in much the same way as to have "standard" Ontologies.

Focus on performance of Speech Acts with respect to program's behavior

The correctness of programs is partly defined in terms of proper performance of the speech acts. Answers should be truthful and responsive and promises should be kept. Sentences of logic expressing these forms of correctness can be generated automatically from the program.

The notion of correctness of a program assumes that a program has to generate a process that terminates with the solution of the problem. If the problem changes during the process – even if the program remembers how it was previously - , it is quite hard to define the notion of correctness. Agents are autonomous, and therefore they may change autonomously their goals during conversations. In the case that programs represent Agents, the notion of correctness should be substituted with the notion of adequateness, i.e. the empirical estimate that the Agent will achieve his goals, i.e. reach within – if possible - each conversation, the subjective decision for the Agent that its current goal – in the conversation – has been satisfied so that the conversation may be considered completed.

Memory model

Elephant source programs may not need data structures, because they can refer directly to the past.

A language that does not need data structures does not need either assignement (cf the programming language Haskell). Thus it is a purely functional language. Notice that McCarthy intended probably "mutable" data structure (thanks to C. Queinnec for this interpretation).

The notion of Stream in STROBE models neatly the evolving components of the conversation. Here Mc Carthy highlights the need for not forgetting as a consequence of assignements and traditional memory models. The reason seems to be that one has to access the whole history of exchanges in order to manage properly a conversational behavior (as confirmed in [27]) .

When attempting to give a synthetic view of Elephant 2000, McCarthy writes:

ξ (t+1) = update (i(t), ξ , t)
where:ξ is the **state vector representing the program**
      ξ(t+1) depends on the whole past, not simply on ξ(t), and:
i(t) = input world(t)
where: *world is the* **state vector representing the world external to the computer**
world (t+1) = worldf (output ξ (t), world, t)
      world(t+1) depends on the whole past, not simply on world(t)

Mc Carthy's paper is rich and dense, and we cannot have the ambition neither to comment every detail, nor to represent his current view. We simply propose in the following how McCarthy's Elephant 2000 programs may be re-interpreted as represented by one of our Agents, emerging from STROBE and Phi Calculus.

5   C+C: Steps towards a Specification

The name C+C comes from the intuition that a new language for Interaction may emerge from observing historical reflections from two sources: Cybernetics as Communication and Control in animals and machines [28] and Philosophy, with the Speech Act Theory pioneered by Austin and Searle and the large contributions, from Aristotle on, towards a definition of rationality in human behavior [29] .

McCarthy self adopts and limits correctly his inspiration from Language philosophers, when he writes: *"... Taking the design stance in the concrete way needed to allow programs to use speech acts tends to new views on the philosophical problems that speech acts pose ... we can incorporate whatever abstract analogs of these notions we find useful ... the philosophical investigations have resulted in ideas useful for our purposes ... ".* Therefore, it seems today healthy and well motivated for a computer scientist – not only for a researcher in Artificial Intelligence (see McCarthy, page 2: *"Elephant 2000 is at the borderline of AI, but the article emphasizes the Elephant usages that do not require AI")* to look at philosopher's work and import whatever may be useful for our purposes. Ironically, what seemed years ago a theoretical exercise far from any potential applicability, becomes more and more the necessary foundation for the most concrete expected evolution of societies worldwide: the availability and the use of the Web.

We envisage C+C to be our proposed language for programming the Web. C+C programs are like Elephant 2000 programs, but they are called Agents because they behave autonomously with respect to any external observer. All observers of C+C Agents are external, except the Agent that builds an Agent: this is an internal observer. Let us call Pagent – Proprietary Agent - the Agent that builds an Agent A. Pagent is the only Agent may verify logically A's behaviour, while he may never verify logically any other Agent's behavior, as in the opposite case we would again fall in the trap of a single memory or authority over the Agent's evolution; the one typical of distributed computing or blackboard expert systems.

C+C Agents, being programs, are each sequential and discrete. The clock that they have is proprietary, and scans operations occurring within the Agent; therefore operations may receive an explicit time tag, that is only recognized by the Agent. A C+C Agent – similarly to an Elephant program – operates in a loop that is active from its birth to its death. The Agent's operation is described by a single formula:

$$\xi(t_\xi +1) = \text{update (input\_from\_world } (t_\xi), \xi, t_\xi); \text{ and output\_to\_world } (t_\xi +1)$$
with: $\xi = \xi_{\text{agent name}}$; t_ξ is the time of operation of Agent ξ

update = function applied by each agent = worldf of Elephant.

There is no difference in representation between a program and the world: both are Agents and both behave asynchronously by exchanging messages.

world = set of distributed, concurrent Agents.

Each Agent may send messages also to Self, thus modelling a kind of "reminder". This feature may be useful, for instance, to be aware of commitments.

input_from_world (0) = start message for each Agent.

STROBE synthetic (functional) representation of Exchange n was as follows.

E_n: i_n		$-$	$((g_n\ i_n)eQn) =>$	o_n	M_nP
$i_{n+1} <= ((f_n\ o_n)ePn)$	$<$			o_n	M_nQ

At time **n** Agent **Q** (Right Hand Side) selects Act i_n from the mailbox, coming from Agent **P** (Left Hand Side), and reacts applying the function g_n in Environment eQn; the resulting Act o_n is sent to Agent **P** that at time $(n + 1)$ applies the function f_n in environment ePn yelding Act i_{n+1} that is sent to Q ...

From the description, one may think that time is a shared variable. The above described formulas may at most model synchronous mutual calls of procedures, possibly represented as synchronous objects. In the formula, there is also not any explicit representation of the input mailbox available to Agents, nor of the potentially multiple sending of messages as a result of the evaluation of a single message. The representation is poor; eventually it may model a two-agent conversation. As reported in [21], however, two-agent conversations may not account for "autonomy", as one may suppose that each Agent communicates synchronously with the partner: if the knowledge available to one Agent may be reduced to the one acquired from the other Agent we return to a closed-world assumption. The minimum for a truly autonomous behaviour of Agents is reached when three autonomous, asynchronous Agents communicate.

In order to depict in a yet simpler and clearer way what our Agent architecture is in C+C, let us consider the Actor's simplified architecture available in [30].

Actors consult the Mailbox at each cycle. Their scheduling algorithm may vary from language to language but it is fixed during the temporal evolution of the Actor's knowledge. They may generate new Actors, replace themselves, send messages to other actors.

From this model, we have produced the Agent's model by implementing a scheduling algorithm that is variable with the evolution of the Agent's behavior. In order to ensure the Agent's autonomy, it is necessary and sufficient to view Agents as Actors with a dynamic scheduling algorithm[31][25].

The difference between Actors and Agents consists of the fact that Agents do not have a fixed, externally defined scheduling algorithm. Thus, the scheduling algorithm of Agents may be represented as a function that selects a message out of the mailbox at the moment the Agent operates, using any information in the Environment that is useful for an autonomously convenient choice.

In terms of functional (Scheme) programming, an Agent applies a function Scheduler to the input mailbox Inbox in Environment Env at each loop; the message selected Msg is passed to the operational Object associated to the Agent, together with the Environment dedicated to the partner that has sent Msg. As Objects may be functionally modelled as a Dispatch function on Selectors of Messages, from the moment that the Agent becomes an Object, all properties of Objects are applicable.

For instance, Selectors may be more than one. In our case we may at least envisage two Selectors in Msg: one for the Ontology and one for the Method.

```
AgentLoop      (Scheduler_A Mailbox_A Env_A) ->
;;;  Phase 1: <selecting the Partner P>
                    (Dispatch_A Msg_P Env_AP ) ->
;;; Phase 2:<selecting Ontology O for the conversation with P>
                    (Dispatch_A Msg_PO Env_APO ) ->
;;; Phase 3:<selecting Method M for the conversation with P to check OntologyO>
                    (Method_M arg1 arg2 ... argn Env_APO) ->
;;; Phase 4:<applying Method M to solve a problem within Ontology O>
                    (send OutMessage(s))
;;; Phase 5:<sending output messages>   and
                    (goto AgentLoop); Env_A transformed into Env_A'
;;; Phase 6=Phase 1<looping>
```

Phase 1: <selecting the Partner P>
  The Agent operates selecting one of the messages (Speech Acts à la KQML or ACL [5]) in the Mailbox. Criteria are private: the selection function applied has full access to the Agent's Environment. Once the message has been selected, it identifies a unique Sender (Partner P). The Partner name and the dedicated Environment

Env_AP are passed to the Phase 2. If P us unknown, A starts a transaction dedicated to the goal to know the new Partner P (an example of laziness in Communication).

Phase 2: <selecting Ontology O for the conversation with P>
  Similarly, the explicit Ontology is selected in the Message. Clearly, this Phase 2 may include a selection of a Language for the Content of the Message, etc. in cascade. Any field in the Message - represented as a formalized Speech Act - may be known to the Agent or unknown. In the latter case, a transaction is initiated by A in order to have sufficient information for continuing to process the Message; the process suspended and later resumed in a co-routine or delegation like behavior. Transactions initiated by A as a result on insufficient information on P message's components are examples of mixed initiative dialogues, that encapsulate sub-exchanges within main exchanges.

Phase 3: <selecting Method M for the conversation with P to check Ontology O>
  The evaluation in this phase includes a verification of potential disagreements (paradoxes) between the expected behavior of the partner and the real behavior such as expressed in the message.

Phase 4: <applying Method M to solve a problem within Ontology O>
  This phase assumes the Agent to have reached the Content of the Message and to be willing to process it in the traditional Object Oriented way. Any information necessary was obtained previously, so that this phase may be modeled as a traditional procedure call, eventually accompanied by send operations. Parameters – as well as

Fields in the Message – may be not known by A, e.g. when an argument is a pointer to a Web Page – an URL -. In our model, arguments with unknown value at the Agent's side are admitted as the evaluation model for functional applications is a lazy one, i.e. values are evaluated when needed. When an argument's value is required, if it is not available in the Agent's Environment, it is required at the Partner's side by starting a specific transaction, embedded in the other one (an example of laziness in control).

Phase 5: <sending output messages>

Sending a Message out means depositing it in an Outbox, where an asynchronous handler cares for the physical transmission to receivers.

5. Discussion

This view of Agents accounts for several apparently separate problems and issues.

The computational nature of Agents. Agents are neither Objects nor Actors: they are "crazy" or "skilled" Actors according to the behaviour emerging from the message selection process. In itself, the process is highly non deterministic: during the time needed for dealing with the Agent's loop, other messages may reach the Mailbox, and there is no certainty to process all of them somehow. The Actor model is that of an Operating Systems, a server of clients, and its objective is to serve fairly the client's needs by delivering services. The Agent's model is the contrary: an Agent serves his own goals, deciding autonomously if and when to dedicate his time to any of the partners.

Agents as looping schedulers. As much as an Object behaviour is totally dependent on its dispatching algorithm, an Agent behaviour depends on its Scheduling algorithm. However, the dispatching algorithm of an Object is fixed, while the scheduling of an Agent may vary with time, intrinsically as an effect of modification in the Environment and extrinsically as an effect of the occurrence of new messages on the Mailbox. An Agent is a totally undetermined computational entity: we know what it is at the beginning, but we cannot foresee what it becomes as a result of interactions.

Ambiguity in Agent's behaviour. The scheduling algorithm is both similar and different from a non deterministic "amb" evaluator [32] that may be a neat model of non deterministic search such as the one realised in the Knowledge Systems literature. The similarity is that one and just one message is chosen at each loop. The difference is that even if the conversation engaged as a consequence of the message selected ends in a failure, selecting other messages does not ensure any "backtracking" as in search, be it with or without dependency or truth maintenance. The past is never forgotten: the effects of a dialogue cannot be undone [1,21]. Thus, assignments to variables must be realised by keeping the history of values, e.g. binding names to streams of values in Environments.

Lazy control and Lazy communication are realised in C+C by admitting non strictness of any component of messages. When some information is not known, a transaction is started aiming at winning the value corresponding to the expression denoting the information. The aphorism is: when in doubt, do not compute, ask (and wait: do something else ...). Someone will resume your suspended evaluation sometimes providing you with what you need in order to go on.

We have described briefly the necessity, not only the convenience, of laziness in Web computing in [7]). The arguments analyse Web Documents observing that tags may be considered explicit types and subtypes of instances of complex data types with a tree structure. From this observation, the link to a dynamically typed language is immediate, thus to a memory model such as our Environment, linking non-typed names with explicitly typed simple or compound data. Yet, functions (constructors, selectors, predicates, ...) proprietary of the ADT relative to Web Documents are not necessarily within the Document, nor at the site of the Agent that needs the document. In order to access and use Web documents, thus, we need not only to access the documents but also to find the ADT definitions that help us in interpreting the document. Notice that by definitions we do not simply mean the definition of the structure (e.g. the DTD in XML), but also any further information necessary to have a semantic model of the document valid for the user – not just for the producer -.

Messages (Speech Act – like) are as well instances of Abstract Data Types, that include a "content" subtype with the specified content of the message. We may distinguish elementary messages and compound messages, i.e. messages that include other messages. Finding out what messages are elementary and what are compound is the most difficult task. We have noticed that programming languages – such as Scheme – do include elementary "speech acts" (see [21]) as well as Excel and any interactive programming or system language, such as the UNIX shell. A deeper study [23] has re-classified KQML Speech Acts as consisting of variations of 3 basic classes: tell-like, query-like and answer-like. However, the "effects on the partner Agent" considered was at the utmost simple level: essentially reading from or writing to Memory. If the considered effects will be enhanced, as it is the case envisaged by Phi Calculus [11-16], then it is necessary to adopt a constructive view of complex messages – Speech Acts, that covers Agent communication phenomena such as those referenced by asserted modalities (can, know, have-to, want, may, hope-wish, believe, ...); negated modalities (not-believe etc.); extended performatives (see McCarthy's Elephant 2000 preliminary list) and time. We will not have a logic approach, however: we know of many logic approaches that brought to unmanageable languages and systems. Rather, we will use a truly conversational approach of joint construction of complex Acts from simpler ones; where simple and traditional principles of software engineering (such as those used in extensible languages) will be used.

Finally, Agents and Messages may be combined in modelling simple, but significant transactions. From the processes generated, more properties of the necessary and sufficient Acts will be discovered / constructed in an experimental cycle reflecting the theoretical framework of Phi Calculus: rationality, adequacy and learning in real situations such as those evaluated by real users.

6   Conclusions

The paper has reported over ongoing research of two groups that have joined their efforts for the ambitious task of offering a generic theoretical and experimental framework for developing interactive software, such as the one necessary for Distance Learning and Electronic Commerce. Focussing on the developments around a new Agent Language, called C+C, the paper has reported about and discussed extensively a foundational paper about a language proposal by J. McCarthy. Inspired by the paper, the previous work of the authors has been reviewed and new directions have been presented for the realisation of C+C.

The essence of the paper consists in specifying the components of C+C as consisting of the traditional Control elements – such as those in Objects -, the "new" Communication elements – such as Speech Acts in messages - and the Interactive supervision ones, such as the interrelation among Communication and Control; into a homogeneous architecture that has a support from a number of simple arguments.

We are convinced that it is not just the final result – the language C+C we wish to develop and use – but the constructive, interactive process that counts in achieving significant scientific results. Therefore, we adopt the role and behaviour that we attribute to our Agents and, having generated the first move towards potential partner Agents, in a Conference, we wait confidently their reactions, that will hopefully help us in better obtaining the envisaged results.

Acknowledgements

The work described in this paper was partially supported by the EU INCO-COPERNICUS project LeARning Foreign LAnguage Scientific Terminology (LARFLAST), by the EU IST projects Multilingual Knowledge-Based European Electronic Marketplace (MK-BEEM) and Support for Mediation And bRokering for Electronic Commerce (SMART-EC), and by the enterprise EURIWARE.

References

1.   McCarthy, J.: Elephant 2000: A Programming Language Based on Speech Acts. Stanford University, Stanford. http://www-formal.stanford.edu/jmc/elephant/elephant.html, appeared: 6 Nov 1998 written: 1989.
2.   Wegner, P.: Why interaction is more powerful than algorithms. Comm. ACM **40, 5** (1997) 80-91
3.   Jennings, N. R.: On Agent-Based Software Engineering. Artificial Intelligence **117, 2** (2000) 277-296
4.   W3C: Extensible Markup Language. http://www.w3.org/XML/ (2000)
5.   Labrou, Y., Finin, T., Peng, Y.: Agent Communication Languages: The Current Landscape. Intelligent Systems **14, 2** (1999) 45-52

6. Ferber, J., Gutknecht, O., Operational semantics of a Role-based Agent Architecture. In: Jennings, N.R., Lesperance, Y., (eds.) Intelligent Agents VI. Agent Theories, Architectures, and Languages, LNCS 1757, Springer Verlag (1999).

7. Franklin, S.,Graesser, A.: Is it an Agent, or just a Program?: A Taxonomy for Autonomous Agents. Presented at Third International Workshop on Agent Theories, Architectures and Languages (1996).

8. Cerri, S. A.: Dynamic typing and lazy evaluation as necessary requirements for Web languages. Presented at European Lisp User Group Meeting. Amsterdam (1999).

9. Cerri, S. A.,McIntyre, A.: Knowledge Communication Systems. Invited paper at 8ème Congres Reconnaissance des formes et Intelligence Artificielle, AFCET. Lyon Villeurbanne, France (1991).

10. Cerri, S. A.,Loia, V.: Knowledge Communication: motivation and foundations. Presented at ACM Workshop on Strategic Directions in Computing Research - Working group on Parallel and Distributed Computation. Cambridge, Mass. (1996).
    http://www-osl.cs.uiuc.edu/sdcr.html

11. Sallantin, J., Castro, E., Liquière, M.: Les rationalités des agents. In: K. Zreik (ed.): Human-Machine Learning, Proc. CAPS'98, Caen; Europia Productions (1998) 29-43

12. Castro, E., Sallantin, J., Koriche, F.: Abduction, induction with rational agents. In: Flach, P. (ed.): Workshop on Abduction and Induction in AI, ECAI'98: The 13th Biennal European Conference on Artificial Intelligence. Brighton (1998) 25-32

13. Castro, E., Gachelin, G., Sallantin, J.: M@int.   LIRMM: CNRS & Un. Montpellier II, Technical Report N. 9729 30132 (1998)

14. Nobrega, G., Castro, E., Malbosse, P., Sallantin, J. and Cerri, S.A.: A Framework for supervised conceptualizing. In: Benjamins, R., A., Gomez-Perez, A., Guarino, N. and Uschold, M. (eds) Workshop on Applications of Ontologies and Problem Solving Methods, ECAI 2000: The 14th Biennal European Conference on Artificial Intelligence. Berlin. (2000) In press.

15. Rodriguez, J. M.,Sallantin, J.: A system for document tele-negotiation (negotiation agents). Presented at COOP'98 3rd International Conference on the Design of Cooperative Systems. Cannes (1998).

16. Castro, E., Sallantin, J., Cerri, S. A.: Paradox and transaction. Presented at International Joint Conference IBERAMIA'2000 and SBIA'2000, Brasil (2000).

17. Garrod, S. C.,Doherty, G.: Conversation, co-ordination and convention: an empirical investigation of how groups establish linguistic conventions. Cognition (1994) 181-215

18. Fabiano, A. S.,Cerri, S. A.: Concurrent, asynchronous search for the availability of knowledge. Applied Artificial Intelligence Journal **10, 2** (1996) 145-161

19. Cerri, S. A.: Computational Mathetics Tool kit: architecture's for dialogues. In: Frasson, C., Gauthier, G., and Lesgold, A. (eds.): Intelligent Tutoring Systems. Lecture Notes in Computer Science , Vol. 1086. Springer-Verlag, Montréal (1996) 343-352

20. Cerri, S. A.: A simple language for generic dialogues: "Speech acts" for communication. In: Gengler, M., Queinnec, C. (eds.): Journées Francophones des Langages Applicatifs - JFLA97. INRIA, Dolomieu, Isère, France (1997) 145-168

21. Cerri, S. A.: Shifting the focus from control to communication: the STReams OBjects Environments model of communicating agents. In: Padget, J. A. (ed.): Collaboration between Human and Artificial Societies, Coordination and Agent-Based Distributed Computing. Lecture Notes in Artificial Intelligence , Vol. 1624. Springer-Verlag, Berlin Heidelberg New York (1999) 71-101

22. Cerri, S. A.,Loia, V.: Emerging Behavior in Fuzzy Evolutionary Agents. Studies in Fuzziness and Soft Computing. Physica-Verlag , Springer, Berlin Heidelberg New York (2000) In press.

23. Benuzzi, M.: A model of collaboration language for autonomous agents. . Dept. of Information Sciences, Univ. of Milano, Milano, Italy: Computer Science, (1997).

24. Dionisi, G.: AL: a language to describe agent-to-agent communication. . Dept. of Information Sciences, Univ. of Milano, Milano, Italy: Computer Science, (1998).

25. Maffioletti, S.: Intelligent agents: the scheduler of messages and the conversations. . Dept. of Information Sciences, Univ. of Milano, Milano, Italy: Computer Science, (1998).

26. Maraschi, D.: JASKEMAL: a language for communicating agents. . Dept. of Information Sciences, Univ. of Milano, Milano, Italy: Computer Science, (1999).

27. Porayaska-Pomsta, K., Mellish, C., Pain, H.: Aspects of speech act categorisation: towards generating teachers' language. Int. J. of AI in Education **11** (2000) In press.

28. Wiener, N.: Cybernetics, or control and communication in the animal and the machine. . John Wiley & Sons, New York (1948)

29. Searle, J.: Speech Acts . Cambridge University Press, Cambridge,UK (1970)

30. Kafura, D.,Briot, J. P.: Actors & Agents. IEEE Concurrency **6** (1998) 24-29

31. Guessoum, Z.,Briot, J.-P.: From Active Objects to Autonomous Agents. IEEE Concurrency **7, 3** (1999) 68-76

32. Abelson, H.,Sussman, G. J.: Structure and Interpretation of Computer Programs 2nd ed. MIT Press, Cambridge, Mass.: (1996)

Efficient Reasoning Using the Local Closed-World Assumption

Patrick Doherty[1*], Witold Łukaszewicz[2], and Andrzej Szałas[2]

[1] Department of Computer and Information Science, Linköping University
S-581 83 Linköping, Sweden,
patdo@ida.liu.se
[2] Institute of Informatics, Warsaw University
ul. Banacha 2, 02-097 Warsaw, Poland
{witlu,szalas}@mimuw.edu.pl

Abstract. We present a sound and complete, tractable inference method for reasoning with localized closed world assumptions (LCWA's) which can be used in applications where a reasoning or planning agent can not assume complete information about planning or reasoning states. This *Open World Assumption* is generally necessary in most realistic robotics applications. The inference procedure subsumes that described in Etzioni et al [9], and others. In addition, it provides a great deal more expressivity, permitting limited use of negation and disjunction in the representation of LCWA's, while still retaining tractability. The approach is based on the use of circumscription and quantifier elimination techniques and inference is viewed as querying a deductive database. Both the preprocessing of the database using circumscription and quantifier elimination, and the inference method itself, have polynomial time and space complexity.

1   Introduction

Traditionally, classical reasoning and planning techniques have been developed for environments in which the reasoning agent is assumed to have complete information about the world in which it is embedded and the only changes to the world are the effects which result from the agent's invocation of actions. Under this assumption, an efficient means of representing negative information about the world in each planning or reasoning state is to apply the *Closed World Assumption* (CWA) [1,16]. In this case, information about the world, absent in a state, is assumed to be false.

In many realistic applications, in particular robotics applications, the assumption of complete information is not feasible and the CWA can not be used. For example, an unmanned aerial vehicle flying over a region can not have a complete model of the region. New objects are continually sensed or encountered and

---

* The authors are supported in part by a basic research grant from the Wallenberg Foundation, Sweden.

S. A. Cerri and D. Dochev (Eds.): AIMSA 2000, LNAI 1904, pp. 49–58, 2000.

agents other than the UAV agent cause change in the region. In applications such as this, an *Open World Assumption* (OWA), where information not known by the agent is assumed to be unknown, is the ontologically right choice to make, but complicates both the representational and implementational aspects associated with inference mechanisms and the use of negative information.

The CWA and the OWA represent two extremes. Quite often, a reasoning agent has information which permits the application of the CWA *locally*. If the UAV agent has a camera sensor, the agent can assume complete information about objects in the focus of attention (FOA) of the camera; for example, the only cars in the FOA are those identified by the image processing module.

The research issue then, is to find maximally expressive, but tractable inference mechanisms for local closed world reasoning which can be integrated with deliberative components, such as planning algorithms, used in applications where the OWA applies. An additional issue is to be able to dynamically modify the degree of closed-worldness relative to the dynamics of the application at hand.

We approach the problem as follows. The starting point is the approach to LCWA described in [9], where the authors present a sound, but incomplete, tractable algorithm for LCWA intended for use in the XII Planner. Briefly, their approach works as follows: Assume an actual world w which can be represented by a complete logical theory. Since the reasoning agent only has incomplete information about that world, but that information is assumed correct, the agent's knowledge can be represented as a set of possible worlds S, where $w \in S$. For reasons of tractability, the approach approximates S by representing it as a set of ground literals, M, where negative information about w known to the agent is represented explicitly. M can be viewed as the agent's knowledge database. Localized closure information is represented in another database, $\mathcal{L}$, as a set of formulas restricted to be conjunctions of literals (not necessarily grounded). For example, $M = \{parent.dir(\text{ecai.tex}, /\text{ecai00}), size(\text{kr.tex}, 100)\}$, $\mathcal{L} = \{LCW(parent.dir(f, /\text{ecai00}))\}$. Although a reasoning agent could not infer that it knows about all the files in all directories and their sizes, it can infer that it knows about all the files in the directory ecai00. In [9], the authors describe an algorithm which encodes a sound, but incomplete inference relation, $M, \mathcal{L} \models_\varepsilon \alpha$, where given M and $\mathcal{L}$, they can determine whether a conjunction of positive ground literals, α, is inferable under partial closure of the theory. Since both $\mathcal{L}$ and α are restricted to be positive conjunctive formulas, the algorithm and its efficiency are based on the use of matching conjunctive queries against a conjunctive database. Note that due to the OWA, for a specific query α, the algorithm may return true, false, or unknown. In the following, we use QLCW to refer to the query language of which α would be an instance.

We substantially extend the approach of [9] by:

- providing a semantics for the case where LCW constraints in $\mathcal{L}$ and queries in QLCW are expressed by arbitrary first-order formulas. The semantics is based on the use of circumscription. The new semantics and the one given in [9] agree on the special case where conjunctions of positive literals are used in $\mathcal{L}$ and QLCW.

- isolating a more expressive language for LCW constraints in $\mathcal{L}$ which subsumes that used in [9], permits limited use of negation and disjunction, and still retains tractability.
- providing a sound **and** complete, tractable deduction method for the more expressive language. Observe that in [9] completeness is not guaranteed even in the case of a language with conjunctions of positive literals only.

Our approach to the problem is based on the use of circumscription to minimize formulas in $\mathcal{L}$ in the context of the theory $\mathcal{L} \wedge M$. Using quantifier elimination techniques, the original circumscribed theory can be reduced to a 1st-order or fixpoint formula. Viewing the reduced theory as a database query, inference relative to M can be viewed as a query to a database. Restricting the expressivity of $\mathcal{L}$ to what we call semi-Horn formulas, M to a conjunction of positive and negative ground literals, and queries in QLCW to semi-Horn formulas, we can show that both the theory reduction technique and querying technique remain tractable and safe. Tractability means that the method allows for efficient (PTIME) computations. Safety means that no inconsistencies are introduced by the method no matter what logical dependencies are used in $\mathcal{L}$.

Note that by first providing a general framework and semantics for structuring the problem in a classical setting and then isolating tractable combinations of fragments of the languages used in M, $\mathcal{L}$, and QLCW, we provide a methodology for generalization of the technique based on the use of results from the knowledge representation and deductive database communities.

2   Preliminaries

We deal with an ordinary first-order language with equality, L_1, over a fixed alphabet A without function constants. By L_2 we denote the second-order language based on an alphabet whose symbols are those of A, together with a denumerable set of n-ary predicate variables (for each $n \geq 0$). These will be denoted by the letters Φ and Ψ, possibly with subscripts and/or primes.

In the sequel, we shall use second-order circumscription. Our definition follows [13].

Definition 1. Let $\overline{P}$ be a tuple of distinct predicate constants, $\overline{S}$ be a tuple of predicate constants disjoint with $\overline{P}$, and let $T(\overline{P}, \overline{S})$ be a finite theory in a language L_1. The *second-order circumscription of $\overline{P}$ in $T(\overline{P}, \overline{S})$ with variable $\overline{S}$*, written $CIRC(T(\overline{P}, \overline{S}); \overline{P}; \overline{S})$, is the sentence (in the language L_2)

$$T(\overline{P}, \overline{S}) \wedge \forall \overline{\Phi} \overline{\Psi}[T(\overline{\Phi}, \overline{\Psi}) \wedge [\overline{\Phi} \leq \overline{P}] \supset [\overline{P} \leq \overline{\Phi}]],$$

where $\overline{\Phi}$ and $\overline{\Psi}$ are tuples of predicate variables similar to $\overline{P}$ and $\overline{S}$, respectively[1], and $\overline{\Phi} \leq \overline{P}$ (resp. $\overline{P} \leq \overline{\Phi}$) stands for $\bigwedge_{i=1}^{n}[\forall \overline{x}.\Phi_i(\overline{x}) \supset P_i(\overline{x})]$ (resp. $\bigwedge_{i=1}^{n}[\forall \overline{x}.P_i(\overline{x}) \supset \Phi_i(\overline{x})]$). □

---

[1] A tuple of predicate expressions $\overline{X}$ is said to be similar to a tuple of predicate constants $\overline{Y}$ iff $\overline{X} = (X_1, \ldots, X_n)$, $\overline{Y} = (Y_1, \ldots, Y_n)$ and, for all $1 \leq i \leq n$, X_i and Y_i are of the same arity.

In the following, we shall often write $CIRC(T; \overline{P}; \overline{S})$ instead of the formula $CIRC(T(\overline{P}, \overline{S}); \overline{P}; \overline{S})$.

Let us now quote the fixpoint theorem formulated and proved in [15] for second-order quantifier elimination.

Theorem 1. Let P be a predicate variable, and $\Psi'(P), \Psi(\neg P)$ be formulas without second-order quantification. Let $\Phi(P)$ be positive w.r.t. P, $\Psi(\neg P)$ be negative w.r.t. P and $\Psi'(P)$ be positive w.r.t. P, then

$$\exists P \forall \bar{y}[\Phi(P) \supset P(\bar{y})] \wedge [\Psi(\neg P)] \equiv \Psi[P \leftarrow \mu P(\bar{y}).\Phi(P)], \tag{1}$$

and

$$\exists P \forall \bar{y}[P(\bar{y}) \supset \Phi(P)] \wedge [\Psi'(P)] \equiv \Psi'[P \leftarrow \nu P(\bar{y}).\Phi(P)], \tag{2}$$

where the above substitutions exchange the variables bound by fixpoint operators by the corresponding actual variables of the substituted predicate. (1), ((2)) is used to minimize (maximize) P. □

The definition of semi-Horn formulas, for which Theorem 1 is applicable, has been introduced in [5]. In what follows we shall consider a restricted version of semi-Horn formulas, where the *recursive* part of the semi-Horn formula is restricted as to the use of universal quantifiers.

Definition 2. By a *semi-Horn formula (w.r.t. Q)* we understand a conjunction of formulas of the form

$$[\Phi(\bar{x}) \supset Q(\bar{x})] \wedge \Psi(\neg Q), \tag{3}$$

and

$$[Q(\bar{x}) \supset \Phi(\bar{x})] \wedge \Psi(Q), \tag{4}$$

where $\Phi(\bar{x})$ is any classical first-order formula positive w.r.t. Q and $\Psi(\neg Q)$ $(\Psi(Q))$ is any first-order formula negative (positive) w.r.t. Q. Formula $\Phi(\bar{x}) \supset Q(\bar{x})$ $(Q(\bar{x}) \supset \Phi(\bar{x}))$ is called the *recursive part* of (3) ((4)) and $\Psi(\neg Q)$ $(\Psi(Q))$ is called the *negative (positive) part* of (3) ((4)).

By a *semi-Horn formula* we understand a semi-Horn formula w.r.t. all predicate symbols occurring in the formula. □

3   Representing an Agent's Knowledge

Suppose W is a complete logical theory formalizing what is true in an actual world state w. Suppose also, that T is a finite first-order theory, i.e. a finite set of sentences from L_1, formalizing an agent's *knowledge* about w. Following [9], we say that an agent has *local closed-world information* w.r.t. a formula α and T iff

$$T \models \alpha\theta \quad \text{or} \quad T \models \neg\alpha\theta \quad \text{for each ground substitution } \theta.$$

It is assumed that any knowledge the agent infers from T is correct in the actual world w. Since T provides only incomplete information about w, not all facts about w are known to the agent. In other words, only some of the information is locally closed relative to T, other information is unknown.

Following [9], we approximate an agent's knowledge about T by a pair $M, \mathcal{L}$, where M is a finite set of positive or negative ground literals and $\mathcal{L}$ is a set of first-order formulas, representing local closed-world assumptions. We assume that if T formalizes the agent's knowledge about the world, then for each formula α

$$M \models \alpha \text{ implies } T \models \alpha.$$

Let $c_1, \ldots, c_n$ be all the constants from the alphabet under consideration. We write $DCA(M)$ to denote the *domain closure* axiom for a theory M. This is the formula

$$\forall x. \bigvee_{i=1}^{n} x = c_i.$$

We write $UNA(M)$ to denote the *unique name assumption* axiom for a theory M. This is the formula

$$\bigwedge_{1 \leq i < j \leq n} c_i \neq c_j.$$

We write $M, \mathcal{L} \models \alpha$ to denote that a formula α follows from a pair $M, \mathcal{L}$. This notion is defined as follows.

Definition 3. Let $M, \mathcal{L}$ be a finite set of ground literals and a set of formulas representing closed-world information, respectively. Suppose that $\mathcal{L}$ consists of formulas $\beta_1, \ldots, \beta_n$. Let $\overline{R} = R_1, \ldots, R_n$ be a set of new predicates symbols similar to $\beta_1, \ldots, \beta_n$.[2] By an *LCW-based extension of M*, denoted by M', we shall understand this to be the theory consisting of formulas of M, augmented by:

- $DCA(M)$ and $UNA(M)$
- the set of formulas $\forall \overline{x}.R_i(\overline{x}) \equiv \beta_i$ $(i = 1, \ldots n)$.   □

The following definition provides us with the semantics of *LCW* as understood in this paper.

Definition 4. Let $\overline{S}$ be the set of all predicate symbols occurring in $\beta_1, \ldots, \beta_n$. Then

$$M, \mathcal{L} \models \alpha \text{ iff } CIRC(M'; \overline{R}; \overline{S}) \models \alpha,$$

where $\overline{R} = (R_1, \ldots, R_n)$.   □

Note that definition 4 provides the general case and semantics for reasoning under the LCWA. The rest of the paper considers restrictions on M, $\mathcal{L}$ and QLCW which make reasoning under the LCWA tractable.

---

[2] A predicate symbol P is similar to a formula α iff the arity of P is equal to the number of free variables of α.

In what follows we divide M' into three parts:

- a *positive part*, denoted by M_+, consisting of positive literals of M; the positive part is intended to gather positive information directly included in the database M
- a *negative part*, denoted by M_-, consisting of negative literals of M; the negative part is intended to gather negative information directly included in the database M
- an *LCW part*, denoted by M_c, consisting of equivalences $\forall \overline{x}.R_i(\overline{x}) \equiv \beta_i$ $(i = 1, \ldots n)$ introduced in Definition 3.

Observe that M_+ is just an extensional database as understood in the field of deductive databases (see, e.g. [1,8]). Also M_- can be easily treated as a part of an extensional database. Now (deductive) queries are represented by M_c embedded in a tractable query language like fixpoint calculus or classical first-order logic (see e.g. [1]). Thus, whenever LCW is polynomially reducible to fixpoint or classical formulas, one has a tractable reasoning mechanism.

In what follows we often call $M_+ \cup M_-$ simply a database.

4   The Main Result

The following theorem provides us with a sufficient condition which guarantees that second-order quantifiers can be eliminated from $CIRC(M'; \overline{R}; \overline{S})$ using the fixpoint theorem (Theorem 1) and some syntactic transformations applied in the DLS algorithm [6].

The main result of this paper, formulated below, shows that the second-order formula resulting from circumscription can be reduced to a fixpoint formula. Thus the complexity of reasoning is polynomial in the size of M. This follows from the fact that the database part of M is not affected by the quantifier elimination process. Only LCW constraints can, in some cases, introduce additional complexity. However the size of the resulting formula is, in the worst case, not greater than $m + O(n^2)$, where n is the size of LCW constraints together with the query and m is the size of the database.

In the proof of the theorem we use second-order quantifier elimination (For surveys of approaches to second-order quantifier elimination consult [6,14]). Because of the space limitations, the proof is not included in the current paper, but is available from the authors.

Theorem 2. Let $CIRC(M'; \overline{R}; \overline{S})$ be defined as in Section 3. If M consists of literals and LCW constraints in $\mathcal{L}$ are defined by means of semi-Horn formulas, then the following conditions hold:

- second-order quantifiers can be eliminated from $CIRC(M'; \overline{R}; \overline{S})$;
- if the size of the database M is m and the size of M_c together with the query is n then, in the worst case, the resulting formula has size $m + O(n^2)$. Moreover M is not affected by the quantifier elimination process.

The second-order quantifier elimination technique applied in the proof of Theorem 2 is based on Theorem 1 and provides us also with definitions of the eliminated predicates. As in [8], this feature is crucial for the approach we present in this paper. More precisely (for details see e.g. [8]):

- in the case of formulas of the form (1), one gets an explicit definition of the least relation P satisfying the first-order part of (1); and
- in the case of formulas of the form (2), one gets an explicit definition of the greatest relation P satisfying the first-order part of (2).

Observe that Theorem 2 can still be generalized using techniques of [6,7,8,14].

Corollary 1. Consider a relational (or deductive) database in which the query language QLCW is the classical first-order logic or monotone fixpoint calculus[3]. If M consists of literals and the LCW constraints in $\mathcal{L}$ are defined by means of semi-Horn formulas, then:

- the time complexity of the quantifier elimination algorithm is polynomial in the size of the input query;
- the formula resulting from the quantifier elimination process is a monotone fixpoint formula, thus time and space data complexity of querying the database is polynomial in the size of the database;
- if all Φ's occurring in recursive parts of semi Horn formulas defined in definition 2 (i.e. in formulas of the form $\Phi(\bar{x}) \supset Q(\bar{x})$ and $Q(\bar{x}) \supset \Phi(\bar{x})$) do not contain Q's then the formula resulting from the quantifier elimination process is a classical first-order formula. Thus assuming that the query language is restricted to the classical first-order logic one obtains polynomial time data complexity and polylogarithmic space data complexity [1,12].

Proof. The first item easily follows from the results provided in [5,8] and from the proof of Theorem 2.

The second item just quotes results well-known from deductive databases (see e.g. [1,12]).

The last item follows from the fact that for such formulas the Ackermann Lemma [2] is applicable - see also [6].

5   The LCW Algorithm

Theorem 2 together with results in [8] provides us with a complete and tractable algorithm for deduction from a database M and LCW database $\mathcal{L}$, assuming that formulas in $\mathcal{L}$ and α are formulated as semi-Horn formulas and M consists of literals. An un-optimized abstract version of the algorithm is shown below:

---

[3] I.e. calculus in which fixpoint are defined on monotone formulas - see e.g. [1].

Function LCWQuery$(\alpha, M, \mathcal{L})$: 3-boolean
    $M_{\mathcal{L}} := M \cup Reduce(\mathcal{L})$
    if $RQuery(M_{\mathcal{L}}, \alpha) \neq \emptyset$ **then return** T
    else if $RQuery(M_{\mathcal{L}}, \neg\alpha) \neq \emptyset$ **then return** F
    else return U;
end.

$Reduce()$ is the quantifier elimination technique described in [8] extended with the result from Theorem 2. It is assumed that $Reduce()$ provides us with definitions of the predicates eliminated from $CIRC(M'; \bar{R}, \bar{S})$.

$RQuery()$ is based on [12] and returns a set of tuples satisfying α. However, CWA is not assumed by $RQuery()$.

6 Related Work

In this section, we show that our approach subsumes the approaches proposed in [9,3] and [10].

In [9] it is assumed that the LCW database, $\mathcal{L}$, consists of formulas that are conjunctions of atoms. We write $M, \mathcal{L} \models_{\mathcal{E}} \alpha$ to denote that a formula α follows from a pair $M, \mathcal{L}$ in Etzioni *et al.* [9] approach. The following theorem holds.

Theorem 3. For all M and $\mathcal{L}$

$$M, \mathcal{L} \models_{\mathcal{E}} \alpha \text{ implies } \mathcal{M}, \mathcal{L} \models \alpha. \qquad \square$$

Similarly, the ψ-forms considered in [3] are simply expressible in the language we deal with. Moreover, the semantics of both approaches is equivalent when restricted to the ψ-forms only.

In fact, the approach presented in [3] is subsumed by the one provided in [10]. In [10] Horn clauses, with additional built-in predicates, are used to express LCW constraints. These are easily expressible in our approach as we deal with semi-Horn formulas that are substantially more expressive than Horn clauses.

Note that the subsumption results are related to reasoning in a static state under the LCWA and not to sequences of dynamic states where updating the LCWA database is an additional issue considered in both [9] and [3].

7 Example

Example 1. The following example demonstrates the versatility of the approach by representing the UAV example in section 1. There are four cars with different signatures based on color. The UAV's focus of attention (FOA) is region r3. In $\mathcal{L}$, we assume complete information about the $ContainedIn()$ relation by minimizing it (6), and the $In()$ relation by maximizing it (5). (7) encodes the following LCWA by maximizing the relation $See()$:

After sensing region r3 *with a camera, we want to assume that we have seen **all** moving vehicles in the FOA (*r3*) except for those with signature* gray.

In querying the database using the LCWQuery algorithm, we can infer that $See(c1, r3)$ holds, but it is unknown whether $See(c2, r3)$, due to its signature; unknown whether $See(c3, r3)$, because it is unknown whether it is moving; and unknown whether $See(c4, r3)$ because it is not in the FOA. Note that the latter queries return unknown and not false due to the incompleteness of the database. In fact, other sensors may contribute to whether the unknown vehicles are seen.

$$\mathcal{L} = \{In(x, r') \supset \neg(In(x, r) \wedge ContainedIn(r, r')), \tag{5}$$
$$ContainedIn(r, r'), \tag{6}$$
$$See(x, r3) \supset \neg(InFOA(r3) \wedge In(x, r3) \wedge Sig(x, s) \wedge$$
$$s \neq \mathsf{gray} \wedge Moving(x))\} \tag{7}$$

$$M = \{In(c_1, r_1), In(c_2, r_2), In(c_3, r_1), In(c_4, r_4),$$
$$Moving(c_1), Moving(c_2), Moving(c_4),$$
$$sig(c_1, \mathsf{blue}), sig(c_2, \mathsf{gray}), sig(c_3, \mathsf{green}), sig(c_4, \mathsf{yellow}),$$
$$ContainedIn(r1, r3), ContainedIn(r2, r3), InFOA(r3)\}$$

In order to understand why the constraints for $In()$ and $See()$ in $\mathcal{L}$ are represented in the manner above, it is important to observe that the relations we want to *minimize* or *maximize* are in fact relations that are varied in the circumscriptive definition used for LCWA. Consequently, the minimization and maximization are achieved indirectly.

Another interesting observation is that the query generated by the quantifier elimination procedure results in a fixpoint formula due to the recursive definition of $In()$.

8   Conclusions

We have extended and subsumed the LCW querying techniques described in [9,3,4], and [10] and presented a tractable algorithm. The technique is based on the use of circumscription and results from the deductive database community and is consequently amenable to generalization. We have demonstrated the versatility of the approach by encoding a relatively complex UAV sensing scenario. We have not yet dealt with the LCW update problem associated with the query mechanism's integration with other planning and state sequential reasoning techniques considered in the other approaches, but are currently pursuing the problem.

References

1. S. Abiteboul, R. Hull, V. Vianu. *Foundations of Databases*, Addison-Wesley Pub. Co., 1996. 49, 54, 55

2. W. Ackermann. *Untersuchungen über das Eliminationsproblem der mathematischen Logik,* Mathematische Annalen, 110, 390-413, 1935. 55

3. T. Babaian, J. G. Schmolze. *PSIPLAN: Planning with ψ-forms over Partially Closed Worlds,* Technical Report. 56, 57

4. T. Babaian, J: G. Schmolze. *PSIPLAN: Open World Planning with ψ-forms,* Proceedings of the 5th Int'l Conference on Artificial Intelligence and Planning (AIPS 2000), 2000. 57

5. P. Doherty, W. Łukaszewicz, A. Szałas. *A Reduction Result for Circumscribed Semi-Horn Formulas,* Fundamenta Informaticae, 28, 3-4, 261-271, 1996. 52, 55

6. P. Doherty, W. Łukaszewicz, A. Szałas. *Computing Circumscription Revisited. A Reduction Algorithm.,* Journal of Automated Reasoning, 18, 3, 297-336, 1997. 54, 55

7. P. Doherty, W. Łukaszewicz, A. Szałas. *General Domain Circumscription and its Effective Reductions,* Fundamenta Informaticae, 36, 1, 23-55, 1998. 55

8. P. Doherty, W. Łukaszewicz, A. Szałas. *Declarative PTIME Queries for Relational Databases using Quantifier Elimination,* Journal of Logic and Computation, 9, 5, 739-761, 1999. 54, 55, 56

9. O. Etzioni, K. Golden, D. S. Weld. *Sound and Efficient Closed-World Reasoning for Planning.* Artificial Intelligence, 89, 113-148, 1997. 49, 50, 51, 52, 53, 56, 57

10. M. Friedman, D. Weld. *Efficiently Executing Information Gathering Plans,* IJCAI-97. 56, 57

11. J. Gustafsson. *An Implementation and Optimization of an Algorithm for Reducing Formulae in Second-Order Logic,* Technical Report LiTH-Mat-Ex-96-04, Linköping University, 1996.

12. N. Immerman. *Relational Queries Computable in Polynomial Time,* Information and Control, **68**, 86-104, 1986. 55, 56

13. W. Łukaszewicz. (1990) *Non-Monotonic Reasoning - Formalization of Commonsense Reasoning,* Ellis Horwood Series in Artificial Intelligence. Ellis Horwood, 1990. 51

14. A. Nonnengart, H. J. Ohlbach, A. Szałas. *Elimination of Predicate Quantifiers,* In: *Logic, Language and Reasoning. Essays in Honor of Dov Gabbay, Part I,* H. J. Ohlbach and U. Reyle (eds.), Kluwer, 159-181, 1999. 54, 55

15. A. Nonnengart, A. Szałas. *A Fixpoint Approach to Second-Order Quantifier Elimination with Applications to Correspondence Theory,* In: *Logic at Work. Essays Dedicated to the Memory of Helena Rasiowa,* E. Orlowska (ed.), Physica Verlag, 89-108, 1998. 52

16. R. Reiter. *On Closed World Databases,* in: *Logic and Databases,* H. Gallaire and J. Minker (eds.), Plenum Press, New York, 55-76, 1978. 49

Least Generalization under Relative Implication

Svetla Boytcheva

Department of Information Technologies, Faculty of Mathematics and Informatics,
Sofia University "St. Kliment Ohridski",
5 J. Bauchier Blvd., 1164 Sofia, Bulgaria,
svetla@fmi.uni-sofia.bg

Abstract. The main operators in Inductive Logic Programming (ILP) are specialization and generalization. In ILP, the three most important generality orders are subsumption, implication and implication relative to background knowledge. The present paper discusses the existence of least generalization under implication relative to background knowledge. It has been shown that the least generalization under relative implication does not exists in the general case, but, as argued in this paper, it exists if the sets to be generalized and the background knowledge satisfy some special conditions.

1   Introduction

Inductive Logic Programming (ILP) is a subfield of Logic Programming and Machine Learning that investigates the problem of inducing clausal theories from given sets of positive and negative examples. An inductively inferred theory must imply all of the positive examples and none of the negative examples. The paper is organized as follows. In section 2 some preliminary definitions of the concepts used in the further discussion will be given. In Section 3 we will discuss existence of least generalization under relative implication and it will be shown that it does not exist in the general case, but exists if the sets to be generalized and the background knowledge (BK) are of some special kind. The most interesting and useful case is to find least generalization under relative implication(LGRI) (which is a set of definite program clauses) for the BK and sets of positive and negative examples that are definite program clauses. In section 3 it will be shown that in this case, after imposing some additional restrictions to the given sets, LGRI exists.

The LGRI exists for many other more particular cases of the given sets (for details see [5,6]). However in most of them the background knowledge is a set of ground clauses or literals. Even the subsumption is weaker than implication, LGRS not exists in the general case both for the clausal language and for a Horn language. LGRS exists only for background knowledge sets of ground atoms.

2   Preliminaries

The definitions of the concepts used in the further discussion are given in this section.

S. A. Cerri and D. Dochev (Eds.): AIMSA 2000, LNAI 1904, pp. 59–68, 2000.

Definition 1: Let Σ be a set of formulas and ϕ a formula. Then ϕ is said to be a *logical consequence* of Σ (written as $\Sigma \models \phi$), if every model of Σ is a model of ϕ. If $\Sigma \models \phi$, we also sometimes say that Σ *logically implies* (or just *implies*) ϕ. If $\Sigma = \{\psi\}$, this can be written as $\psi \models \psi$.

Definition 2: Let Σ and Γ be sets of formulas. Γ is said to be a *logical concequence* of Σ(written as $\Sigma \models \Gamma$), if $\Sigma \models \phi$, for every formula $\phi \in \Gamma$. We also sometimes say that Σ *(logically) implies* Γ.

Definition 3: Let Γ be a set and R be a binary relation on Γ.

1. R is *refflexive* on Γ if xRx for every $x \in \Gamma$.
2. R is *transitive* on Γ if for every $x, y, z \in \Gamma$, xRy and yRz impies xRz.
3. R is *symmetric* on Γ if for every $x, y \in \Gamma$, xRy impies xRy.
4. R is *anti-symmetric* on Γ if for every $x, y \in \Gamma$, xRy and xRy, implies $x = y$.

If R is both reflexive and transitive on Γ we say R is a *quasi-order* on Γ. If R is both transitive and anty-symmetric on Γ we say R is a *partial order* on Γ. If R is reflexive, transitive and symmetric on Γ we say R is a *equivalence relation*.

Definition 4: Let Γ be a set of clauses, $\geq$ be a quasi-order on Γ, $S \subseteq \Gamma$ be a finite set of clauses and $C \in \Gamma$. If $C \geq D$ for every $D \in S$, then we say that C is a *generalization* of S under $\geq$. Such a C is called a *least generalization (LG)* of S under $\geq$ in Γ if we have $C' \geq C$ for every generalization $C' \in \Gamma$ of S under $\geq$.

Dually, C is a *specialization* of S under $\geq$, if $D \geq C$ for every $D \in S$. Such a C is called a *greatest specialization (GS)* of S under $\geq$ in Γ if we have $C \geq C'$ for every specialization $C \in \Gamma$ of S under $\geq$.

Theorem 1 (Deduction Theorem): Let Σ be a set of formulas and ϕ and ψ be formulas. Then $\Sigma \cup \{\psi\} \models \phi$ iff $\Sigma \models (\psi \rightarrow \phi)$.

Preposition 1: Let Σ be a set of formulas and *phi* be a formula. Then $\Sigma \models \phi$ iff $\Sigma \cup \{\neg\phi\}$ is unsatisfiable.

Definition 5: Let B be background knowledge (set of clauses) and C and D be clauses. We will say that C *logically implies* D *relative to* B if $\{C\} \cup B \models D$ and we denote as $C \models_B D$.

Definition 6 (Concept learning problem): Given background knowledge B and given sets of positive and negative examples P and N, the induction task of a concept learning problem is to find a concept description in the form of a logic program T that satisfies the following conditions:

1. $T \cup B \models A$ for all $A \in P$ (posterior sufficiency)
2. $T \cup B\neg \models A$ for all $A \in N$ (posterior satisfiability)
3. $B\neg \models A$ for all $A \in N$ (prior satisfiability)
4. $B\neg \models A$ for all $A \in P$ (prior necessity)

Every such program T is called a *target program*.

Definition 7: Let H and B be sets of clauses and D be a clause. H is a *least generalization of D under relative implication(LGRI) to background knowledge B*, if $H \models_B D$ and for each set of clauses C, such that $C \models_B D$ is valid $C \models_B H$.

Definition 8: Let C and D be a clauses and Σ be a set of clauses. We say that C *subsumes* D, denote $C \geq D$ if there exists a substitution θ such that $C\theta \subseteq D$.

Definition 9: Let L be a first-order language. The *Herbrand universe U_L* for L is the set of all ground terms, which can be formed out of the constants and function symbols appearing in L. In case L does not contain any constants, we add one arbitrary constant to the alphabet to be able to form ground terms.

Definition 10: Let L be a first-order language. The *Herbrand base B_L* for L is the set of all ground atoms, which can be formed out of the predicate symbols in L and the terms in the Herbrand universe U_L.

Definition 11: Let L be a first-order language. The *Herbrand pre–interpretation* for L is the pre-interpretation J consisting of the following:

1. The domain of the pre-interpretation is the Herbrand universe U_L.
2. Constants in L are assigned to themselves in U_L. $J(a) = a$, a-constant
3. Each n-arity function symbol f in L is assigned the mapping J_f from U_L^n to U_L, defined by $J_f(t1, \ldots, tn) = f(t1, \ldots, tn)$.

Definition 12: Let L be a first-order language and J a Herbrand pre-interpretation. Any interpretation I, such that $J \subseteq I$ is called a *Herbrand interpretation*.

Definition 13: Let L be a first-order language, Σ a set of formulas of L, and I a Herbrand interpretation of L. If I is a model of Σ, it is called a *Herbrand model* of Σ.

Definition 14: Clause C *subsumes* (or is more general than) clause D with respect to logic program P if for any Herbrand interpretation I (for the language of at least P, C, D) such that P is true in I, and for any atom A, C covers A in I whenever D covers A. This is denoted $C \geq_P D$. C is referred to as a *generalization* of D, and D as a *specialization* of C.

All other concepts used above have the standard definitions. For more details see [1,2,3,5,6].

3   Existence of Least Generalization under Relative Implication

In this section we will discuss the existence of least generalization under relative implication.

For general clauses, the LGRI-question has a negative answer. We will sketch the counter example given in [5,6].

3.1   Example for Non-existence of LGRI in the General Case

Example 1: Even if S and the background knowledge Σ are both finite sets of function-free clauses, a LGRI of S relative to Σ does not necessarily exist. Let $D_1 = P(a)$, $D_2 = P(b)$, $S = \{D_1, D_2\}$ and $\Sigma = \{(P(a) \vee \neg Q(x)), (P(b) \vee \neg Q(x))\}$. We will show that S has no LGRI relative to Σ.

Suppose C is a LGRI of S relative to Σ. Note that if C contains the literal $P(a)$, then the Herbrand interpretation that makes P(a) true and which makes all other ground literals false would be a model of $\Sigma \cup \{C\}$ but not of D_2, so we have $C \not\models_\Sigma D_2$. Similarly if C contains $P(b)$ then $C \not\models_\Sigma D_1$. Hence C cannot contain $P(a)$ or $P(b)$.

Now let d be a constant not appearing in C. Let $D = P(x) \vee Q(d)$. Then $D \models_\Sigma S$. By the definition of the LGRI, we should have $D \models_\Sigma C$. Then by Subsumption Theorem [5], there must be a derivation from $\Sigma \cup \{D\}$ of a clause E, which subsumes C. The set of all clauses which can be derived (in 0 or more resolution-steps) from $\Sigma \cup \{D\}$ is $\Sigma \cup \{D\} \cup \{(P(a) \vee P(x)), (P(b) \vee P(x))\}$ but none of these clauses subsumes C, because C does not contain the constant d or the literals $P(a)$ and $P(b)$. Hence $D \not\models_\Sigma C$ contradicts the assumption that C is a LGRI of S relative to Σ.

Thus, in general LGRI of S relative to Σ need not exist.

3.2   Analyses of Some Properties of the Given Sets

Where is the weak point? Let's look again on the background knowledge set $\Sigma = \{(P(a) \vee \neg Q(x)), (P(b) \vee \neg Q(x))\}$. We can present this set in the following equivalent form $\Sigma = \{(Q(x) \to P(a)), (Q(x) \to P(b))\}$. The BK set Σ consists of Horn clauses and we can represent it as the program:

```
p(a):-q(X).
p(b):-q(X).
```

We can see that two different ground instances ($P(a)$ and $P(b)$) of the predicate $P(x)$ can be inferred from an arbitrary grounding of $Q(x)$ inferences. One of the possible generalizations of the given set relative to the BK is:

```
p(Y):-q(X).
```

But there is no dependency between the variables X and Y, and this is not a useful generalization, because it is not generative. Thus, some restrictions on the BK and the set to be generalized must be made to ensure the existence of a LGRI. Some examples of cases when a LGRI does exist will be given and after analysing them we will formulate the requirements for the BK and the initial set. Let the BK $\Sigma = \{C_1, C_2, \ldots, C_m\}$ be a finite set of clauses and $S = \{D_1, D_2, \ldots, D_n\}$ be a finite set of clauses. Additionally we suppose that:

- a substitution θ, such that $C_{ibody}\theta = C_{jbody}$, for $i \neq j$ does not exist
- a predicate A such that $A' \in C_{ihead}$ and $A'' \in C_{jhead}$, where A' and A'' are ground instances of A, does not exist.

Example 2: Consider the following set of positive examples:

```
C1 = food(X):-tasty(X),strawberry(X).
C2 = food(X):-tasty(X), not_poisonous(X), mushroom(X).
```

The most obvious way to generalize them is to take their least generalization under implication, which is the rather general and not very useful clause:

```
D = food(X):-tasty(X).
```

Suppose we have the following definite program $\Sigma = \{B_1, B_2, B_3\}$, expressing background knowledge:

```
B1 = plant(X):-mushroom(X).
B2 = plant(X):-strawberry(X).
B3 = not_poisonous(X):-strawberry(X).
```

Taking Σ into account, we may also find the more informative generalization clause:

```
D' = food(X):- tasty(X), not_poisonous(X), plant(X).
```

D' together with Σ implies both examples, but without the BK our clause D' does not imply the examples. For instance, not everything that has delicious taste is eatable, some things can be poisonous or harmful for people.

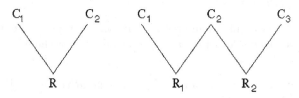

Fig. 1. The main view of the V-operator and the W-operator

In their article [7], Muggleton and Buntine described two operators based on inverting resolution steps: the V- and the W-operator (fig.1).

Given C_1 and R, the V-operator finds C_2 such that R is an instance of a resolvent of C_1 and C_2. Thus the V-operator generalizes $\{C_1, R\}$ to $\{C_1, C_2\}$. The W-operator combines two V-operators, and generalizes $\{R_1, R_2\}$ to $\{C_1, C_2, C_3\}$, such that R_1 is an instance of a resolvent of C_1 and C_2, and R_2 is an instance of a resolvent of C_3 and C_2. In addition the W-operator is able to invent new predicates.

Going back to the example described above it is easy to see, that D' is a result of consecutively applying V- (see Fig.3) and W-operators(see Fig.2) under C_1, C_2 and clauses of Σ.

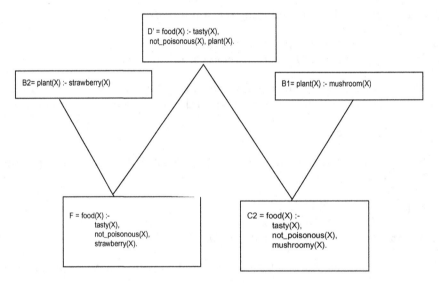

Fig. 2. The W-operator applyed on C_2, B_1, B_2 and F

Let D is the result of the W-operator applyed on C_2, B_1, B_2 and F. D is the LGRI of $\{C_1, C_2\}$ under $\{B_1, B_2, B_3\}$.

Let F_1 is the result of the V-operator applied on C_1 and B_3.

3.3   More Definitions

These two operators require some restrictions on the type of the given clauses. The following definitions will help us to describe some of them.

Definition 15: Let C be a clause. C is a *generative clause* if all variables in C_{head} are contained in C_{body}.

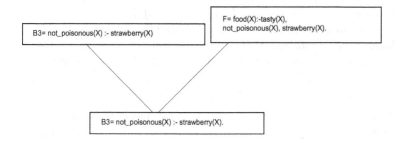

Fig. 3. The V-operator applied on C_1 and B_3

Definition 16: Let C be a clause and Σ be a set of clauses. Let C contain n different variables. C is a *determined clause* with respect to Σ if after binding $n-1$ variables of C with terms of Σ for the remining variable of C there exists a unique substitution that binds this variable with a term contained in Σ.

Definition 17: Let $\Sigma = \{C_1, C_2, \ldots, C_m\}$ and $S = \{D_1, D_2, \ldots, D_n\}$ be finite sets of clauses. S has an *absolute model* under Σ if for each $D_i \in S$ and for each literal $L \in D_i body$ there exists a clause $E = \{some\ C_j \in \Sigma\ or\ some\ D_j \in S\}$, and a substitution σ such that $L\sigma \in E$.

For a clause C_2 to exist, the V-operator requires C_1 and R to be generative clauses.

For clauses C_1, C_2 and C_3 to exist, the W-operator requires R_1, R_2 to be generative clauses. The found clause C_3 is generative and determined with respect to the set $\{R_1, R_2, C_1, C_2\}$.

The clauses R_1, R_2 have one and the same head, hence the clause C_3 will have the same head and the clause C_2 will be a generalization of the set of clauses $\{R_1, R_2, C_1, C_3\}$.

Suppose that R_1, R_2 are members of the given set of clauses, that we would like to generalize and C_1 and C_3 are clauses from the background knowledge. We can consider C_2 as a generalization under implication of R_1, R_2 relative to background knowledge set $\{C_1, C_3\}$.

The clause C_2 is a LGRI of R_1, R_2 because it is generated by one resolution step.

If the set that will be generalized has an absolute model under background knowledge then we can easily combine clauses from the given set and the BK in V- and W-operators.

The previous discussion enables the formulation of the following theorem.

3.4   Theorem of Existence of LGRI in Limited Case

Theorem 2: *Let $\Sigma = \{C_1, C_2, \ldots, C_m\}$ be a finite set of function-free definite program clauses and $S = \{D_1, D_2, \ldots, D_n\}$ be a set of function-free definite program clauses and all D_i have the same predicate symbol in their heads and at least one of them is non-tautologous. If S has an absolute model under Σ and all the clauses of S are generative and $\Sigma \not\models S$, then a LGRI of S relative to Σ exists.*

Proof: Let $\Sigma = \{C_1, C_2, \ldots, C_m\}$ be a finite set of function-free definite program clauses and $S = \{D_1, D_2, \ldots, D_n\}$ be a set of function-free definite program clauses and all D_i have the same predicate symbol in their heads and at least one of them is non-tautologous. The LGRI T of S relative to Σ exists if for every $C_i, C_j \in \Sigma$ there does not exist a substitution θ such that $C_{ibody}\theta = C_{jbody}$, and there does not exist a predicate A such that $A' \in C_{ihead}$ and $A'' \in C_{jhead}$, where A' and A'' are ground instances of A and for every $D_i \in S$ and for every literal $L \in D_i$ there exists clause $E = \{some\ C_j \in \Sigma\ or\ some\ D_j \in S\}$ and a substitution σ such that $L\sigma \in E$.

Then $T \not\models_\Sigma D_i$ iff $\{T\} \cup \Sigma \models D_i$ iff $T \models D_i \cup \neg\Sigma$. It remains to be shown that $D_i \cup \neg\Sigma$ is a set of function-free clauses and at least one of them is non-tautologous. Then by the theorem for existence of the least generalization under implication (LGI) [5,6], it will follow that a generalization H exists. The clauses of the set $D_i \cup \neg\Sigma$ are function-free, as required in the condition of the theorem. Since each $D_j \in S$ has the same predicate in its head, each clause in $T = \{(D_1 \cup \neg\Sigma), (D_2 \cup \neg\Sigma), (D_n \cup \neg\Sigma)\}$ will contain the same predicate in its head.

Because of the conditions of the theorem, each of the elements of T is a definite program clause.

It remains to show that $T = \{(D_1 \cup \neg\Sigma), (D_2 \cup \neg\Sigma), (D_n \cup \neg\Sigma)\}$ contains at least one non-tautologous clause. Suppose that all clauses in T are tautologous. From the definition of tautologous clause we conclude that every interpretation is a model of the clauses in T, in other words $\models D_i \cup \neg\Sigma$, hence $\Sigma \models D_i$ for each $D_i \in S$, hence $\Sigma \models S$, but this is a contradiction with the theorem conditions.

So, T is a set of definite program clauses and at least one of them is non-tautologous. From the theorem for existence of LGI (see [5,6]), we obtain that there exists a LGI H of T and H will be a LGRI of S relative to Σ.

Why do we need the sets' restrictions in the theorem 2? Are they too strong or not?

Most of the restrictions are necessary, because of the V- and W-operators requirements for the existence of the generalization clause and its computability.

The restriction $\Sigma \not\models S$ is imposed by the definition of the concept learning problem (prior necessity).

The restriction of the set S to contain one and the same predicate symbol in their heads is imposed by the necessity for the obtained LGRI of S under BK to be a program, that gives the definition of the concept, coded by this predicate symbol.

The other restrictions come from the analysis of the contradiction example mentioned above and from the requirement for the background knowledge to be consistent.

3.5 Computability of LGRI

This LGRI is computable because, it is a kind of LGI, which is computable. There are exists algorithm for construction of LGI of given sets. This algorithm is not very efficient. A more efficient algorithn may exist but since implication is harder than subsumption and the computation of an LGS is already quite expensive we should not put our hopes too hight. Nevertheless the existence of the LGI-algorithm does establishe the theoretical point that the LGI of any finite set of clauses containing at least one non-tautologous function-free clause is effectively computable.

4   Conclusion

The presented case of existence of a least generalization under relative implication helps us to search for generalizations of the concepts presented by most natural and often used types of sets and background knowledge. In the concept learning problem, usually examples are presented as ground literals and/or definite program clauses, and the background knowledge is a program. It is reasonable to expect that the LGRI of these sets will be a program too.

The contribution of this paper is the discovery of a more general (than those described in the literature) case of existence of least generalization under relative implication. This result can be used for several applications in the field of Machine learning, such as automated generation of concept definitions, improvement of predicate definitions and other kinds of concept generalization.

In the further work a simpler algorithm for finding the least generalization under relative implication will be presented concerning the described cases.

Another line of research is to find other cases of existence of LGRI.

Acknowledgements

I would like to thank Zdravko Markov and Ani Nenkova for their comments, which helped to improve this paper.

References

1. W. Buntine, Generalized Subsumption and Its Applications to Induction and Redundancy, Artificial Intelligence, 36(2),149-176, (1988). 62

2. P. van der Laag, An anlyses of refienment operators in inductive logic programming, Ph.D thesis, Tinberg Institute Research Series, Rotherdam, (1995). 62
3. J. W. Lloyd, Foundations of Logic Programming, Springer-Verlag Berlin Heidelberg, (1984). 62
4. Z. Markov, Machine Learning, Softex, (1996) (in Bulgarian).
5. S.-H. Nienhuys-Cheng and R. de Wolf, Foundations of Inductive Logic Programming, Springer-Verlag,Berlin Heidelberg, (1997). 59, 62, 66
6. S.-H. Nienhuys-Cheng and R. de Wolf, Least generalizations and greatest specializations of sets of clauses, Journal of Artificial Intelligence, 4:341-363, (1996). 59, 62, 66
7. S. Muggleton and W. Buntine, Machine invention of first-order predicates by inverting resolution. In J.Laird editior, Proceedings of the 5th International Conference on Machine learning (ICML-88),pages 339-352, Morgan Kaufman, San Mateo, CA, (1988). 64

Theorem Proving for Constructive λ-Calculus

Allan Ramsay

Dept of Language Engineering, UMIST
PO Box 88, Manchester M60 1QD, UK
Allan.Ramsay@umist.ac.uk
http://www.ccl.umist.ac.uk/staff/allan

Abstract. This paper presents a theorem prover for a combination of constructive first-order logic and the λ-calculus. The paper presents the basic theorem prover, which is an extension of [6]'s model generation theorem prover for first-order logic, and considers issues relating to the compile-time optimisations that are often used with first-order theorem provers.

1 A Constructive Intensional Logic

For various reasons, the idea of a language which allows you to construct abstractions and apply them to terms, as in the λ-calculus, and to combine these operations with the truth functional connectives of predicate logic, is extremely tempting. It is well known, however, that simply adding the λ-calculus and predicate logic together opens the way to the paradoxes of negative self-reference – the Liar, Russell's set, and so on.

The classical way out of this is to place restrictions on what can be said [11,8,3]. [9] approaches the matter by allowing you to *say* whatever you want, but then placing constraints on what can be proved. The current paper follows this general approach, but uses entirely different constraints.

Turner takes a classical treatment of first-order logic and adds λ-abstraction and β-reduction to it (or at any rate, operations which look extremely like λ-abstraction and β-reduction). In order to avoid the paradoxes, however, he constrains the circumstances under which you are allowed to perform λ-abstraction. The constraints he chooses are enough to make the underlying logic consistent (in other words, to avoid the paradoxes), and makes the paradoxes UNSTABLE [2]. The current paper takes a constructive treatment of first-order logic, allows unrestricted use of both λ-abstraction and β-reduction, but avoids the paradoxes by placing constraints on the assumptions that can be used in a well-founded proof.

The logic which we will use, which we will call $\Lambda(C)$ for constructive λ-calculus, extends first-order logic as follows:

$\Lambda(C)$-1 If A is a formula of first-order logic then it is a formula of $\Lambda(C)$, and if t is a term of first-order logic then it is a term of $\Lambda(C)$.

S. A. Cerri and D. Dochev (Eds.): AIMSA 2000, LNAI 1904, pp. 69–79, 2000.

$\Lambda(C)$-2 If A is a formula of $\Lambda(C)$, possibly including free occurrences of x, then $\lambda x A$ is a term of $\Lambda(C)$.

$\Lambda(C)$-3 If t and t' are terms of $\Lambda(C)$ then $t.t'$ is a formula.

The proof theory for $\Lambda(C)$ is obtained by adding the rules in Fig. 1 to a standard set of natural deduction rules, which I will refer to as ND (these rules are omitted here for space reasons, but any standard text on contructive logic will provide such a set, e.g. [10]).

(λ-intro:) $\alpha \vdash [\ldots, A, \ldots] \Longrightarrow \alpha \vdash [\ldots, (\lambda x A').t, \ldots]$
    ($[\ldots, A, \ldots]$ is any formula containing A as a subformula or a term, and $[\ldots, A', \ldots]$, the formula that is obtained from $[\ldots, A, \ldots]$ by replacing 0 or more instances of t in A by x.)
(λ-elim:) $\alpha \vdash [\ldots, (\lambda x A).t, \ldots] \Longrightarrow \alpha \vdash [\ldots, A_{t/x}, \ldots]$

Fig. 1. Natural deduction rules for $\Lambda(C)$

(λ-intro) and (λ-elim) add λ-abstraction and β-reduction to ND. Theorem 1 shows that we can do this without introducing proofs of $\bot$.

Theorem 1. *Soundness of $\Lambda(C)$*
If there is no proof of $\bot$ from α using ND then any proof of $\bot$ from α using all the rules of $\Lambda(C)$ introduces some irreducible instance of $(\lambda x A).t$[1].

Proof.
Suppose that $\alpha_0 \vdash A_0, \alpha_1 \vdash A_1, \ldots, \alpha_n \vdash \bot$ is a proof of $\bot$ from α_0 using the rules $\Lambda(C)$, where α_0 contains no irreducible λ-applications and there is no proof of $\bot$ from α_0 just using ND; and that there is no proof of $\bot$ from any set β which also satisfies the conditions but which contains fewer applications of λ-elim and λ-intro.

Consider the first use in this proof of $\bot$ from α_0 of either (i) λ-elim to change some formula $(\lambda x A).t$ into $A_{t/x}$, or (ii) λ-intro to change some formula $A_{t/x}$ into $(\lambda x A).t$ (there must be one, since otherwise α_0 would have supported a proof of $\bot$ from ND alone). In case (i) we can obtain a proof of $\bot$ from $\alpha \cup A_{t/x}$, and in case (ii) we can obtain one from $\alpha \cup (\lambda x A).t$, each of which omits the relevant step, and hence involves fewer applications of these rules, contradicting the assumption (note that $(\lambda x A).t$ is irreducible iff. $A_{t/x}$ is, so that the first step which adds either of these to α will not introduce an irreducible formula unless there was already one there) $\square$

The point of this theorem is that any proof of $\bot$ from a set which is consistent under the first-order rules must introduce some irreducible formula (since otherwise every subproof would satisfy the conditions of the theorem). If we take the constructive view of λ-applications as promissory notes for proofs, or for

---

[1] $(\lambda x A).t$ is irreducible if there is no sequence of applications of λ-elim which will produce a term with no occurrences at all of $(\lambda y B).s$.

programs that would produce proofs [10], then irreducible formulae are promises that can never be fulfilled.

Caveat emptor: Theorem 1 shows that the logic is sound so long as you avoid formulae with irreducible applications of λ-terms. It does *not* prevent you from saying things which would have been better left unsaid. It is perfectly easy to ask whether the property $\lambda x(\neg x.x)$ holds of itself, and to conclude that it both does and doesn't. But $(\lambda x(\neg x.x)).(\lambda x(\neg x.x))$ is irreducible, and hence there is no reason to suppose that it can investigated safely.

2   Satchmo for $\Lambda(C)$

The theorem prover we will present for $\Lambda(C)$ is developed by extending [6]'s first-order theorem prover Satchmo. The original presentation of Satchmo is very effective for puzzles (where all the information that is present is required for solving the problem, but it is hard to see how to use it), but can perform very poorly on problems where a lot of the information that is present is irrelevant. [7] and [5] show how to avoid some of the pathological behaviour of the basic Satchmo algorithm in such circumstances: unfortunately these techniques, like most other optimisations for first-order theorem provers [4] [1], rely on a static analysis of the problem. Optimisations that rely on static analysis of the initial problem statement do not work for intensional logics. Section 3 shows how to recover such optimisations dynamically.

The original presentation of Satchmo is unsuitable for our purposes, since it assumes a classical version of predicate logic, so that you can prove P by showing that $\neg P$ is unsatisfiable, and you can also use equivalences such as $((P \rightarrow Q) \rightarrow R) \leftrightarrow ((Q \rightarrow R)\&(P \; or \; R))$ which are not available in constructive logic. We therefore need to adapt it so that it does work properly for ND.

We do this in two stages: first we have to convert our problem into an appropriate normal form, and then we have to adapt the basic Satchmo engine to work constructively with this normal form.

Normal form:

The construction of a normal form proceeds in three stages.

(i) We start by making very straightfoward textual changes, to make standard logical form look a bit more like Prolog and to get rid of existential quantifiers.

NF-1 Replace (A & B) by (A', B') and (A or B) by (A'; B'), where A' and
       B' are the normal forms of A and B.
NF-2 Replace not(A) by (A' => absurd)
NF-3 Replace P => (Q => R) by ((P & Q) => R)'.
NF-4 Skolemise away existential quantifiers, and remove all universal quantifiers.

(ii) Separate the result of (i) into Horn and non-Horn clauses, and convert the Horn clauses to ordinary Prolog.

PL-1 If the normal form of P is atomic then assert it as a Prolog fact.

PL-2 If the normal form of P is (Q, R) then deal with Q and R individually.

PL-3 If the normal form of P is (Q;R) then assert `split(Q, R)` as a Prolog fact.

PL-4 If the normal form of P is (K => Q) where Q is atomic then assert Q :- K as a Prolog rule.

PL-5 If the normal form of P is (K => (Q, R)) then deal with (K => Q) and (K => R) individually.

PL-6 If the normal form of P is (K => (Q; R)) then assert `split(Q; R)` :- K as a Prolog rule.

(iii) Perform any optimisations that you can on these. We will return to this in Section 3.

Constructive Satchmo

Once we have the problem converted to normal form, we can use the following adaptation of the basic model generation algorithm.

MG-1 If you can prove A by using Prolog facts and rules then you can prove it.

MG-2 If you can prove `split(P, Q)` and you can show that you could prove A if you had either P or Q then you can prove A. This step corresponds to *or*-elimination.

MG-3 In order to prove (A => B), you have to add A to your set of Prolog facts and rules and then show that you can prove B. This corresponds to →-introduction.

Steps (1) and (2) are exactly as in the original presentation of Satchmo, except that since Satchmo works by trying to show that the hypotheses + the negation of the goal are unsatisfiable it always tries to prove **absurd**, whereas a constructive version has to show that the goal itself is provable from the hypotheses. Step (3) is introduced because Satchmo relies on the classical equivalence between $((P \rightarrow Q) \rightarrow R)$ and $(Q \rightarrow R)\&(P \text{ or } R)$ when constructing normal forms. This equivalence is no longer available: if we want to prove $P \rightarrow Q$ we have to use →-introduction. Fig. 2 provides a skeletal implementation of this.

The only non-cosmetic differences between this and Satchmo are that (i) this version implements a constructive version of first-order logic rather than a classical one, and (ii) it is slightly more direct when faced with clauses of the form $((P \rightarrow Q) \rightarrow R)$. Most of the work in Satchmo is performed in the backward chaining phase where the Prolog facts and rules are being used to prove specific goals. By converting $((P \rightarrow Q) \rightarrow R)$ to R :- (P => Q), we ensure that this rule is activated when it is required, at the cost of having to prove P => Q by asserting P and showing that Q follows from it. If we convert $((P \rightarrow Q) \rightarrow R)$ to R :- Q and `split(R; P)`, we end up having to explore the consequences of asserting P anyway.

2.1   Adding Abstraction and λ-Reduction

According to λ-intro and λ-elim, $(\lambda x A).t$ and $A_{t/x}$ are equivalent, and according to Theorem 1 there is no problem with this so long as none of your assumptions

```
% You can prove A either directly
prove(A) :-
    A.

% or by proving (P or Q), (P => A) and (Q => A)
prove(A) :-
    split(P; Q),
    \+ (P; Q), % check you haven't tried this already
    prove(P => A),
    prove(Q => A).

% To prove (P => A), assert P and try to prove A
% (with some funny bookkeeping to tidy up after yourself)
(P => A) :-
    assert(P),
    (prove(A) -> retract(P); (retract(P), fail)).
```

Fig. 2. Basic constructive Satchmo

or hypotheses contain irreducible instances of $(\lambda x P).t$. We would therefore like to add the following step to the normal forming process:

NF-5 Replace `lambda(X, P):T` by $P_{T/X}$.

This would eliminate all instances of $(\lambda x A).t$ before we ever started trying to use the underlying inference engine, so that including such expressions in our problem statement would have no effect whatsoever on the performance of the theorem prover. Unfortunately, the definition of $\Lambda(C)$ also allows formulae of the form $x.y$, where x and y are variables. If it did not, then the language would not really be all that different from ordinary first-order logic. But since it does, we have a problem with producing the correct normal form for such cases. We need one final normal form rule:

PL-7 If the normal form of P is `Q => (X:A)`, where X is a variable, then replace it by `split(X:A) :- Q`.

We also have to extend the inference engine to take account of these new cases, as shown in Fig. 3. The new clause for `prove(A)` reflects the decision that clauses with λ-applications involving uninstantiated functions as their heads should be used forwards, like clauses with disjunctive conclusions. The point here is that since we do not know what the conclusion of such a clause is, we have no way of telling whether it is likely to be useful. We therefore leave them out of the backwards chaining part of the proof procedure, and simply allow them to emerge when there is nothing more obvious to try.

The clause for proving `(P:T)` says that if you know what P is then you should actually work with the β-reduced version. This is guaranteed to work precisely

```
% you can also prove A if (lambda(X, P):T) => A
% and you can prove P(T/X)
prove(A) :-
    split(P:T),
    nonvar(P),
    fully_reduce(P:T, R),
    (R => A).

% To prove (P:T), try proving P(T/X) instead
(P:T) :-
    nonvar(P),
    fully_reduce(P:T, R),
    prove(R).
```

Fig. 3. Extending Satchmo to cover λ-intro and λ-elim

because if (P:T) were provable from the original problem statement then we will have either replaced it directly by $P_{T/X}$ during the normal forming process, or we will eventually do so when we explore the consequences of split(P:T).

The program outlined above provides a sound and reasonably efficient theorem prover for $\Lambda(C)$. The soundness is guaranteed by Theorem 1 and Theorem 2. The reasonable efficiency is inherited from Satchmo, together with the fact that by proving $(\lambda x A).t$ from $A_{t/x}$ we start working backwards as soon as we possibly can. Completeness is any case unavailable, since even first-order logic is only semi-decidable, as is the task of deciding whether a λ-application is reducible (see [10]).

Theorem 2. *The algorithm outlined in Fig. 2 and Fig. 3 is sound.*

Proof.
Suppose that the algorithm is not in fact sound, i.e. that there is a proof of absurd from some set of clauses {A1, ..., An} using the algorithm in Fig. 2 and Fig. 3 which would not have led to such a proof just using the algorithm in Fig. 2. At some point the proof must have either (i) used a splitting rule to derive $P_{T/X}$ from lambda(X, P):T, or (ii) proved lambda(X, P):T by proving $P_{T/X}$. In case (i) we could have proved absurd from {A1, ..., An, lambda(X, P):T}, and in case (ii) we could have proved it from {A1, ..., An, $P_{T/X}$}. In either case we have a proof of absurd using one less application of the relevant rule. We can repeat this until there are no applications of either of the rules from Fig. 3, in which case we have a set {A1, ..., An, K1, ..., Km} which supports a proof of absurd just using the rules in Fig. 2.   □

3   Optimisations

The program described above is 'reasonably efficient' – as efficient, that is, as something based on Satchmo could be expected to be. As noted earlier, however,

Satchmo is very effective for certain kinds of problem, less so for others. There are known optimisations for Satchmo, particularly for lessening the impact of irrelevant disjunctive clauses. We will consider a number of these in the context of the extension of Satchmo to deal with $\Lambda(C)$.

3.1   Deleting and Reinstating Pure Literals

The first move is to introduce [4]'s notion of 'pure literals'. Suppose that we have a clause of the form `p(X, Y) :- p1(X, Y), ..., pk(X, Y), ..., pn(X, Y)`, but there is no clause with `pk(U, V)` as its head. Then clearly there is no point in using this rule when attempting to prove `p(a, b)`, since the k-th subgoal is bound to fail. So we may as well remove it from our clause set. The subgoal `pk(U, V)` is said to be PURE.

But this might be the only clause which supports proofs of `p(U, V)`. In that case, removing it may well make it possible to delete some other clause, which may ...   Kowalski shows how this kind of 'gangrene' can lead to quite dramatic reductions in the problem statement. The effect tends not to be quite so dramatic in the context we are working in (meaning postulates for lexical semantics in natural language), but there are in any case two problems with it.

(i) Kowalski's original presentation marked a literal L as being pure if there was no clause containing a complementary literal L' which would unify with it. We, however, are working with equality as well as intensionality. Suppose our initial problem consists of the following:

$$\begin{array}{|l|}
\hline
male(f) \\
male(f) \& parent(f,a) \rightarrow father(f,a) \\
parent(j,a) \\
f = j \\
\hline
\end{array}$$

Fig. 4. Rule set with an apparently pure literal

It seems as though there is nothing which could support $parent(f,a)$, since the only potentially relevant literal, $parent(j,a)$, does not unify with it. This suggests that we can delete the rule for proving $father(f,a)$. This is clearly too strong, since the presence of the equality means that we *can* prove $parent(f,a)$, so that we should not delete this rule. We are therefore restricted to saying that we can delete a rule if it contains a subgoal `g(t1, t2)` for which there is no clause whose head has `g` as its functor and arity 2. This is weaker than Kowalski's notion, and hence is less likely to lead to drastic reductions in the search space.

(ii) To make matters worse, however, the fact that we have clauses with completely underspecified heads means that we actually have no idea at all what literals might actually be provable. We therefore cannot simply throw away clauses with pure literals, since it is entirely possible that a literal may become *impure* as a result of the forward application of some clause resulting from a formula with an intensional consequent. The best we can do is to put them to one side until they become impure, and then reinstate them. Thus instead of deleting a clause whose antecedent contains pure literals, we store it in such a way that it can easily be reinstated. Fig. 5 shows the form in which `father(f, a) :- male(f), parent(f, a)` would be stored if `parent(f, a)` was pure, and we include an extra step in the treatment of conditional proofs, as in Fig. 6.

```
impure(parent(X, Y),
         (father(f, a) :- male(f), parent(f, a))).
```

Fig. 5. Storing a clause with a pure literal for later reinstatement

```
prove(A => B) :-
     assert(A),
     impure(A, CLAUSE),
     assert(CLAUSE),
     (prove(B) ->
         retract(A);
         (retract(A), retract(CLAUSE), fail)).
```

Fig. 6. What to do when a literal becomes impure

Split rules transform themselves into conditional proofs, since in each case the result of a split rule is to introduce a request for a proof that the new information would lead to a proof. Fig. 2 dealt with such requests by adding the antecedent of the clause to the set of facts and then attempting to show that the goal is provable under these new circumstances. Fig. 6 simply makes sure that anything that the new facts would help with is made available before the proof continues.

This introduces many of the benefits of pure literal deletion in a context where clauses containing pure literals may suddenly become available as a result of moves which could not have been predicted. The cost is a small fixed time search for reinstatable clauses every time you undertake a conditional proof.

3.2   Relevance

Satchmo can be made to perform very poorly if you include disjunctive clauses where one of the disjuncts is irrelevant. The problem is that each use of such a clause, say $A \rightarrow B \ or \ C$, introduces two conditional proofs, namely $B \rightarrow G$ and $C \rightarrow G$, where G is the top-level goal you are trying to prove. If B is not going to contribute to a proof of G then $B \rightarrow G$ will be provable precisely if G itself is, and likewise for $C \rightarrow G$. But then at least one of the branches introduced by using $A \rightarrow B \ or \ C$ is at least as hard as just proving G without using this clause.

[7] and [5] show that you can deal with this problem by banning the use of a split clause until it has been shown that its consequents *will* contribute to a proof of G. The current implementation continues to take the approach of dynamically reinstating such a clause when at least one of its disjuncts has shown up in a failed attempted proof. The key is that instead of including such a clause in the database directly, we assert a rule which will itself add the clause when its consequents have been shown to be relevant. If we had, for instance, a clause like split(p(X); q(X)) :- g1(X), ..., gn(X) we would replace it by the clauses shown in Fig. 7.

```
p(_Y) :-
    \+ clause((split(p(X); q(X)) :- g1(X), ..., gn(X))),
    assert((split(p(X); q(X)) :- g1(X), ..., gn(X))),
    fail.

q(_Y) :-
    \+ clause((split(p(X); q(X)) :- g1(X), ..., gn(X))),
    assert((split(p(X); q(X)) :- g1(X), ..., gn(X))),
    fail.
```

Fig. 7. Relevance checking

The first of these says that if you find yourself trying to prove p(t), and you don't already have this split clause available to you, then add it to the database, and likewise for q(t). This provides a very cheap way of implementing the requirement that at least one of the disjuncts should be potentially relevant to something that you actually want to prove. It is less easy to provide a cheap test to ensure that both disjuncts are desirable – you have to choose between a cheap test that may still allow a some undesirable cases through [7], and a more expensive one which is more rigorous [5].

4 Conclusions

The table in Fig. 8 the effects of the various optimisations discussed in Section 3 on the performance of the system when applied to a specific task from our NLP domain (space precludes a detailed discussion of the particular task: what matter here is the effect of the various optimisations). It turns out that pure literal deletion and relevance checking interact in unexpected ways[2]. Strong purification corresponds to deleting clauses if they contain literals for which there is no relevant Horn clause, weak purification corresponds to deleting them if there is no relevant clause at all. If you use strong purification with the relevance check from Section 3.2 then clauses will be deleted because their only support comes

---

[2] Well I didn't expect it, and it took a lot of tracking down!

from some disjunctive clause; but disjunctive clauses are now only triggered if they would be helpful. The problem is that the clauses that the disjunctive clauses would have been helped by (which are their triggers) will have been purified, and hence will never be accessed.

	+groundedness	-groundedness
Unoptimised	1.62	1.98
Strong purification	0.38	0.42
Relevance checking	1.55	2.04
Weak purification	0.54	0.59
Relevance + weak pur.	0.52	0.59

Fig. 8. Relative effects of optimisations

The two columns marked $\pm$ groundedness show the effect of blocking repeated proofs of the same ground fact.

The key observation is that the optimisations do improve the performance. It's what optimisations are supposed to do, of course, but it's always reassuring when they do. It is striking, however, that the effect of relevance checking with this particular problem is extremely marginal. If we simply add relevance checking to the basic system, we get a small improvement, if we add it to the weak form of purification we get a small improvement, but the best performance comes from the strong version of purification, which *cannot* be combined with relevance checking. It seems likely the relative effectiveness of different combinations will depend on the exact mix of sequents in the problem statement. The move to a dynamic version of pure literal deletion was forced on us by the fact that we are working in an intensional context, where it is not possible to permanently delete clauses, since they may be impurified at any time. It turns out to work very nicely with Satchmo, since it means that we can be much more ruthless about what we delete.

References

1. W Bibel, R Letz, and J Schumann. Bottom-up enhancements of deductive systems. Technical report, Technische Universitat München, 1987. 71
2. H Herzberger. Notes on naive semantics. *Journal of Philosophical Logic*, 11:61–102, 1982. 69
3. T J Jech. *Lectures in Set Theory, with Particular Emphasis on the Method of Forcing*. Springer Verlag (Lecture Notes in Mathematics 217), Berlin, 1971. 69
4. R Kowalski. A proof procedure using connection graphs. *JACM*, 22(4):572–595, 1975. 71, 75
5. D W Loveland. Near-horn Prolog and beyond. *Journal of Automated Reasoning*, 7:1–26, 1991. 71, 77

6. R Manthey and F Bry. Satchmo: a theorem prover in Prolog. In *Proc. 9th Inter. Conf. on Automated Deduction (CADE-9), LNAI 310*, pages 415–434, 1988. 69, 71

7. A M Ramsay. Generating relevant models. *Journal of Automated Reasoning*, 7:359–368, 1991. 71, 77

8. R. H. Thomason, editor. *Formal Philosophy: Selected Papers of Richard Montague*. Yale University Press, New Haven, 1974. 69

9. R Turner. A theory of properties. *Journal of Symbolic Logic*, 52(2):455–472, 1987. 69

10. R Turner. *Constructive Foundations for Functional Languages*. McGraw Hill, London, 1991. 70, 71, 74

11. A N Whitehead and B Russell. *Principia Mathematica*. Cambridge University Press, Cambridge, 1925. 69

Classification with Belief Decision Trees

Zied Elouedi[1], Khaled Mellouli[1], and Philippe Smets[2]

[1] Institut Supérieur de Gestion de Tunis
41 Avenue de la liberté, cité Bouchoucha, 2000 Le Bardo, Tunis, Tunisia
zied.elouedi@isg.rnu.tn
khaled.mellouli@ihec.rnu.tn
[2] IRIDIA, Université Libre de Bruxelles
50 av., F. Roosvelt, CP194/6, 1050 Brussels, Belgium
psmets@ulb.ac.be

Abstract. Decision trees are considered as an efficient technique to express classification knowledge and to use it. However, their most standard algorithms do not deal with uncertainty, especially the cognitive one.
In this paper, we develop a method to adapt the decision tree technique to the case where the object's classes are not exactly known, and where the uncertainty about the class' value is represented by a belief function. The adaptation concerns both the construction of the tree and its use to classify new objects characterized by uncertain attribute values.

1 Introduction

Decision trees are among the well known machine learning techniques. They are widely used in a variety of fields notably in artificial intelligence applications. Their success is explained by their ability to handle complex problems by providing an understandable representation easier to interpret and also their adaptability to the inference task by producing logical rules of classification.

Several methods [1,5,7] have been proposed to construct decision trees. These algorithms have as inputs the training set composed by instances where each one is described by the set of attribute values and its assigned class. The output is a decision tree ensuring the classification of new instances.

A major problem faced in the standard decision tree algorithms results from the uncertainty encountered in the data. This uncertainty can appear either in the construction or in the classification phase. Ignoring it can affect the efficiency of the obtained results.

In order to overcome this drawback, probabilistic decision trees have been developed by Quinlan [6]. This kind of trees presents small extensions over the standard one and its use remains limited since it only deals with statistical uncertainty induced by information arisen from random behavior.

The objective of this paper is to develop what we call a belief decision tree, a classification method adapting the decision tree approach to uncertain data, where the uncertainty is represented by belief functions as defined in the Transferable Belief Model (TBM). The choice of the TBM seems appropriate as it

S. A. Cerri and D. Dochev (Eds.): AIMSA 2000, LNAI 1904, pp. 80–90, 2000.

provides a convenient framework [2] for dealing with limited and uncertain information, notably those given by experts.

This paper is organized as follows: section2 provides a brief description of standard decision tree algorithms. In section3, the basics of the belief function theory are recalled. Our approach regarding a belief decision tree is described in section4. Both the construction and classification procedures will be detailed. Finally, an example explaining these two procedures is proposed in section5.

2   Basics of Decision Tree Algorithms

Several algorithms have been developed for learning decision trees [1,5,7]. In the artificial intelligence community, the most used is based on the TDIDT[1] approach. In that approach, the tree is constructed by employing a recursive divide and conquer strategy. Its steps can be defined as follows:

- By using *an attribute selection measure*, an attribute will be chosen in order to partition the training set in an *"optimal"* manner.
- Based on *a partitioning strategy*, the current training set will be divided into training subsets by taking into account the values of the selected attribute.
- When *the stopping criterion* is satisfied, the training subset will be declared as a leaf.

In the literature many attribute selection measures are proposed in [3,5,7]. Among the most used, we mention the information gain used within the ID3 algorithm [5]. The information gain of an attribute A relative to a set of objects S measures the effectiveness of A in classifying the training data. It is defined as follows:

$$Gain(S, A) = Info(S) - Info_A(S) \text{ where}$$

$$Info(S) = -\sum_{i=1}^{n} p_i.log_2 p_i \text{ and } Info_A(S) = \sum_{v \in Domain(A)} \frac{|S_v^A|}{|S|}.Info(S_v^A)$$

where p_i is the proportion of objects in S belonging to the class C_i (i = 1..n) and S_v^A is the subset of objects for which the attribute A has the value v.

Although, it has shown good results, this measure has a serious limitation. It favors attributes with large number of values over those with few number of values [7]. To overcome this shortcoming, Quinlan [5,7] suggests another selection attribute measure called the gain ratio and defined by:

$$Gain \text{ ratio}(S, A) = \frac{Gain(S,A)}{Split \ Info(A)} \text{ where}$$

$$Split \ Info(A) = \sum_{v \in Domain(A)} \frac{|S_v^A|}{|S|}.log_2 \frac{|S_v^A|}{|S|}$$

---

[1] Top-Down Induction of Decision Tree

Split Info(A), measures the information content of the attribute A itself [5]. The gain ratio is the information gain calibrated by Split Info. Note that when the ratio is not defined, this criterion selects attributes among those with an average or better information gain [5].

Once constructed, the decision tree is used to classify new objects. For a new instance, we start with the root, we evaluate the relative test attribute and we take the branch corresponding to the test's outcome. This process is repeated until a leaf is encountered. The new object belongs to the class labeling the leaf.

3   Belief Function Theory

In this section, we briefly review the main concepts underlying the theory of belief functions [8,10,11].

3.1   Definitions

Let Θ be a finite set of elementary events called frame of discernment. The basic belief assignment (bba) is a function m: $2^{\Theta} \to [0,1]$ such that $\sum_{A \subseteq \Theta} m(A) = 1$.

The value m(A) represents the part of belief supporting exactly that the actual event belongs to A and nothing more specific. The subsets A in Θ such that m(A) > 0 are called focal elements.

Associated with m is the belief function [10] defined for $A \subseteq \Theta$ as: $bel(A) = \sum_{\emptyset \neq B \subseteq \Theta} m(B)$. The degree of belief bel(A) given to a subset A of the frame Θ is defined as the sum of all the masses given to subsets that support A.

The representation of total ignorance is nicely achieved in the belief function theory. It is represented by the so-called vacuous belief function [8], i.e., the belief function which bba satisfies m(Θ) = 1 and m(A) = 0 for all A $\neq \Theta$.

3.2   Rules of Combination

Let m_1 and m_2 be two basic belief assignments induced from two distinct pieces of evidence. These bbas can be combined either conjunctively or disjunctively.

1. *The Conjunctive Rule:* When we know that both sources of information are fully reliable then the bba representing the combined evidence satisfies [12]:

$$(m_1 \wedge m_2)(A) = \sum_{B,C \subseteq \Theta : B \cap C = A} m_1(B).m_2(C) \text{ for } A \subseteq \Theta$$

2. *The Disjunctive Rule:* When we only know that at least one of the sources of information is reliable but we do not know which is reliable, then the bba representing the combined evidence satisfies [12]:

$$(m_1 \vee m_2)(A) = \sum_{B,C \subseteq \Theta : B \cup C = A} m_1(B).m_2(C) \text{ for } A \subseteq \Theta$$

3.3   Vacuous Extension of Belief Functions

Let X and Y be two sets of variables such that $Y \subseteq X$. Let m^Y be a bba defined on the domain Θ_Y of Y. The extension of m^Y to Θ_X, denoted $m^{Y\uparrow X}$ means that the information in m^Y is extended to a larger frame X [4]:

$$m^{Y\uparrow X}(A \times \Theta_{X-Y}) = m^Y(A) \text{ for } A \subseteq \Theta_Y$$

$$m^{Y\uparrow X}(B) = 0 \text{ if B is not in the form } A \times \Theta_{X-Y}$$

3.4   Pignistic Transformation

The decision making problem is solved in the TBM framework by using the pignistic probability function defined and fully explianed by [10]:

$$BetP(\theta) = \sum_{A \subseteq \Theta, \theta \in A} \frac{m(A)}{|A|.(1-m(\emptyset))}, \text{ for all } \theta \in \Theta$$

It is the only transformation between belief functions and probability functions that satisfies some natural rationality requirements. The major one is described as follows: Suppose two contexts C_1 and C_2, suppose your beliefs in context C_i is represented by m_i and that the choice of the context obeys to some random process, with $P(C_1) = p$ and $P(C_2) = q$ with $p + q = 1$. Let Γ denotes the operator that transforms a bba into a probability function. We want that it satisfies:

$$\Gamma(p\ m_1 + q\ m_2) = p\ \Gamma(m_1) + q\ \Gamma(m_2).$$

This translates the property that transforming the belief held before knowing the context that will be selected is the same as combining the conditional probability functions one would have obtained if the context had been known. Full details can be found in [10]. The probability function so obtained is then used to compute the expected utilities needed for optimal decision making.

4   Belief Decision Tree

In this section, we define the structure of the decision tree within the belief function framework, called belief decision tree then we present the notations that will be used in this paper. Next, we develop the two major procedures of a decision tree: the construction and the classification procedures.

4.1   Decision Tree Structure in the Belief Function Context

Any decision tree is constructed from a training set of objects based on successive refinements. Due to the uncertainty, the structure of the training set may be different from the traditional one. In fact, we assume that the uncertainty is lying only on classes of training instances. That is, our training set is composed by objects where the value of each attribute is known with certainty, whereas there is some uncertainty regarding its corresponding class.

We propose to associate for each training instance I_j, $j = 1..p$, a bba, denoted $m^\Theta\{I_j\}$, defined on the set of the possible classes Θ to which the object I_j can belong, and representing the beliefs given by an expert (or several experts) on the actual class of the object I_j. This representation is also appropriate to describe the classical case where the object's class is exactly known.

Once the structure of the training set is defined, our belief decision tree is composed by the same elements as in the traditional tree. However, due to the uncertainty in training instances' classes, the structure of the leaves will change. Instead of assigning a unique class to each leaf, it will be labeled by a bba expressing a belief about the actual class of the objects belonging to the leaf.

4.2   Notations and Assumptions

In this paper, we use the following notations:
- S: a given set of objects,
- I_j: an instance (object, case, example),
- $\mathbf{A} = \{A_1, A_2...A_k\}$: a set of k attributes,
- $D(A_i)$: the domain of the attribute $A_i \in \mathbf{A}$,
- $A(I_j)$: the value of the attribute A for the object I_j,
- $S_v^A = \{I_j : A(I_j) = v\}$: the subset of objects which value for attribute $A \in \mathbf{A}$ is $v \in D(A_i)$
- $\Theta = \{C_1, C_2, ..., C_n\}$: the frame of discernment involving the possible classes related to the classification problem.
- $C(I_j)$: the actual class of the object I_j,
- $m_g^\Theta\{I_j\}[A](C)$ denotes the conditional bba given to $C \subseteq \Theta$ relative to object I_j given by an agent g that accepts that A is true. Useless indices are omitted.

4.3   Procedure for Constructing a Belief Decision Tree

As mentioned the algorithm to construct a decision tree, also called the induction task, is based on three major parameters: the attribute selection measure, the partitioning strategy, the stopping criterion. These parameters must take into account the uncertainty encountered in the training set.

Attribute Selection Measure. Our attribute selection measure has to take into account the bba of each object in the training set. The idea is to adapt the gain ratio proposed by Quinlan [7] to this uncertain context.

In order to define the gain ratio measure of an attribute A over a set of objects S within the TBM framework, we propose the following steps:

1. For each object I_j in S, we have a bba $m^\Theta\{I_j\}$ that represents our belief about the value of $C(I_j)$. Suppose we select randomly and with equi-probability one object in S. What can be said about $m^\Theta\{S\}$, the bba concerning the actual class of that object selected in S?

$m^\Theta\{S\}$ is the average of the bbas taken over the objects in the subset S:

$$m^\Theta\{S\}(C) = \frac{\sum_{I_j \in S} m^\Theta\{I_j\}(C)}{|S|} \quad \text{for } C \subseteq \Theta \tag{1}$$

2. Apply the pignistic transformation to $m^\Theta\{S\}$ to get the average probability $BetP^\Theta\{S\}$ on each singular class of this randomly selected instance.
3. Perform the same computation for each subset S_v^A, we get $BetP^\Theta\{S_v^A\}$ for v $\in D(A)$, $A \in \mathbf{A}$.
4. Compute Info(S) and $Info_A$(S) as done initially by Quinlan, but using the pignistic probabilities. We get:

$$Info(S) = -\sum_{i=1}^{n} BetP^\Theta\{S\}(C_i).log_2 BetP^\Theta\{S\}(C_i) \tag{2}$$

$$Info_A(S) = \sum_{v \in D(A)} \frac{|S_v^A|}{|S|} Info(S_v^A)$$

$$= -\sum_{v \in D(A)} \frac{|S_v^A|}{|S|} \sum_{i=1}^{n} BetP^\Theta\{S_v^A\}(C_i) log_2 BetP^\Theta\{S_v^A\}(C_i) \tag{3}$$

Once computed, we get the information gain provided by the attribute A in the set of objects S such that:

$$Gain(S, A) = Info(S) - Info_A(S) \tag{4}$$

5. Using the Split Info, compute the gain ratio relative to each attribute A:

$$Gain \text{ Ratio}(S, A) = \frac{Gain(S, A)}{Split \text{ Info}(A)} \tag{5}$$

In each decision node, the attribute having the highest gain ratio will be selected as the root of the corresponding decision tree.

Partitioning Strategy. For the selected attribute, assign a branch corresponding to each attribute value. Thus, we get several training subsets where each one is relative to one branch and regrouping objects having the same attribute value.

Stopping Criterion. It allows to stop the development of a path and to declare the treated training subset as a leaf. Three strategies are proposed:

1. There is no more attribute to test.
2. The treated training subset contains only one object.
3. The values of the gain ratio relative to the remaining attributes are equal or less than zero.

Once the stopping criterion is fulfilled, the current node is declared as a leaf characterized by a bba defined on Θ. The leaf's bba is equal to the average bba taken over the objects belonging to the same leaf.

Constructing Algorithm. Our algorithm presents an extension of the ID3 algorithm to the uncertain context. It is composed by the following steps:

1. Create the root node of the decision tree including all the objects of the training set T.
2. Verify if this node satisfies or not the stopping criterion. If it is fulfilled, declare it as a leaf node and compute its corresponding bba.
3. Otherwise, look for the attribute having the highest gain ratio. This attribute will be designed as the root of the tree related to the whole training set T.
4. Divide the training set according to the partitioning strategy.
5. Create a root node relative to each training subset.
6. For each node created, repeat the same process from the step 2.

If the bbas over the classes for every instance in the training set are described by a certain bba, i.e., there is no uncertainty about the actual class for all the objects in the training set, then we get the same results as the ID3 algorithm of Quinlan [7] based on the gain ratio.

4.4   Procedure of Classifying New Instances

Once constructed, the belief decision tree will be used to ensure the classification of new instances in this uncertain framework. These instances may present some uncertainty regarding the value of one (or several) of its attributes. In fact, the uncertainty related to each attribute A_i can be defined by a bba m^{A_i} on the set Θ_{A_i} of all the possible values of the attribute. For those, where the value is known with certainty, it would correspond a certain bba having as a focal element only this value. Besides, if an attribute value is unknown, it would be expressed by a vacuous bba.

We have to find the bba expressing beliefs characterizing the different attributes' values of the new instance to classify. To ensure this objective, we have to apply the following steps:

1. Extend the different bbas m^{A_i} to the global frame of attributes Θ_A.
2. Combine the extended bbas $m^{A_i \uparrow A}$ by applying the conjunctive rule:

$$m^{\Theta_A} = \wedge_{i=1..k} m^{A_i \uparrow A} \qquad (6)$$

m^{Θ_A} represents beliefs on the combinations of the attributes of the given instance. We then consider individually the focal elements of this bba . Let x be such a focal element. The next phase is to compute the belief functions $\mathrm{bel}^\Theta[x]$.

1. If the treated focal element x is a singleton (only one value for each attribute), then $\mathrm{bel}^\Theta[x]$ is equal to the average belief function corresponding to the leaf to which this focal element is attached.
2. If the focal element x is not a singleton (some attributes have more than one value), then we have to explore all the possible paths relative to this combination of values. Two cases are possible:
   - If these paths lead to one leaf, then $\mathrm{bel}^\Theta[x]$ is equal to this leaf's bel.

– If these paths lead to distinct leaves, then $bel^{\Theta}[x]$ is equal to the result of the combination of each leaf's bel by applying the disjunctive rule.

Finally the belief functions computed with each focal element x are averaged [9] using the m^{Θ_A}:

$$bel^{\Theta}[m^{\Theta_A}](\theta) = \sum_{x \subseteq \Theta_A} m^{\Theta_A}(x).bel^{\Theta}[x](\theta) \text{ for } \theta \in \Theta \qquad (7)$$

Note that we have to apply the pignistic transformation in order to take a decision on the class of the instance to classify.

5 Example

Let's illustrate our method by a simple example. Assume that a bank wants to develop a loan policy for its clients by taking into account a number of their attributes. Let T be a training set (see Table 1) composed of eight instances (clients) characterized by three symbolic attributes: - *Income* with possible values $\{no, low, average, high\}$,

- *Property* with possible values $\{less, greater\}$ that is to express if the property's value is less or greater than the loan expected by the client,
- *Unpaid-credit* (denoted by Unp-c) with possible values $\{yes, no\}$ in order to know if the client has another credit unpaid or not.

Three classes may be assigned to clients ($\Theta = \{C_1, C_2, C_3\}$): C_1 for whom the bank accepts to give the whole loan, C_2 for whom the bank accepts to give a part of the loan and C_3 for whom the bank refuses to give the loan.

Table 1. The training set T

Income	Property	Unp-c	Class
High	Greater	Yes	$m^{\Theta}\{I_1\}(C_1) = 0.7; m^{\Theta}\{I_1\}(\Theta) = 0.3;$
Average	Less	No	$m^{\Theta}\{I_2\}(C_2) = 0.5; m^{\Theta}\{I_2\}(C_1 \cup C_2) = 0.4; m^{\Theta}\{I_2\}(\Theta)=0.1$
High	Greater	Yes	$m^{\Theta}\{I_3\}(C_1) = 0.8; m^{\Theta}\{I_3\}(\Theta) = 0.2;$
Average	Greater	Yes	$m^{\Theta}\{I_4\}(C_2) = 0.5; m^{\Theta}\{I_4\}(C_3) = 0.2; m^{\Theta}\{I_4\}(\Theta) = 0.3$
Low	Less	Yes	$m^{\Theta}\{I_5\}(C_3) = 0.8; m^{\Theta}\{I_5\}(C_2 \cup C_3) = 0.1; m^{\Theta}\{I_5\}(\Theta)=0.1$
No	Less	Yes	$m^{\Theta}\{I_6\}(C_3) = 1; m^{\Theta}\{I_6\}(\Theta) = 0$
High	Greater	No	$m^{\Theta}\{I_7\}(C_1) = 1; m^{\Theta}\{I_7\}(\Theta) = 0$
Average	Less	Yes	$m^{\Theta}\{I_8\}(C_3) = 0.6; m^{\Theta}\{I_8\}(\Theta) = 0.4$

Contrary to the 'traditional' training set where it includes only instances which classes are known with certainty, this given training set T is characterized by uncertainty relative to some instances'classes and which is represented by bbas. The training set T offers a more generalized framework than the tradional one. Thanks to our belief decision tree algorithm, we are able to generate the corresponding tree by taking into account this uncertainty.

Construction Procedure. Let's now try to construct the induced belief decision tree relative to the training set T. The first step is to find the root of the decision tree. Hence, we have to compute the gain ratio relative to the three attributes by taking into account the uncertainty embedded in instances' classes.

Let's illustrate briefly the computation of the gain ratio relative to the property attribute. Let $m^\Theta\{T\}$ be the average bba relative to T, $m^\Theta\{T_{greater}^{property}\}$ and $m^\Theta\{T_{less}^{property}\}$ be the average bbas relative to the sets of objects in T having as a value of the property attribute respectively greater and less. These bbas are computed by using the equation (1), then their corresponding pignistic probabilities $BetP^\Theta\{T\}$, $BetP^\Theta\{T_{greater}^{property}\}$ and $BetP^\Theta\{T_{less}^{property}\}$ have to be calculated.

Once computed, we get Info(T) = 1.535; Info$_{property}$ = 1.17 and Split Info (property) = 1. So Gain ratio(T, property) = 0.365; By applying the same process, we get Gain ratio(T, income) = 0.405; Gain ratio(T, unpaid-credit) = 0.214

The gain ratio criterion favors the income attribute since it presents the highest value. Thus, it will be chosen as the root of the decision tree and branches are created for each of its possible values (high, average, low, no).

The same steps of the algorithm will be applied recursively. The belief decision tree induced is represented by Fig. 1:

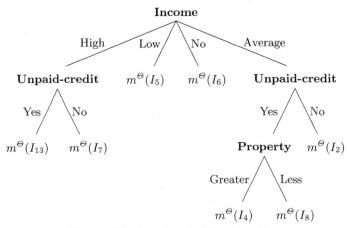

Fig. 1. The Final Belief Decision Tree

Note that the leaf labeled by $m^\Theta\{I_{13}\}$ is the average bba of the set involving the objects I_1 and I_3 defined as: $m^\Theta\{I_{13}\}(C_1) = 0.75$; $m^\Theta\{I_{13}\}(\Theta) = 0.25$;

Classification Procedure. Once the belief decision tree relative to the training set T is constructed (see Fig. 1), suppose that we would classify an instance characterized by certain and exact values for its income and unpaid-credit attributes which are respectively the values average and yes. However, there is some uncertainty in the value of the property attribute defined by: $m^{property}(greater) = 0.4$; $m^{property}(less) = 0.3$; $m^{property}(\Theta_{property}) = 0.3$;

Once the attributes' bba are extended to Θ_A ($\Theta_A = \Theta_{income} \times \Theta_{property} \times \Theta_{unpaid-credit}$), we apply the conjunctive rule. We get a joint bba m^{Θ_A} on singular or subsets of instances such that: $m^{\Theta_A}(\{(average, greater, yes)\}) = 0.4$; $m^{\Theta_A}(\{(average, less, yes)\}) = 0.3$; $m^{\Theta_A}(\{average\} \times \Theta_{property} \times \{yes\}) = 0.3$;

Next, we have to find beliefs on classes (defined on Θ) given the values of the attributes characterizing the new instance to classify. Three belief functions have to be defined where for each one, we take into account one focal element of m^{Θ_A}. According to the induced belief decision tree (see Fig. 1), we get: $bel^{\Theta}[\{(average, greater, yes)\}] = bel_4$; $bel^{\Theta}[\{(average, less, yes)\}] = bel_8$; $bel^{\Theta}[\{average\} \times \Theta_{property} \times \{yes\}] = bel_4 \vee bel_8$.

Hence, these belief functions will be averaged then computing its corresponding BetP. As a result, we obtain that the new instance to classify has respectively 0.14, 0.38 and 0.48 as probability to belong to the classes C_1, C_2 and C_3. So, it seems most probable to refuse the loan expected by this client.

As we note, our classification method using the induced belief decision tree is able to ensure the classification of new instances characterized by certain attribute values (like in the case of the standard decision tree). It has also the advantage (over the standard tree) to classify instances characterized by uncertain attribute values.

6   Conclusion

In this paper, we have developed a classification method providing a formal way to handle uncertainty in decision trees within the belief function framework. In fact, the construction procedure of the belief decision tree is ensured by taking into account the uncertainty about the actual classes of training objects. Then, we have proposed a classification procedure allowing to classify objects characterized by uncertain attributes. This method ensures the classification of instances with certain attributes or even those presenting some missing attribute values.

The major interest of the proposed method is that it can be applied to training sets where the instance classes are uncertain. Belief function theory offers a perfect representation of any form of uncertainty, from total knowledge to total ignorance, in particular more flexible than what probability theory can achieve. The most obvious case where belief decision trees will show their power is encountered where the instance classes are only known to belong to some subsets of the class domain.

References

1. Breiman, L., Friedman, J. H., Olshen, R. A., Stone, C. J.: Classification and regression trees. Belmont, CA: Wadsworth, (1984) 80, 81

2. Elouedi, Z., Mellouli, K., Smets, P.: Decision trees using the belief function theory. To appear in the Proceedings of the International Conference on Information Processing and Management of Uncertainty IPMU'2000 (2000) 81
3. Lopez De Mantaras, R.: A distance-based attribute selection measure for decision tree induction. Machine learning **6** (1991) 81–92 81
4. Mellouli, K.: On the propagation of beliefs in network using the Dempster-Shafer theory of evidence. Ph.D dissertation University of Kansas Lawrence KS (1987) 83
5. Quinlan, J. R.: Induction of decision trees. Machine learning **1** (1986) 81–106 80, 81, 82
6. Quinlan, J. R.: Decision trees as probabilistic classifiers. Proceedings of the Fourth international Machine Learning (1987) 31–37 80
7. Quinlan, J. R.: C4.5: Programs for machine learning. Morgan Kaufmann San Mateo Ca (1993) 80, 81, 84, 86
8. Shafer, G.: A mathematical theory of evidence. Princeton University Press (1976) 82
9. Smets, P.: Belief functions : the disjunctive rule of combination and the generalized bayesian theorem. International Journal of Approximate Reasoning **9** (1993) 1–35 87
10. Smets, P., Kennes, R.: The transferable belief model. Artificial Intelligence **66** (1994) 191–234 82, 83
11. Smets, P.: The transferable belief model for quantified belief representation. D. M. Gabbay and Ph. Smets (eds.) Handbook of Defeasible Reasoning and Uncertainty Management Systems **1** Kluwer Doordrecht (1998) 267–301 82
12. Smets, P.: The Application of the transferable belief Model to Diagnostic Problems Int. J. Intelligent Systems **13** (1998) 127–158 82

A Temporal Many-Valued Logic
for Real Time Control Systems

Gonzalo Escalada-Imaz

Artificial Intelligence Research Institute (IIIA)
Spanish Scientific Research Council (CSIC)
Campus UAB, s/n 08193 Bellaterra, Barcelona (Spain)
gonzalo@iiia.csic.es

Abstract. Control of Systems in different real world fields such us
Chemistry, Medicine, Robotics, etc. has been tackled for decades with
approaches developed in the classical Control Systems field. In this paper, we will propose a Real Time controller relying on a Knowledge Based
System with a Temporal Multi-valued Language. The proposed controller
deals with the typical features of a Real Time framework such as imprecision produced by the sensors, smart and continue changes of the physical
variables and it sends the required control signals in bounded time. This
is a major restriction that must be fulfilled by a real time controller.

Keywords: Automated Reasoning, Computational Complexity, Real
Time, Temporal Reasoning, Many-valued Logic, Control Systems.

1 Introduction

The interesting features shown by the Expert Systems together with the mature
theoretical basis existing currently to model and process uncertain and temporal
information, were the original technical points for envisaging new applications
inside the field of Control Systems by a part of the research community in Artificial Intelligence.

The mentioned new applications have in common their strong time restrictions in supplying actions in real time. In other words, to the existing difficulties
of representing uncertain and temporal knowledge, a technical step ahead begun
to be considered aiming at developing Artificial Intelligence techniques to cope
with time restrictions as well.

Thus, new theoretical material and schemes were developed progressively till
such Artificial Intelligence techniques turned out to be an important alternative
to perform Real Time control of complex processes.

One of the challenges of these new techniques is to represent and to process
inexact information, more specifically, imprecise, fuzzy, incomplete and noisy information. Thus, several languages have been proposed and deeply analysed to
model such types of inexact information. Here we propose a Multi-valued Logic
that, as we will argue later, allows to model imprecise and incomplete information

S. A. Cerri and D. Dochev (Eds.): AIMSA 2000, LNAI 1904, pp. 91–100, 2000.

both being necessary to tackle in Automatic Control Systems. Indeed, imprecision is inevitably introduced by sensors while incomplete information can be due to the bad functioning of some hardware or software elements in an input chain of a source information. Currently, many theoretical results on Multi-valued Logic have been found and real applications have been developed [10].

Another aspect in the representation and process of real time signals is their continuous changes. In order to deal with this temporal dimension, we extend the multi-valued language to a Temporal Multi-valued logic. Thus, the proposed KBS controler is modeled by a set of *Multi-valued Temporal Propositional Rules*.

The controler inputs are the outputs of the physic system and the control signals are the outputs of the KBS controller. The control strategy is established by a human expert or it is generated by a program computer taking into account the difference between the desired and the current state of the process. The control signals must be sent to the physical system within a bound time after the reception of some variation in an input signal meaning that the physic process has changed of state. This property is called Reactivity.

Thus, we shall analyse the involved algorithms in the proposed KBS interpreter and we shall show that the final complexity is in $O(1)$.

Summarising we propose in this paper a KBS controller based on 1) a Propositional Temporal [1] Many-valued Logic to account for state changes and certain kind of uncertainty; 2) an acyclic representation of the Rule Base of the KBS, namely logical literals can be ranked in levels; 3) a bottom-up interpreter algorithm with $O(1)$ on-line complexity; and 4) some methods to automatic validation of the KBS.

The plan of the article is the following. After the related work, we give an example to show that applications fit the hypothesis done in the design of the proposed KBS controller. Section 3 introduces the syntax and semantics of our Knowledge Based System. Section 4 discusses knowledge representation issues. Afterwards, we describe the Logical Calculi. Section 6 describes the main characteristics of our KBS and its associated interpreter. Finally, section 8 analyses the complexity issues.

2   Related Work

In this section, we briefly point out some works connecting Artificial Intelligence techniques with Real Time control process. To our knowledge, there is not attempts to design KBS with our features mentioned in the previous section.

In [16,17] is studied the connection between Real-Time processes and Artificial Intelligence techniques.

Reactivity is analysed for instance in [21,11]. In [12,18] necessary conditions that a KRBS interpreter must fulfill to posses the reactivity has been stated.

In [15] some issues relating incomplete information, precision in the answer and time response are addressed.

---

[1] The proposed logic is propositional and hence, it is not aimed at tackling with the frame problem and other famous problems in Temporal Reasoning

The idea of anytime algorithm have turned out of remarkable relevance in designing algorithms supplying answers in any time of the processing [3].

Search space problems with bounded computational time and where the quality of the heuristic is linked to the relative approximation of the answer to a global optimal are studied in [14,13].

Diagnosis and control in real time is a major field in Artificial Intelligence in Medicine, see for instance the special issue entitled "Computational Intelligent Diagnostic Systems" of [2] and more particularly, it has special relevance in the subfield intensive heart cure, see for instance the special issue entitled "KBS in cardiovascular medicine" of [1].

Bi-dimensional systems representing and reasoning with temporal and uncertainty information have appeared also in [9,7,6,19].

Finally, an alternative to classical control systems for complex systems is the so called Fuzzy control which is based also in KBSs. These systems operate by handling uncertainty but without temporal raisoning. For a survey of this topic and its applications see for instance [4,20].

3   A Real World Example

The described problem is part of a project aiming to implement a Real Time KBS at the Clinical Hospital of Barcelona (Spain) to execute automatically the required reactive actions in a Pediatric Intensive Care Unit (PICU). The main difference between reactivity in PICU with respect to any other ICU is that temporal constraints are stronger due to the *fragile nature* of new borns. Physicians in a ICU must perform both classical diagnosis and reactive diagnosis. Indeed, one main feature of patients in ICU's is that they are in critical states which could evolve dangerously to unstable states with dramatical outcomes.

Before computer technologies were available, the evolution of critical patients was sensored by means of analogical material and all patient bio-signals were under continuous supervision of medical personal. However, this continuous supervision provoke a natural tireness of the medical personal implying an unavoidable lost of the dynamical pursuit of the monitored signals during some moments. Unfortunately, within these unsupervised intervals dangerous pathological tendencies can appear and thus, the emergence state is detected with some delay. This delay could seriously aggravate the critical state of the patient and may render impossible to control the danger.

Thus, automatising the monitoring, supervision, diagnostic and therapeutic steps will avoid such severe drawbacks existing in manual operations.

The way of physicians reason in a PICU is compatible with the construction of the well known KBS applied in Medicine.

4   Syntax and Semantics

Let us start by the classical boolean logic to better grasp a straightforward extension called boolean multi-valued logic. This logic is then generalised to take into account the temporal dimension. In Real Time Knowledge Based Systems we deal with Horn Theories. A set of facts models a state and a set of implication rules allow to deduce implicit information associated to the states.

4.1   Syntax

Definition 1. Boolean Bi-valued Logic BBL. *It has two possible semantic values $\{0,1\}$ for each propositional variable. Classically, these literals are noted p and $\neg p$ respectively. According to our Many-valued notation, they would be noted $\{1\}$:p and $\{0\}$:p respectively.*

Definition 2. Boolean Multi-valued Logic. *It is a straightforward extension of the BBL, the only change relies on the cardinality of the set N of truth values that an interpretation can assign to a proposition p. Thus, a literal in BML is noted S:p and its complemented literal N/S:p. N:p is a tautology.*

Remark A large class of applications relies on this logic [10], but its suitability for Real Time Systems has not been considered yet.

Definition 3. Temporal Multi-valued Logic. *A TML literal is a triple (T, S, p), where S and p are as defined before and T is an interval [lb up]. If lb=up, the literal represents instantaneous information.*

Definition 4. Knowledge Based System. *A KBS is composed by a set of facts and rules. Facts and literals in rules are TML literals. The antecedent of a rule is a conjunction of TML literals and its consequent is a TML literal.*

Example 1. An example of a rule expressed in our language would be:

$$([t - 1h, t], (high), P) \wedge ([t - 1h, t], (high), Q) \rightarrow ([t, t + 2h], (very - high), R)$$

where t is the current instant and 1h stands for one hour. The rule models a particular situation in which if P and Q are high for the last hour then R will be very high in the next two hours.

4.2   Semantics

Definition 5. Interpretation *An interpretation is a map of the set of propositions to the paires of time intervals S_T and value intervals S_S:*

$$I : P \rightarrow S_T \times S_S$$

Definition 6. Literal Satisfiability. *An interpretation I satisfies a literal (T,S,p) if $I(p) = (T_p, S_p)$ and $T \subseteq T_p$ and $S_p \subseteq S$.*

Definition 7. Rule Satisfiability. *An interpretation satisfies a rule if it does not satisfy at least one literal antecedent or satisfies its literal consequent.*

Definition 8. Logical Consequence *A literal is a Logical consequence of a KBS if all the interpretation that satisfy the KBS satisfy also the literal.*

5   Representation Issues

Reasoning without considering imprecision and/or missing information could lead to erroneous decisions and hence provoke considerable pains. Indeed, the controller could lost the control of the process. We discuss briefly below the sources of these inexact information as well as some few concepts related to it.

The source of imprecision could be due to the analytical or digital sensors and the way experts reason in its expertise domain, because of the use of the so called linguistic labels appearing in the statements employed to explain the relationship among physical variables.

5.1   Sensor Imprecision

Imprecision is a feature inherent to sensors. The resolution of a sensor indicates the minimal variation of the signal perceptible by a particular sensor. Namely, a variation smaller than the resolution sensor has no effects in the output of the sensor.

Unaccurate Information. The existence of a sensor resolution entails that the output value of the sensor, which is possibly the input to the information process, is not the real input value. More precisely, if SR is the sensor resolution value, then its output value is related to the real physic value by:

$$val(physic) \in [val(sensor) - SR, val(sensor) + SR]$$

Digital Sensor. As we address here the control by means of a computer, the output sensor must be digital. If the computer processes data represented by at most n bits, then $SR = 1/2^n$.

5.2   Imprecision Due to Linguistic Labels

Some inputs to the system can be provided by an expert. For example, in medicine the physician can provide some informations relative to the clinical story of a patient, the dynamic of a certain illness, the relationship among particular parameters (cardiac rhythm, blood pressure, body temperature, etc.) and so on. Thus, an expert can provide his knowledge stating for instance "if a variable is between high and very high then ...". This is, firstly the expert *qualifies* the quantitative values of a variable mapping its real values to a limit set of the so-called Linguistic Labels (low, average, high, very-high,...) and second, he refers to it by mentioning intervals, for instance [high very-high]. In such situation, one has:

$$LB(val(var)) \in [LB_1 \ LB_2]$$

where LB(val(var)) stands for the linguistic label associated to val(var) and LB_1 and LB_2 are two linguistic labels, the first one associated to smaller values than those associated to the second one.

Unaccurate information modeling. The effect of the Sensor resolution can be captured easely by a TML literal (T,S,p) doing:

$$S = [val(sensor) - SR, val(sensor) + SR]$$

5.3   Incomplete Information

The controler sequentially reads the input signals, makes a certain reasoning and afterwards sends the output signals. A sensor breakdown or a connection problem during a certain time can cause that a particular physic variable was not measured when the automatic controler needed it. Similarly, the human expert for some reason can omit or unknow certain information at one determined moment and then do not supply it to the automatic controler. These situations can be covered by a literal $(T, Dom(p), p)$ where Dom(p) is the whole domain of possible values of the unknown variable.

6   Logical Calculi

The Inferences rules are two: One corresponding to a direct extension of the Modus Ponens to our Logic and another refering to the intervals of values and time.

Intervals Rule (IR)

$$\frac{(T, S, p), T \supseteq T', S' \supseteq S}{(T', S', p)}(\text{IR})$$

Temporal Multivalued Modus Ponens (TMMP)

We note $L = (T, S, p)$ and $I(L) = (T', S', p)$, with $T \supseteq T', S' \supseteq S$. Hence, $L \vdash I(L)$.

$$\frac{L_1, \ldots, L_k, I(L_1) \wedge \ldots \wedge I(L_k) \rightarrow (U, V, q)}{(U, V, q)}(\text{TMMP})$$

Theorem 1. Soundness *Let us note $\vdash_{\{IR,TMMP\}}$ the logical calculi formed by the IR and TMMP rules. $\vdash_{\{IR,TMMP\}}$ is a sound calculi.*

Theorem 2. Completeness *If $KBS \models L$ then $KBS \vdash_{\{IR,TMMP\}} L$*

7   KBS Design Issues

Notation We will distinguish between input Variables I, output variables O and state variables S.

In control Systems the dynamic of systems is mathematically well established by:

$$S(t) = f(I(t), S(t-1), S(t-2), \ldots, S(t-k))$$

$$O(t) = g(I(t), S(t))$$

The control in real time imposes that the computation of $g(I(t), S(t))$ may take at most $O(1)$ time to fulfill the Reactivity property.

Each output control variable o is associated with a set of rules whose consequent is a literal of kind $(., ., o)$.

Each input signal i coming from a sensor is associated with literals appearing in rule antecedents of kind $(., ., i)$.

Other literals are defined by the expert who needs to declare intermediate deduction. The set of intermediate deduced variables are the consequent literals of a set of rules. The different values of these variables taken in different instants conform the state of the controler. Intuitively, this state is related to the diagnostic of the external process. Thus, according to the combination of these values, the control signals O are defined to maintain the system continuously under control.

In order to design the Knowledge Based System the expert must have clear in mind:

The domain of each input variable, the set of different diagnostic of the physical state or similarly, a proper classification of physic states and the action to be pursued in each diagnosed state. Experience with Expert Systems, Control Fuzzy and other KBS technologies have proved that for many cognitive fields there exists a Rule Base System whose interpretation by an algorithm in an on-line process matches the suitable properties of a efficient control.

Although the design of KBS has be done till now in an ad-hoc way, recently, see for instance [8], some attempts have been proposed to design a KBS in a systematic way. The aim of this methodology is to bridge the gap between a specification of a problem in natural language and a specification in a declarative programming language.

In this article, we are proposing a language and the required algorithms that enable the existence of such KBS in order to have an adequate controler. As mentioned, KBS have arisen since several decades as a serious alternative to control when the system to be controled is very difficult to be modeled.

We consider three types of rules:

- *Input rules*: all their antecedent literals are associated to input sensors.
- *Output rules*: its consequent literal is associated to an output control signal.
- *Deduction rules*: they are not output rules, i.e. the consequent represents deduced information used by the expert.

The KBS is associated to a graph AND/OR as usual. Each node corresponds to a propositional variable. Each rule to an AND connector. The set of connectors whose literal consequent contains the same propositional variable defines an OR connector. The literals that do not have descendent connectors are input literals. The literals that do not have ascendent connector are associated to output control signals. Nodes having ascendent and descendent are intermediate deduced variables that corresponds to state variables S. As mentioned, they help the expert to make a diagnosis of a part of the physic system and also they provide a preliminary information required by the expert before stating with confidence the diagnostis and its corresponding control signals.

Human experts do not associate to each infinite combination of the input variable a different diagnostic and hence a different control. What an expert does it is to qualify the values of variables with infinite or big number of possible values and classify the values in a finite set (between three and ten) of values. Each set is refered to by a linguistic label.

Intuitively, this is because a part of the hyper-space of values corresponds to a same qualitative situation. Namely, although the state of the system is not exactly the same for two different values of the same region, the variation is not significant enough to change the qualitative diagnostic.

The values of the state variable are also qualified and then these values take a limit number of variables that usually goes from three

$$< Yes, unknow, Not >$$

to for example ten

$$< very - low, low, ..., very - high >$$

To each value of a qualified variable corresponds a virtual range of values in a numerical reference.

To take into account the variations of the signal with respect to time, a propositional variable $v(t)$ is stored as an array:

$$t => v(t) : v(t-1) : \ldots : v(t-k)$$

In order to keep a record of these values in the next instant is enough to execute a simple shift of the set of consecutive memory cells and to add the new value $v(t+1)$:

$$t+1 => v(t+1) : v(t) : \ldots : v(t-k+1)$$

The principle of the algorithm consists in propagating the value of the antecedents of a rule to the consequent. This propagation begins by the input signals and ends in the signal control accomplishing therefore a bottom-up strategy.

8   Complexity Issues

The forward algorithm is a straightforward extension of the algorithm [5], designed for the propositional case, to our temporal multi-valued language.

In our case, we assume that the connectors must be ranged in levels. Connectors of level 1 are those whose antecedents are all input variable. Connector of level k+1 are those whose antecedents are at most of level k and at least there is a literal with level k.

Linearity The linear complexity O(n) of the algorithm in [5] enable to design an interpreter with linear complexity:

 - Connectors are processed by levels and each connector is computed at most once.

– To determine if a rule can be fired each antecedent must have a truth evaluation in the current instant. To check this, one needs to match each literal (T,S,p) with the input or deduced correspondent literal (T_d, S_d, p). Thus (T,S,p) is true whenever $T \subseteq T_d$ and $S_d \subseteq S$.

Reactivity. Now, as the complexity of the algorithm is O(n), by definition of big "O", we know that the maximal time elapsed by the propagation process is $k_1.n + k_2$, where k_1 and k_2 are experimental constants. Knowing that, once the KBS is definitive and not modified anymore, n is fixed, the maximal time to compute the output signals is fixed and it can be determined experimentally. In other words, with n fixed, the complexity of the algorithm is $O(1)$ verifying in this way the reactivity property.

Coarse Parallelism. The reactivity time can be reduced using parallelism. Thus, with a coarse granularity in a multiprocessor architecture of p processors, the reactivity time can be reduced to up $K' < K$ and $K' > K/p$.

Fine Parallelism. If we use a fine granularity architecture with one processor per each variable and interval and one per each connector, this is O(n) processors, we can achieve a parallel complexity of $O(D.logR)$, where D is the number of levels in the KBS and R is the maximal cardinality of the antecedents of the rules. Hence, $K'' < K'$.

9 Conclusion

In this article we have proposed a language and an interpreter to perform control of physic systems in real time. This method relies on the Knowledge Based System paradigm. The language underlying our approach is a temporal multivalued language which cope with two major issues in representing knowledge: on the one hand, imprecise and incomplete information, and on the other hand, temporal information.

Thus our proposed method is an alternative to develop control in real time when the physic process is difficult to model, escaping in this way to the mathematical line attached to the Control Systems field.

Many advantages of our KBS devise have been pointed out and the strict restrictions in computing the output signal demanded by a real time control loop has been showed to be fulfilled.

Acknowledgements

This work has been supported by the project TAP 99-1086-C03-02.

References

1. *Artificial Intelligence in Medicine,* 10(1), 1997. 93
2. *International Journal of Intelligent Sytems,* 8(1-2), 1998. 93

3. M Boddy and T. Dean. Deliberation scheduling for problem solving in time-constrained environments. *Artificial Intelligence,* 67:245-265,1994. 93

4. P. Bonissone, Y. Chen, K. Goebel, and P. S. Khedkar. Hybrid soft computing systems: Industrial and comercial applications. In *Proceedings of the IEEE International Conference on Fuzzy Systems,* September 1999. 93

5. W. F. Dowling and J. H. Gallier. Linear-time algorithms for testing the satisfiability of horn propositional formulae. *Journal of Logic Programming,* 3:267-284, 1984. 98

6. D. Dubois, H. Fargier, and H. Prade. Possibility theory in constraint satisfaction problems: handling priority, preference and uncertainty. *Applied Intelligence,* 6:287-309, 1996. 93

7. P. Felix, S. Fraga, R. Marin, and S. Barro. Linguistic representation of fuzzy temporal profiles. *International Journal of Uncertainty. Fuziness and Knowledge Based Systems,* 7(3): 243-257. 93

8. M. Gelfond and A Gabaldon. Building a knowledge base: an example. *Annal of . Mathematics and Artificial Intelligence,* 25(3-4): 165-169, 1999. 97

9. L. Godo and L. Vila. Possibilistic temporal reasoning based on fuzzy temporal constraints. In Chris S. Mellish, editor, *Proceedings of the Fourteenth International Joint Conference on Artificial Intelligence.,* volume 2, pages 1916-1922, 1995. 93

10. R. Hahnie and G. Escalada-Imaz. Deductions in many-valued logics: A survey. *Mathware and Soft Computing,* 4(2):69-97, 1997. 92, 94

11. M. H. Klein, T. Ray, B. Pollack, R. Obenza, and M. Gonzalez-Harbour. *A prac-Honor's handbook for real-time analysis. Guide to Rate Monotonic Analysis for real-time systems.* Kluwer Academic Publisher, 1993. 92

12. E. Kligerman and A. D. Stoyenko. Real-Time Euclid: A language for reliable real-time sytems. *IEEE Trans. on Softw. Enginer.,* SE-12(9):941-949, 1986. 92

13. R. E. Korf. Depth-limited search for real-time problem solving. *Real-Time Systems,* 2(1-2):7-24, 1990. 93

14. R. E. Korf. Real-time heuristic search. *Artificial Intelligence,* 42(2-3):189-211, 1990. 93

15. R. Michalski and P. Winston. Variable pricision logic. *Artificial Intelligence,* 29(2):121-146, 1986. 92

16. D. J. Mulsliner, E. H. Durfee, and K. G. Shin. CIRCA: A cooperative intelligent real-time control architecture. *Trans. on Sytems, Man and Cybernetics,* 23(6): 1561-1574, 1993. 92

17. D. J. Mulsliner, J. A. Handler, E. H. Durfee, J. K. Strosnider, and C. Paul. The challanges of real-time artififcial intelligence. *Computer IEEE,* 28(1):58-66, 1995. 92

18. P. P. Puschner and C. Koza. Calculating the maximum execution time of rela-time programs. *Real-Time Systems,* 1(2): 160-176, 1989. 92

19. D. Qian. Representation and use of imprecise temporal knowledge in dynamic systems. *Fuzzy Sets and Systems,* 50:59-77. 93

20. E. H. Ruspini, P. P. Bonissone, and W. Pedycz. *Handboook of Fuzzy Computation.* 93

21. J. A. Stankovic and K. Ramamritham. What is predictability for real-time sytems? *Real Time Sytems,* 2(4):247-254, 1990. 92

Propositional Contexts

Christo Dichev, Trendafil Madarov*

Department of Computer Science,
North Carolina A&T State University
Greensboro, NC 27411
e-mail: *dichev@ncat.edu*

*Faculty of Mathematics and Informatics,
Sofia University, Sofia, Bulgaria
e-mail: *tmadarov@nemetschek.bg*

Abstract. A number of formalizations of contexts has been proposed since the seminal paper of J. McCarthy on contexts [8]. Despite considerable research efforts over the last two decades aimed at formalizing contexts, there are still a number of important aspects from a formal point of view that have not been sufficiently studied. This paper is a part of a more general study of several classes of multicontext systems aimed at characterizing them with respect to their languages. The present paper addresses the simplest multicontext systems, with propositional languages. Hilbert-style syntax is introduced as well as a context version of modal Kripke semantics. Correctness and completeness of the propositional multicontext systems are proved as well as their decidability.

1 Introduction

In many different domains the notion of context plays an important role. Intuitively, the notion of context is used to capture the meaning of all relevant factors in the environment that can affect an agents's behavior and help him to reduce the number of unexpected situations. In AI, contexts are used to overcome the problems resulting from huge knowledge bases (KBs) and also to tackle the problems related to "generality" [8]. The alternative suggested by the contextual approach is based on structuring the original knowledge base into a subset of smaller and easier manageable units. An essential aspect in such a partitioning is that the knowledge in each subset is assumed to be grouped based on given features, e.g. they might be grouped based on the problem being solved or based on a particular sub-domain. The next important aspect related to the partitioning of the global KB is to provide "local reasoning" in each unit or context. This property would enable us to localize the search for a solution within a particular context rather than searching the global knowledge base. However, partitioning the global KB into a subset of units does not solve the problem associated with the complexity of knowledge manipulation. The units of the global KB must be provided with "channels of communication" so that some facts derived in one of the units may be made accessible to the other units. It is important also that

S. A. Cerri and D. Dochev (Eds.): AIMSA 2000, LNCS 1904, pp. 101-110, 2000.

the interactions between contexts be based on reliable (justified) information. In a way, a system of contexts can be viewed as a set of "local" contexts connected with channels of communication into a network of contexts, i.e. into a *multicontext system.*

A number of formalizations of contexts have been proposed [1,5,6,7] since the seminal paper of J. McCarthy on contexts [8]. One possible approach of representing contexts is based on the notion of *logical formal system.* Each logical system can be viewed as a compound system with three components: a language, defining which sequences of symbols of a given alphabet are well formed formulas; a set of axioms asserting a collection of facts assumed to be true in the system; and a set of inference rules inferring new facts from already proven facts. If we associate each context from a given set of contexts with a particular logical formal system and introduce further new rules that enable us to infer new facts in a context from premises derived in some other contexts, then we arrive at the notion of a multicontext system. In the following considerations, the notion of context and the notion of logical formal system will be used as synonyms.

Despite considerable research efforts over the last two decades aimed at formalizing contexts, there are still a number of important aspects from a formal point of view that are not understood sufficiently. This paper is a part of a more general formal study of contexts. It addresses the simplest type of multicontext systems, with propositional languages, namely, *propositional contexts* and studies their properties from a formal point of view. The paper starts with definitions of some basic notions, which enable us to give a formal definition of a multicontext system and derivability in it. In the second part we introduce a Hilbert style syntax as well as a context version of the modal Kripke semantics. In the following part correctness and completeness of the propositional multicontext systems, are proved as well as their decidability.

2   Basic definitions

Following [6] in this section we introduce some basic definitions related to the multi-context systems and derivability in them.

Definition 1. *A context c_i is a triple $c_i = \langle L_i, A_i, \Delta_i \rangle$, where L_i is the language of c_i, A_i is the set of axioms of c_i and Δ_i is the set of inference rules.*

Each context describes the world from its specific point of view, based on its expressive and reasoning capabilities.

Definition 2. *A multicontext system (MCS) is defined as a pair $\langle \{c_i\}_{i \in I}, BR \rangle$, where I is a set of indices, $\{c_i\}_{i \in I}$ is a set of contexts and BR is a set of bridge rules.*

If $\varphi \in L_i$, then $c_i : \varphi$ is a *context formula*, that is any context formula contains the name of its context as a label. Thus $c_i : \varphi$ denotes the formula φ and the fact that φ is a formula of the context c_i. In addition we extend the set of context formulas, by adding one more rule for constructing new formulas. If $c_i : \varphi$ is a context formula, then $c_j : ist(c_i, \varphi)$ is also a context formula for all $j \in I$. Intuitively the formula $c_j : ist(c_i, \varphi)$ is used to express the fact that c_j is "aware" that φ is true in c_i.

To make a distinction between the two types of inference rules, the inference rules that belong to Δ_i are called *internal inference rules* or simply inference rules, while the inference rules that belong to BR are called *bridge rules*. The inference rules specify the "local deduction" in c_i, while the bridge rules specify the interaction and constraints between contexts. In fact the bridge rules make a collection of contexts a MCS. In general the bridge rules are of the following types

$$\frac{c_1 : \alpha_1 \ldots c_n : \alpha_n}{c : \alpha} I$$

or

$$\frac{c_1 : \alpha_1 \ldots c_m : \alpha_m \quad c_{m+1} : \alpha_{m+1} \quad \cdots \quad c_n : \alpha_n}{c : \alpha} II$$
$$\overset{[c'_{m+1} : \beta_{m+1}] \qquad [c'_n : \beta_n]}{}$$

The most popular type of bridge rules are the reflection up bridge rules and the reflection down bridge rules [6]. The following are instances of reflection up and reflection down bridge rules termed by us correspondingly *ist-inferring bridge rules* and *ist-eliminating bridge rules*.

An *ist*-inferring bridge rule such as

$$\frac{c_j : A}{c_i : ist(c_j, A)} Iist$$

enable us to infer in a given context c_i that in some other context c_j formula A is true based on the fact that this formula is proven to be true in the second context.

An *ist* -eliminating- bridge rule

$$\frac{c_i : ist(c_j, A)}{c_j : A} Eist$$

enable us to infer in a given context c_j that a given formula A is true, based on the fact that in some other context c_i the formula $ist(c_j, A)$ has been derived.

Notice, that in the previous example it is assumed that all contexts have the same language, i.e. each wff in a context c_i is also wff in any other context c_j.

The following definition introduces the notion of derivability (entailment) in multicontext systems. Each proof is a tree structure, whose elements are context formulas obtained by the following rules

Definition 3. *(Proof of a formula depending on a set of assumptions)*

(a) If $\alpha \in A_i$, then $c_i : \alpha$, is a proof of $c_i : \alpha$, depending on $\emptyset$.

(b) If $\alpha \neg \in A_i$, then $c_i : \alpha$, is a proof of $c_i : \alpha$, depending on $\{c_i : \alpha\}$.

(c) If Π_k is a proof of $c_k : \alpha_k$, depending on Γ_k for each k, such that $1 \leq k \leq n$, then

$$\frac{\Pi_1 \dots \Pi_n}{c : \alpha} \iota$$

is a proof of $c : \alpha$, depending on Γ, where

$$\Gamma = \bigcup_{1 \leq k \leq n} \Gamma_k,$$

assuming that the applied rule ι is of the type I, or

$$\Gamma = \bigcup_{1 \leq k \leq m} \Gamma_k \bigcup (\bigcup_{m < k \leq n} (\Gamma_k \setminus \{c_k' : \beta_k\}))$$

assuming that the applied rule ι is of the type II.

Definition 4. *A context formula $c : \alpha$ is derivable in a given multicontext system from a set of context formulas Γ if there exists a proof of $c : \alpha$ depending on Γ. By $\Gamma \vdash c : \alpha$ we denote the fact that $c : \alpha$ is derivable from Γ. A formula $c : \alpha$ is a theorem in a given multicontext system if $\emptyset \vdash c : \alpha$, denoted also by $\vdash c : \alpha$.*

One fundamental difference between our approach to formalizing contexts [2,3] and the other authors such as the work done by Giunchiglia and his colleagues [5,6] is in the type of bridge rules that are used. While most of the MCS defined in [6] introduce two types of bridge rules - reflection down and reflection up bridge rules, in this paper we restrict our considerations to a class of multicontext systems based on a reflection up bridge rules of the type

$$\frac{c_i : \phi}{c_j : ist(c_i, \phi)}$$

termed by us *ist-inferring bridge rules*.

One motivation for addressing multicontext systems limited to *ist*-inferring bridge rules is grounded on our observation that the multicontext systems extended with a reflection down *(ist-eliminating)* type bridge rule such as

$$\frac{c_j : ist(c_i, \phi)}{c_i, \phi}$$

are in a sense more vulnerable to inconsistencies compared to the former class. In MCS provided with *ist-eliminating (Eist)* bridge rules any inconsistency derivable in one context is propagated to the other contexts of the system:

$$\frac{\dfrac{c_i:\perp}{c_i:ist(c_j,\perp)}}{c_j \ : \ \perp} Eist$$

It turns out that it is possible to overcome this shortcoming by limiting our consideration to MCS with *ist*-inferring bridge rules. As a result of the elimination of the *ist*-eliminating bridge rules we achieve a locality of inconsistency, that is any inconsistency of a given context is its internal property and it can not be imported from outside. However, the consequences of such restrictions are not only beneficial. One problem with contexts limited to *ist*-inferring interactions is that it is possible from a given context c_i to derive facts such as $c_i \vdash ist(c_j,\varphi)$, while φ is not derivable from c_j. Thus it is possible a context c_i to assert that a formula φ holds in some other context c_j, while it does not. Such *ist*-assertions make c_i *incorrect for* c_j. For detecting and studying contexts with such properties we have introduced the notion of *importing context* [3]. Intuitively importing contexts are contexts where the ist-eliminating bridge rule is a derivable property. By elimination of the ist-eliminating bridge rules we arrive naturally to the possible world semantics which is demonstrated in the present paper for the propositional case of multicontext systems.

In the following sections we study the simplest class of multicontext systems, where all contexts are defined in a propositional language. We introduce a Hilbert-style syntax as well as a context version of a modal Kripke semantics. The correctness and completeness of the inference system has been proved and has its decidability.

3   Propositional multicontext systems

3.1   Syntax

Let *VAR* be a countable set of propositional variables and C be an at most countable set of context constants.

Definition 5.   *1. If $c \in C$, then $c : \perp$ and $c : \top$ are formulas.*
2. If $p \in VAR$ and $c \in C$, then $c : p$ is formula.
3. If $c : A$ is formula, then $c : \neg A$ is also formula.
4. If $c : A$ and $c : B$ are formulas, then $c : A \vee B$, $c : A \wedge B$, $c : A \to B$ are formulas
5. If $c : A$ is a formula and $c' \in C$, then $c' : ist(c, A)$ is also formula.

The following is the set of axioms of the multicontext system, including:

A context version of the classic propositional axioms:

$Ax_1 : \ c : \alpha \to (\beta \to \alpha)$

$Ax_2 : c : (\alpha \rightarrow \beta) \rightarrow ((\alpha \rightarrow (\beta \rightarrow \gamma)) \rightarrow (\alpha \rightarrow \gamma))$
$Ax_3 : c : \alpha \rightarrow (\beta \rightarrow \alpha \wedge \beta)$
$Ax_4 : c : \alpha \wedge \beta \rightarrow \alpha$
$Ax_5 : c : \alpha \wedge \beta \rightarrow \beta$
$Ax_6 : c : \alpha \rightarrow \alpha \vee \beta$
$Ax_7 : c : \beta \rightarrow \alpha \vee \beta$
$Ax_8 : c : (\alpha \rightarrow \gamma) \rightarrow ((\beta \rightarrow \gamma) \rightarrow (\alpha \vee \beta \rightarrow \gamma))$
$Ax_9 : c : (\alpha \rightarrow \beta) \rightarrow ((\alpha \rightarrow \neg\beta) \rightarrow \neg\alpha)$
$Ax_{10} : c : \neg\neg\alpha \rightarrow \alpha$

The following is K axiom in its context version:

$$c : ist(c', \alpha \rightarrow \beta) \rightarrow (ist(c', \alpha) \rightarrow ist(c', \beta))$$

And the axiom $\neg\bot$:

$$c : \neg ist(c', \bot)$$

In the following sections we examine two separate multicontext systems that result correspondingly from the inclusion and the exclusion of the axiom $\neg\bot$.

The following two expressions define the inference rules included in both multicontext systems.

Modus ponens (MP):

$$\frac{c : \alpha \quad c : \alpha \rightarrow \beta}{c : \beta}$$

$Iist$ brige rule:

$$\frac{c : \alpha}{c' : ist(c, \alpha)}$$

Thus we have defined a class of multicontext systems using Hilbert-style axioms for its axiomatization. The following are some basic definitions related to derivability.

Definition 6. *Let X be a set of formulas and $c : A$ be a formula. The formula $c : A$ is said to be derivable from X if there exists a finite sequence of formulas $c_1 : A_1, c_2 : A_2, ..., c_n : A_n$ such that*

    1. $c_n = c$ and $A_n = A$, and

    2. each element of the sequence is either an axiom or element of X or is obtained from the previous elements by applying any of the two inference rules.

The sequence of formulas $c_1 : A_1, c_2 : A_2, ..., c_n : A_n$ is called a proof of $c : A$, from X. The fact that $c : A$ is derivable from X is denoted by $X \vdash c : A$.

Definition 7. *Any formula that is derivable from $\emptyset$ is called a theorem. The fact that $c : A$ is a theorem is denoted by $\vdash c : A$.*

3.2   Semantics

Definition 8. *Let $U \neq \emptyset, R \subseteq C \times U \times U$. Then (C, U, R) is called a Kripke context structure.*

Definition 9. *Any mapping $v : C \times VAR \times U \longrightarrow \{0, 1\}$ is called a truth assignment function.*

Let (C, U, R) be a Kripke structure and v be a truth assignment function in it. The following is an extension of the truth assignment function to a truth assignment of any formula:

$$v(c : \bot, x) \stackrel{def}{=} 0$$
$$v(c : \top, x) \stackrel{def}{=} 1$$
$$v(c : \neg A, x) = 1 \stackrel{def}{\Leftrightarrow} v(c : A, x) = 0$$
$$v(c : A \vee B, x) = 1 \stackrel{def}{\Leftrightarrow} v(c : A, x) = 1 \text{ or } v(c : B, x) = 1$$
$$v(c : A \wedge B, x) = 1 \stackrel{def}{\Leftrightarrow} v(c : A, x) = 1 \text{ and } v(c : B, x) = 1$$
$$v(c : A \rightarrow B, x) = 1 \stackrel{def}{\Leftrightarrow} v(c : A, x) = 0 \text{ or } v(c : B, x) = 1$$
$$v(c : ist(c' : A), x) = 1 \stackrel{def}{\Leftrightarrow} \forall y \in U((c : x, y) \in R \rightarrow v(c' : A, y) = 1)$$
$$v(c : ist(c' : A), x) = 0 \stackrel{def}{\Leftrightarrow} \exists y \in U((c : x, y) \in R \text{ \& } v(c' : A, y) = 0)$$

Definition 10. *(C, U, R, v) is said to be Kripke context model. A formula $c : A$ is true in this model, if for each $x \in U$ we have $v(c : A, x) = 1$.*

A formula $c : A$ is true in a Kripke context structure (C, U, R), if it is true in any model (C, U, R, v) of this structure.

If Σ is a set of Kripke context structures, then the formula $c : A$ is true in Σ if and only if it is true in each structure of Σ.

3.3   Correctness and completeness

Definition 11. *By Σ_0 we denote the set of all Kripke context structures (C, U, R), such that $\forall c \in C \; \forall x \in U \; \exists y \in U \; : \; (c, x, y) \in R$. A relation R and context structure (C, U, R) with this property are said to be a serial relation and a serial context structure respectively.*

Theorem 1. *(correctness)*

1. *Each theorem in a multicontext system without the axiom $\neg\bot$ is true in each Kripke context structure.*
2. *Each theorem in a multicontext system with the axiom $\neg\bot$ is true in each Kripke context structure that belongs to Σ_0, that is, in each Kripke serial context structure.*

Definition 12. *A set of formulas X is called a theory if it satisfies the following conditions:*

1. *If $c : A$ is a theorem, then $c : A \in X$*
2. *If $c : A \in X$ and $c : A \to B \in X$, then $c : B \in X$ (X is closed with respect to MP).*

Definition 13. *A Theory X is a maximal theory, if:*

1. *X is consistent.*
2. *If Y is a consistent theory and $X \subseteq Y$ then $X = Y$.*

Lemma 1. *(Lindenbaum) If X is a consistent theory and $c : A$ is a formula, that does not belong to X, then there exists a theory $Y : X \subseteq Y$ and $c : A \notin Y$.*

Lemma 2. *Let X be a maximal theory. Then*

1. *$c : \neg A \in X \Leftrightarrow c : A \notin X$*
2. *$c : A \wedge B \in X \Leftrightarrow c : A \in X$ and $c : B \in X$*
3. *$c : A \vee B \in X \Leftrightarrow c : A \in X$ or $c : B \in X$*
4. *$c : A \to B \in X \Leftrightarrow c : A \notin X$ or $c : B \in X$*

Corollary. If $c : A$ is not a theorem, then there exists a maximal theory X: $c : A \notin X$.

Notice that the following property that is true in propositional and predicate calculus and in modal logic as well is not true any more in the multi-context case.

If X is a theory that does not contain given formula, then there exists a maximal theory containing X, but not containing the formula.

Definition 14. *Let X be a set of formulas. Then we denote $Ist^{-1}(c, X) = \{c' : A \mid c : ist(c', A) \in X\}$*

Lemma 3. *If X is a theory, then $Ist^{-1}(c, X)$ is also a theory.*

Lemma 4. *If X is a consistent theory, then $Ist^{-1}(c, X)$ is also a consistent theory.*

Definition 15. *The Kripke context structure (C_k, U_k, R_k) is said to be Kripke canonic context structure if U_k is the set of all maximal theories and for R_k holds*

$$x, y \in U_k : (c, x, y) \in R_k \Leftrightarrow Ist^{-1}(c, x) \subseteq y$$

Lemma 5. *Let $x \in U_k$. Then for any formula $c : ist(c', A)$ holds:*

$$c : ist(c', A) \in x \Leftrightarrow (\forall y \in U_k)((c, x, y) \in R_k \to c' : A \in y)$$

Definition 16. (C_k, U_k, R_k, v_k) *is said to be canonic context model if* $p \in VAR, c \in C$ *and* $x \in U_k$, *then*

$$v_k(c : p, x) = 1 \overset{def}{\Leftrightarrow} c : p \in x$$

where v_k *is extended to a truth assignement of any formula as described earlier.*

Lemma 6. $v_k(c : A, x) = 1 \Leftrightarrow c : A \in x$

Theorem 2. *(for the canonic model)*
   $c : A$ *is a theorem* $\Leftrightarrow c : A$ *is true in the canonic model.*

Theorem 3. *(completeness)* $c : A$ *is true in* $\Sigma_0 \Leftrightarrow c : A$ *is a theorem.*

4   Decidability

Consider a multicontext structure with the axiom $\neg\bot$ and finite number of contexts.

Definition 17. *Let* (C, U, R, v) *be a context model and* Γ *is a set of formulas closed under the subformula relation (i.e. if* $c : A \in \Gamma$ *and* $c' : B$ *is a subformula of* $c : A$, *then* $c' : B \in \Gamma$). *Let* $x, y \in U$. *We denote*

$$x \equiv y \overset{def}{\Leftrightarrow} (\forall c : A \in \Gamma)(v(c : A, x) = v(c : A, y))$$

Lemma 7. *The relation* $\equiv$ *is an equivalnce relation.*

Definition 18. *The context model* (C, U^*, R^*, v^*) *is said to be a filter of the context model* (C, U, R, v) *with respect to* Γ, *a set of formulas closed under the subformula relation, if:*

1. $U^* = [U]$
2. $\forall x, y \in U \; \forall c \in C$
   a) *If* $(c, x, y) \in R$, *then* $(c, [x], [y]) \in R^*$
   b) *If* $(c, [x], [y]) \in R^*$ *then for any formula* $c : ist(c', A) \in \Gamma$ *it holds: If* $v(c : ist(c', A), x) = 1$, *then* $v(c' : A, y) = 1$.
3. $v^*(c : p, [x]) = v(c : p, x)$ *for all* $p \in VAR, c : p \in \Gamma$ *and* $x \in U$

Theorem 4. *Let* (C, U^*, R^*, v^*) *be a filter of the context model* (C, U, R, v) *with respect to* Γ. *Then for any formula* $c : A \in \Gamma$ *and for all* $x \in U$ *it holds:*

$$v(c : A, x) = v^*(c : A, [x])$$

Lemma 8. *If* (C, U, R, v) *is a context model and* Γ *is a set of formulas closed under the subformula relation, then there exists a filter of the model with respect to* Γ.

Lemma 9. *Each filter of a serial context model is also a serial context model.*

Theorem 5. *The multicontext system with the axiom* $\neg\bot$ *has the finite model property, i.e. if* $c : A$ *is not a theorem then there exists a finite model in which* $c : A$ *is not true.*

Theorem 6. *(decidability) The multicontext system with the axiom* $\neg\bot$ *is decidable.*

5   Conclusion

The importance of formalizing contexts has motivated considerable research efforts over the last two decades. However the work done so far is not sufficient for understanding some important aspects of contexts from a formal point of view. This paper addresses a number of key logical properties of propositional multicontext systems. In fact the propositional contexts are an instance of a family of multicontext systems with respect to their languages. A similar study has been done for first order multicontext systems. In contrast to the propositional contexts, there are still open questions regarding both the completeness and decidability of first order MCS. This two types of multicontext systems cover a class of comparativly simple multicontext systems with respect to their languages. It is interesting to compare the results obtained for the latter MCS with a similar study of "mixed" multicontext systems, whose contexts are different logical formal systems.

REFERENCES

1 Buvač S. 'Quantificational Logic of Context'. In Proceedings of the Thirteenth National Conference on AI. Menlo Park, Calif.: AAAI, 1995.

2. Dichev Ch. Contexts as communicating theories. *AI Communications - The European Journal on Artificial Intelligence*, No 10(3), 1997.

3. Dichev C., Multicontext systems and importing contexts, *Proceedings of the 8th International Conference on Artificial Intelligence: Methodology, Systems, Applications (AIMSA'98)*, LNAI, Springer-Verlag, 1998, pp. 209-220.

4. Ghidini, C. and Serafini L., A Context-based Logic for Distribution Knowledge Representation and Reasoning. In Proceedings CONTEXT'99, Trento, Italy, September 1999 LNAI, volume 1688, Springer-Verlag.

5. Giunchiglia, F., Contextual reasoning. *Proc. of the IJCAI'93 Workshop on "Using knowledge in context"*, 1993, pp. 39-50.

6. Giunchiglia, F., L. Serafini. Multilanguage hierarchical logics or: how we can do without modal logics. *Artificial Intelligence*, 65:29-70, 1994.

7. Guha,R.V. Contexts: a formalizations and some applications, *PhD Thesis, Stanford*, 1991.

8. McCarthy J. Generality in Artificial Intelligence. In *Communication of ACM*, 30(12):1030-1035, 1987.

An Alternative Approach to Dependency-Recording Engines in Consistency-Based Diagnosis

Belarmino Pulido and Carlos Alonso

Grupo de Sistemas Inteligentes. Dpto. de Informática. Universidad de Valladolid
Edificio Tecnologías de la Información y las Telecomunicaciones
47011. Valladolid (Spain)
{belar,calonso}@infor.uva.es

Abstract. Consistency-based diagnosis is a main research area in Model-based diagnosis. Many approaches to consistency-based diagnosis need to compute the set of conflicts to generate diagnosis candidates. Possible conflicts are introduced as an alternative to dependency-recording engines for conflict calculation. Given a qualitative representation of system description, then search for those subsystems capable to generate predictions, and hence, capable to become conflicts. We define this concept for static systems, and later on we extend the definition to deal with continuous dynamic environments. Moreover, we explain how to do consitency-based diagnosis using possible conflicts.

1 Introduction

Consistency-based diagnosis uses only the description of the structure of a system and model of the intended behaviour of its constituents to localize malfunctioning components. Several techniques have been proposed to implement this theoretically sound theory. Probably the GDE approach[8] has been the most successful one. Nevertheless, several drawbacks have been reported when it was applied to dynamic systems[4, 7]. Perhaps, the most important problem is the presence of feedback loops, which appears due to the use of dependency-recording engines in the GDE framework.

Morevoer, in the field of continuous processes usually the number of sensors and its location is fixed in advance. Hence, candidate refinement stage in a GDE approach is more difficult.

As an alternative to dependency-recording engines for diagnosis of continuous processes, in this paper we extend and formalize the *possible conflict* concept[13] which reduce computation effort of on-line diagnosis in those environments where the number of available measurement points is fixed beforehand.

This work is organized as follows: first we introduce the concept of *possible conflict* for static systems. Second, we extend the concept to cope with dynamic systems, showing results in a case study. Later on we describe how to use that concept in classical consistency-based diagnosis. Finally, we compare our approach to related work.

S. A. Cerri and D. Dochev (Eds.): AIMSA 2000, LNAI 1904, pp. 111–121, 2000.
© Springer-Verlag Berlin Heidelberg 2000

2   The Possible Conflict Concept

In the GDE paradigm, diagnoses are obtained in an iterative cycle of behaviour prediction, conflict detection and candidate generation or refinement. A conflict is a set of correctness assumptions for system components that contradicts current observations. Moreover, the set of minimal conflicts characterizes the set of minimal diagnoses[8]. However, conflict calculation is not a trivial step and requires additional computation effort. In fact, GDE-like systems usually rely on dependency-recording engines to find them.

To avoid problems related with these engines, we propose the following insight: not every node in the conflict lattice can be a conflict. There are topological and behavioral restrictions that limit subsystems capable to become conflicts, assuming that no bridge-faults are present. To find these subsystems we work with a qualitative representation of system description.

From now on, *model* refers to a set of relations among variables describing a component or subsystem behaviour. And *model evaluation* denotes the search of values for one or more variables in a subsystem, given a model and a set of known variables, and using only local resolution techniques.

In the qualitative representation we propose, only system variables and relations among them are considered. The term *relation* applies to any constraint among system variables (physical laws, expertise knowledge, or control algorithms) whatever the form they adopt (quantitative or qualitative, algebraic equation or tabular function, linear or not). In this way, system description may be represented as a hypergraph.

2.1   System Description as a Hypergraph

System description, SD, defines a hypergraph $H = \{V, R\}$:

- $V = \{v_1, v_2, \ldots, v_n\}$ are system variables.
- $V = OBS \cup NOBS$. OBS is the set of observed, i.e. measured, variables, and $NOBS$ is the set of non observed variables.
- $R = \{r_1, r_2, \ldots, r_m\}$ is a family of subsets in V and it identifies the set of relations among system variables.

To avoid the use of dependency-recording engines, we must localize those subsystems in SD able to become conflicts. But conflicts are linked to discrepancies between observed and predicted values or between two predicted values. Therefore, we must search for those subsystems able to predict one value for an observed variable or to predict two values for a non-observed variable, that is, subsystems which can be evaluated[11]. We have called them *evaluable chains*.

Definition 1. *Given H, an evaluable chain is a partial subhypergraph $H_{ec} = \{V_{ec}, R_{ec}\}$, $V_{ec} \subset V$, and $R_{ec} \subset R$, verifying:*

1. *H_{ec} is connected.*
2. *$V_{ec} \cap OBS \neq \emptyset$.*

3. $\forall v_{no} \mid v_{no} \in (V_{ec} \cap NOBS) \supset d_{H_{ec}}(v_{no}) \geq 2$.
4. Let $X = V_{ec} \cap NOBS$ be the set of unknown variables in V_{ec} and let $G(H_{ec})$ be the bipartite graph whose set of nodes corresponds in one hand to the $x \in X$ and in the other hand to the $r_{i_{ec}} \in R_{ec}$, where nodes are linked by an edge iff $x \in r_{i_{ec}}$. Then, $G(H_{ec})$ has a matching of maximum cardinality $m' = |X|$ and $|R_{ec}| \geq m' + 1$.

The second point states for the need of, at least, one measured variable to diagnose. The third point is a necessary condition for local propagation[1], while the fourth point guarantees that the subsystem defined by H_{ec} has redundancy, which is a necessary condition to perform diagnosis.

As a result of this definition, an evaluable chain represents a set of relations whose variables might be either measured or evaluated using adjacent relations.

Definition 2. *An evaluable chain, H_{ec}, is minimal if no partial subhypergraph $H'_{ec} \subset H_{ec}$ is an evaluable chain.*

From now on, we will only consider minimal evaluable chains, since minimal diagnosis can be characterized from the set of minimal conflicts.

2.2   How to Do Predictions from Evaluable Chains

H_{ec} represents a necessary condition for a subsystem to be evaluable. However this does not suffice. We must consider the different ways a relation r_i can be locally solved. This information is usually available or can be computed. And it must be introduced to figure out **how** evaluable chains can be evaluated.

We create an AND-OR graph, the *evaluable model*, associated to each evaluable chain. Each edge in the evaluable chain provides with one or more AND-OR arcs the AND-OR graph, representing the different ways variables can be locally propagated to evaluate the relation. An AND arc implies that every variable in the tail of the arc must be measured or previously estimated to get the value of the variable in the head. An OR arc represents the need of the value of any variable in the tail of the arc to get the value of the variable in the head.

Different resolution methods, using only local propagation criterion, will provide different, if any, evaluable models for each evaluable chain.

We introduce two concepts needed to interpret the AND-OR graph:

Definition 3. *i is a leaf node iff $\hat{\Gamma}_i^{-1} = 0$.*

Definition 4. *i is a possible discrepancy node iff*
$$(d_{\overline{H_m}}(i) = 2 \wedge i \in NOBS) \vee (d_{\overline{H_m}}(i) = 1 \wedge i \in OBS).$$

That is, a leaf node has no predecessor[2]. And, possible discrepancy nodes represent variables which are either estimated twice because they are not measured, or estimated once because they are measured[3].

---

[1] $d_H(i)$ is the degree of node i.

[2] $\hat{\Gamma}_i^{-1}$: set of predecessors of node i.

[3] $d_{\overline{H_m}}$: inward demi-degree of the node i in graph G_m.

Proposition 1. *Let be $H_m = \{V_m, R_m\}$ the AND-OR graph induced by local propagation criterion on H_{ec}, where:*

1. $V_m = V_{ec}$
2. $\forall r_i \in R_{ec} \supset \exists r_{ik} \in R_m, k \geq 1$

Then, $r_i \in R_{ec}$ induce a partition in R_m.

$r_{ik} = \{x_{i_1}, x_{i_2}, \ldots, x_{i_l}\}, k \geq 1$ represents the k different ways r_i can locally compute x_{i_1} using $\{x_{i_2}, \ldots, x_{i_l}\}$.

Proof. Each $r_i \in R_{ec}$ induces an equivalence class in R_m. Hence, by definition, it induces a partition in R_m.

This is the first step towards the identification of evaluable models.

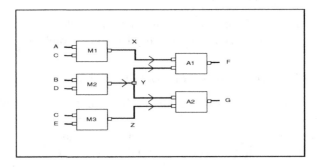

Fig. 1. A classical example. M_1, M_2 and M_3 are multipliers. A_1 and A_2 are adders. $OBS = \{A, B, C, D, E, F, G\}$. $NOBS = \{X, Y, Z\}$

Definition 5. *A partial AND-OR graph in H_m, $H_{em} = \{V_{em}, R_{em}\}$ is an evaluable model iff:*

1. H_{em} *is connected.*
2. R_{em} *is a minimal hitting-set for the partition induced by $r_i \in R_{ec}$ in R_m.*
3. $(\forall x_i \mid x_i \in V_{em}$ *and x_i is a leaf node) $\supset x_i \in OBS$.*
4. $\exists_1 x_i \in V_{em} \mid x_i$ *is a discrepancy node.*

The second point guarantees that every relation in the evaluable chain provides only one AND-OR arc to the evaluable model. The third point states the need of measurements to start local propagation. Finally, the fourth point imposes that a unique node may be the origin of a discrepancy.

We have analyzed the system in figure 1 looking for evaluable chains and evaluable models. To differentiate among components and relations in their models, we use uppercase and lowercase letters respectively. If needed, indices will distinguish different relations in the same model.

In upper left corner of figure 2, we can see its related hypergraph. In the upper right corner, we show the set of minimal evaluable chains obtained from the hypergraph:$\{m_1, m_2, a_1\}$, $\{m_2, m_3, a_2\}$, $\{m_1, a_1, a_2, m_3\}$. Also, we represent all the possible ways of local propagation allowed for model of the adder behaviour in the lower left corner. Finally, selected evaluable models, in the lower right corner, are:

$$F = X + Y \ \text{ where } \ X = A + C, \ \text{ and } \ Y = B + D$$
$$G = Z + Y \ \text{ where } \ Z = C + E, \ \text{ and } \ Y = B + D$$
$$Y = G - Z \ \text{ and } \ Y = F - X \ \text{ where } \ X = A + C, \ \text{ and } \ Z = C + E$$

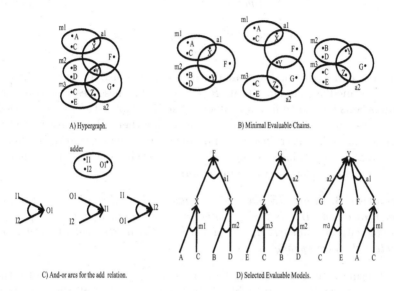

Fig. 2. Minimal evaluable chains and related evaluable models in the adder-multiplier example

2.3   Possible Conflicts and Their Relation with Real Conflicts

Summarizing, we can identify, off-line, those subsystems capable to become conflicts. However, it is obvious that conflicts can not be detected without real observations. Therefore we call these sets of relations *possible conflicts*.

Definition 6. *A possible conflict is the set of relations found in each evaluable chain containing at least one evaluable model.*

Since each relation is provided by one component, it is straightforward to obtain the set of components involved in each possible conflict.

To finish possible conflicts characterization, we compare them with conflicts obtained using dependency-recording engines.

First, we understand by $MODEL(C)$ a set of relations characterizing C behaviour, not only as an unique relation.

Let be:

- $P(S)$ the set of subsets of a given set S.
- $R = \bigcup_{H_{ec} \in SD} R_{ec} \in H_{ec}$.
- $MOD : COMPS \rightarrow P(R), C \rightarrow MOD(C) = \{r_i \in MODEL(C)\}$
- $COM : R \rightarrow P(COMPS), r_i \rightarrow COM(r_i) = \{comp \mid r_i \in MOD(com)\}$

Proposition 2. *If a GDE-like system finds a minimal conflict, co, from a discrepancy in v, there is a minimal evaluable chain $H_{ec} = \{V_{ec}, R_{ec}\}$, such that:*

$$v \in V_{ec} \text{ and } co = \bigcup_{r_i \in R_{ec}} COM(r_i)$$

The method searching for evaluable chains is exhaustive. Hence, it finds any over-constrained system such that $|R_{ec}| = m' + 1$. These describe the minimal set of relations needed to find a conflict: while the knowledge about one variable in the over-constrained system is suspended, another value is estimated using the remaining well-constrained system. Since dependency-recording engines find the set of well-constrained systems able to do predictions[9], our method finds these systems too, as stated in proposition 2.

Proposition 3. *If a GDE-like system finds a minimal conflict, co, from a discrepancy in v, and H_{ec} is the minimal evaluable chain verifying proposition 2, and all the evaluable models H_{em} obtained from H_{ec} are equivalent, then any H_{em} will detect the discrepancy in v.*

Furthermore, an evaluable model represents one of the ways to solve the set of relations in a minimal evaluable chain. On one hand, if all the ways to solve the well-constrained system, using local propagation alone, are equivalent (as in static linear systems) only one evaluable model suffices to detect conflicts. On the other hand, when solutions obtained from different evaluable models may differ depending on the initial starting point, we might fail to detect a conflict. Therefore, our set of diagnoses may be suboptimal, w.r.t. the number of conflicts used to compute diagnosis candidates.

Revisiting the example in figure 1, and assuming that the set of observable variables remain unchanged, any single or multiple fault will produce one or more of the following conflicts: $\{M_1, M_2, A_1\}$, $\{M_2, M_3, A_2\}$, or $\{M_1, A_1, A_2, M_3\}$. And they correspond to the set of components associated to each possible conflict.

Finally, what would happen if cycles were present? We have found two cases. If we have an observable value within the cycle, we can do estimations (see figure 4. Hence we have an evaluable model. Otherwise, local propagation alone can not be used, and the evaluable model is not valid. As reported in [9] this problem can be solved with the super-component alternative. Nevertheless, this last problem is out of the scope of this paper.

3   Possible Conflicts in Dynamic Environments

Let's now consider those systems whose components have state. In order to model dynamics[4], system description include relations involving time derivatives. As others have done[2, 7], we distinguish two kinds of relations (a) instantaneous, and (b) differential. The former kind describes static behavior and is represented as a solid edge in the hypergraph. The latter applies to relations containing time derivatives and are represented as dashed edges. In the previous section, only instantaneous relations were used.

The presence of differential relations in the models does not change significantly the main idea behind the possible conflict concept. However, we impose that (a) v_i and dv_i/dt, or v_i' for short, must be identified as different variables, and (b) only relations (v_i, v_i') will be allowed. This last relation means that we can estimate the value of the variable v_i at time t, if we know or we can estimate the value of v_i' and v_i at time $t-1$.

This last condition classify our approach as an *integration method*[2], and forces a slightly different interpretation of the evaluable models. If differential relations are present, the evaluation process has two stages. Initially, these relations together with variable values at time $t-1$ are used to estimate several variable values at time t. Afterwards, these values, together with current observations, are used to estimate the rest of variables at time t. To proceed in this way, we have assumed that the initial state of the process is known (i.e. the values of state variables at the start of simulation).

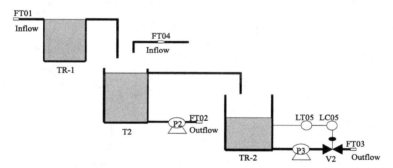

Fig. 3. The system to be diagnosed. $\{TR1, T2, TR2\}$ are tanks, $\{P2, P3\}$ are pumps, and $\{V2\}$ is a valve. We measure the flows $FT01, FT02, FT03, FT04$, the level $LT05$, and the control signal to valve $V2$: $LC05$

To illustrate these concepts we will use the system shown in figure 3, which contains elements common in many continuous industrial processes. Their models were obtained from first principles laws, and typical control algorithms, such

---

[4] In this context dynamic does not mean time-varying.

as a PID controller:

$$tr1_2 \equiv f_{10} = Cv_{10} \cdot \sqrt{\rho^2 \cdot g \cdot h_{TR1}} \qquad tr1_3 \equiv h_{TR1_t} = \int_{t-1}^{t} h'_{TR1}\, dt + h_{TR1_{t-1}}$$

where f_i applies for flow in line i, h_T for the height in tank T, ρ is density, g is the gravity force, and Cv_i is a parameter for pipe i.

In this system, we have found four possible conflicts:

$$\{tr1_1, tr1_2, tr1_3, t2_1, t2_2, t2_3, t2_4, p2_1, p2_2, p2_3\}, \ \{tr2_2, p3_1, p3_2, v2_1, v2_2\},$$
$$\{t2_2, t2_4, p2_1, p2_2, tr2_1, tr2_3, p3_3, v2_2\}, and$$
$$\{tr1_1, tr1_2, tr1_3, t2_1, t2_2, t2_3, p2_3, tr2_1, tr2_3, p3_3, v2_2\}$$

Figure 4 shows the steps to find the first possible conflict. In the left hand scheme the minimal evaluable chain is represented. In the right hand scheme its related evaluable model is shown. The conflict includes relations from models of components: $\{TR1, T2, P2\}$ and predicts the evolution of $FT02$.

Since solid and dashed arcs have different temporal indices, they break apparent loops in figure 4, i.e. $\{tr1_1, tr1_2, tr1_3\}$. In fact, loops become spirals[7]. This implies that we can not find a diagnosis in the precise moment its symptoms manifest. Instead, it will be localized in the last monitored period (as described in the next section).

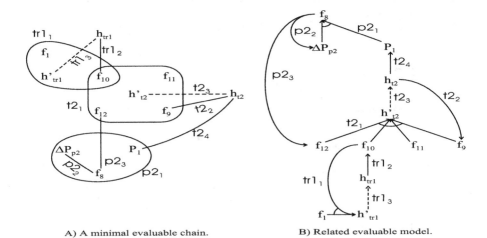

A) A minimal evaluable chain.   B) Related evaluable model.

Fig. 4. Two steps towards identifying possible conflicts. Represented variables are: flows (f), heights(h), and pressures (P). f_1, f_8, and f_{11} are measured variables

4 Consistency-Based Diagnosis Using Possible Conflicts

Consistency based diagnosis of dynamic systems is a complex task, because prediction and comparison of dynamic behaviour is required. Nevertheless, several diagnosis systems have coped with these problems in different ways [4, 7]. In this section we explain how the possible conflict approach can be used in consistency based diagnosis. It can be summarized as follows:

1. Identify every minimal evaluable chain.
2. Select one evaluable model by minimal evaluable chain, and reject evaluable chains with no evaluable model. Each model produces a possible conflict: $pc_1, \ldots, pc_k$.
3. Build models as described by its evaluable model for each pc in SD: SD_{pc_i}.
4. Iterate 4a to 4e:
    (a) feed each model SD_{pc_i} with system observations, OBS_{pc_i}. SD_{pc_i} produces a set of estimations $PRED_{pc_i}$,
    (b) check for discrepancy: $\parallel PRED_{pc_i} - OBS_{pc_i} \parallel > \delta$,
    (c) for each pc_i which finds a discrepancy, confirm pc_i as a real conflict,
    (d) introduce the set of components in each confirmed conflict SD_{pc_i} in the set of conflicts,
    (e) compute the set of candidates to diagnosis.

In the field of continuous processes, 4b and 4e usually can not be implemented in a straightforward manner. The presence of dynamics and the lack of accuracy in the models makes infeasible a simple point to point comparison between predictions and observations, hence we must compare their trends. Moreover, to discriminate among competing diagnosis candidates, we can not select new measurable points, because they are fixed in advance. Therefore, we propose to do consistency based diagnosis as a combination of monitoring plus fault detection. Periodically, we feed the possible conflict models with data series from the plant. Afterwards, each model estimates the trajectory of several system variables in the monitoring period. Both trajectories, measured and predicted, are compared by means of a Dynamic Time Wrapping algorithm, which give us a numeric estimation of the global distance between both series. This similarity measurement is compared against a fixed threshold. In this way, a fault is detected only when this value surpasses the threshold.

5 Discussion

Different approaches have analyzed system structure searching for a reduction in the computational effort of on-line model-based diagnosis. Nevertheless, this work is not intended for logical characterization of diagnoses[5], and we do not use any kind of heuristic information to help discrimination among diagnosis candidates once conflicts were detected[11]. Conceptually, we follow a similar pathway to that of structural residues generation[1]. However we do not analyze residual in a process control approach to model-based diagnosis[12]. Instead, we look for subsystems able to become conflicts in a consistency-based approach to diagnosis.

Moreover, the analysis required to find out possible conflicts can be done off-line instead of going back and forward in a causal graph once a discrepancy was found[10]. [6] reported a similar work for high observable, well structured discrete-events systems. Nevertheless, our focus mechanism does not split the system based only on observations and topology. We decompose it depending on relations among magnitudes too. Hence, possible conflicts can share components, as can be seen in figure 4.

Although information from conflicts may be used in the candidate rejection phase[14, 3], this role of possible conflicts is out of the scope of this introductory paper and it is considered as further work.

Main contributions of this work are a) the possible conflict approach is suitable for on-line diagnosis, because it avoids the computational burden related with dependency-recording engines, and b) it overcomes the feedback loop problem associated to dependency-recording engines in dynamic systems.

Acknowledgments

This work has been partially funded by the Spanish M.E.C. by means of CICYT grants TAP98-0828 and TAP99-0344.

References

[1] J. P. Cassar and M. Staroswiecki. A structural approach for the design of failure detection and identification systems. In *Proc. of the IFAC-IFIP-IMACS Conference on Control of Industrial Processes*, Belfort, France, 1997. 119

[2] M. J. Chantler, T. Daus, S. Vikatos, and G. M. Coghill. The use of quantitative dynamic models and dependency recording engines. In *Proc. of the Seventh Intl. Workshop on Principles of Diagnosis*, pages 59–68, Val-Morin, Quebec, 1996. NRC-CNRC, Canada. 117

[3] L. Chittaro, G. Guida, C. Tasso, and E. Toppano. Functional and teleological knowledge in the multimodeling approach for reasoning about physical systems: A case study in diagnosis. *IEEE Transactions on Systems, Man and Cybernetics*, 23, No. 6:1718–1751, 1993. 120

[4] P. Dague, P. Devs, P. Luciani, and P. Taillibert. Analog systems diagnosis. In *Proc. 9th Eur. Conf. on Artificial Intelligence*, pages 173–178, Stockholm, Sweden, 1990. Also appears in Readings in Model-based Diagnosis, pg. 229-234. 111, 119

[5] A. Darwiche. Model-based diagnosis using structured system descriptions. Technical Report 97-07, Department of Mathematics American University of Beirut, 1997. 119

[6] A. Darwiche and G. Provan. Exploiting system structure in model-based diagnosis of discrete-event systems. In *Proc. of the Seventh Intl. Workshop on Principles of Diagnosis*, pages 93–105, Val-Morin, Quebec, 1996. NRC-CNRC, Canada. 120

[7] O. Dressler. On-line diagnosis and monitoring of dynamic systems based on qualitative models and dependency-recording diagnosis engines. In *Proc. of the European Conference on Artificial Intelligence, ECAI96*, pages 461–465. John Wiley & Sons, Ltd., 1996. 111, 117, 118, 119

[8] W. Hamscher, L. Console, and J. de Kleer(Eds.). *Readings in Model based Diagnosis*. Morgan Kaufmann, 1992. 111, 112

[9] G. Katsillis and M. J. Chantler. Can dependency-based diagnosis cope with simultaneous equations? In *Proc. of the Eigth Intl. Workshop on Principles of Diagnosis*, pages 51–59, Le Mont Saint Michel, France, 1997. 116

[10] P. J. Mosterman. *Hybrid dynamic systems: a hybrid bond graph modeling paradigm and its applications in diagnosis*. Phd in electrical engineering, Vanderbilt University, Nashville, Tennessee, May 1997. 120

[11] P. Nooteboom and G. B. Leemeijer. Focusing based on the structure of a model in model-based diagnosis. *Int. J. Man-Machine Studies*, 38:455–474, 1993. 112, 119

[12] R. Patton, P. Frank, and R. Clark. *Fault Diagnosis in Dynamic Systems. Theory and Applications*. Prentice Hall International, 1989. 119

[13] B. Pulido and C. Alonso. Possible conflicts instead of conflicts to diagnose continuous dynamic systems. In *Proceedings of the Tenth Intl. Workshop on Principles of Diagnosis, DX99*, pages 234–241, Loch Awe, UK, 1999. 111

[14] L. Travé-Massuyès and R. Milne. Gas-turbine condition monitoring using qualitative model-based diagnosis. *IEEE Expert*, pages 22–31, 1997. 120

An Open Approach to Distribution, Awareness and Cooperative Work

Walter Balzano[1], Antonina Dattolo[2], and Vincenzo Loia[3]

[1] Dipartimento di Informatica ed Applicazioni, Università di Salerno,
via S. Allende, 84081 Baronissi (SA), Italy
[2] Dipartimento di Matematica ed Applicazioni, Università di Napoli "Federico II"
Via Cinthia 45, 80126 Napoli, Italy
[3] Dipartimento di Matematica ed Informatica, Università di Salerno,
via S. Allende, 84081 Baronissi (SA), Italy

Abstract. In this paper we present CoHyDe (Collaborative Hypermedia distributed Design), an open and strongly distributed hypermedia model that supports distributed workgroups. The architecture is based on the metaphor of the actor model and is structured in three layers, each represented as populations of autonomous and independent actors that cooperate in order to achieve common goals. The model supports temporally and geographically distributed workgroups and a current web-based implementation proves its applicability and functionality.

1 Introduction

An open collaborative framework should favour activities performed by geographically and temporally distributed groups, supporting (a)synchronous work, notification of events and awareness tools. In order to achieve these goals, a distributed groupware needs to address four important issues:

- *Distribution.* People in a work group may be distributed geographically, thus the models must adequately manage distribution of data and tasks, not only at the human level, but also at the software level.
- *Communication* refers to the basic ability to exchange information in any required form for the collaboration process between the involved parties.
- *Coordination* focuses on the scheduling and ordering tasks performed by the parties involved.
- *Cooperation* focuses on working on shared tasks in both asynchronous and synchronous ways.

This work proposes an open, distributed collaborative framework, CoHyDe (Collaborative Hypermedia distributed Design) modeled on the actor metaphor [1]. CoHyDe represents the extension of a previous adaptive hypermedia model, HyDe [4,5,6,7], towards a Web-level platform designed to support the working activities of the partners of a large scale project[1]. The remainder of this paper is

---

[1] European Raphael project "Pompeii, Regio I: Conservation Project", REF 96/412143 (A/IT/6).

S. A. Cerri and D. Dochev (Eds.): AIMSA 2000, LNAI 1904, pp. 122–131, 2000.
© Springer-Verlag Berlin Heidelberg 2000

organised in this way: section 2 describes the CoHyDe model and discusses in a detailed way the role of the actor-based layers that constitute its internal architecture. Section 3 is devoted to the Web-based prototype. A short comparison of our approach with related works is outlined in the conclusion together with some proposal of future works.

2   The Architecture of CoHyDe

The CoHyDe model is fully described in terms of autonomous and distributed actors. Each actor [1] is a computational agent living with autonomous knowledge and performing duties in a distributed and cooperative environment. Figure 1 shows the CoHyDe architecture, devoted to the collaboration activities; it is organized in three layers (*Coordination, Access* and *Work*). Each layer performs activities of distribution, communication, coordination and cooperation during the interaction with the other layers.

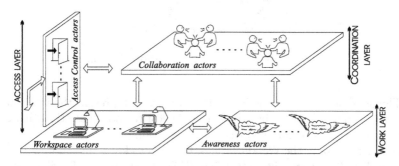

Fig. 1. Architecture of CoHyDe

2.1   Coordination Layer

The Coordination layer contains *Collaboration* actors (shortly *C* actors). For each collaboration activity there exists a unique **C** actor, but it can encompass several sub-collaborations (identified as *sessions*), restricted to its subsets of tasks and co-workers.

Each participant to a collaboration can create a cooperative session. All the sessions created within a collaboration are managed and coordinated from the same **C** actor and from it they inherit data and functionality. As shown in Figure 2, the **C** actor is a composite entity and can be viewed as the organization of internal data/scripts and of a collection of sessions that evolve in time. A Session actor inherits from the **C** class a subset of tasks, a subset of users, and specific constraints and abilities.

A description of the **C** class is shown in Figure 3, highlighting the two separate sections containing respectively acquaintances and scripts.

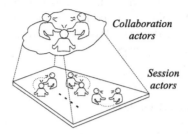

Fig. 2. The sessions represent a meaningful part of each **C** actor

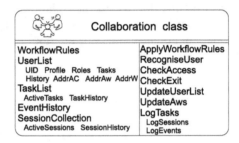

Fig. 3. Description of the Collaboration class **C**

The acquaintances, on the left part of Figure 3, represent the internal data, while the scripts, on the right, enable the **C** actor to coordinate the other actors, performing local tasks and cooperating with them.

In order to apply the WorkflowRules, **C** needs to know and to update the list of co-workers (UserList), their identifiers (UID), their profiles (Profile), their roles (Roles), the list of their tasks (which can evolve over time) (Tasks), the history of their personal interactions during the collaboration (History).
C manages in a distributed and coordinated way:

- the access control functionality, by direct cooperation with the Access layer;
- the private and shared workspaces and the event notifications;
- the history of all the cooperative processes;
- its sessions.

2.2   Access Layer

This layer is composed from *AC Access Control* actors (shortly, **AC** actors). A unique **AC** exists for each user. **AC** is responsible for initializing collaboration activities, maintaining and updating roles and access rights of co-workers. In order to manage this dynamic knowledge, **AC** maintains an active communication with the Coordination layer and a continuous cooperation with the user workspace. Figure 4 lists acquaintances and scripts related to this actor population.

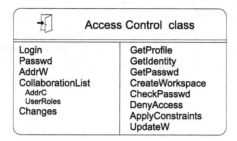

Fig. 4. Description of the Access Control class **AC**

AC actor knows the user, the address of his or her workspace and the addresses of collaborations where the user is involved and the roles of the user in each of them. Also, **AC** is responsible for creating the workspace for a newly accepted co-worker; successively, when the co-worker demandes a joint collaboration (or session), **AC** verifies the access and then communicates its consensus (or not) to **C**.

2.3   Work Layer

The Work layer is composed from two populations of actors, Workspace and Awareness (**W** and **Aw**).

Workspace level W manages the interface between the system and the user, by distinguishing private from shared activities.

Virtual workspaces [11] improve the abstraction from the specific time constraints and provide for simultaneous interaction of local and remote teams as well as rapid acquisition of feedback on material that must be reviewed by the whole group. Figure 5 lists acquaintances and scripts related to this actor population.

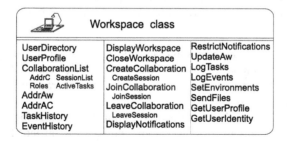

Fig. 5. Description of the Workspace class **W**

W contains private and shared knowledge of each co-worker: references to the storage, user profile, specific features related to his or her collaborations. **W** updates access rights of its co-worker thanks the cooperation with the **AC** actor. Further, **W** maintains logs of tasks, events, settings and enables the co-worker to send files or message and to get info about other co-workers.

Awareness level CoHyDe supports some consolidated types of awareness [14,15]:

- *Organizational awareness.* It represents the knowledge of how the work group fits in with the larger purposes of a project or society.
- *Structural awareness.* It is related to the roles, tasks and purposes of the people involved in the collaboration.
- *Workspace awareness.* It maintains the collection of up-to-the minute knowledge a person holds about the state of another's interaction with the workspace. In this typology of awareness is enclosed *presence awareness* and *event awareness* [2].

Furthermore, CoHyDe includes another typology of awareness, not taken into consideration by the current literature:

- *Domain awareness.* It is constituted by the information and tools that are specific to the application domain, and helps the user to better understand the actions and choices of the other co-workers.

CoHyDe provides a unique **Aw** actor for each user. In this way there is a one-to-one correspondence between **Aw** and **W** actors and a bi-directional communication flow between them:

- **W** → **Aw**. Any time that a user performs an action on his or her workspace, the workspace **W** informs its **Aw**, in such a way **Aw** that it can acquaint (by means UpdateC, Figure 6) with the same event the coordinator **C** that in turn communicates (in multi-casting) the occurred event to the **Aw**$_s$ that participate in the collaboration.
- **W** ← **Aw**. The aim of the previous cooperation is to inform all the users of the occurred event. For this reason, the **Aw**$_s$ send a point-to-point event notification (by means UpdateW, Figure 6) to their **W**$_s$. We note that this notification action is performed on the workspaces of both active and absent users.

Figure 6 lists the acquaintances and scripts related to this actor population.

The main role of **Aw** is the communication of new events to **W** (addressed by AddrW) during the collaborations (recorded in CollaborationList) (and sessions, SessionList) to which the user belongs.

The major part of its scripts are devoted to notification and log activity, in order to realize the first three types of awareness described earlier. These actions are carried out from the scripts NotifyActions, NotifyActivity, ..., LogNotifications.

The last script in Figure 6 (ApplyDomainAw) is a descriptive label that includes a more general set of domain-specific tools that make the collaboration process more effective.

![icon] Awareness class		
AddrW	UpdateC	NotifyNewRole
CollaborationList	UpdateW	NotfyNewSession
SessionList	NotifyActions	NotfyNewTask
NotificationHistory	NotifyActivity	NotifyNewUser
ReceivedNotifications	NotifyChange	NotifyOperation
SendNotifications	NotifyEvent	NotifyPresence
Action	NotifyIdentity	NotifyProfile
Activity	NotifyMessage	LogNotifications
	NotifyNewAccess	ApplyDomainAw

Fig. 6. Description of the Awareness class **Aw**

3   A Web Application of CoHyDe

The Web-based CoHyDe prototype has been implemented on the top of the
Web, using HTML, Java and Javascript. The interface of virtual workspaces is
organized as multi-layer HTML frame-sets. The browsing of the vector files is
enabled by the use of the WHIP, a public domain plug-in [17]. It supports multi-
layer vector images, the automated localization of predefined views, interactive
operations of pan and zoom on the images.

3.1   The Application Domain

The working context project, the European Raphael project, aims to favour
the interactions between persons of different European states, with very specific
skills, in order to preserve the cultural heritage of Pompeii. Many experts from
different backgrounds (essentially, archaeologists, programmers, computer scientists and architects) are working on the restoration and preservation of some
houses of Pompeii ruins. The experts need to work on a relief of walls (or on a
map of houses), to superimpose often a vector relief (or map) with the corresponding wall (or aerial) photo, to fill specific forms for any interesting particular,
the so-called contexts[2] and to discuss their results in such a way as to generate
scientific documentation on the houses (and parts of them).

3.2   An Example of Cooperation

Figure 7 shows a snapshot of the Web-based CoHyDe interface.
    The right part is automatically updated from the system on the basis of
the user actions, preferences and choices, while the left part of the window is
dedicated to the direct actions of the co-workers.
The right part provides meaningful information about:

1. the collaboration and session names (in the example, the users are working
   on the definition of the contexts related to the walls E-N-S-W (East, North,

---

[2] Context can be a door, a window, a hole, a plaster trace.

Fig. 7. A snapshot of CoHyDe interface during the cooperation process

South and West) of the room number 5 in the house 3, indicated in Figure 7 with the label Contexts - h3r5wE-N-S-W;
2. the co-workers, their state (present, absent, temporally absent) and their features;
3. the list of tasks related to the current session (Define context names ..., ...);
4. the log of meaningful events and activity, recorded in the Awareness frame.

The left part of Figure 7 contains:

5. on the bottom, a discussion area, on which co-workers can discuss in a synchronous way.
6. a graphical area organized for browsing on vector (or raster) images. A layer of this frame is supported by WHIP plug-in [17] and enables co-workers to see vector images and perform a set of localization functions (pan, zoom, etc.) as highlight by the pop-menu shown in Figure 7.
7. some speed-reference buttons that enable user to perform actions such as connect and disconnect, join, leave or create a session, show the list of co-workers with their profiles, identities, roles, tasks and home page addresses.

In Figure 7 and in the next two figures, the workspace shown belongs to the co-worker Antos.
In Figure 7, after a collaborative discussion, co-workers decide to concentrate their attention on context 2 (the second door on the relief); for this reason Helen zooms on it and extends her action to all the group.

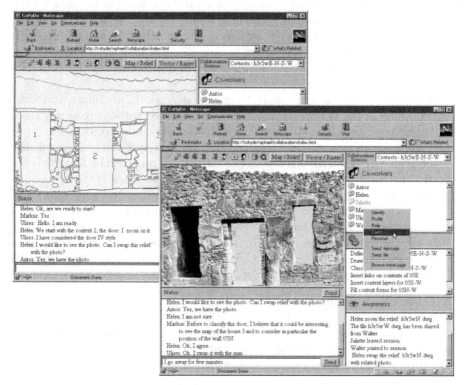

Fig. 8. Swapping between vector and corresponding raster image

The zoomed image is shown in left window of Figure 8. The difficulty to define the style of the door 2 presses co-workers to swap the relief with its related photo, clicking on the button Vector/Raster. The second window in the same Figure 8 shows the photo.

4   Conclusion

The CoHyDe approach proposes a distributed and cooperative model to support collaboration on the Web. It supports (a)synchronous cooperation activities, it is platform and browser independent, it provides very general solutions to the classical collaboration issues and manages group awareness abilities beyond the current page.

The current literature proposes a number of systems that support collaborative applications:

– CHIPS [9], DCWA [3], GroupKit [12] do not support session management, mechanisms for accessing shared information, tools for application-specific message exchange, access control, but there have not specific support tool for the development and integration of these important concepts in the Web.

- Alliance [13] is a Web-level authoring environment: it accomplishes distributed document management, communication and cooperation among distributed authors, but is provides only asynchronous collaboration support.

BSCW [2] offers basic support for cooperative work, providing a modular extension of the WWW's client-server architecture, without requiring modifications to Web clients (required by CoHyDe), servers or protocol, but it provides poor awareness tools, that actually are managed as asynchronous lists of occurred events. An attempt in this direction is proposed by MetaWeb [16], that extends the BSCW system with continuous feedback of the actions (activity awareness) and availability of co-workers (presence awareness).

GroupWeb [8] and CoWeb [10] allow interaction over several pages in a group, but provide, differently by CoHyDe, no awareness of other users beyond the current page. Also, GroupWeb is browser dependent (it is based on a specialized browser), and CoWeb relies on functionality only available in a now obsolete alpha release of Java and the HotJava browser.

Currently we are improving the synchronization mechanism and we are dedicating our research activity to model a new module that provides CoHyDE of more specific authoring tools; a requirement in this direction has been stimulated by the partners during the established collaborations on the Pompeii ruins domain.

Acknowledgments

This work has been partially supported by the European Social Fund of European Communities.

References

1. G. Agha. *Actors: A Model of Concurrent Computation in Distributed Systems.* MIT Press, Cambridge, MA, 1986. 122, 123
2. R. Bentley, T. Horstmann, J. Trevor. The World Wide Web as enabling Technology for CSCW: the Case of BSCW. *Computer Supported Cooperative Work, the Journal of Collaborating Computing*, vol.6, pp. 111-134, 1997. 126, 130
3. K. H. Chang, L. Murphy, J. D. Fouss, T. F. Dollar II, B. G. Lee, Y. Chang. Software Development and Integration in a Computer Supported Cooperative Work Environment. *Software-Practice and Experience*, vol. 28, n. 6, pp.657-679, 1998. 129
4. A. Dattolo, V. Loia. Collaborative Version Control in an Agent-based Hypertext Environment *Information Systems*, vol. 21, n. 2, pp.127-145, 1996. 122
5. A. Dattolo, V. Loia. Active distributed framework for adaptive hypermedia. *International Journal of Human-Computer Studies*, vol. 26, n. 5, pp.605-626, 1997. 122

6. A. Dattolo, V. Loia. A Distributed, Self-Adaptive Model of Hypermedia System. *Proc. of the 30th Annual Hawaii Intern. Conf. on System Sciences*, Wailea, Hawai'i, January 7-10, pp.167-176, 1997. 122

7. A. Dattolo, V. Loia. Distributed Information and Control in a Concurrent Hypermedia-oriented System. *International Journal of Software Engineering and Knowledge Engineering*, vol. 10, n. 6, December, 2000. 122

8. S. Greenberg, M. Roseman. GroupWeb: A Web Browser as Real-Time Groupware. *Proc. of the CHI96*, Vancouver, Canada, April 13-18, 1996. 130

9. J. M.Haake, W. Wang. Flexible Support for Business Processes: Extending Cooperative Hypermedia with Process Support. *Proc. of the Inter. ACM SIGGROUP Conf. on Supporting Group Work - GROUP97*, November 16-19, Phoenix, Arizona, USA, pp. 271-280, 1997. 129

10. S. Jacobs, M. Gebhardt, S. Kethers, W. Rzasa. Filling HTML forms simultaneously: CoWeb - architecture and functionality. *Proc. of the 5th Inter. World Wide Web Conf. - WWW96*, Paris, May 6-10, pp. 1385-1395, 1996. 130

11. N. C. Romano, Jr, J. F. Nunamaker, J., R. O. Briggs. User Driven Design of a Web-based Group Support System. *Proc. of the 30th Annual Hawaii Intern. Conf. on System Sciences - HICSS-30*, Wailea, Hawai'i, Jan. 7-10, vol. II, pp. 366-375, 1997. 125

12. M. Roseman, S. Greenberg. GroupKit: A Groupware Toolkit for Building Real-Time Conferencing Applications. *Proc. of the Conf. CSCW92*, Toronto, Oct. 31-Nov.2, pp. 43-50, 1992. 129

13. M. R. Salcedo, D. Decouchant. Structured Cooperative Authoring for the World Wide Web. *Computer Supported Cooperative Work, the Journal of Collaborating Computing*, vol.6, pp. 157-174, 1997. 130

14. J. Schlichter, M. Koch, M. Bürger. Workspace Awareness for Distributed Teams. *Proc. Workshop on Coordination Technology for Collaborative Applications*, Singapore, W. Conen (ed.) *LNCS*, 1997. 126

15. M. Sohlenkamp, L. Fuchs, A. Genau. Awareness and Cooperative Work: the POLITeam Approach. *Proc. of the 30th Annual Hawaii Intern. Conf. on System Sciences - HICSS-30*, Wailea, Hawai'i, Jan. 7-10, vol. II, pp. 549-558, 1997. 126

16. J. Trevor, T. Koch, G. Woetzel. MetaWeb: Bringing synchronous groupware to the World Wide Web. *Proc. of the 5th European Conf. on CSCW*, 7-11 September 1997, Lancaster, UK, pp.65-80, 1997. 130

17. WHIP: the Free Viewer for Drawing on Any Network. http://www.autodesk.com/products/whip/index.htm 127, 128

How to Schedule a Job Shop Problem through Agent Cooperation

Khaled Ghédira and Meriem Ennigrou

High Institute of Management
Research Unit of Artifical Intelligence for Information Systems and Simulation
41, Rue de la Liberté, Cité Bouchoucha, 2000 Le Bardo, Tunis, Tunisia
Khaled.ghedire@isg.rnu.tn

Abstract. Scheduling is an important aspect of automation in manufacturing systems. It consists in allocating a finite set of resources or machines over time to perform a collection of tasks or jobs while satisfying a set of constraints. One of the most known and hardest scheduling problems is the Job Shop, to which a distributed approach is proposed in this paper based on agent cooperation. There are essentially two types of agents: Job agents and Resource agents. Different agent behaviours based on heuristics are proposed and experimentally compared on randomly generated examples.

Keywords: Scheduling, Job Shop, Multi-Agent systems.

1 Introduction

The Job Shop Scheduling Problem (JSSP) is one of the hardest [12] and most commonly encountered scheduling problems. Because JSSP is NP-hard, a wide range of approaches have been proposed for its solving. These approaches fall into two classes: the exact or complete methods which provide optimal solutions but explode with problem size, such as [1,2,3,4], and the approximate methods that provide "near-optimal" solutions but with a "reasonable" time, such as [6,9,10,14,15]. In spite of all this panoply of approaches, the m×n Job Shop scheduling problem remains difficult to solve. Hence, other issues have been considered like the distributed ones based on multi-agent systems, where the scheduling is carried out by a collection of agents. Among them we can state [5,11,10]. Scheduling consists in allocating a finite set of resources or machines over time to perform a collection of tasks or jobs while satisfying a set of constraints. Each job is composed of one or several operations that can also be processed by one or several machines. The order of its operation processing defines its *process routing*, according which we distinguish essentially three types of factory scheduling problems: *Flow Shop* (same process routings for all jobs), *Job Shop* (different process routings) and *Open Shop* (unspecified process routings). The $m \times n$ Job Shop, in which we are interested in this paper, is defined as follows: -n jobs $\{J_1, \dots, J_n\}$ have to be achieved on a set of m resources $\{M_1, \dots, M_m\}$. -Each job J_k, k=1, ..., n, is composed of n_k operations performed

S. A. Cerri and D. Dochev (Eds.): AIMSA 2000, LNAI 1904, pp. 132–141, 2000.

according to a predefined order specified by its process routing. This order defines the *precedence constraint* between its operations. Let $O_{k,j}$ and $O_{k,j+1}$ be two given operations of a job J_k: $O_{k,j+1}$ can start only when $O_{k,j}$ has already been completed. -Preemption is not tolerated; i.e.; once started, an operation cannot be interrupted until it finishes. -Each job has its release date and its due date that specify its *temporal constraints*. -Each operation can be processed by one or several resources, and have a processing time depending on the resource chosen. -Each resource can process only one operation at a time. This condition is more known as *disjunctive constraint*.

2   The Multi-agent Approach

2.1   Multi-agent Architecture

Job Shop scheduling involves two kinds of constraints: on the one hand, precedence and temporal constraints relative to jobs, and on the other hand, disjunctive constraints relative to resources. That's why we define two classes of agents: Job agents and Resource agents. The former are responsible for the satisfaction of precedence and temporal constraints under their jurisdiction whereas the latter are responsible for enforcing their disjunctive constraints. In addition, Job agents are responsible for allocating their operations to one of their resources and to fix for them a start time. Nevertheless, these two classes are insufficient, an interface between this collection of agents and the user is needed in order to: -create the collection of agents needed for solving the Job Shop problem, -recognize whether the problem has been solved by the agents and -inform the user of the result. Consequently, a third agent class composed of a single component is added, the Interface agent. The latter doesn't intervene in the dialogue between Job agents and Resource agents. The proposed model relies on the Eco-problem solving one [7] enriched by [8], a Multi-Agent system where each agent has acquaintances (agents that it knows and with which it can communicate), a local memory composed of its static and dynamic knowledge and its own mailbox where it stores the received messages that it will later process one by one. Moreover, each agent, independently of its type, has a behaviour based on satisfaction search with priority to message processing.

Job Agents Each Job agent has as acquaintances the Resource agents that may perform its operations and the Interface agent. Its static knowledge consists of its release date, its due date, its process routing and for each one of its operations the list of possible resources with the corresponding processing times. Its dynamic knowledge consists, for each operation, of the currently assigned resource with the associated start time, the temporal slack and the resource penalities. The temporal slack of an operation is the time interval that spans between the current finish time of its previous operation and the current start time of its next operation minus its greatest processing time comparing to the worst case. It indicates the temporal range within which the operation may be assigned to without causing precedence constraint conflicts. Concerning the resource penalty, it indicates the number of times the resource has been solicited for that operation but has failed in finding a location for it. A Job agent is satisfied when all its operations are assigned and all its precedence and temporal constraints are satisfied and in this case it doesn't anything. Otherwise, it tries to assign its operations not yet allocated. In the following, we will call, for a given job, *its operations*, the operations under its responsibility and *its resources*, the resources which are likely to achieve its operations. In the same way, we call, for a given operation, *its job*, the job it belongs to and *its resources*, the resources that may perform it.

Resource Agents Each Resource agent has as acquaintances the Job agents whose operations are likely to be fulfilled by it and the Interface agent. Its static knowledge consists of the list of potential operations that it might perform with the correlated processing times. Its dynamic knowledge consists of the list of currently allocated operations along with their start times. A Resource agent is satisfied when its disjunctive constraint is satisfied and in this case it doesn't anything. Otherwise, it solves all disjunctive constraint conflicts as described in §2.2. In the following, we will call, for a given resource, *its operations*, the operations that it may perform.

Interface Agent The Interface agent has as acquaintances all Job agents and Resource agents. Its static knowledge consists of the list of jobs to realize and the list of available resources in the shop. Its dynamic knowledge consists of the schedule found and its makespan (i.e. the length of the time interval between the start time of the first operation achieved to the finish time of the last operation completed). Interface agent is satisfied when all the agents are satisfied, in this case it provides the found-solution to the user. Otherwise, it doesn't anything.

2.2   Global Dynamic

Before starting the distributed solving process, the Interface agent asks the Job and the Resource agents to initialize their environments (tables 1 and 2 line 3), namely their local memory and their acquaintances. Furthermore, each Job agent J_k determines an initial allocation for each one of its operations, that satisfies its precedence and temporal constraints and initializes penalities to zero for each one of its resources. An initial allocation, for a given operation, consists in choosing one of its resources and selecting a start time such that: *"If j=1 then start_time $(O_{k,j})$ = release_date (J_k) else start_time $(O_{k,j})$ = finish_time $(O_{k,j-1})$"*. Then, J_k sends these initial allocations to the selected resources to be checked (message *"Check $(O_{k,j}$, start_time, processing_time"* table 1 line 4). Such allocations do satisfy precedence and temporal constraints but not necessarily the disjunctive ones. A conflict between two operations assigned to a resource R_i occurs when these operations are overlapping. Such conflict is named an *overlapping conflict*. Hence, each unsatisfied Resource agent R_i proceeds to its own satisfaction by solving its overlapping conflicts one by one: it selects $O_{k,j}$, one of two operations involved in a given overlapping conflict (table 1 line 7), and sends the message "$Select\_Temporal\_Locat$ $(O_{k,j})$" (table 1 line 8) to itself in order to insert $O_{k,j}$ by choosing a new start time satisfying the three following conditions (function "$insertion\_succeeded$ $(O_{k,j})$" table 1 line 11): -C_1: R_i must be available during a period starting from the new start time and greater than or equal to the processing time of $O_{k,j}$ in order to satisfy its disjunctive constraint. -C_2: the new start time must belong to $O_{k,j}$'s temporal slack in order to satisfy precedence constraint of J_k. -C_3: the finish time of $O_{k,j}$ mustn't exceed the due date of J_k in order to satisfy temporal constraint of J_k. In addition, it updates its overlapping conflicts by side-effect (function "$update\_conflicts$" table 1 line 9). "$insertion\_succeeded$ $(R_i, O_{k,j})$" is a function that returns "$false$" if it fails to find a start time for $O_{k,j}$ satisfying C_1, C_2 and C_3, otherwise, it returns "$true$". In the "$false$" case, $O_{k,j}$ is ejected and sent to its Job J_k in order to find a new location (message "$Select\_Spatial\_Locat$ $(O_{k,j})$" table 1 line 11). At the reception of this message (table 2 line 4), J_k firstly penalizes this resource (table 2 line 5) and then chooses a resource R_i (table 2 line 8), the less penalized among $O_{k,j}$'s resources (when two or more resources have the same less penality, J_k selects a resource according to one of the heuristics described in §4). If all its possible resources have reached a predefined threshold, called "$first\_threshold$", J_k sends the message "$Create\_Temporal\_Locat$ $(O_{k,j})$" (table 2 line 9) to R_i in order to build a free location satisfying both J_k's constraints and R_i's constraints. Otherwise, it sends the message "$Select\_Temporal\_Locat$ $(O_{k,j})$" (table 2 line 10) to R_i asking it to find a location satisfying also both J_k's constraints and R_i's constraints. If R_i fails in either placing the operation or creating a location, it sends the message "$Select\_Spatial\_Locat$ $(O_{k,j})$" (table 1 lines 11 and 19) to J_k and so on. When all resources reaches another predefined threshold, called "$last\_threshold$", J_k sends an interruption message (table 2 line 6) to the Interface agent informing it that it has failed in allocating one of its operations. At the reception of this message, the Interface agent stops all the other agents and informs the user of the absence of solutions for the problem.

To create a free location, R_i firstly saves the current context (function $save\_current\_context$" table 1 line 13), namely the start times of its operations, and secondly shifts to the right a subset S_{op} of them of a duration d (function "$shift\_operations$" table 1 line 17), so as it will be available along a sufficient period greater than or equal to $O_{k,j}$'s processing time. An operation O belongs to S_{op} if it verifies one of the following conditions (let O_{prev} be the operation performed by R_i before O): -O is involved in an overlapping conflict with $O_{k,j}$ on R_i. -Start time of O minus finish time of $O_{k,j}$ is less than d. -O_{prev} belongs to S_{op} and start time of O minus finish time of O_{prev} is less than d. The procedure "$Shift\_Operations$ (S_{op},d)" shifts the operations of S_{op} of a duration equal to d. It returns a boolean value, which is set to "$false$" if there exists at least one operation in S_{op} that cannot be shifted, otherwise, it is set to "$true$". Shifting an operation to the right consists in replacing it such that its new start time is equal to its old start time plus the duration d. This new start time must satisfy the three conditions C_1, C_2 and C_3. Besides, shifting an operation to the right may lead to the shifting of its next operations (according to the process routing of its job) in order to not violate precedence constraints. If R_i fails in finding a new location for $O_{k,j}$ it restores the old context (function "restore_old_context" table 1 line 18). Before giving an example illustrating agent dynamic, we describe here the syntax used in tables 1 and 2: -sendMsg (receiver, sender, "message"): "message" is sent by "'sender" to "receiver". -getMsg (MailBox):retrieves the first message stored in Mailbox.

Table 1. Message processing relative to Resource agent R_i

1. m ←getmsg(mailBox);
2. case m of
3. Initialize_Environment: initialize_environment(R_i)
4. Check($O_{k,j}$, start_time, processing_time):
5.   Conflicts ←determine_list_of_conflicts(R_i);
6.   For each conflict of Conflicts do
7. $O_{k,j}$ ← select an operation of conflict;
8.   sendMsg(itself, itself, "Select_Temporal_Location($O_{k,j}$)");
9.   update_conflicts
10. Select_Temporal_Location($O_{k,j}$):
11.   if 7insertion_succeeded(R_i,$O_{k,j}$) then
11.   sendMsg(J_k, R_i, "Select_Spatial_Location($O_{k,j}$)");
12. Create_Temporal_Location($O_{k,j}$):
13.   save_current_context;
14. S_{op} ← subset of operations assigned to R_i;
15. O_{next} ← the next operation performed by R_i after $O_{k,j}$;
16.   d ← start_time($O_{k,j}$)+processing_time($O_{k,j}$,Ri)-start_time(O_{next});
17.   if 7(shift_operations(S_{op},d) and insertion_succeeded(R_i, $O_{k,j}$)) then
18.   restore_old_context;
19.   sendMsg(J_k, R_i, "Select_Spatial_Location($O_{k,j}$)");

2.3 Illustrative Example

Let the 4×3 Job Shop problem defined as follows: let J_1, J_2, J_3, J_4 be four jobs with respectively $(O_{11}, O_{12}, O_{13}, O_{14})$, (O_{21}, O_{22}, O_{23}), (O_{31}, O_{32}), (O_{41}, O_{42}) their subsets of operations. Let R_1, R_2, R_3 be three resources. Suppose that the penalization threshold is equal to 5. Table 3 summarizes the operation processing times of a subset of operations according to the used resources. Figure 1a shows the Gantt-chart of the current state of the 4×3 Job Shop problem. In addition, the current penality of resource R_2 for operation O_{22} is 5, the one of resource R_1 for operation O_{31} is 2 and the one of resource R_2 for operation O_{31} is 2. The Resource agent R_2 is unsatisfied because operations O_{11} and O_{31} are overlapping. So, it chooses among them one operation to reallocate, suppose

Table 2. Message processing relative to Jobagent J_k

1. m ←getmsg(mailBox);
2. case m of
3. Initialize_Environment: initialize_environment(J_k);
4. Select_Spatial_Location($O_{k,j}$):
5.   increase_penality(sender(m));
6.   if all penalities¿less penalized resources then
6.   sendMsg(Interface, J_k, "Interruption");
7.   else
8.   Ri ← less penalized resource for $O_{k,j}$;
9.   if all penalities ¿ first_threshold then
9.   sendMsg(R_i,J_k,"Create_Temporal_Location($O_{k,j}$)");
10.   else sendMsg(Ri,Jk,"Select_Temporal_Location(Ok,j)");

Table 3. Operation starting times

	O_{11}	O_{13}	O_{14}	O_{22}	O_{31}	O_{32}	O_{41}	O_{42}
R_1	4	3	3	-	4	5	2	2
R_2	2	4	2	-	2	3	-	4
R_3	-	1	-	1	-	2	2	3

that is O_{31}. Because there is no possible place on resource R_2 satisfying all the problem constraints, the Resource agent R_2 ejects O_{31} and sends the message "*Select_Spatial_location (O_{31})*" to its Job agent J_3 in order to find another location. When Job agent J_3 receives this message, it, firstly, increases the penality of R_2 to 3 and, secondly, selects the less penalized resource for O_{31}, in this case R_1 to which it sends the message "*Select_Temporal_location(O_{31})*" since its penalization is still below the penalization threshold. The latter is available during the time interval [2 ; 6] so O_{31} will be placed on R_2. Similarly, R_3 is unsatisfied because operations O_{22} and O_{42} are overlapping. Let us suppose that it chooses O_{22} to reallocate. Because there is no possible place on resource R_3 satisfying all the problem constraints, the Resource agent R_3 ejects O_{22} and sends the message "*Select_Spatial_location (O_{22})*" to its Job agent J_2 in order to find another location. Since R_3 is the only possible resource for O_{22} and the penality of R_2 is equal to 5, the Job agent J_2 will send the message "*Create_Temporal_location (O_{22})*" to R_3 asking it to create a free location for O_{22} such that all the problem constraints are satisfied. For this reason, R_3 shifts operations O_{42} and O_{13} of a duration equal to 1, in order to make R_3 available for O_{22}. O_{42} is shifted because it is involved in an overlapping conflict with O_{22} whereas O_{13} is shifted because O_{42} is shifted and the start time of O_{13} minus the finish time of O_{42} (5-5=0) is less than 1, the processing time of O_{22}. However, O_{32} isn't shifted because the start time of O_{32} minus the finish time of O_{13} (8-6=2) is greater than 1. Shifting O_{13} involves shifting O_{14} in order to satisfy precedence constraints relative to Job agent J_1. The obtained state after the above modifications is represented by

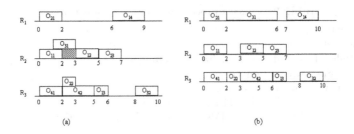

Fig. 1. Current state and the solution found

figure 1b where all agents are satisfied, so there is no more dialogue between the agents and the process has reached the end at this step. The interface agent will then provide this solution to the user.

3   Heuristic Adding

Two families of heuristics have been added to the basic model described earlier: the first one concerns Job agents and the second one concerns Resource agents. The first family consists in selecting the best resource to assign to a given operation. The second one consists in selecting the best operation to replace among the operations overlapping.

3.1   Job Agent Heuristics

Let $O_{k,j}$ be an operation to replace by its Job agent J_k. J_k will then select a resource according to one of the following heuristics: -Heuristic H1: J_k selects randomly a resource among the set of possible resources of $O_{k,j}$. -Heuristic H2: J_k selects the less loaded resource in the interval in which $O_{k,j}$ is likely to be assigned. -Heuristic H3: J_k selects the resource that performs the operation with the minimum processing time. Let J_k be a job and $O_{j,k}$ be the operation that it tries to place on R_i within the interval $[t_1 ; t_2]$, where t_1 corresponds to the earliest start time of $O_{k,j}$ and t_2 corresponds to the latest finish time of $O_{k,j}$. The load of R_i relatively to $[t_1 ; t_2]$ is obtained by summing the processing times of the operations already assigned to R_i in $[t_1 ; t_2]$ and dividing by the number of these operations.

3.2   Resource Agent Heuristics

Let $O_{k,j}$ and $O_{x,y}$ be two operations involved in an overlapping conflict. The Resource agent R_i will then select an operation according to one of the following heuristics: -Heuristic H4: R_i chooses randomly an operation between $O_{k,j}$, $O_{x,y}$. -Heuristic H5: R_i chooses the operation with the minimum processing time between $O_{k,j}$, $O_{x,y}$.

4   Experimentation

The goal of our experiments is to compare six versions, resulting from the different heuristics above-defined. In order to find the best version that provides the best performances in terms of Makespan and run time. The six versions are presented in table 4.   The experiments are performed on randomly generated ex-

Table 4. The different versions

Name Version	Resource selection	Operation choice
RANDOM	H1	H4
RANDMIN	H1	H5
LESSLOADRAND	H2	H4
LESSLOADMIN	H2	H5
LESSTIMERAND	H3	H4
LESSTIMEMIN	H3	H5

amples. The generation is guided by the following four parameters: -Complexity degree P corresponds to the probability that two operations will be involved in an overlapping conflict. $P \in \{0.1, 0.3, 0.5, 0.7, 0.9\}$. -Number of jobs $Nj \in \{5, 10, 15\}$. -Number of operations per job $No \in \{5, 10, 15, 20\}$. -Number of resources $Nr \in \{10, 20\}$. Consequently, 120 configurations (P, Nj, No, Nr) are obtained. Due to the non deterministic character of our model, we have generated, for each configuration, 10 examples and we have taken the average. Therefore, the total number of examples that have been generated is 1200. The performance of the six versions is assessed by the the two following measures: -Makespan: the length of the interval between the start time of the first operation achieved and the finish time of the last operation completed. -Run time (CPU time) requested for solving the problem instance. Two families of experimental comparisons have been selected among several ones to show the different versions' performances in terms of makespan and run time. The first one has the total number of operations (Nj × No denoted Tn_{op}) that varies but keeps complexity degree (P) constant equal to 0.5 and the number of resources (Nr) constant equal to 10 (figure 2). The second one has complexity degree (P) that varies but keeps the total number of operations (Tn_{op}) constant equal to 100 (figure 2).

5   Conclusion and Perspectives

In this paper we have proposed a Multi-Agent model for solving the m×n Job Shop scheduling problem. Two classes of agents have been defined: Job agents responsible for satisfying their respective precedence and temporal constraints and Resource agents responsible for satisfying their respective disjunctive constraints.

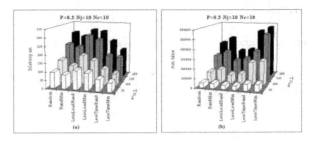

Fig. 2. Makespan and run time with P=0.5 and Nr=10

Each Job tries to allocate its associated operations in cooperation with its Resource acquaintances such that all their constraints are satisfied. The choice of Resource (resp. operation) to allocate (resp. to instantiate) is very important for model performances, namely makespan and run time. Thus, six versions based on heuristics have been proposed and compared on randomly generated examples: the "*LessTimeMin*" version (minimum processing time for both operation and resource) provides the best makespan whereas the "*LessLoadMin*" version (less loaded resource and operation with the minimum processing time) requires the less run time. Moreover, the makespan and the run time corresponding to these versions vary with complexity degree in a linear way. Furthermore, experimentation has shown a linear tendency for makespan varying with the number of operations and a late appearance of the exponential aspect (from 150 operations for 10 resources).

As far as our future work is concerned, other heuristic combinations and other experimentation based on compromise makespan/run time are foreseen. In addition, we shall extend our model to the optimisation aspect and to compare it with similar models.

References

1. Applegate, D., Cook, W.: A computational study of the job-shop scheduling problem. ORSA Journal on Computing (1991) 149 – 156
2. Baptiste, P., Le Pape, C.: A Constraint-Based Branch and Bound Algorithm for preemptive Job Shop Scheduling Problem. In Proceedings of the International Workshop on Production Planning and Control, Mons, Belgium (1996)
3. Blazewicz, J., Sterna, M., Pesch, E.: A Branch and Bound algorithm for the Job Shop scheduling problem. (A Drexl and A. Kimms, eds.) Beyond Manufacturing Resource Planning (MRP II). Springer Verlap, Berlin (1998) 219 – 254
4. Carlier, J., Pinson, E.: An algorithm for solving the job shop scheduling problem. Management Science (1989) 164 – 176
5. Cardon, A., Galinho, T., Vacher, J. P.: A Multi-Objective Genetic Algorithm in Job-Shop Scheduling Problem to Refine an Agents' Architecture. In Kaisa Miettinen, Marko M. Makela, Pekka Neittaanmaki, and Jacques Periaux, editors, Proceedings of EUROGEN' 99, Jyvaskyla, Finland (1999)

6. Dorndorf, U., Pesch, E., Phan Huy, T.: Recent Developments in Scheduling. In Operations Research Proceedings, Springer (1998)
7. Ferber, J., Jacopin, E.: The framework of eco problem solving. In Decentralized artificial intelligence. Editions North Holland, vol. 2 (1990)
8. Ghédira, K.: Partial Constraint Satisfaction by a MA approach combined with a Simulated Annealing Process. International Conference on AI, Paris (1994)
9. Ghedjati, F., Pomerol, J.Ch.: Résolution du problème d'ordonnancement de type Job-Shop généralisé par des heuristiques dynamiques. Rapport de Recherche LIP6 1997 / 005, Laboratoire d'informatique de Paris6, (1997)
10. Lin, S. C., Goodman, E. D., Punch, W. F.: Investigating Parallel Genetic Algorithms on Job Shop Scheduling Problems. In Proceedings of Seventh International Conference on Genetic Algorithms, Morgan Kaufmann Publishers, San Fransisco (1997) 481 – 488
11. Liu, J., Sycara, K.: Emergent Constraint Satisfaction through Multi-Agent Coordinated Interaction. In Pre-proceedings of the 5th European workshop on Modeling autonomous agents in a multi-agent world (1993)
12. Tsujimura, Y., Cheng, R., Yen, M.: Improved genetic algorithms for Job Shop Scheduling Problems. Engineering Design and Automation 3(2) (1997) 133 – 144
13. Wellner, J., Dilger, W.: Job Shop Scheduling with Multiagents. In workshop planen und Konfigurieren (1999)
14. Yamada, T., Nakano, R.: Job Shop Scheduling by Simulated Annealing Combined with Deterministic Local Search. Kluwer academic publishers MA, USA (1996) 237 – 248
15. Yen, B. P., Wan, G.: Solving the Job Shop Problem using Taboo Search with Fuzzy Reasonning. Proceedings of the 3rd Annual International Conference on Industrial Engineeering theories, Applications and Practice, PN 35. 1 - PN 135. 9, Hong Kong (1998)

Revisable Analysis and Design throughout Actors Interaction

Hassen Kriaa and Guy Gouarderes

Laboratoire LIA, IUT de Bayonne
3 Avenue Jean Darrigrand, 64100 Bayonne France
{kriaa,Gouarde}@larrun.univ-pau.fr

Abstract. This paper describes a method of multi-agent analysis and design for reactive, real-time information systems, relating to complex and risk-bearing applications. The fundamental principle consists of using a series of models in "cascade" to shift from an abstract representation of the problems to a formal one of the directly programmable agent (in Java for example). The first basic idea is not to have fixed goals or tasks, but rather for them to be gradually released from the analysis of the interactions between the actors (human or artifacts). The second idea, aims at integrating the space-time constraints according to an individual and collective point of view in a concurrent way. The last one, proposes neither to process on a hierarchical basis nor to laminate the final architecture of the interactions between agents but to, on the contrary define the acquaintance rules and their evolution according to the context. This paper details the various stages of this approach and compares them with other current work.

1   Introduction

The analysis of complex risk-bearing systems is directed towards information systems centered on the processes, whose architecture is built on network or distributed according to the various actors viewpoint. Thus in Wooldridge's work [1] an agent oriented analysis and design methodology for distributed and evolutionary information systems is presented. This method is based on predefined agents roles. Then an analysis of interactions between those various roles is implemented to account for the collective aspect of the system.

Kinny's Work [2] also suggests an agent oriented methodology which uses modeling techniques of individual agents based on the beliefs -desire – intention paradigm. Thus, it seems interesting for us to define an hybrid approach (individual and collective) one to design agents and systems based on agents like those mentioned in [3], [4] and [5].

Following Jennings's work [4], it proved interesting to try and improve the interactive complex systems making them more easier to use, quicker, more robust and easy to conceive and implement.

S. A. Cerri and D. Dochev (Eds.): AIMSA 2000, LNAI 1904, pp. 142-151, 2000.
© Springer-Verlag Berlin Heidelberg 2000

The models and the context specification are described here below and illustrated with an example.

2   Why an Agent-Oriented Method?

For several years, a great number of object analysis and design method have been developed. We will quote to Cauvet [6] and Rumbaugh [7] works for a quick layout. They have in common, the limits of the actors behavior representation, the re-use of the knowledge obtained by these actors (knowledge re-engineering) and a poor real time specification of space-time constraints.

In an intuitive way we think that an agent-oriented method is initially a reasoning step with phases, stages, etc., a dynamic phase which can mitigate some of those inconveniences. To represent that dynamic phase, we use some techniques and models. This representation favors the emerge of dynamic associations (reasoning parts or "chunks "). These are evolutionary concepts and thus revisable to be encased in formalization steps, allowing checking and coherence. Then we will implement them in an agent form with evolutionary programming tools such as : a real-time object languages, logical objects (CLIPS) or dynamic entities (SCHEME) or an agent framework such as Madkit [8].

Now, we introduce some approaches such as Use Case [9], Dano work's and an intuitive agent-oriented one. The Use Case approach consists in looking at the system to be built from the outside, from the user's point of view and from the expected features. The Use Case is addressed to an actor who is going to request the system and expect a measurable service from it. This request creates the notion of external event which calls for the system. The use Case regroup a sequence of actions to be created by the system.

The approach proposed in Dano's work [10] is a general method of acquisition and conceptualization of the necessities which focuses on the static aspects and then on dynamic one. That approach is based on Use Case and on Statecharts [11]. The innovation concerns the integration of the formalization within the development process of the object software.

An agent-oriented approach, according to our point of view begins with the actors interactions analysis in a informal way throughout a defined process pending to the indexation of the process into a triggering device. Then, we use a human-computer interaction modeling methods or techniques such as the GOMS method "Goal Operator Method and Selection rules" [12] to model activities and behavior. A formal specification is elaborated thanks to formal methods for example the ETAG grammar one "Extended Task Action Grammar" [13]. This level allows the specification of tasks matching activities and the description of behavior of individual and collective organizations for each of them. Then, conception is made up with classification and grouping of specifications. This conception brings to the foreground the individual and collective dimension which requires a mode of communication such as the STROBE "STRean OBject Environment" model for example [14]. Finally an implementation in an object language is created.

Unlike the approach proposed in [10] chich defines the Use Case and scenarios, we think that during the analysis step scenarios are going to develop progressively and that the agents cannot be identified by direct analogy with the actors in the studied process. So, in order to determine the agents, we need to analyze the activities, not through the actors of real world but through internal and external events which give rhythm to process.

We may note that these events are not only dependent on changes of state (states are not yet specified because we still have no tasks). They are relative to changes observed in the process. These changes observed in the process have for origin the speech-act [15]. They are in fact here generalized in any kind of exhange among the actors involved in the process, the process it self and the spatio temporal context. The chart below summarizes briefly the approach expressed.

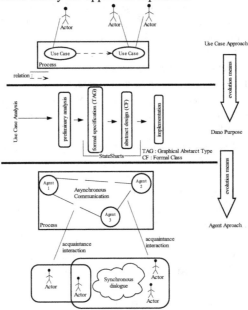

Figure 1 Three approach summarize

We think that an agent-oriented method won't be able to base itself on Use Case from a predefined scenarios. It will be based on a dynamic observation and events from speech-act among the actors. So the method described in the next paragraph introduces the various steps to cross speech-act to the agents who implement them.

3   A Preliminary Study

The agent paradigm is a popular among researchers although it is progressively introduced in certain professional application (as the web). The role of the agent-oriented methodology is to assist and to manage agent application during the whole life cycle step. For that, we distinguish three approach as :

Extension of object-oriented methods and techniques – Burmeister [16], Jenning [1] and Kinny [2]. This approach take its advantage from the similarity between agents and objects and the experience of the objects technologies. The major disadvantage is not only the lack of the social dimension of the agent but also the cognitive one (mental state).

Extension of the knowledge engineering method – MAS-CommonKADS [17] and CoMoMAS [18] which re-uses the defined ontology library and tools released from knowledge engineering methods. The disadvantage of this extension that it's a centralized design and they don't tackle the social and distributed aspect of agent.

The third approach gathers all other works, as one uses formal approach (DESIRE framework) [19], or the hybrid one which is based on dialogue analysis and interaction applied to the medical domain [20] or the approach to conceive cooperative information agent.

4   General Framework

When the behaviour of the human is being taken into account it lead us to consider that the dialogue between actors is a dynamic design source of the process itself. The activity is then defined as a generic unit of representation, with a distributed control and a purpose to be a vector of interaction between the constraints of the system (event-driven). The adaptation of the system to the user and its reciprocity is made possible with the revision in real time of the scheduling and the activities.

Rather than analysing individual and collective dynamics system separately, a convergent interactive analysis as in Barber work's [21] allows us to better articulate them, by including the distributed aspect thanks to the multi-agents concept. The objective is then to provide a methodological approach of agents specification and design which can perceive the environment, interpret it and act on it.

The starting point is based on the analysis of the dialogues for goals identification released from activities. The tasks identification and their regrouping allows a dynamic design and a structural and functional composition of the system components. During this stage, the architecture and the component are revised by rules (conflict resolution) not as a Guided Use Case [22] approach but with a Case Base Reasoning [23] type of resolution.

4.1   Process

The first step of our approach consists of dialogue analysis. So we construct manually the basic set of goals required by the system. To do that we extract from the dialogue exchanged between the actors of the system the set of the necessary triggers. For each one we associate it with the adequate goals. Then we set up the integrated class of activity launched. An example is given (see case study below).

The second step is the dialogue and action reification. It's the analysis step which is made up of two sub-steps. The first sub-step allows us to elaborate scripts for each goal. To do that, we analyze with the GOMS method each class of integrated activity. By this way, we begin the build up of the agent body. The second sub step is carried out in a parallel way and allows us to set up the basic task bases for the system. This sub step uses the ETAG grammar. To do that, we specify for each method, a function or a step the set of required objects, states, events, tasks and interaction diagrams. By this way, we begin the construction of the collective model. An example is given in the case study section to illustrate this step.

The third one is the design step. It consists of the construction of different entities needed by the system throughout aggregation and classification. Then, we use the STROBE model as a proof communication tool between the different entity taken two by two to determinate the agent. Then, we assigned for each agent the resource extracted from the different ontology of the system. These resources are differently instantiated according to the context. Finally all the agents are implemented with JAVA. An example of some agent is given in the case study section. During the second and the third steps some conflicts are detected so a knowledge and task revision is performed for each step to avoid error. The chart below summarizes those steps.

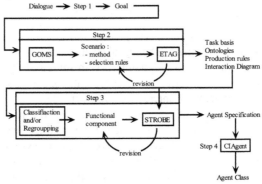

Figure 2 Step summary

4.2   Concepts

The concept used by our approach are process, trigger, activity, goal, script, task, individual model and collective model. Here are some definitions of the basic concepts :

–   Trigger : not only an event which launches a group of activities to accomplish a goal, but also any change taking into effect within the context.
–   Activity : it's a generic unit of representation. It can be considered as an interaction vector between all the constraints of the system.
–   Goal : a gathering of facts which describes the objective to reach.
–   Agent : autonomous (self-sufficient) software by the meaning of the STROBE model [24].

4.3   Models

The basic models that emerge from our approach are :
Activity model : this model allows us to identify the whole integrated activity of the system. An activity is to be done by the actor in a voluntary or non way to accomplish

goal. An activity is characterized by used method and it will be specified by a semi formal method "GOMS".

Task model : this model allows us to describe the task composition assigned to one or more actors under a time constraint imposed by the speech act between actors. This task basis will be formally represented by ETAG grammar.

Agent model (individual) : it represents the basic characteristics of the agent. Moreover, it includes goals, services, reasoning mechanism, communication modules, etc. The goal of that model is to provide a description for all the agents used by the system. An agent will be defined by all the tasks and services associated for each one.

Organizational model (collective) : this model represents agents organization. It describes the architecture which is made up of agents and the relations among them, plus their environment. This model itself is composed of a coordination model and a communication model.

5   Case Study

To illustrate our approach, we will study the emergency health care. Our system is composed of those actors : the doctor, the nurse, the reception and orientation nurse, a personal computer and the patient. All these actors cooperate to accomplish the main goal : a good assumption and awareness of the patient care. In this case study we detail steps of our method.

Step 1 : speech act analysis
Here we will construct manually the bulk of the triggering device as well as released goals then we set up the associated activities. For that we consider $D = \{D1, D4\}$:

D1 : "patient arrival alone or not "
Some released goal to accomplish are :
For D1 (A1, A2), the goal is "admission of a patient"
For these triggering device here are some associated activities :
For D1 :   A1 : "reception of a patient", A2 : "orientation of a patient"

Step 2 : analysis
step 2-1: GOMS specification
This step is performed to specify the task bodies. GOMS is the tool to construct the individual agent model and its body. To do that, we consider :
Rules: R2 : rule to accomplish "admission of a patient"
    If (new patient) then (accomplish "admission new patient")
    Return with goal accomplished
According to this rule we found some script :
S1 : method for goal "admission new patient"
  step1 : social allowances (M1)
  step 2 : visual allowances (M2)
  step 3 : method for goal : "create file" (M3)
  step 4 : method for goal : "move to care unit" (M4)
  step 5 : validation (M5)
  step 6 : return goal accomplished (M6)

Step 2-2 : ETAG formlalisation

It's a formal approach to describe task hierarchy by event, independently from the agent body. It's a tool to detect the event that generates acquaintance for the collective model.

Type [object = identification]

Value set : traumatology | medical

End object

Type [object = box]

Value set : occupied | non occupied

End object

Entry 1 :

[*task* > identification patient] , [*event* > patient], [*object* > patient = *P]

t1 [event > new patient],[OBJECT > patient = p]

   "identification new patient"

Entry 3 :

[*task* > box attribution] , [*event* > patient] , [*object* > patient = *P], [*object* > Box = *B]

t4 [event > patient], [*object* > patient = p], [*object* > Box = "non occupied "]

   "attribute a box to a patient"

Step 3 : Design

In this step we classify and regroup the system components depending on internal and external events. For the components we apply the STROBE model to qualify it as agent or not. The chart below illustrate an example of STROBE communication between "Box" and "SaisieOrientation" components.

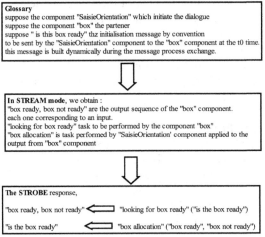

Figure 3 Communication with STROBE model

Step 4 : Implementation

Here we gives the specification of the retained agent using the CIAgent framework [25]. The chart 5 describes the prototype implemented in JAVA.

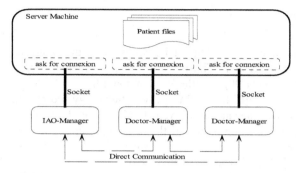

Figure 4 General framework of our prototype

6   Conclusion and Perspectives

We have presented an agent-oriented analysis and design method for the implementation of complex systems based on agents. That method articulates around four essential phases: the analysis of the dialogue itself among actors, the semi-formal and formal specification of the dynamics, the revisable and concourant design of components and the implanting phase.The main purpose of this paper is the definition of an agent based stage methodology which is based on the upstream analysis of the dialogue itself among the system actors.

For the "RADAI" method we assert as a significant result, the combination of the convergent ascending interactive analysis based on multiple points of view with the specification and the downward implementation of agents. This generates a flexibility based on revisability and autonomy, whereas Jennings's work [1] presents a strict and rigid methodology based on predefined agents throughout their specific roles. However, we lose many of the advantages acquired by this flexibility by the CIAgent framework that we used and which is based on the adaptation of agents by rules with poor mechanisms of inference. Thus, we may consider some improvements such as the use of a training mechanism to implement agents, like the results in Baron's work [26] on knowledge revision by genetic algorithms, or those with mutant agents [27].

On the other hand, we noted that the used methods (GOMS and ETAG) to specify tasks and activities are way too simple, too heavy and limited. Then we plan to adopt a more powerful and richer formalization method, such as the DESIRE framework of Brazier's work [19]. Moreover, agent must have a superior agility therefore the actual framework. For that, evolutionary or/and anticipative model developed by Ekdalh and Astor [28]or the FOCALE project [29] explore different possible solutions. The prototype which we developed is a real simulator, which allows to test, to verify, to update and to complete forthcoming knowledge in the process of emergency health care. The agents foreseen in the system cover learning, tracking, cooperation, help(assistant) and accreditation control aspects.

References

1. M. Wooldridge, N. Jennings et D. Kinny. a Methodology for Agent-Oriented Analysis and Design. Third International Conference on AUTONOMOUS AGENTS (Agents '99), Seattle, Washington, May 1-5 1998.
2. Kinny D., Georgeff M., and Rao A. A methodology and modelling technique for systems of BDI agents. In W. van de Velve and J. W. Perram, editor, Agent Breaking Away : proceeding of the seventh european workshop on modelling autonomous agents in a multi-agent world, (LNAI volume 1038), pages 56-71. Springer-Verlag : Berlin, Germany. 1996
3. Jennings, N.R. Agent Software. In proc. Of UNICOM Seminar on Agent Software, pages 12-27, London, UK. 1995
4. Jennings, N.R. et Wooldridge, M. (1995). Applying agent technologie. Applied artificial Intelligence, 9(6) : 357-370.
5. Müller, H.J. (Multi)-agent systems engeneering. In Second Knowledge Engeneering Forum, Kalsruhe. 1996.
6. Corine Cauvet, Colette Rolland. Object-Oriented Conceptual Modelling. CISMOD 1992.
7. Rumbaugh J. What is a method ? Journal of Object Oriented Programming, 1995, pp. 10-16 and 26. 1995
8. Ferber, J. http://www.lirmm.fr/madkit/.1998
9. Jacobson I., Christerson M., Jonsson P. et Overgaard G. Object- Oriented Software Engineering - A Use Case Driven Approach. Addison- Wesley. 1992.
10. Dano B: Une démarche d'ingénierie des besoins orientée objet guidée par les cas d'utilisation. Thèse, université de Nantes. 1997
11. Harel D. Statecharts: A visual formalism for complex systems. SCI. Computer Program, 8:231-247. 1987.
12. Card, S.K., Moran, T.P. and Newell, A. The Psychology of Human–Computer Interaction. Lawrence Erlbaum Ass., Hillsdale, New Jersey, 1983.
13. De Haan, G. ETAG-based Design: User Interface Design as Mental Model Specification". In: Palanque, P. and Benyon, D. (eds.) Critical Issues in User Interface Systems Engineering. Springer Verlag, London, 81-92. 1996.
14. Cerri S, Loia V, Maffioletti S, Fontanesi P et Bettinelli A: Serendipitous acquisition of Web Knowledge by Agents in the context of Human Learning. THAI-ETIS, Varese, Italy; june 21-22. 1999.
15. Searle J.P (ed) : Speech act – an Essay in Philosophy of Language, Cambridge University Press. 1969.
16. B. Burmeister. Models and methodology for agent-oriented analysis and design. In K Fischer, editor, Working Notes of the KI'96 Workshop on Agent-Oriented Programming and Distributed Systems. DFKI Document D-96-06. 1996.
17. C. A. Iglesias, G. Mercedes, J. C. Gonzalez, et J. R. Velasco. Analysis and design of multiagent systems using MAS-CommonKADS. In AAAI'97 Workshop on Agent Theories, Architectures and Languages, Providence, RI, July. ATAL. (An extended version of this paper has been published in INTELLIGENT AGENTS IV: Agent Theories, Architectures, and Languages, Springer Verlag, 1998.

18. Norbert G. Contribution to Knowledge Modelling in a Multi-Agent Framework (the CoMoMAS Approach). PhD thesis, L'Universtit'e Henri Poincaré, Nancy I, France, November. 1996.
19. Brazier, F.M.T, Dunin Keplicz, B.M, Jenning, N.R. and Treur, J. DESIRE : Modelling multi-agent systems in a compositional formal framework. In M. Huhns, M. Singh, (Eds), International Journal of Cooperative Information Systems, special issue on Formal Methods in Cooperative Information Systems : Multi-Agent Systems. 1997.
20. Kriaa H., Gouardères G. Revisable Analysis and Design by Actors Interaction : Emergency Case Study. Knowledge and information Systems, International Journal, B. W. Wah Editor, ISSN 0219-1377 – Springer-verlag – Berlin, (à paraître). 2000.
21. Barber, K. S., Graser, T. J., Jernigan, S. R. and McGiverin, B. Features of the Systems Engineering Process Activities (SEPA) Methodology. Accepted to AAAI's Special Interest Group in Manufacturing Workshop on Artificial Intelligence and Manufacturing: State of the Art and State of Practice (SIGMAN Workshop 1998), Albuquerque, NM. 1998.
22. Colette Rolland, Carine Souveyet, Camille B. Achour: Guiding Goal Modeling Using Scenarios. TSE 24(12): 1055-1071, 1998.
23. Millet S, Gouardères G: Approche qualitative de la ré-ingénierie d'un système tuteur intelligent à partir d'une méthodologie d'évaluation. 3° International Conference on Intelligent Tutoring Systems
-ITS'96- ACM/AFCET/SIGART/SIGCUE/IEEE - Montréal - Canada. 1996.
24. Cerri, S. Cognitive environments in the STROBE Model. European Conference on Artificial Intelligence in Education - Euro-AIED'96 - Lisbon - Portugal. 1996.
25. Bigus J.P and Bigus J. Constructing Intelligent agent with java. A programmer's guide to smarter applications. Wiley computer publishing, Toronto. 1998
26. Baron, C. et Gouardères, G. Diagnostic et filtrage par algorithme génétique pour l'aide à la décision dans la conception de mécanismes. 3ème Congrès International de génie industriel. Du 25 au 28 mai, Montréal, Canada. 1999
27. Gouardères G., Canut M.F., Sanchis E. From Mutant to Learning Agents. Different Agents to Model Learning. A symposium at the 14th European Meeting on Cybernetics and Systems Research - EMCSR'98, Vienna, Austria. 1998.
28. Ekdahl B., Astor E., Davidsson P. Toward Anticipatory Agents», In M. Woolridge and N.R. Jennings, editors, Intelligent Agents - Theories, Architectures, and Languages, Lecture Notes in Artificial Intelligence 890, pp. 191-202, Springer Verlag, 1995
29. Courant M., Le Peutrec S., «From virtual instruments to real control», Proceedings of the Eleventh Congress of World Organisation of Systems and Cybernetics, Uxbridge, England, August 23-27, 1999.

Simulation and Multi-agent Environment for Aircraft Maintenance Learning

G. Gouardères[1], A. Minko[1,2], and L. Richard[2]

[1]Equipe MISIM - Laboratoire d'Informatique Appliquée –
IUT de Bayonne, 64100 Bayonne – France
`Guy.Gouarderes@iutbay.univ-pau.fr`
[2]Interactive STAR Rue Marcel Issartier 33700 Mérignac – France
`{Anton.Minko,Luc.Richard}@STAR-IMA.com`

Abstract: This paper presents the earlier results of the CMOS project prototype including an embedded multi-agents ITS (Intelligent Tutoring Systems) aimed to help efficiently the learner who faces troubleshooting maintenance tasks. This environment gives responses dedicated to aeronautical training sessions according to a three-step principle: first to «introduce», second to «convince» and, finally, to get to do. We emphasize two main characteristics: a real-time full simulation of the technical domain, which works with a tutoring multi-agent architecture, ASITS. ASITS is supplied with reactive and cognitive agents to track the learner's performance, to detect inherent negative effects (the learner's "cognitive gaps"), and as a feedback issue, to identify some deficiencies that current training simulator lacks. Therefore, as the measuring of gap values with quantitative rules keeps sometimes hazardous, the concept of simulation has to be extended to a Qualitative Simulation approach.

Keywords: Interactive Learning Environments, Real-time Simulation, Intelligent Tutoring Systems, Multi-agent Systems, Graphical Interface, Diagnostic Reasoning.

1 Introduction

This paper describes why the « intelligent » desktop simulators for individual learning and/or team training rely on social aspects of distributed artificial intelligence. This reflection leads us to study computationally intelligent behavior using specifically tailored architecture for multi-agents ITS (ASITS, Actor System for ITS) [7, 8].

This architecture has been applied in a simulation-based learning environment in order to allow the instructors to perform an anytime assessment [2] by tracking the learner in real time (Progressive Assessment). As a feedback issue, we show how specialized cognitive agents can contribute to model the interaction design of a

S. A. Cerri and D. Dochev (Eds.): AIMSA 2000, LNAI 1904, pp. 152-166, 2000.
© Springer-Verlag Berlin Heidelberg

learning session in an Intelligent Desktop Trainer. In multi-agent based ITS, this perspective raise three major problems: (i) the definition of the communication standards for exchanging real-time information between the agents, (ii) the indexing of expertise to facilitate 'know-how' tracking within all the relevant domains and (iii) the cognitive interaction design.

To resolve the problems raised before, agents must integrate adaptable strategies to monitor the user's actions and his level of attention and to provide him the adequate help in the same way as an ITS does.

In order to detect inherent negative effects (i.e. the learner's"cognitive gaps") brought into the learning process both by imperfect or incomplete immersion in simulation and by insufficient learner expertise for pedagogical strategy in ITS [7], we have developed a prototype1 as a fully runnable maintenance simulator [13]. In this system, the "full-simulation" principle is supported by an embedded architecture built on three simulation layers: Real-time Kernel (free-play mode), distributed simulation (individual or team learning of procedure) and qualitative simulation (evaluating cognitive gaps from the learner).

This architecture matches exactly the procedural learning (aeronautical maintenance) and lets to control all the three phases of learning - (i) the learner is firstly introduced in the exercise in instructor-assisted mode, (ii) the he/she can try to repeat training sequences in step-by-step mode in order to understand the knowledge acquired and to get convinced (the agents follow the learner and correct him/her immediately), (iii) finally, the learner does all exercises in free-play mode (agents don't show their reaction during the exercise, but they sum up all learner's activities and deliver a summary sheet for further debriefing with the instructor).

Finally, the system was designed with the capacity to detect immediately (it runs in real-time environment) changes in the cognitive profile of the learner. This aspect can be estimated (positively or not) depending on three learning mode identified as a, b, c mechanisms (§4.3) and using a typology of primitive cognitive gaps (tunnel effect, dropping or context gaps). The paper focuses on how aspects of user's behavior can be monitored by a gap evaluator agent.

2   New Concepts for Simulation Training in Aeronautics

2.1   Key Concepts for the Design of Task-Oriented Activities

Degani & Wiener [5] and Boy [4] have focused on the manner in which pilots use the checklists in normal situations. As new research issues from this previous work we emphasize the search for tools more adapted to human operators, aimed to improve the reliability of the human-system tandem. We have shown that the learner cannot be considered as a simple "executant". He/she has to be trained to take real time decisions from concurrent activities: understanding of checklists and correct execution of prescribed operations. Also, when users do not apply procedures as

---

¹ CMOS (Cockpit Maintenance Operation Simulator) [13] - supported by Airbus Training - is a an advanced prototype for aeronautical maintenance operators (A340).

expected, it is important to ask it should be considered as an error (i) if the non application is an attempt to adapt procedures because the operational situation is rarely identical to the expected situation or (ii) if the non application is a result of improper procedure design.

They have to be mastered in reverse mode as a dual control of each other by a specific ITS strategy, the "reverse assessment": free learner's interaction with the real time kernel of the simulator in fact, is tightly coupled with an evolving checklist window which traces and monitors the learner in ITS mode -and vice versa- (fig. 2).

2.2   Different Approaches for Training Simulation

A fair model of classical ITS simulator is Sherlock II, a learning-by-doing system for electric fault diagnosis for F15 fighter aircraft [10]. With Sherlock the progressive assessment of learner's competency became a prominent goal for future in ITS. In the same way, the concept of "full-simulation" has integrated recent advances on desktop trainers [13] - by merging three paradigms:

- Full Fidelity Simulation targets at a quality insurance given by a very fine grain for represented knowledge issued from simulation modules, each one is devoted to a specific aircraft system (Hydraulics, Engines, Electricity...) and they act together as reactive agents in the Real Time Kernel of the simulator,
- Networked Simulators dynamically split on different stations zoomed processes of the previous modules allowing the learner to focus on precise point with an important cognitive unballasting ,
- Qualitative Simulation analyze monitors the interaction between the learner and the simulator in terms of positive or negative effects when assessing the learner's performance [6, 11].

When the previous functions act together on a desktop trainer, the issued realistic feed-back can be qualified of "Full-Simulation" in spite of the lack of an effective immersive interface.

3   A Prototype for "Full-Simulation"

3.1   Human Factors in Aeronautical Training

Trainers' developers usually seek to minimize human information processing and cognitive demands on the user when they learn on simulators, and more often in safety-critical sequences or procedures. However, the way of achieving this goal differs greatly with the aim to avoid different classes of cognitive difficulties (task load, cognitive gaps...). For this primary work, we have used a reduced framework for classifying different cognitive task loads:

1. Concurrent mastering of three layers of simulation: kernel, checklists, ITS (see 3.2)
2. Splitting learner activity into two alternate but equivalent interactions between hypertext document and window simulation; and

3. Possibility of joint interaction from multiple learners acting on networked station as in the simulator.

The methods we used to perform task analysis in # 1 are HCI related ones adapted to man-machine interaction [4], in which *reactive agents* for detecting cognitive task loads and learner's misses will be paramount. Detecting gaps during the task analysis for # 2 needs *planned agents* for recording the distributed design process and replaying some portions of it if necessary. For # 3 we have developed tools and techniques to assess how users will work and perform with *cognitive agents* in distributed engineering environments [8].

This will require the creation of novel methods and interfaces for real-time tracking of learner's activity with adaptive agents operating at any time.

3.2   Proposed Solution: Layered Architecture for the "Full Simulation"

The concept of the full simulation, as defined above, makes us to propose the three-layered architecture for the training environment.

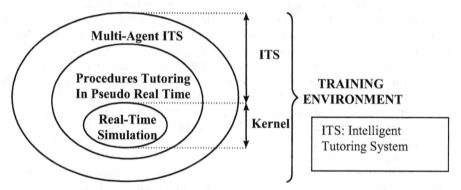

Figure 1. "Full simulation": different layers

The approach of the "full simulation" in three layers imposes an architecture of the ITS, which is itself distributed between these 3 layers:

- in the center, the kernel of simulation represents the physical object of simulation (an aircraft); this layer is exposed to the constraints of real-time actions/stimulations
- the layer of the simulation follow-up is added above (so as to save a trace, a chronology of the activated commands). This level corresponds to the description of the "profession", ie to the constraints related to the norms of the profession taught (checklists, procedures etc.),
- the third layer completes the system by adding a cognitive validation to the pedagogical assessment of the diagnostics made on the previous layer.

These three levels form together an environment of the "full-simulation", and involve different agents such as reactive agents in pseudo real-time of the kernel, planned agents of error corrections in procedures, and cognitive agents which need heuristics in order to proceed to the gaps evaluation.

3.3   Qualitative Monitoring of the Learner's Operations

The learner can operate in free-play mode (as in a Full Flight Simulator) but the real-time kernel of the simulator cannot assume a quantitative comparison of the value of expert solution with the value of student solution. It can just signalize if «cockpit» equipments and indicators run properly or not. This is why the qualitative simulation is necessary to monitor the progressive assessment of the learner by detecting gaps.

4   Multi-agent ITS (ASITS)

In multi-agent based ITS, this perspective raises three major problems: (i) the definition of the communication standards for exchanging real-time information between the agents, (ii) the indexing of expertise to facilitate 'know-how' tracking within all the relevant domains and (iii) the cognitive interaction design.

In order to resolve the problems rose before, agents must integrate adaptable strategies to monitor the user's actions when mastering two concurrent activities: understanding of checklists and correct execution of prescribed operations. These two activities have to be managed in reverse mode as a dual control of each other by a specific ITS strategy, the "reverse assessment": a- free learner's interaction with the real time kernel (pseudo free play) is tightly coupled with b- an evolving checklist window (aeronautical procedures) which monitors the learner in ITS mode. This strategy must be applied to study maintenance procedures (AMM tasks) together with the practice of tracking and troubleshooting procedures (TSM tasks)[2]. So, defining the curriculum consists mainly in choosing a precise set of "key-tasks" in order to give the learner a general knowledge of the structure of the complete course and a documentation handling experience. The structure of the meta-help window is an hypertext active document (see "Layer2" on the figure 2).

The interaction between the three layers is not strictly planned before. During the practice of the task, the trainee can choose between acting directly on a flight-deck pushbutton (layer 1, fig. 2), checking an item on the checklist (top left window layer 2, in fig. 2) or even asking the ITS to trace step by step this task (layer 3).

Problem can occur when analyzing conflicts in reasoning steps and attempts to track possible issues that bridges the gap between the ITS and learner reasoning. In agent-based simulation, different agents play specific roles to achieve these goals [7]: at the first level, pedagogical agents (learner, tutor...) acts in different learning scenarios, at the second level, gap detector agents trace their reasoning and at the third level, cognitive evaluator agents detect and solve conflicts to improve new strategy.

4.1   General Presentation of Multi-agent ITS

Three main components of an ITS (the student model, the knowledge model, and the pedagogical model) have been formerly built in a form of the intelligent agent architecture as in the Actor's agent [7]. It is possible to limit the number of actors and the casting of roles by (i) viewing learning as a reactive process involving several

---

[2] AMM = Aircraft Maintenance Manual, TSM = Trouble Shooting Manual

partners (human, simulated functions, pedagogical agents...), (ii) adapting each advising agent to various learning strategies co-learner, advisor,...[7].

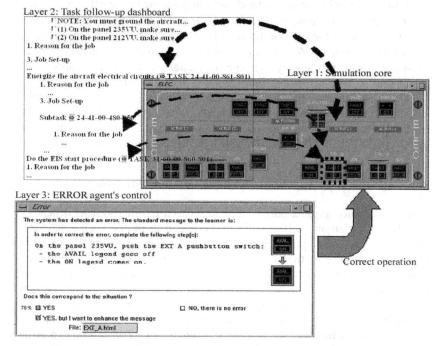

Figure 2. Three-layered learner's interaction during a maintenance task

4.2 Typology of Pedagogical Agents in the Simulation-Based Multi-agent ITS

According to the "users in the loop" concept [8], general characteristics of the used agents used are the following:

– Cognitive Agents: consider different strategies and learning styles, establish learning objectives, create, locate, track and review learning materials, e.g., diagnostic and assessment instruments, learning modules, mastery tests, etc...,
– Planned Agents: register changes and review/track students' progress and manage student-tutors communications both asynchronously and synchronously,
– Reactive Agents: assign appropriate materials to students, manage student-ITS communications synchronously (when needed) and evaluate student needs.

The remaining problem is how to classify cognitive interactions amongst a society of cognitive agent acting together in shared initiative (or not) with the learner(s).

4.3 Classification of Cognitive Interactions

We need to have agents, which mimic human behavior in learning situations. From the previous multi-agent ITS experiments, we have classified three levels of abstraction depending on the functional aspects of learner's practice:

- (a-mechanism): learning as replication, where agents can provide instructional data, representation of pedagogical strategy, and one of them, the Tutor, is devoted to mimic the teacher acting in the classroom (learning is a reactive mechanism),
- (b-mechanism): learning by tautology, where demonstrations can be designed to guide the learner through the learning process with the help of specialized agents as Tutor, Companion, Adviser... (learning as an adaptive or planned mechanism),
- (c-mechanism): learning by dynamic interactions and shared initiative, where the computer is more active and information is not only provided by the system, but can be modified and generated by the learner (learning is a cognitive mechanism).

At the second stage, which is the related current phase of the work, the ASITS architecture allows to detect in real-time the emergence of deviant behaviors and cognitive misses from the learner. What we do call cognitive gaps of the learner.

4.4   Cognitive Gaps Typology: Dropping Gap & Context Gap

However, the success of a pure multi-agent based tutoring system depends on the learner's motivation and self-discipline. We intend to profile such behavior by just using three types of cognitive gaps: -the 'context gap' at the points of divergence between the purpose of the tasks performed within an ITS and the purpose of the predicted solutions expected by the pedagogue (that needs a b-mechanism - the 'dropping gap' (i.e., the rate of renunciation due to the lack of motivation and help) which implies a c-mechanism approach. Thereby, this method for weakening the "dropping gap" inevitably introduces the 'context gap' restraint jointly with the shared initiative problem between the learner and the system. The solution to reduce the dropping gap by agents' auto-adaptation introduces often the context gap, which breaks the initiative share between the learner and the system. Such conflict limitation needs a specialized type of actor - the gap evaluator agent.

4.5   Cognitive Agents as Gap Evaluators

The "instructor assistant" plays the role of a collaborator and his help is more and more useful because he observes captures and generalizes decision help made by other agents. The learning of activities by agents was limited to two simple mechanisms: (i) learning by the needs satisfaction (individual), such as the agents of two levels (reactive and planned) with the planner agent for beliefs and presupposes, (ii) learning by satisfaction of contradictions (collective), which uses a genetic algorithm in the aim to resolve antagonist constraints between the evolution of each agent and the operation of the whole system.

5   Architecture for Gap-Tracking in the Multi-agent System

The following scheme displays the organization of different agents, which form a part (tracking system) of the general ITS architecture based on ASITS principles.

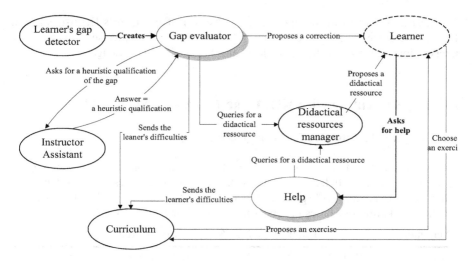

Figure 3. Cognitive agents managing interactions with the learner

5.1   Cognitive Agents Role

Cognitive agents are present permanently in the environment: they are created at the launch of application and "live" until its end. Each is represented by one specimen.

Learner's gap detector agent supervises interactions of the learner with the system. It is based on the know-how model in order to detect each gap of the learner. This gap detection does not evaluate the gap (severity level of the error).

Curriculum agent controls the progression of the learner within the whole course. Synthesizing different problems encountered by the learner, it is responsible for organizing learning sessions and for individualizing the progression in difficulties.
Depositor of Instructor's Experience agent collects preferences in order to guide the learner according to the personal instructor's style. It must, on the demand of Gap Evaluator agent, analyze this gap and propose a heuristic issue for qualification.

5.2   Reactive Agents Role

Reactive agents have a different lifetime. They are created by another agent (cognitive or reactive) and are killed when their objective is completed. Depending on situation, each type of reactive agents is represented by 0 to n specimen.
Gap evaluator agent is created by Learner's gap Detector agent in order to find the real signification of the gap (negligible gap, notable, important, major error...).
Learner Assistant agent offers requested help when on the learner's demand. The only interaction of this agent with the environment is produced when the learner, after numerous indexes or helps, can't correct his/her error. In this case, Assistant agent realizes, step-by-step, a demonstration of the correction.

The Learner's Gap Evaluator agent creates observer of Instructor's Heuristics agent. It uses machine-learning techniques in order to collect precise and heuristic interventions of the instructor but it stores also the acquired knowledge.

6   Experimenting with KQML and CIAgent Agents [1]

6.1   General Architecture for "gap detector" Agents

The general architecture of an agent in CMOS is framed on six slots (Know-how, Curriculum Vitae, Beliefs, Acquaintances). Reactive procedures are coded in slots "Beliefs", "Acquaintances", planned functions in "Nature" and "Script", cognitive functions as knowledge bases in "know-how" and "Curriculum Vitae".

Agent model   Instance: *Learner's gap evaluator Agent*

Know-how	{Eval_gap,Build_correction,Query_didactical_ressource}
Curric.Vitae	{ Eval_gap, Build_correction }
Nature	Aperiodic
Script	Evaluate the gap→ *Instructor_Agent*, Compute final gap
Beliefs	{ (Error_level, 0.3), (Back, 0.9), (Jump, 0.2) }
Acquaintances	{ *Gaps_detector, Didactical_ress_manager,Curriculum.* }

Figure 4. General framework for ASITS agents

6.2   Agent Classes

The ASITS architecture supports autonomous agents defining a generic class of agent-supervisor named CIAgent3, which monitors six principal agents:
– Ag.I: initialization agent (not presented in fig.6) because it is not permanent
– Ag. LGD: Learner's Gap Detector
– Ag.DRM : Didactical Ressources Manager
– Ag.IA : Instructor's Assistant
– Ag.C : Curriculum
– Ag.GE#n : Gap Evaluator
In addition, these five agent types are cognitive; they are represented by a unique instance. The last agent is reactive, the whole system can have dynamically from 0 up to n agents of this type, and it perishes (Dead state) at the end of their script.
The architecture presented needs really autonomous agents. However, the problem of autonomy was not completely resolved. But the agents developed by Tim Finin using KQML [13], give a correct answer to CMOS project's design and enrich the basic CIAgent architecture.
One of the remaining problems is the correct handling of what S. Cerri call access to "multiples contexts"[3]. In fact, each agent, before activate oneself, has to examine

---

[3] CIAgent = Constructing Intelligent Agent.

with "real autonomy" if the context needs or not its immediate engagement. As there is no effort in KQML to model agents with multiple viewpoints, we have to embeds some rules to determine when an agents takes the initiative (see § 6.3)

The agents' reasoning is constructed on the basis of reasoning rules. In the beginning, only a minimum set of rules is presented in the memory of the agent (agent applies his reasoning rules to the procedures). The instructor can get an agent to take in account him/her own particularities or training approach - the instructor can teach rules to the system, following the procedure and making consequently an action, which is still correct (from the instructor's point of view) but doesn't explicitly written in the procedure. The system detects an anomaly and requests the validation: whether the action performed was correct (to be recorded as a new additional rule in order to become more flexible for the learner) or not (just instructor's mistake). After the validation, the new rule is recorded in the rule base and, when the learner repeats the same action, the system is ready to respond and doesn't record this action as a mistake (such analysis is realized by Gap Evaluator Agent).

A better solution to this problem can be currently carried on by using an interpreter of KQML messages in Scheme, as suggested in the STROBE model [3] and then compile the issued Scheme algorithm into Java code.

Another pending problem is what we call the "any time" activation of agents in accordance with the different unsynchronized value of the three "real-time" referrals: real-time simulation, procedures tutoring and ITS evaluation of gaps. Real-time activation of agents can be embedded with a correct interoperability into the CIAagent version of the CMOS prototype by using the CTJ[4] library but this package cannot handle different time referrals and we are restricted to the poor alternative of accessing multiple context to determine the correct activating time for each agent.

6.3   Results

At the beginning, the only initialization agent (Ag.I) is awake. Its only task consists in arousing other agents (LGD, DRM, IA et C) before going to slep itself. A series of creations is performed by the agent I. In response to each message of t[...]ed receive the «Wake up !» signal :

Ag.I: Create Ag.LGD
Ag.LGD: Wake up !
Ag.I: Create Ag.DRM
Ag.DRM: Wake up !
Ag.DRM: Didactical ressource chosen = AMM page
Ag.I: Create Ag.IA
Ag.IA: Wake up !
Ag.IA: Run mode = learner's mode
Ag.I: Create Ag.C
Ag.C: Wake up !
Ag.C: Storing 'the learner is starting a new exercise'
Ag.I: Falling asleep
New procedure 24-24-00-710-801
6 0: Action: EXT A   IMPULSED

Actions: didactical ressources manager (DRM) chooses an AMM task, which will point to the associated didactical ressource in order to propose this exercise to the learner.

Instructor's Assistant (IA) identifies the current mode of functioning – « learner mode »,

Curriculum (C) records the fact that the llearner begins a new exercise on the active

---

[4] «Communicating Threads for Java» [9]

Ag.LGD: Learner's interaction detected
10 0: Action: BAT 1
Ag.LGD: Learner's interaction detected
10 2: Action: APU BAT   PU
Ag.LGD: Learner's interaction detected
6 0: Action: EXT A   IMPU
Ag.LGD: Learner's interaction detected
Ag.LGD: Gap detected
Ag.LGD: Create Ag.GE
Ag.GE: Wake up !
Ag.GE: Gap evaluation
Ag.GE: Gap = Learner's error
Ag.GE: Notifying learner's error to Curriculum
Ag.C: Storing learner's error
Ag.GE: Dead
6 0: Action: EXT A   IMPULSED
Ag.LGD: Learner's interaction detected
Ag.LGD: Gap detected
Ag.LGD: Create Ag.GE
Ag.GE: Wake up !
Ag.GE: Gap evaluation
Ag.GE: Gap = Learner's correction of the error
Ag.GE: Notifying learner's correction to Curriculum Agent
Ag.C: Storing learner's correction
Ag.GE: Dead
10 1: Action: BAT 2   PUSHED
Ag.LGD: Learner's interaction detected
2 2: Action: UPPER potentiometer Superieur a
Ag.LGD: Learner's interaction detected
2 3: Action: LOWER potentiometer Superieur
Ag.LGD: Learner's interaction detected
4 2: Action: HYD/GREEN/ELEC   IMPULS
Ag.LGD: Learner's interaction detected
Ag.LGD: Gap detected

Normal learner's progression in the current task. Only the Learner's Gap Detector agent (LGD) produces internal notifications at each learner's action (it shows clearly the transparent real-time learner's follow-up). But in 6.0, the learner makes a gap related to the normal procedure.

(LGD remarks it, and then creates a Gap Evaluator agent (GE). GE qualifies the gap as a learner's mistake. GE notifies curriculum of it.

Immediately after making a mistake, the learner is informed on it and tries to correct this error at once

The rest of this chronicle shows the normal progression of learner before he makes a new mistake in 4.2 (pushing start button of hydraulic pump HYD/GREEN/ELEC, which action is outrun by the learner). The hypothesis to verify is whether this is a context gap

Ag.LGD: Create Ag.GE
Ag.GE: Wake up !
Ag.GE: Gap evaluation
Ag.GE: Gap = Learner's error
Ag.GE: Notifying learner's error to Curriculum Agent
Ag.C: Storing learner's error
Ag.GE: Dead
4 2: Action: HYD/GREEN/ELEC   IMPULSE
Ag.LGD: Learner's interaction detected
Ag.LGD: Gap detected
Ag.LGD: Create Ag.GE
Ag.GE: Wake up !
Ag.GE: Gap evaluation
Ag.GE: Gap = Learner's correction of the error
Ag.GE: Notifying learner's correction to Curriculum Agent
Ag.C: Storing learner's correction
Ag.GE: Dead
1 0: Action: Ecam   C/B

The same mecanisms as in the action 6.0 are launched in order to guide always the learner as efficiently as possible. But this time, it doesn't work, because the learner is "displaced". He needs to re

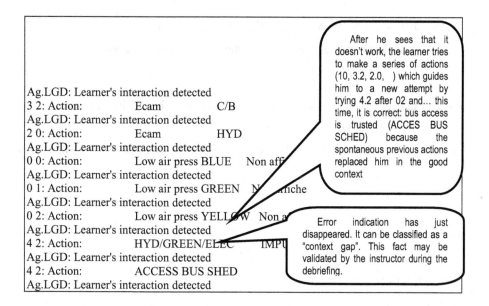

6.4   Example of Cognitive "know how" for the Learner Gap Detector Agent

Contextual gap detection is based on the idea that an agent should have explicit knowledge about contexts in which it may find itself, then use that knowledge when acting in those contexts. In our approach, this knowledge is represented as contextual schemas (Turner, 1994). Each contextual schema (c-schema) is 2-uple :

```
<TL=Task List> : <LA=Learner's situated Actions>
```

Therefore, the local detection of a learner gap is restricted to a given context <TL:LA>, more generally <c', c> is evaluated by a logic function f . This context is evolving in real-time and must be evaluated "any time" (i.e. at each learner action). Let c, c' a n-uple of distinct contexts and f as a functional evaluation of action in context :

```
<c', c>: f          f true for c is true for c'
```

$$\text{Let } \sigma = <\chi_{1,} \ldots_{,}\chi_{n}> \text{ with } \forall i \in (1,\ldots.,n) \quad \chi_{i} \in C$$

σ is a sequence in the set of contexts Σ constructed as symbolic expression on C (set of context symbols). A language L_{seq} to identify sequences (as contexts) can be defined by:

```
if   φ ∈ Lp , σ ∈ Σ    →    σ: φ L_seq
```

A context change is denoted by:

$$e: \qquad L_{seq} \quad \rightarrow \quad L_{seq}$$
$$\sigma_{x}: \quad \phi_{x} \quad \rightarrow \quad \sigma_{y}: \quad \phi_{y}$$

with $\sigma_x \in \Sigma$, $\sigma_y \in \Sigma$,   and ϕ_x , $\phi_y \in Lp^5$

and the associate functional expression of the corresponding c-schema is

$$\sigma_y: \quad \phi_y \ = \ e(\sigma_x: \quad \phi_x)$$

A contextual learner's behavior can be represented by n changes in the context

$$b = (e1, e2,...en)$$

To compare and evaluate these changes, an LGD agent can uses three basic axioms and three logic functions :
- Axioms :

1 - $\sigma: \quad \phi$

2 - $\sigma:$ ist $(\chi, \phi \to \psi)$ $\to$ (ist $(\chi, \phi \to (\chi, \psi))$

3 - $\sigma:$ ist (χ, ϕ) $\to$ $\neg$ ist $(\chi, \_\phi)$

- Logic functions :

Modus Ponens

$$|- \sigma: \quad \phi \quad |- \ \sigma: \quad \phi \to \psi \ \Rightarrow \ |-\sigma: \quad \psi$$

Rule as precondition to enter into a new context :

$$|- <\chi_1, ...,\chi_n> : \ \text{ist} \ (\chi, \phi) \qquad \Rightarrow \qquad <\chi_1, ...,\chi_n, \chi> : \ \phi$$

Rule as postcondition to quit an identified context :

$$<\chi_1, ...,\chi_n, \chi> : \ \phi \qquad \Rightarrow |- \ <\chi_1, ...,\chi_n> : \ \text{ist}(\chi, \phi)$$

Equipped with this basic knowledge an LGD agent detects the following changes :

For Action 10 1 in § 6.2 :

  `<c1, c2>: BAT2 state unknown` $\to$ `<c1, c2>: BAT2 pushed`

(No learner's error or gap detected)

For Action 4 2 : with context σ= (1 0, 3 2, 2 0, 0 0, 0 1, 0 2)
The context change detected by the LGD agent is

  σ_x : `HYD/GREEN/ELEC state unknown` $\to \sigma_x$: `HYD/GREEN/ELEC` impulsed

(No learner's error or gap detected)

Continuing 4 2 but with changed context σ = (1 0, 3 2, 2 0, 0 0, 0 1, 0 2, 4 2)
The context change detected by the LGD agent is

σ_{x+1} : `ACCESS BUS none` $\to \sigma_{x+1}$: `ACCESS BUS SHED`

---

[5] Propositional logic

(This correct action is error free and allows the learner to access data from the simulator for the next task)

7   Conclusion

We began the experiments of this prototype, at first with the senior engineers and instructors all along the development cycle. Nowadays, we make them with novice learners: students from the Institut de Maintenance Aéronautique at Bordeaux and from the Institut Universitaire de Technologie at Bayonne with the aim to classify the different cognitive task loads during learner's interactivity.

Depending on three functional aspects of learning identified as a, b, c mechanisms and with a rather primitive cognitive gaps typology (Tunnel Effect, Dropping, and Context Gaps), we have shown what aspects of a user's behavior are possible to be monitored by a gap evaluator agent.

Implemented with a Java repository of agents (CIAgent), the deliberately limited actor's architecture, and the Gap Evaluator agent. This Gap Evaluator agent is responsible for qualifying the gap: from "nothing important" to "major misunderstanding" for a given type of gap – dropping, context or tunnel – in a, b, c mechanism).

The major scientific obstacle consists in identifying learner's behavioral aspects, which can be captured, controlled and learned by different cognitive (or not) agents in shared initiative between the learner and the system.

We plan to extend rather poor capabilities of learning within the current cognitive agents. Another promising way to investigate is the improvement of man-machine interaction by immersing the learner in virtual reality interfaces. This may originate a new spread of influent cognitive discrepancies or shifts that need to identify new types of distinctive gaps.

References

1.   Bigus J.P., Bigus J., « Constructing intelligent agents with Java», Wiley Computer Publishing, 1997.
2.   Beck J.E., Woolf B. Park, « Using a Learning Agent with a Student Model», Fourth International Conference on Intelligent Tutoring Systems -ITS'98- San Antonio. USA- August 1998., Lecture Notes in Computer Science, 34, Springer.
3.   Cerri S.A., A simple language for generic dialogues: ``speech acts" for communication. Proceedings of JFLA97, Journées francophones des langages applicatifs, Collection Didactique de l'INRIA, Marc Gengler et Christian Queinnec (eds.), pag. 145-168 (1997) Computer Science, 34, Springer.
4.   Boy G., « Cognitive Function Analysis. Ablex, Stanford», CT, 1998.
5.   Degani A., Wiener E.L. "Cockpit Checklists: Concepts, Design and Use" Human Factors, Ashgate, 35, 327-365, 1993
6.   Forbus K.D., « Qualitative process theory: twelve years after», Artificial Intelligence 59, pp. 115-123, 1993

7.   Frasson C., Mengelle T., Aïmeur E, Gouardères G., « An Actor-based Architecture for Intelligent Tutoring Systems», Third International Conference ITS'96, Montreal, Lecture Notes in Computer Science, June 1996, Springer

8.   Gouardères G., Frasson C., « On effectiveness of distance learning using LANCA», Workshop on Pedagogical Agents. Fourth International Conference on Intelligent Tutoring Systems -ITS'98- San Antonio. USA- 1998.

9.   Hilderink G., Broenink J., Vervoort W., Bakkers A., «Communicating Java Threads« WoTUG-20 conference 13-16 April 1997, Enschede The Netherlands, Proceedings of the 20th World Occam and Transputer User Group Technical Meeting, pp. 48-76, ISBN 90 5199 336 6, IOS Press, The Netherlands.

10. Katz, S. Lesgold, A. Eggan, G. Greenberg, L., « Towards the Design of More Effective Advisors for Learning-by-Doing Systems», Lecture Notes in Computer Science, Springer. Intelligent Tutoring Systems, Third International Conference, ITS '96, pp. 641-649, Montréal, Canada, 1996.

11. Kuipers B.J., « Reasoning with qualitative models», Artificial Intelligence 59, pp. 125-132, 1993.

12. Munro A., Surmon D., Johnson M., Pizzini Q., Walker J. «An open architecture for simulation-centered tutors 9th Int. Conf. on AIED -Le Mans, pp. 578-585, - ISSN: 0922-6389- IOS Press - Amsterdam- The Netherlands, 1999

13. Richard L., Gouarderes G., « An Agent-operated Simulation-based Training System», Proceedings of the 9th Int. Conf. on AIED -Le Mans, pp. 578-585, - ISSN: 0922-6389- IOS Press - Amsterdam- The Netherlands, 1999

14. Richard L., Gouarderes G., «Human Centered designed ITS for Aircraft Maintenance Training System», 2d International Conference HCI Aeronautics - ACM SIGCHI - Montréal, 1998.

15. Turner. R.M. Context-Mediated Behavior for Intelligent Agents. International Journal of Human-Computer Studies, 48(3):307--330, March 1997.

Improving WWW Access - from Single-Purpose Systems to Agent Architectures?

D. Sramek, P. Berka, J. Kosek, and V. Svatek

Faculty of Informatics and Statistics, The University of Economics, Prague
W. Churchill Sq. 4, Prague, Czech Republic
{sramek,berka,kosek,svatek}@vse.cz

Abstract: Sophisticated techniques from various areas of Artificial Intelligence can be used to improve the access to the WWW; the most promising ones stem from Data Mining and Knowledge Modeling. We describe the process of building two experimental systems: the VSEved system for intelligent meta-search, and the VSEtecka system for navigation support. We discuss our experience from this process, which seems to justify the hypothesis that the Multi-Agent paradigm can improve the efficiency of web access tools, in the future. With this respect, we outline a web-oriented multi-agent architecture.

Keywords: WWW Access, Data Mining, Knowledge Modeling, Meta-Search, Navigation Support, Agent Architecture.

1   Introduction

During the last few years, the World-Wide Web has become one of the most widespread technologies of information presentation. Making the enormous amount of information on the web really useful is inconceivable without intelligent assistance, both for end users and for maintainers of large sites. From this point of view, we can distinguish two basic groups of tasks that are frequently attacked by web applications:

The most important user-oriented tasks are probably:

1. search (retrieval) of relevant documents, using one-shot queries
2. filtering a stream of new documents against stable profiles
3. navigation, i.e. support for the user during the browsing session
4. question-answering, i.e. extraction of relevant low-grained data relevant to the user questions (see e.g. [Gaisauskas, Humphreys, 2000]); a particular form of question-answering is passage retrieval, which is rather similar to document retrieval.
   As maintainer-oriented tasks, we can view especially:
1. overall site auditing and maintenance
2. low-level marketing tasks such as market-basket analysis of customers' access.

S. A. Cerri and D. Dochev (Eds.): AIMSA 2000, LNAI 1904, pp. 167-178, 2000.
© Springer-Verlag Berlin Heidelberg

A number of techniques can be used to solve these tasks (cf. e.g. [Chakrabarti, 2000]): statistically-grounded information retrieval methods, computational linguistics and natural language processing methods, as well as more ad-hoc artificial intelligence (AI) techniques. Within AI, the dominating paradigms seem to be those of *data mining* and *knowledge modeling*.

1.1   WWW and Data Mining

Zaiane and Han [Zaiane, Han, 1998] gave a nice taxonomy of data mining in the web environment, to say, *web mining*. They distinguish web content mining, web structure mining and web usage mining.

The goal of *web content mining* is to extract knowledge from the web pages itself. The tasks related to this goal can be:
– web search and meta-search (find pages relevant to the user's query), or filtering (recognize pages relevant to the user's profile); this is the question of information retrieval,
– text mining (find knowledge "hidden" in the pages); this is the question of information extraction or question answering.

While the goal of *information retrieval* is to find relevant pages (strictly speaking, to find a set of pages with high precision and high recall), the goal of *information extraction* is to extract information from these pages. Text mining can be applied e.g. for discovering associations in collections of textual documents [Feldman, 1997].

Web structure mining means extracting knowledge from web structure and hyperlinks. An observation has been made that web space is not homogeneously interconnected. There are pages (called hubs) pointing to a large number of other pages; there are pages (called authorities, i.e. referential for some areas of interests) pointed to by large number of pages. Doing web structure mining we can e.g. look for some regular patterns of links between such types of pages [Tomkins, 2000]. The information about the structure can be useful for navigation. Methods from the graph theory are suitable for performing such kind of analysis.

The goal of *web usage mining* [Srivastava, 2000] is to discover access patterns (form web server logs) and find paths frequently traversed by users. This task is very similar to market basked analysis performed in standard data mining; what are the goods (pages) frequently purchased (visited) by the customers. The results of web usage mining can be used in marketing (Amazon uses such approach when recommending similar books) and for reorganizing the web site (pages frequently visited during one log should be linked together).

1.2   WWW and Knowledge Modeling

The hot topics in up-to-date knowledge modeling are *ontologies* and *problem-solving methods*, namely their construction, sharing and reuse.

The Web environment, containing a huge, diverse collection of textual documents, is highly favorable for experiments in ontological engineering. Most research has concentrated on the development of ontologies (hierarchical collections of concepts, their relations and other elements) as a background for semantic unification of the web content, in particular of *metadata*. In addition to „terminological" ontologies (or, thesauri) used by digital libraries to annotate documents (such as the Dublin Core set [Weibel et al., 1998]), more sophisticated „knowledge" ontologies [1] have emerged as a results of efforts within the AI community. The two seminal projects most widely discussed are SHOE [Luke et al., 1997] and Ontobroker [Fensel et al., 1998]. The central issue of both is the use of ontologies by authors of web pages, in specifying knowledge annotations (i.e. richly structured metadata) for the pages and their parts; the difference between them lays in the construction and management of ontologies (distributed in SHOE, centralized in Ontobroker). Ontologies are also used as a conceptual grounding for *factual knowledge bases*, describing the (interesting parts of) the web at the level of instances, for *inferential knowledge bases* [2]describing recurring patterns in web data, as well as for *data mining* tasks aiming at discovery of inferential knowledge.

In contrast, hardly any attention has been paid to web-specific *problem-solving methods*. In the project outlined in this paper, we plan to fill this gap via defining skeletal action plans for web access tasks, which will be refined and executed part-by-part by different agents in a multi-agent environment.

There is a number of single-purpose systems oriented on particular tasks described above. In our paper we present a slightly different attempt of using multi agent architecture to solve more tasks simultaneously.

The paper is organized as follows. Section 2 describes the experimental VSEved system developed for „intelligent" information retrieval (using the meta-search technology). Section 3 describes another system named VSEtecka - a browsing assistant, which is currently being developed in order to support the navigation in the web space via a collection of meta-information and links to associated pages. Section 4 compares different tasks with respect to the (largely overlapping) input data they require. Finally, section 5 discusses the pros and cons of agent architecture, and suggests an agent-based model for the WWW information access, and section 6 summarizes the whole work.

2   The VSEved Meta-search System

2.1   Search and Meta-search

Due to the enormous growth of the web, finding information about a specific topic can be extremely demanding. Search engines attempt to automate this task by means of building (off-line; manually - e.g. Yahoo, or automatically - e.g AltaVista) inverted indices of WWW pages, which can be then searched according to words/phrases given by the user. However, the use of search engines themselves entails significant

---

[1] See e.g. [Uschold, Gruninger 1996] for an elaborate typology of ontologies.
[2] See e.g. [Harmelen, Fensel, 1999] for a discussion on conceptual, inferential and factual knowledge on the web.

difficulties for a common (inexperienced) user. There is a vast number of search engines at different locations, each with its own way of user interaction - the user thus has to know which one to choose, how to reach it and how to utilize it. Moreover, each engine is constrained by its own index, which usually covers only a small fraction of the whole WWW space.

The idea of WWW *meta-search* has subsequently emerged to help users to find more relevant information in a more convenient way. The essence of all meta-search systems consists in giving access to more than one search engine, while their other features may vary. The typical models of meta-search are as follows:

- the user selects himself which search engine is to be queried (e.g. in the All-in-One system: `www.albany.net/allinone`)
- the system itself queries all accessible search engines (e.g. the MetaCrawler system [Etzioni, 1997])
- the system itself selects the most promising search engines to be queried (e.g. the SavvySearch system [Howe, 1997])
- the system queries both its local database of frequently asked questions, and some remote search engines (e.g. the AskJeeves system: `www.askjeeves.com`).

As the main advantages of meta-search we can view:

- simultaneous submission of the query to different search engines
- exploitation of search engines possibly unknown to the user
- single interface on the user's side
- merging and sometimes further post-processing of returned information (lists of hits).

2.2   Overview of the VSEved System

We have developed an experimental system named VSEved, which combines usual WWW meta-search with Artificial Intelligence techniques. In the former, VSEved has been inspired mostly by AskJeeves, in particular in

- directing the queries both to (multiple) remote search engines and to a *local database* of „direct answers"
- *linguistic preprocessing* of the query, which can be written in natural language.

The local database of VSEved's answers contains links to pages judged as interesting with respect to the particular community of the users of the system (it has been used mainly by university campus users). Linguistic preprocessing in VSEved consists in language recognition (English or Czech) simple lemmatization (for Czech), and extraction of linguistic Boolean operators (for Czech).

In addition, the hit lists returned by search engines are *post-processed* by means of a *rule–based expert system*, which accounts for their „cleaning" (removing duplicities and dead links), integration, re-ordering (according to a „quality" criterion based on query-term coverage) and structuring, in order to provide more concise and informative output to the user. Unlike other document-structuring systems that perform unsupervised clustering [Zamir, Etzioni, 1998], [Honkela et al., 1996], we have decided to use assignment to pre-defined categories (page types). Typological categorization is one of the display options of the system, besides *linear ordering* according to quality and (URL-) *domain-based* grouping. The process of typological categorization will be described in more detail in the next two subsections; more details of the VSEved systems can be found in [Berka et al., 1999].

2.3   VSEved and Knowledge Modeling

The design of VSEved's typological categorization has been grafted on previous knowledge modeling (ontological engineering) efforts. An ontology named *WEB-ONT*, covering different aspects of the web (websites, logical documents, physical pages, tag structures, addressing etc.) had been elaborated [Simek, Svatek, 1998] and implemented in several languages (incl. e.g. SHOE). A part of this ontology, dealing with page typologies, has been reused for constructing the categories that could be assigned to the search hits retrieved (and thus to the pages referenced, respectively).

The three typologies are, in turn:

- *Bibliographic* categorization, operating on concepts like „article", „bibliography", „image", „pricelist„ or „newsgroup message". This categorization was essentially borrowed from the existing Dublin Core metadata system [Weibel et al., 1998] (element ResourceType), which had been previously embedded into the WEB-ONT ontology.
- Categorization according to the *sphere of origin*, such as „commercial", „academic", „governmental", „non-profit" or „private".
- Categorization according to *technological type*, such as „plain text", „form" or „index".

The operational rulebase (written in the CLIPS language) capable of recognizing (to a certain extent) these categories, has been constructed using, essentially, data-mining approaches.

2.4   VSEved and Data Mining

In the data-mining part of the VSEved project, we have attempted to build a rulebase relating web document types to the following information:

- Terms from and structure of the URL - this part of the rulebase is generally applicable (i.e. not only for meta-search, but also for navigation, filtering etc.).
- Other information returned by search engines (name, size, date and textual „snippet" of the page) - this part is specific for the meta-search task. Using this information can lead to reduction of ambiguity in the categorization.

Due to the structural nature (overall hit structure, plus linear structure of the URL, name and „snippet") of the data, *Inductive Logic Programming* (ILP) seems to be a good choice for the learning approach. However, due to the high computational complexity of ILP, we have decided to use

- fast and straightforward *frequency analysis* of terms, pairs of terms and specific symbols from a large set of URLs, in the overall type-assignment task (the details of the frequency-analysis process can be found in [Svatek, Berka, 2000])

– sensitive but costly *ILP*, in the specific subtasks for which frequency analysis alone lead to ambiguous models - this was the case e.g. for the URL terms „art", „pub", „cat" or „bio".

The overall rulebase thus consists of two layers: pure URL-based rules (applicable for various categorization tasks) and rules encompassing general features identifiable in search results (applicable for the meta-search categorization only). We have shown in [Svatek, Berka, 2000] that even the first layer, consisting of a few dozens of pure URL-based rules, can more-or-less successfully assign some generic category to approx. 70-90% (depending on the language and query-specificity settings) of pages retrieved by search engines; 25-50% of the assignments account for Dublin-Core-like bibliographic categories. Future experiments will show the impact of the newly-introduced, ILP-based disambiguation on these figures.

3   The VSEtecka System for Navigation Support

3.1   Searching vs. Browsing

Today's web search engines clearly separate the phases of searching and using (i.e. reading pages) information stored in „Web Space". You must specify your query to search engine as much precisely as you can. Search engine returns you list of pages which may be of your interest. Then you manually browse through this result. If founded pages are not exactly on your subject, you must go back to search engine, precise your query and hope that search results would be closer to your expectations.

Above described approach is used by most of today's search engines. But if we tighter integrate intelligent search process with browsing, we will get environment which is much more effective, user-friendly and intuitive for users. Our aim is to develop navigation support system VSEtecka which will provide useful information related to actually viewed page.

3.2   Navigation-Support Information

After finishing VSEtecka will provide the following information in an easily-accessible way:

Meta-information about the current page: Useful information related to the current page alone, such as like author, title, keywords and so on. The meta-information set of VSEtecka will also include the same information as delivered by the VSEved meta-search system, see previous section.

Links to similar pages: The links to similar pages are categorized according several similarity criteria, such a content similarity, structural similarity and so on. This functionality will allow to traverse similar pages without the need for explicit web search service.

Associations: Almost every web page is a part of a larger document or web-site. Not all pages are well designed and, as a result, they do not contain very helpful navigation links. This part of the system will automatically provide the links (if appropriate) to the previous and next page in a sequence, to the table of contents of the document, to a relevant home page, and so on. This should prevent the user from getting lost on badly designed sites.

User definable filter: Filtering is an effective way of narrowing the scope of pages offered in the similar and associated pages' sections. Only the pages which fit to restrictions set on the author's name, page title, subject etc. (basically, any of the meta-information fields can be used here) will be supplied to the user.

Domain-specific information: In many domains, specific page categories and relations among them are important for the user's understanding of the site structure, in addition to generic ones (which are listed under „associations"). This may be the case e.g. for course, lecturer and department pages in an academic environment (see e.g. [Craven et al., 1998]), or for company homepage, pricelist and press–releases' page in a business environment.

3.3   Notes on Implementation and Data Input

For the system to operate conveniently on-line, the responses to user's actions must be fast. Navigation information on the pane has to be updated in a few seconds after a new page has been loaded into the browser. This makes the option of collecting necessary data on-line for each request rather problematic. Instead, we assume that the system will mostly rely on a web-crawler that will scan a pre-defined subspace of the web: currently, we index the pages on (a huge number of) web-servers within the campus of the University of Economics, Prague. The information will be extracted from this pages using a synergy of AI methods, and stored in a factual knowledge-base (FKB), analogical to the knowledge base currently built within the WebKB project. The existence of the FKB will guarantee fast response to requests from the users aiming within its scope. For the requests outside its scope, the system will either have to perform on-line document retrieval and analysis, or will rely on limited information, such as URLs and anchor text of links (see [Svatek, Berka, 2000]) in a similar way as the VSEved system.

4   Search, Navigation and Beyond: Overlap of Web-Mining Tasks

The experience with the running prototype of the meta-search system, as well as the design of the (not finished yet) navigation support system have led us to the conclusion that the requirements of input data vary but significantly overlap for different web-related tasks. Let us enumerate the most characteristic information resources, as identified by us and others (e.g. [Chakrabarti, 2000], [Craven et al., 1998]), in the rough order of increasing grain-size:
– Elementary data types, which (in particular, the first two) appear in different places and situations around the „web-world"; these mainly amount to

1. text in a natural language
2. URLs.
3. images and other multimedia information
– Static data structures:
1. tag structure of pages, expressing (namely, HTML in the common way of use) display formatting and/or logical structure
2. explicit, more-or-less standardized metadata on pages
3. frequency count of linguistic terms, tag structures and non-text objects, as well as more abstract concepts (such as „personal names" or „downward links"), within pages
4. topology on the space of pages, induced by interconnecting links
– Dynamic data structures:
1. user-access data (web server or proxy logs)
2. search queries and their results

Let us then match the data with the (somewhat refined) list of web-related tasks from section 1:

– Meta-search with „limited information" post-processing, as performed by the above described VSEved system, uses URLs, page titles, and, possibly, short (usually almost worthless from the point of view of linguistic analysis) text snipped from the beginning of the page.
– Common search engine indexing, as well as some other off-line tasks such as filtering, process page fulltexts, thus yielding word frequencies, but possibly also linguistic, HTML and link structures; some search engines also rely on information about the users' choice.
– Navigation support as well as all site-maintenance oriented tasks put stress on the link structure; the latter are often based on usage mining, i.e. exploitation of user access data.
– Marketing-related tasks always require user access data.

The overlap of lower-level data analysis tasks is, in our opinion, a strong incentive for the development of modular (agent) architectures for web analysis and access.

5   Analyzing and Accessing the Web Using Agents - Discussion

Earlier in this paper, we have mentioned several powerful techniques which make it possible to exploit information hidden in the web more effectively. Somewhat surprisingly current search engines incorporate quite a few of them. The most often used method for web search is still the ancient word or term indexing. Current success of Google search engine [Chakrabarti, 2000] (in particular gaining Altavista users) proves that using more sophisticated techniques can provide a competitive advantage.

The following reasons may slow down the implementation of modern algorithms:

– Each technique may require different data representation
– User still expects integrated result (therefore the result aggregation must be implemented)
– Sophisticated algorithms are likely to require a lot of computer power

How can we build an integrated, powerful and efficient system? We are constrained by the need of several different data representations. For example we use a word index for classical fulltext search but a kind of an associative net for storing information about web structure. It is difficult to predict all possible representations required in the future. For each data representation we require a different kind of processing. This led us to consideration of many agents, each specialized for a specific web searching or mining task. As a first step we plan to develop a multi-agent architecture which should enable:
1. Bottom up development model
2. Possibility of gradual evolution of the system and easy adding of new features
3. Natural decomposition of the system based on data representation
4. Communication framework for query decomposition and result aggregation

In addition we believe that competition or cooperation of the specialized agents can bring better results than a single process, single representation system.

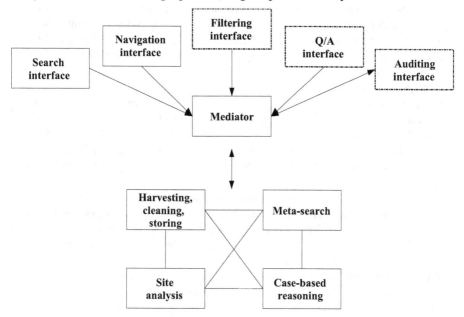

Schema 1: current preliminary version of the multi-agent system

Basically there are several classes of agents:
1. Data harvesting / preprocessing / storing in a standardized format
2. Query decomposer and dispatcher / result aggregator
3. Analytical agents (performing specific tasks)
4. Helpers (performing useful common tasks like linguistic analysis)

As we want the analytical modules to focus just to their task we provide a standardized data format. For example all harvested web pages are checked for errors and converted to canonical XML. The meta-information about pages is also saved in the pre-defined format. In the future the web-harvesting module should also serve as a cache for requested documents which are temporary inaccessible (which is not a rare case).

For the same reason we develop helper agents which should resolve common requests from analytical agents e.g. a specialized text parsing or linguistic processing.

The analytical agents can be classified by a generality of task for which they are responsible. For example the structure-analyzing agent can solve rather wide area of tasks (e.g. find the nearest neighbors by mutual hyperlinks or by similar hyperlinks to other pages). On the other hand it should be possible to add an agent for such a specific task like answering who is the chair of the department X of the university Y (which can be implemented as filling this pattern by standard methods of IE). Currently we are finishing specifications of the analytical agents which should be implemented first to check the agent model features. A brief example of basic agents is included further in this paper.

One of the most difficult parts of implementing the suggested multi-agent system will be designing the agent responsible for communication with a user. This task represents understanding the user query and dispatching it to the right analytical agents. On the other hand the results of the specific agents must be aggregated to the qualified answer. We believe that quality of answers is the most important goal of the described system.

Examples of analytical agents

- Word indexing agent – the basic agent which can answer questions like: What documents do contain the word X? Which document is the most relevant to the word X? In the most basic version this is nothing new but it will serve mainly for testing the communications among agents. In the future this agent will be upgraded to work with terms or possibly concepts and will use the text parsing and linguistic agents.

- Structure analyzing agent – will answer questions like: What pages are near to this page in terms of number of clicks needed to get there? What pages cite the same addresses as this page does? This agent should store the web structure in the form of multidimensional hypergraph. Its answers can be used for example to sorting final results by number of citations.

We anticipate some drawbacks of suggested solution. In particular:

1. The agent communication leads to overhead in processing time
2. The different data representations lead to overhead in data store
3. It is difficult to make global optimizations of query processing

We expect that the possible problems will arise as soon as we start to test the minimal prototype with just a few analytical agents and the basic dispatcher agent. We expect that most of the problems can be solved and the system can be tuned up in this minimal setting. We plan exploit the experience to design maximally robust and efficient architecture which could be used as a framework for building powerful search engines and a testbed for testing modern and sophisticated AI techniques in exploiting the information richness of the Internet.

6   Conclusions

We have analyzed the problem of improving the WWW access using AI techniques, with stress on most common web-related tasks. For two of these tasks we have designed experimental systems: the VSEved system for intelligent meta-search, and the VSEtecka system for navigation support. We discuss our experience from this process, which seems to justify the hypothesis that the Multi-Agent paradigm can improve the efficiency of web access tools.

In the future, we would like to verify this hypothesis via implementing such modular architecture, which will embed also the components for the above mentioned meta-search and navigation systems.

Acknowledgements

This work is partially supported by the grant MSMT VS 96008.

References

[Berka et al, 1999] Berka,P., Sochorová,M. - Svátek,V. - Šrámek,D.: The VSEved System for Intelligent WWW Metasearch. In: Proc. IEEE Conf. On Intelligent Engineering Systems INES'99

[Craven et al. 1998] Craven M., DiPasquo D., Freitag D., McCallum A., Mitchell T., Nigam K., Slattery S.: Learning to Extract Symbolic Knowledge from the World Wide Web. In: Proc. of 15th AAAI, Madison, WI, 1998.

[Etzioni, 1997] Etzioni,O.: Moving Up the Information Food Chain. AI Magazine Vol. 18, No. 2, 1997.

[Faloutsos, 1996] Faloutsos, Christos—Oard, Douglas: A Survey of Information Retrieval and Information Filtering Methods. College Park, University of Maryland 1996.

[Feldman, 1997] R. Feldman and H. Hirsh. "Finding Associations in Collections of Text, " In Methods and Applications of Machine Learning, Data Mining and Knowledge Discovery, R.S. Michalski, I. Bratko, and M. Kubat (eds.), John Wiley and Sons, Ltd., 1997, 20 pages.

[Fensel et al., 1998] Fensel, D. - Decker, S. - Erdmann, M. - Studer, R.: Ontobroker: Or How to Enable Intelligent Access to the WWW. In: Proc. of the 11th Banff Knowledge Acquisition for Knowledge-Based System Workshop (KAW98), Banff, Canada.

[Gaisauskas, Humphreys, 2000] Gaisauskas, R. - Humphreys, K.: A combined IR/NLP approach to question answering against large text collections. In: (Mariani, J. - Harman, D.:) RIAO2000 - Content-Based Multimedia Information Access, Paris, 2000, 1288-1304.

[Harmelen, Fensel, 1999] van Harmelen, F. - Fensel, D.: Practical Knowledge Representation for the Web. In: IJCAI-99 Workshop on Intelligent Information Integration.

[Honkela et al., 1996] Honkela T.,Kaski S., Lagus K., Kohonen T.: Newsgroup Exploration with WEBSOM Method and Browsing Interface, Report A32, Helsinky University of Technology, ISBN: 951-22-2949-8, January 1996

[Howe, 1997] Howe,A. - Dreilinger,D.: SavvySearch - A Metasearch Engine That Learns Which Search Engines to Query. AI Magazine Vol. 18, No. 2, 1997.

[Chakrabarti, 2000] Chakrabarti, S.: Data Mining for Hypertext: A Tutorial Survey. *SIGKDD Explorations*, Vol.1, Issue 1, 2000.

[Joachims, 1997] Joachims,T. - Freitag,D. - Mitchell,T.: WebWatcher: A Tour Guide for the World Wide Web. In: Proc. IJCAI'97, 1997.

[Luke, 1997] Luke, S. - Spector, L. - Rager, D: Ontology-Based Knowledge Discovery on the World-Wide Web. In: AAAI96 Workshop on Internet-based Information Systems.

[Simek, Svatek, 1998] Šimek, P. - Svátek, V.: An Integrated Ontology for the WWW. Tech.Rep. LISp-98-06, Laboratory of Intelligent Systems, Prague, 1998.

[Spertus, 1997] Spertus,A.: ParaSite: Mining Structural Information on the Web. In: Proc. 6th International World Wide Web Conference, Santa Clara, 1997.

[Srivastava et al., 2000] Srivastava, J. - Cooley, R. - Deshpande, M. - Tan, P.: Web usage mining: discovery and applications of web usage patterns from web data. *SIGKDD Explorations*, Vol.1, Issue 1, 2000.

[Svatek, Berka, 2000] Svátek V., Berka P.: URL as starting point for WWW document categorisation. In: (Mariani J., Harman D.:) RIAO'2000 - Content-Based Multimedia Information Access, CID, Paris, 2000, 1693-1702.

[Tomkins, 2000] Tomkins,A.: Hyperlink-Aware Mining and Analysis of the Web. In: (Terano, Liu, Chen, eds.) Proc. PAKDD2000, LNAI 1805, Springer, 2000, 4.

[Uschold, Gruninger, 1996] Uschold, M. - Gruninger, M.: Ontologies: principles,

[Weibel et al., 1998] Weibel,S. - Kunze,J. - Lagoze,C. - and Wolf,M.: Dublin Core Metadata for Resource Discovery, IETF#2413, The Internet Society, September 1998.

[Zaiane, Han, 1999] Zaiane,O. - Han,J.: WebML: Querzing the World-Wide Web for Resources and Knowledge. In: Proc. Int. Workshop on Web Information and Data Management WIDM'98, Bethesda, 1998, 9-12.

[Zamir, Etzioni, 1998] Zamir O., Etzioni O.: Web Document Clustering: A Feasibility Demonstration. In: SIGIR'98, Melbourne, Australia, 1998.

methods and applications. *The Knowledge Engineering Review*, Vol.11:2, 1996, 93-136.

A General Architecture for Finding Structural Regularities on the Web

P. A. Laur[1], F. Masseglia[1,2], P. Poncelet[1], and M. Teisseire[1]

[1] LIRMM UMR CNRS 5506
161, Rue Ada, 34392 Montpellier Cedex 5, France
{laur,massegli,poncelet,teisseire}@lirmm.fr
[2] Laboratoire PRiSM, Université de Versailles
45 Avenue des Etats-Unis, 78035 Versailles Cedex, France

Abstract. With the growing popularity of the World Wide Web, the number of semistructured documents produced in all types of organizations increases at a rapid rate. However the provided information cannot be queried or manipulated in the general way since, although there is some structure in the information, it is too irregular to be modeled using a relational or an object-oriented approach. Nevertheless, some semistructured objects, for the same type of information, have a very similar structure. In this paper we address the problem of finding such regularities and we propose a general architecture based on a very efficient data mining technique.

1 Introduction

With the growing popularity of the World Wide Web (Web), the number of semistructured documents produced increases at a rapid rate. While in classical database applications we first describe the structure of data, i.e. type or schema, and then create instances of that type, in semistructured data, data has no absolute schema and each object contains its own structure [Wor97]. Nevertheless, some semistructured objects, for the same type of information, have a very similar structure. Analysis of such regularities in such semistructured objects can provide significant and useful information for restructuring a Web site for increased effectiveness [WL98], for improving any meaningfull query for Web documents [KS95], for providing a guideline for building indexes and views [Abi97], etc.

The groundwork of the approach presented in this paper is the problem of mining structural regularities in a large set of semistructured objects extracted from the Web. More precisely, we want to discover, using data mining techniques, graph structures appearing in some minimum number of objects. We have to pinpoint that this approach is very different from those on extracting the structure of a single individual object since we consider in the following that we are provided with a large collection of graph structures [Wor97].

The rest of this paper is organized as follows. In section 2, the problem is stated and illustrated. The approach is described in section 3. Related work is briefly presented in section 4. Finally section 5 concludes the paper.

S. A. Cerri and D. Dochev (Eds.): AIMSA 2000, LNAI 1904, pp. 179–188, 2000.

2   Problem Statement

In this section we give the definition of the structural association mining problem. First we formulate the semistructured data which widely resumes the formal description of the Object Exchange Model (OEM) defined for representing structured data [AQM⁺97,ABS00]. Second we look at the structural association mining problem in detail. A concrete example is also provided.

2.1   Preliminary Definitions

The data model that we use is based on the OEM model designed specifically for representing semistructured data. We assume that every object o is a tuple consisting of an *identifier*, a *type* and a *value*. The *identifier* uniquely identifies the object. The type is either *complex* or some identifier denoting an atomic type (like integer, string, gif-image, etc.). When type is complex then the object is called a *complex object* and value is a set (or list) of *identifiers*. Otherwise the object is an *atomic object*, and its value is an atomic value of that type. As we consider set semantics as well as list semantics, we use a circle node to represent an identifier of a set value and a squared node to represented an identifier of a list value. We can thus consider an OEM graph as a graph where the nodes are the objects and the labels are on the edges. In this paper we assume that there is no cycle in the OEM graph.

We also require that: (i) *identifier(o)* and *value(o)* denotes the identifier and value of the object o; (ii) *object(id)* denotes the unique object with an identifier *id*; (iii) Each atomic object has no outgoing edges; (iv) if two edges connect the same pair of nodes in the same direction then they must have different label. We thus assume that we are provided with a labeling function $F_E : E \rightarrow L_E$ where L_E is the domain of edge labels.

Figure 1 shows a segment of information about a collection of three persons [ABS00]. Each circle along with the text inside it represents an object and its identifier. The arrows and their labels represent object references. For instance *value(&o5) = "Mary"* and *value(&o2)="setof"*, standing that *name*, *age*, *child* and *child* may be unordered. The stuctures are thus composed in the following way:

```
{person: &o1 {name:  Mary,     person: &o2 {name:   John,
             age:    45,                    age:     17,
             child: &o2,                    child : &o2,
             child: &o3},                   relatives: {mother: &o1,
                                                        syster: &o3}},
 person: &o3 {name:   Jane,
             country : Canada,
             mother: &o1}
}
```

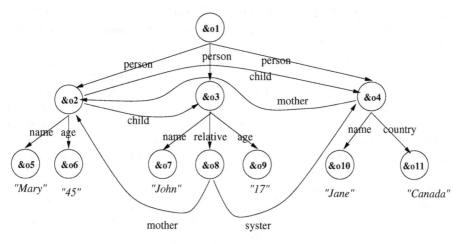

Fig. 1. An OEM graph

A single path in the graph is an alternating sequence of objects and labels $< o_1l_1o_2...o_{k-1}l_{k-1}o_k >$ beginning and ending with objects, in which each label is incident with the two nodes immediately preceding and following it. Such a path p_k is called a *path expression*. The number of labels from the source object to the target node in a path, k, is the length of the path. As we consider nested structures, we can consider that the length is similar to the nested level of the structure. Let P_k the set of all paths p where the length of p is k. We now consider multiple path defined as follows: a *multiple path expression* (or *path* for short) is a set of single paths such as the source object is the same in all the single paths[1]. The length of the multiple path is the maximal length of all single paths. As we are only interested in structural regularities, in the following we do not consider atomic values anymore and we use symbol $\bot$ in order to denote an atomic value in the graph.

Example 1 Let us consider figure 1. From the object &o5, we have the following path expression: { *name* : $\bot$, *age* : $\bot$, *child* : {*name* : $\bot$, *age* : $\bot$}, *child* : { *name* : $\bot$, *country* : $\bot$}}.

A multiple path expression p_m is a *sub-path expression* of another multiple path expression p_n if every object of p_m is included in p_n where the inclusion is defined as follows. If the object is a set value, such as $\{x_1, ...x_l\} \subseteq p_m$ and $\{x'_1, ...x'_k\} \subseteq p_n$ then the object of p_m is included in the object of p_n if and only if every x_i is a subset of some x'_j. If the object is a list value, such as $< x_1, ...x_l > \subseteq p_m$ and $< x'_1, ...x'_k > \subseteq p_n$ then the object of p_m is included

---

[1] In fact, we may consider that a multiple path expression is an OEM graph where the root of the graph is the source object of single paths embedded in the multiple path expression.

in the object of p_n if and only if there exist integers $i_1 < i_2 < ... < i_n$ such that $x_1 \subseteq x'_{i_1}$, $x_2 \subseteq x'_{i_2}$ ... $x_2 \subseteq x'_{i_n}$. Furthermore we assume that an atomic value is included in itself.

Let DB be a set of transactions where each transaction T consists of transaction-id and a multiple path expression embedded in the OEM graph and involved in the transaction. All transactions are sorted in increasing order and are called a *data sequence*. Figure 2 gives an exemple of transactions embedded in DB. A support value ($supp(s)$) for a multiple path expression in the OEM graph gives its number of actual occurrences in DB. In other words, the support of a path is defined as the fraction of total data sequences that contain p. A data sequence contains a path p if p is a sub-path expression of the data sequence. In order to decide whether a path is frequent or not, a minimum support value ($minSupp$) is specified by user, and the multiple path expression is said *frequent* if the condition $supp(s) \geq minSupp$ holds.

Problem statement: Given a database DB of customer transactions the problem of regularity mining, called *Schema mining*, is to find all maximal paths occurring in DB whose support is greater than a specified threshold (minimum support). Each of which represents a *frequent path*.

From the problem statement presented so far, discovering structural association sequential patterns resembles closely to mining association rules [AIS93,AS94,BMUT97,FPSSU96,SON95,Toi96] or sequential patterns [AS95,SA96]. However, elements of handled association transactions have structures in the form of a labeled hirearchical objects, and a main difference is introduced with partially ordered references. In other word we have to take into account complex structures while in the association rules or sequential patterns elements are atomics, i.e. flat sets or lists of items.

Trans_id	path expressions
t_1	$person : \{identity: \{name: \perp, \ address; \perp\}\}$
t_2	$person : \{identity: \{name: \perp, \ address: < street: \perp, zipcode: \perp >,$ $company: \perp, director: < name: \perp, firstname: \perp >\}\}$
t_3	$person : \{identity: \{id: \perp, address: < street : \perp, \ zipcode : \perp >\}\}$
t_4	$person : \{identity: \{name: \perp, \ address: \perp, \ company: \perp\}\}$
t_5	$person : \{identity: \{name: \perp, \ address; \perp\}\}$
t_6	$person : \{identity: \{name: \perp, \ address: < street: \perp, zipcode: \perp >,$ $director: < name: \perp, firstname: \perp >\}\}$

Fig. 2. A transaction database

An Example: In order to illustrate the problem, let us consider the base D given in figure 2, reporting transactions about a population merely reduced to six. Let us assume that the minimum support value is 50%, thus to be considered as frequent a path must be observed for at least 3 transactions. Let us now

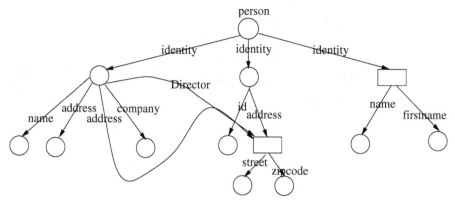

Fig. 3. An OEM graph

consider the associated OEM graph given in figure 3. The only frequent paths, embedded in the DB are the following: *identity*: {*name*: ⊥, *address*: ⊥} and *identity*: {*address*: < *street*: ⊥, *zipcode*: ⊥ >}. The fist one is discovered because it matches with the first transaction t_1 while being detected for t_4 and t_5. In the same way *identity*: {*address*: < *street*: ⊥, *zipcode*: ⊥ >} is supported by transactions t_2, t_3 and t_6. For instance the multiple path expression *identity*: {*name*: ⊥, *address*: < *street*: ⊥, *zipcode*: ⊥ >, *director*: < *name*: ⊥, *firstname*: ⊥ >} is supported by transaction t_2 and t_6 but it is not frequent since the number of data sequences supporting this path does not verify the mininum support constraint.

3   Principles

For presenting our approach, we adopt the chronological viewpoint of data processing: from collected raw data to exhibited knowledge. We consider that the mechanism for discovering regularities on semistructured data in a large database is a 2-phase process. The starting point of the former phase is semistructured objects extracted from sources on the Web and collected in a large file.

From such a file, the mapping phase performs a transformation of original data. It results in a new populated database containing the meaningful remaining data. From such a database, data mining technique is applied in order to extract useful regularities on graph structures. The architecture of our approach is depicted in figure 4.

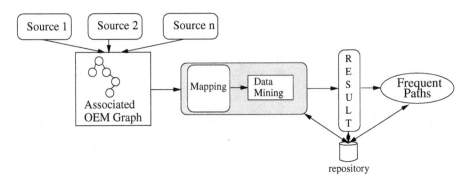

Fig. 4. General Architecture

3.1   Data Extraction

The structure of each object embedded in the source must be extracting during this phase. First of all, a data filtering step is performed in order to filter out irrelevant semistructured data such as image, video, sound, etc. Furthermore, according to the end user view point not interesting substructures are also prunned out.

In order to perform such an extraction, we assume that the end user is provided with a parser or a wrapper. Of course, this parser requires the implementation of efficient algorithms for extracting graph structure. During our experiments, we assumed that such extraction has been done. For instance, in [HGMC+97], a very efficient tool for extracting semistructured data from a set of HTML pages and for converting the extracted information into an OEM graph is addressed. This extraction is done on differents sources in order to provide a large collection of graph structure where we want to discover substructures appearing in some number of graph structures.

3.2   Knowledge Discovery

From the data yielded by the extraction phase, data mining technique is applied for fully meeting the analyst needs.

We split the problem of mining structural association of semistructured data in a large database into the following sub-phases: mapping and data mining.

Mapping phase: The transaction database is sorted with transaction id as a major key and values embedded in a set-of are sorted according to the lexicographic order. In order to efficiently find structural regularity among path expressions, each path expression is mapped in the following way. If the object value is a part of a *set-of* value, then we merge an 'S' to the label (resp. a 'L' for a *list-of* value). Furthermore, in order to take into account the level of the label into the transaction, we append to the label an integer standing for the level of the label in the nested structure. When two labels occur at the same level and if the first one directly follows the second one, they are grouped together in the same set otherwise they form a new set of labels. The ordering of the *list-of* value is taken into account by creating a new set of labels. The "composite" transaction which results from the union of such sets obtained from original transaction describe a *sequence of label* and the ordering of such a sequence may be seen as the way of navigating through the path expression.

This step converts the original original database into a database D of data-sequences where each data-sequence describes the ordering of labels into the transaction according to the path expression.

Figure 5 describes the database of our previous example after the mapping phase.

Trans_id	path expressions mapped
t_1	$(Sidentity_1)$ $(Sname_2\ Saddress_2)$
t_2	$(Sidentity_1)$ $(Sname_2\ Saddress_2)$ $(Lstreet_3)(Lzipcode_3)$ $(Scompany_2\ Sdirector_2)$ $(Lname_3)$ $(Lfirstname_3)$
t_3	$(Sidentity_1)$ $(Sid_2\ Saddress_2)$ $(Lstreet_3)$ $(Lzipcode_3)$
t_4	$(Sidentity_1)$ $(Sname_2\ Saddress_2\ Scompany2)$
t_5	$(Sidentity_1)$ $(Sname_2\ Saddress_2)$
t_6	$(Sidentity_1)$ $(Sname_2\ Saddress_2)$ $(Lstreet_3)$ $(Lzipcode_3)$ $(Sdirector_2)$ $(Lname_3)$ $(Lfirstname_3)$

Fig. 5. A transaction database mapped

Mining Phase: From the database obtained from the mapping phase, the problem resembles closely to mining association rules (also known as *market-basket* proble) which was initially introduced in [AIS93] where association could be seen as relationships between facts, embedded in the database. Nevertheless our problem is quite different since we have to take into account hierarchical structure. In fact, our approach is very similar to the problem of sequential pattern which is introduced to capture typical behaviour over time, i.e. behaviours sufficiently repeated by individuals to be relevant for the decision maker [AS95]. In this context, we assume that we are given a database D of customers' transactions, each of which having the following characteristics: sequence-id or customer-id, transaction-time and the items involved in the transaction. Such a database is called a base of data sequences (C.f. Fig. 2). For aiding efficiently decision making, the aim is discarding non typical behaviours according to user's viewpoint. Performing such a task requires providing data sub-sequence s in the DB with a support value ($supp(s)$) giving its number of actual occurrences in the DB. In order to decide whether a sequence is frequent or not, a minimum support value (σ) is specified by user, and the sequence s is said frequent if the condition $supp(s) \geq \sigma$ holds.

The interested reader could refer to [AS95,SA96,MCP98] in which approaches for exhibiting sequences are presented and compared.

Our approach for mining structural regularities fully resumes the fundamental principles of sequential pattern problem. In order to improve the efficiciny of retrievals we use an algorithm, called PSP, that we defined for mining sequential patterns. It resumes the principles of GSP [SA96] but it makes use of a different intermediary data structure which is proved to be more efficient than in GSP. Due to lack of space we do not detail the algorithm but interested reader may refer to [MCP98,MPC99].

As illustration, when running our algorithm on the database of the figure 5 with a support value of 50%, we obtain the following frequent paths: $< (Sidentity_1) (Sname_2 Saddress2) >$ and $< (Sidentity_1) (Sname_2) (Lstreet_3) (Lzipcode_3) >$. These results may thus be transformed according to information obtained from the mapping phase and we are thus provided with the following semistructured graphs: $identity$: $\{name: \perp, address: \perp\}$ and $identity$: $\{address: < street: \perp, zipcode: \perp >\}$.

The data mining algorithm is implemented using Gnu C++ and preliminary results show that the approach is efficient. In the following figure, we report experiments conducted on the Internet Movies Database [WL99]. We got informations about actors (500 differents actors were examined). When applying our approach, we obtain the following results (C.f. figure 6). For instance, we can notice that more than 250 actors have a name, a date of birth and a filmography as well as a notable apparition on tv.

Support	frequent paths
20%	* $\{actor : \{name, birthname, dateofbirth, filmography_as : \{title, notabletv\}\}\}$ * $\{actor : \{name, dateofbirth, dateofdeath, filmographyas : \{title, notabletv\}\}\}$ * $\{actor : \{name, dateofbirth, minibibliography, filmographyas : \{title, notabletv\}\}\}$ * $\{actor : \{name, dateofbirth, sometimescreditas : \{name\}, filmographyas : \{title\}\}\}$ * $\{actor : \{name, dateofbirth, trivia, filmographyas : \{title, notabletv\}\}\}$ * $\{actor : \{name, sometimescreditas : \{name\}, filmographyas : \{title, notabletv\}\}\}$
30%	* $\{actor : \{name, birth_name, dateofbirth, filmographyas : \{title\}\}\}$ * $\{actor : \{name, dateofbirth, filmographyas : \{title, notabletv\}\}\}$ * $\{actor : \{name, trivia, filmographyas : \{title\}\}\}$
40%	* $\{actor : \{name, dateofbirth, filmographyas : \{title, notabletv\}\}\}$
50%	* $\{actor : \{name, dateofbirth, filmographyas : \{title, notabletv\}\}\}$

Fig. 6. result of experiments on the Internet Movie Database

4   Related Work

To the best of our knowledge there is few work on mining such a structural regularity in a large database. Nevertheless, our work is very related to the problem of mining structural association of semistructured data proposed in [WL98,WL99] where a very efficient approach for mining such regularities is provided. The author propose a very efficient approach and solutions based on a new representation of the search space. Furthermore they give some pruning strategies in order to improve the candidate generation. Nevertheless our work has some important differences. Unlike their approach we are insterested in all structures embedded in the database while they are interested in mining tree expression which are defined as a path from the root of the OEM graph to the atomic values. According to this definition of the tree expression they cannot find regularities such as *identity*: {*address*: < *street*: ⊥, *zipcode*: ⊥ >}. In fact, when parsing the database in order to find frequent tree, they are only provided with maximal tree and when only a part of the tree is frequent it is not discovered.

5   Conclusion

In this paper we present an approach for mining regularities of semistructured objects in a large database. This approach is based on a data mining technique and preliminary results show that such a technique may be useful in order to discover schema regularities on the Web. We have defined the problem and proposed a very efficient approach to solve it.

References

Abi97.   S. Abiteboul. Querying Semi-Structured Data. In *Proceedings of International Conference on Database Theory (ICDT'97)*, pages 1–18, Delphi, Greece, January 1997. 179

ABS00.   S. Abiteboul, P. Buneman, and D. Suciu. *Data on the Web*. Morgan Kaufmann, 2000. 180

AIS93.   R. Agrawal, T. Imielinski, and A. Swami. Mining Association Rules between Sets of Items in Large Databases. In *Proceedings of the 1993 ACM SIGMOD Conference*, pages 207–216, Washington DC, USA, May 1993. 182, 185

AQM+97.   S. Abiteboul, D. Quass, J. McHugh, J. Widom, and J.L Wiener. The Lorel Query Language for Semi-Structured Data. *International Journal on Digital Libraries*, 1(1):68–88, April 1997. 180

AS94.   R. Agrawal and R. Srikant. Fast Algorithms for Mining Generalized Association Rules. In *Proceedings of the 20th International Conference on Very Large Databases (VLDB'94)*, Santiago, Chile, September 1994. 182

AS95.   R. Agrawal and R. Srikant. Mining Sequential Patterns. In *Proceedings of the 11th International Conference on Data Engineering (ICDE'95)*, Tapei, Taiwan, March 1995. 182, 185

BMUT97.   S. Brin, R. Motwani, J. D. Ullman, and S. Tsur. Dynamic Itemset Counting and Implication Rules for Market Basket Data. In *Proceedings of the International Conference on Management of Data (SIGMOD'97)*, pages 255–264, Tucson, Arizona, May 1997. 182

FPSSU96.   U. M. Fayad, G. Piatetsky-Shapiro, P. Smyth, and R. Uthurusamy, editors. *Advances in Knowledge Discovery and Data Mining*. AAAI Press, Menlo Park, CA, 1996. 182

HGMC⁺97.   J. Hammer, H. Garcia-Molina, J. Cho, R. Aranha, and A. Crespo. Extracting Semistructured Information from the Web. In *Proceedings of the Workshop on Management of Semistructured Data. See [Wor97]*, Tucson, Arizona, May 1997. 184

KS95.   D. Konopnicki and O. Shmueli. W3QS: A Query System for the World-Wide Web. In *Proceedings of the 21 st International Conference on Very Large Databases (VLDB'95)*, pages 54–65, Zurich, Switzerland, September 1995. 179

MCP98.   F. Masseglia, F. Cathala, and P. Poncelet. The PSP Approach for Mining Sequential Patterns. In *Proceedings of the 2nd European Symposium on Principles of Data Mining and Knowledge Discovery (PKDD'98), LNAI, Vol. 1510*, pages 176–184, Nantes, France, September 1998. 185, 186

MPC99.   F. Masseglia, P. Poncelet, and R. Cicchetti. An Efficient Algorithm for Web Usage Mining. *Networking and Information Systems Journal*, 2(5-6):571–603, December 1999. 186

NUWC97.   S. Nestorov, J. Ullman, J. Wiener, and S. Chawathe. Representative Objects: Concise Representations of Semistructured, Hierarchical Data. In *Proceedings of the 13th International Conference on Data Engineering (ICDE'97)*, pages 79–90, Birmingham, U. K., April 1997.

SA96.   R. Srikant and R. Agrawal. Mining Sequential Patterns: Generalizations and Performance Improvements. In *Proceedings of the 5th International Conference on Extending Database Technology (EDBT'96)*, pages 3–17, Avignon, France, September 1996. 182, 185, 186

SON95.   A. Savasere, E. Omiecinski, and S. Navathe. An Efficient Algorithm for Mining Association Rules in Large Databases. In *Proceedings of the 21 st International Conference on Very Large Databases (VLDB'95)*, pages 432–444, Zurich, Switzerland, September 1995. 182

Toi96.   H. Toivonen. Sampling Large Databases for Association Rules. In *Proceedings of the 22nd International Conference on Very Large Databases (VLDB'96)*, September 1996. 182

WL98.   K. Wang and H. Q. Liu. Discovering Typical Structures of Documents: A Road Map Approach. In *Proceedings of ACM SIGIR Conference on Research and Development in Information Retrieval*, pages 146–154, Melbourne, Austrialia, August 1998. 179, 187

WL99.   K. Wang and H. Liu. Discovering Structural Association of Semistructured Data. *IEEE Transactions on Knowledge and Data Engineering*, 1999. 186, 187

Wor97.   Work97. The Workshop on Management of Semistructured Data. In *www.research.att.com/s̃uciu/workshop-papers.html*, Tucson, Arizona, May 1997. 179, 188

Web Personalization Using Extended Boolean Operations with Latent Semantic Indexing

Preslav Nakov

Sofia University, Faculty of Mathematics and Informatics and Rila Solutions
preslav@rila.bg

Abstract. The paper discusses the potential of the usage of Extended Boolean operations for personalized information delivery on the Internet based on semantic vector representation models. The final goal is the design of an e-commerce portal tracking user's clickstream activity and purchases history in order to offer them personalized information. The emphasis is put on the introduction of dynamic composite user profile constructed by means of extended Boolean operations. The basic binary Boolean operations such as OR, AND and NOT (AND-NOT) and their combinations have been introduced and implemented in variety of ways. An evaluation is presented based on the classic Latent Semantic Indexing method for information retrieval using a text corpus of religious and sacred texts.

1 Introduction

The pre-Internet era imperative stated that more data means better chance to find the information needed. Internet has imposed new standards and new way of thinking. In 1994 the World Wide Web Worm received an average of about 1500 queries per day, in November 1997 only one of the top four commercial search engines finds itself (returns its own search page in response to its name in the top ten results) and nowadays the AltaVista search engine serves hundreds of millions queries per day. With the enormous growth of the information available on the Web the goal has changed and the main efforts are directed towards the limitation of the information presented to the user. [5] The first that felt the problem were of course the search engines and they offered the users several possibilities for advanced query refinements. Unfortunately their usage remained highly limited, since as Marchionini argued: "End users want to achieve their goals with a minimum of cognitive load and a maximum of enjoyment. ... humans seek the path of least cognitive resistance and prefer recognition tasks to recall tasks; most people will trade time to minimize complexity". [17] The problem of the relevance of information presented to the users was well understood by the commercial Internet sites. When people find some magazine irrelevant to their information expectations they simply stop to buy it. It is the same with the Web sites: if the information presented does not meet the customers' needs they never return there. The limited volume of the magazines does not permit to include everything people would find relevant and they tend to specialize in

S. A. Cerri and D. Dochev (Eds.): AIMSA 2000, LNAI 1904, pp. 189–198, 2000.

a particular area. People buy only those magazines that are relevant to their specific interests. The Web sites and portals are a different case because there are no so strong limitations of the amount of information to be published. The biggest Internet portals like those of Yahoo!, MSN or Netscape can offer almost all a customer may need. The problem is how to organize the site in order to help the users find what they are actually looking for.

2   The Idea of the User Profile

The most valuable decision is the development of a dynamic model of the interests for the specific user. The first attempt in the development of the profile was to ask the user to enter some words that best describe his or her interests. Another possibility is the selection of the relevant ones among a set of articles. Each of them can be assigned a list of key words that will be used to limit the information presented to the user. For example, a personalized search engine could return information only from the field of interest to the user. The same way a well-personalized Web site changes dynamically its content in order to present to the user only relevant information, news or advertisements, according to the previously created profile. [10]

Asking explicitly the users for some kind of relevance feedback may not always be the best way to create their profiles. This is especially the case when using key words. As Furnas, Landauer, Gomez and Dumais have shown in [11], people use the same words to describe the same subject in $10 - 20\%$ of the time (see also [4]). The relevance feedback when using whole articles may not be correct too, because of the influence of some subjective factors like novelty, informativeness or familiarity to the user.

Some sites/portals offer the customers the opportunity to receive a free "passport". The users are asked to fill a form and answer a set of common questions that will be used as a primary source for the construction of their profiles. This may be of great importance and can lead to significant improvements. The problem is that people tend to get annoyed when asked to do something in order to help the System. That is why several business sites/portals developed specialized mechanisms for automatic user's profile construction. Some of the recent studies and applications in the field include the automatic tracking and recording of the user's activity when browsing on the site: e.g. page visited, button clicked, hyper link followed, search query entered etc. The information collected this way is called clickstream and is stored in specially designed clickstream data marts and *Data Webhouses*. Thus, the Web site/portal retains a full history of the user's activity that permits the construction of a more effective and objective profile. [13,14,15,21] For almost all the cases the user profile has a dynamic character and changes over time since new information becomes available. The general sources of additional information are the raw details of the recorded user activity: the clickstream. Most of the systems use a vector representation of the user profile. This is very convenient and, as we will show later, simplifies its creation, support and usage. Although there are several different techniques for vector generation of the type described, we have chosen the Latent Semantic Indexing for several reasons the primary of which is that it is a well-studied classic method that will allow us to concentrate on the specific details of the profile creation and usage we want to study.

3 Latent Semantic Indexing

The *Latent Semantic Indexing* (LSI) is a powerful statistical technique for a fully automatic indexing and retrieval of information. LSI is generally applied to texts and represents a two-stage process that consists of (see [7,9,16] for details): off-line construction of document index, and on-line respond to user queries. The off-line part of the process is the training part when LSI creates its index. First a large word-to-document matrix X is constructed where the cell (i,j) contains the frequencies of occurrence of the i-th word into the j-th document. After that, a *singular value decomposition* (SVD) is performed which results in the compression of the original space in a much smaller one where we have just a few number of significant factors (usually $50 - 400$). Each document is then represented by a meaning vector of low dimensionality (e.g. 100). The on-line part of LSI receives the query (pseudo-document) user typed and finds its corresponding vector into the document space constructed by the off-line part using a standard LSI mechanism. Now we can measure the degree of similarity between the query and the indexed documents by simply calculating the cosine between their corresponding vectors.

4 Extended Boolean Operations

We return now to the automatic creation of the vector representation of the user's profiles. Consider an e-commerce portal tracking users' clickstream activity as have been discussed above. The information collected can be used in variety of ways including analysis of the quality of the Web site structure and organization, etc. ([13]) There are several things we are interested in when constructing the users' profiles among which the most important are:

- Which sections/pages on the site the customer visits most frequently? What do they content?
- Which pages are "session killers" for our customer?
- How long time does the customer spend on the site?
- Who is our customer? How often he or she visits the site?
- Has the customer purchased something and what, if any? What kind of products?
- Is it a complaining customer that often returns back our products?

Having collected information like this will allow us to create a sophisticated high quality user profile that will permit offering him or her personalized news, advertisements, banners etc. We would like to create a profile vector that is closely aligned to the vectors of the pages the user is interested in and is far from those which seem to be uninteresting. A page of interest for the user may be a page where he or she goes often or spends a long time. The longer the user stays on the page, the more relevant it may be to his or her interests. On the other hand we must beware not taking too seriously the extremely long times (the user has just left the browser open) giving at the same time higher weights for the pages related to the user's purchases, if any. So, we would like to combine the vectors of the relevant pages, weighted according to the frequency of the visits and the duration of the time spent there, in order to obtain the profile vector. This implies the need for a weighted OR similarity measure. We would like also to exclude the pages that seem to be strongly uninteresting for the user: e.g. those where he or she (often) cancels the session or those, we know he or she not interested in, according to a relevance feedback, possibly taken from the user "passport" registration information supplied. This implies the need for excluding NOT (MINUS) Boolean operation. These examples show that the extended Boolean operations play a major role in the process of user's profiles creation.

Another possibility is to design a composite profile by keeping several different vectors whose weighted combination gives the profile vector. This results in improved performance since we can manage the different vectors the profile is built of separately and combine (some of) them only when needed. This allows the creation of a dynamic profile that may be recalculated when needed and with changed weights. For example, we may like to drop some elements of the user profile that are no longer relevant (because are old), or at least reduce their weights.

Consider we have collected a complete history of the customers' purchases and clickstream activity, and want to send the users several advertisements by e-mail or show them on the Web when browsing the site/portal. We have already developed LSI index based on the text description of each product. We can think of the purchases/clicks as query components and of the advertisement as a new document in the same space. We need some kind of similarity function that will give us a measure of the similarity between our advertisements and the user's profile. Let us define $d_1, d_2, ..., d_n$ as distances (in LSI sense) between the ad and the n components of the query. The classic LSI algorithm calculates the cosines between the vectors in order to find the degree of their similarity. Most of the similarity measures for the Boolean operations we propose below are based on Euclidean distances, although we can use some other distances (angle, Manhattan, Chebishov's, power, etc.).

There are several similarity measures we have experimented with:

OR-similarity measure. This measure depends only on the minimal distance between the document and the query components and has the following general representation: $S_{or} = f(min(g(d_1), g(d_2), ..., g(d_n)))$, where $f(x)$ and $g(x)$ are some one-argument functions. In case we have more information for the query we can add weights to the query components and change $g(x)$ to $g(x, w)$. So the formula is: $S_{or} = f(min(g(d_1, w_1), g(d_2, w_2), ..., g(d_n, w_n)))$. OR

Fig. 1. OR similarity for two- and three-component query

similarity measure has well separated picks at the query components vectors. The similarity measure for two- and three-component query, $f(x) = 1/(1+x)$, $g(x) = x$ are shown on figure 1.

AND-similarity measure. This measure depends only on the sum of distances between the document and query components. It has the following general representation: $S_{or} = f((g(d_1, w_1)+g(d_2, w_2)+...+g(d_n, w_n)))$ Usually this measure can be thought of as a superposition of distinct similarity measures of the query components. The similarity measure for two- and three-component query, $f(x) = 1/(1+x)$, $g(x) = x$ are shown on figure 2.

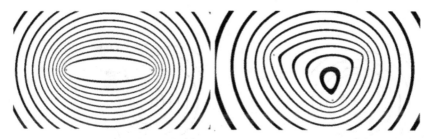

Fig. 2. AND similarity for two- and three-component query

Combination of the previous two (AND-OR). This similarity measure is a combination between the previous two: $S_{and-or} = f(S_{and}, S_{or})$. We can use linear combination between S_{or} and S_{and} measures. $S = k.S_{or} + (1 - k).S_{and}$, where k is constant and $0 <= k <= 1$. Figure 3 shows the two- and three-component query results for $k = 0.5$. We still have two distinct parts like the OR-similarity function but higher values in the middle region between them just like the AND-similarity function.

MINUS and Binary NOT (AND-NOT)-similarity measure. In case we want to exclude a vector we can apply two different similarity measures: MINUS and NOT. For the MINUS similarity measure, if the vector considered is more similar to the exclude vector it will receive a similarity measure of 0 (see the second clause below). Otherwise we return a similarity measure that takes

Fig. 3. Combined similarity for two- and three-component query, k=0.5

in account the distance to the *include vector only*. We can use the following MINUS-measure: $S_{not} = d_1$, when $d_1 < d_2$, and $S_{not} = 0$, else. The result is shown on the left of figure 4.

The problem with this measure is that it takes in account d_2 only when deciding whether to cut the value. A more sophisticated implementation may be used: the NOT (AND-NOT) similarity measure. If the document is more similar to the exclude document text it will receive a similarity measure of 0, but otherwise we return a similarity measure between 0 and 1 that takes in account the distances to *both* documents. Example: We can use the following NOT-measure: $S_{not} = 1 - d_1/(1 + d_2)$, when $d_1 < d_2$, and $S_{not} = 0$, else. The result is shown on the right of figure 4.

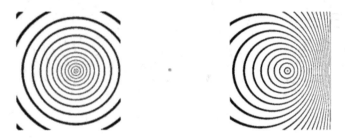

Fig. 4. MINUS and NOT (AND-NOT) similarity measures

5   Application to Religious and Sacred Texts

The first step toward the construction of the dynamic user profile is the development of the appropriate extended Boolean operations. We have experimented the performance of the Extended Boolean Operations presented above on a large number of different corpuses containing thousands of documents by thousands of words and hundreds of megabytes. We will demonstrate how the functions we introduced above work on a small corpus of religious and sacred texts we found at: `http://davidwiley.com/religion.html`. We selected 196 different religious and sacred texts from 14 categories: apocrypha (acts, apocalypses, gospels, writings), Buddhism, Confucianism, Dead Sea scripts, The Egyptian Book of Dead, Sun Tzu: The Art of War, Zoroastrianism, The Bible (Old and New Testaments), The Quran and The Book of Mormons. The experiments were made in a 30 dimensional space with a preliminary to SVD replacement of the frequencies in X (196 documents and 11451 words) with their logarithms. Figure 5 illustrates the inter-document similarities given by the correlation matrix (196x196), shown in 5 different colors for the five correlation intervals: black $(87, 5 - 100\%)$, dark gray $(75 - 87, 5\%)$, gray $(62, 5 - 75\%)$, light gray $(50 - 62, 5\%)$ and white $(0 - 50\%)$. The dark rectangles in the main diagonal show the high correlation between texts belonging to the same religion.

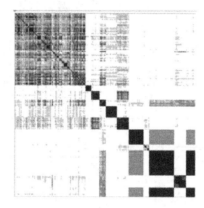

Fig. 5. Correlation between religious texts (196 x 196)

We developed several specialized software command line tools supporting both the on-line and off-line LSI stages using the standard SVDPACKC library routines for the singular value decomposition [4]. A LSI based natural language query search engine has been developed based on these tools and exposed on the Web at `http://nlp.rila.bg`.

Below are presented eight different tables that contain experimental results obtained for two example texts from the corpus belonging to different well-separated clusters (religions): the first chapter of the Sun Tzu's Art of War (`suntzu1.txt`) and the first chapter of the Confucianism religious texts (`conf1.txt`). The first table contains the ranked top list of the documents similar to the first chapter of the Sun Tzu's Art of War with the corresponding degree of similarity. Then follow seven tables containing the results from the application of different Boolean operations. Consider the user's clickstream activity shows he or she is interested in information common to both the documents. The system needs to perform a Boolean AND operation on the LSI vectors of those documents and to produce a ranked document list in order to choose the relevant documents. The results are shown in the second table. The following two tables contain the results of the application of two different excluding operations: NOT and MINUS, whose behavior has been discussed above. Then follow four tables showing the results of the application of four different types of OR operations for different values of k (see above).

```
Z:\>new_doc suntzul.txt

SUNTZU1.TXT:  1.00000000
SUNTZU10.TXT: 0.96812259
SUNTZU8.TXT:  0.96652910
SUNTZU11.TXT: 0.93972055
SUNTZU8.TXT:  0.93858290
SUNTZU9.TXT:  0.93604917
SUNTZU5.TXT:  0.93365826
SUNTZU2.TXT:  0.93192063
SUNTZU6.TXT:  0.93054489
SUNTZU4.TXT:  0.92828905
SUNTZU7.TXT:  0.92593509
CONF2.TXT:    0.91226262
SUNTZU3.TXT:  0.91114359
SUNTZU12.TXT: 0.85816521
CONF1.TXT:    0.82958573
CONF5.TXT:    0.78001097
CONF3.TXT:    0.75975322
CONF8.TXT:    0.75835731
CONF9.TXT:    0.74499495
PLNSENCA.HTM: 0.73306848
CONF7.TXT:    0.71974991
CONF4.TXT:    0.71070083
COMRULE.HTM:  0.68268537
CONF6.TXT:    0.68213084
APCTHOM.HTM:  0.65737315
TOMCNTND.HTM: 0.65597126
REPORTPL.HTM: 0.64527600
ACTPTNPL.HTM: 0.64414208
REPTPILT.HTM: 0.63537118
BKS.HTM:      0.63271447
CONSTITU.HTM: 0.60308042
```

```
Z:\>new_doc_bool
suntzul.txt confl.txt AND

CONF2.TXT:    0.93506011
SUNTZU1.TXT:  0.91479286
CONF1.TXT:    0.91479286
SUNTZU13.TXT: 0.90802675
SUNTZU8.TXT:  0.90745685
SUNTZU10.TXT: 0.89604427
SUNTZU2.TXT:  0.88122315
SUNTZU3.TXT:  0.87397853
SUNTZU11.TXT: 0.86994911
CONF5.TXT:    0.85956386
SUNTZU6.TXT:  0.85553152
CONF3.TXT:    0.85421266
CONF8.TXT:    0.84673427
SUNTZU5.TXT:  0.84201628
CONF9.TXT:    0.83800404
SUNTZU4.TXT:  0.83730812
SUNTZU9.TXT:  0.83378707
SUNTZU7.TXT:  0.82986823
CONF7.TXT:    0.82701671
CONF4.TXT:    0.80956085
CONF6.TXT:    0.78754286
SUNTZU12.TXT: 0.77238908
PLNSENCA.HTM: 0.71858016
COMRULE.HTM:  0.65251025
TOMCNTND.HTM: 0.64263567
SENTANCE.HTM: 0.60424740
BKS.HTM:      0.58734007
APCTHOM.HTM:  0.57461640
FGAPCPT.HTM:  0.57040597
GOSMARY.HTM:  0.56554976
MYSTERY.HTM:  0.56087279
```

```
Z:\>new_doc_bool
suntzul.txt confl.txt NOT

SUNTZU1.TXT:  1.00000000
SUNTZU10.TXT: 0.98252302
SUNTZU8.TXT:  0.98189181
SUNTZU11.TXT: 0.96651472
SUNTZU5.TXT:  0.96605616
SUNTZU9.TXT:  0.96306676
SUNTZU2.TXT:  0.96280884
SUNTZU5.TXT:  0.96209854
SUNTZU6.TXT:  0.96099163
SUNTZU4.TXT:  0.95893613
SUNTZU7.TXT:  0.95728178
SUNTZU13.TXT: 0.95335401
SUNTZU12.TXT: 0.91590555
PLNSENCA.HTM: 0.84335849
COMRULE.HTM:  0.80440870
TOMCNTND.HTM: 0.78884876
APCTHOM.HTM:  0.77033574
BKS.HTM:      0.76180693
REPORTPL.HTM: 0.75937276
ACTPTNPL.HTM: 0.75767365
REPTPILT.HTM: 0.75380184
FGAPCPT.HTM:  0.73594581
MARTBART.HTM: 0.73030361
CONSTITU.HTM: 0.72582505
MYSTERY.HTM:  0.72447034
ACTJNTHB.HTM: 0.71790911
APCJMS1.HTM:  0.71604588
ACTMAT.HTM:   0.71421530
REVSTEV.HTM:  0.71192762
NAGHAM6.HTM:  0.70218790
DEATHPLT.HTM: 0.70177880
```

```
Z:\>new_doc_bool
suntzul.txt confl.txt MINUS

SUNTZU1.TXT:  0.99999999
SUNTZU10.TXT: 0.84153095
SUNTZU8.TXT:  0.83314816
SUNTZU9.TXT:  0.79360580
SUNTZU11.TXT: 0.78726789
SUNTZU5.TXT:  0.78655673
SUNTZU3.TXT:  0.78331581
SUNTZU4.TXT:  0.77882682
SUNTZU7.TXT:  0.77748381
SUNTZU6.TXT:  0.77582141
SUNTZU2.TXT:  0.76678133
SUNTZU13.TXT: 0.70645429
SUNTZU12.TXT: 0.70273529
APCTHOM.HTM:  0.58777081
PLNSENCA.HTM: 0.58703387
ACTPTNPL.HTM: 0.58462459
REPORTPL.HTM: 0.58416049
REPTPILT.HTM: 0.57669034
COMRULE.HTM:  0.57378553
CONSTITU.HTM: 0.56559168
BKS.HTM:      0.56207412
REVJON2.HTM:  0.56055113
ACTMAT.HTM:   0.55897387
ACTPHIL.HTM:  0.55627470
APCPETE.HTM:  0.55580713
MARTBART.HTM: 0.55501092
TOMCNTND.HTM: 0.55428700
YASNAB.TXT:   0.55068365
REVSTEV.HTM:  0.55059070
AVENGSAV.HTM: 0.54946890
ACTANM.HTM:   0.54908653
```

```
Z:\>new_doc_bool
suntzul.txt confl.txt OR 0

SUNTZU1.TXT:  0.99999997
CONF1.TXT:    0.99999993
CONF2.TXT:    0.82317039
SUNTZU8.TXT:  0.72128584
SUNTZU10.TXT: 0.69019913
SUNTZU13.TXT: 0.68069817
SUNTZU2.TXT:  0.61376306
SUNTZU3.TXT:  0.60314637
SUNTZU11.TXT: 0.59609037
CONF5.TXT:    0.57673504
CONF3.TXT:    0.57598572
SUNTZU6.TXT:  0.56392683
CONF8.TXT:    0.55314244
SUNTZU5.TXT:  0.54518708
CONF9.TXT:    0.53777290
SUNTZU9.TXT:  0.53540358
SUNTZU4.TXT:  0.53511372
CONF7.TXT:    0.52538150
SUNTZU7.TXT:  0.52381202
CONF3.TXT:    0.49115954
CONF6.TXT:    0.46332613
SUNTZU12.TXT: 0.44084160
PLNSENCA.HTM: 0.38921508
COMRULE.HTM:  0.35047941
TOMCNTND.HTM: 0.34533693
SENTANCE.HTM: 0.32821505
BKS.HTM:      0.32180010
APCTHOM.HTM:  0.31799264
FGAPCPT.HTM:  0.31500315
GOSMARY.HTM:  0.31317246
REPORTPL.HTM: 0.31256336
```

```
Z:\>new_doc_bool  suntzul.txt
confl.txt OR 0.5

SUNTZU1.TXT:  0.99999999
CONF1.TXT:    0.99999996
CONF2.TXT:    0.89051399
SUNTZU8.TXT:  0.84390747
SUNTZU10.TXT: 0.82916086
SUNTZU13.TXT: 0.79592088
SUNTZU2.TXT:  0.77284184
SUNTZU3.TXT:  0.77086463
SUNTZU11.TXT: 0.76790546
CONF3.TXT:    0.76232891
CONF5.TXT:    0.75792590
SUNTZU6.TXT:  0.74723586
CONF8.TXT:    0.74412684
SUNTZU5.TXT:  0.73942267
SUNTZU9.TXT:  0.73572637
CONF9.TXT:    0.73439302
SUNTZU4.TXT:  0.73170138
CONF7.TXT:    0.72983250
SUNTZU7.TXT:  0.72487356
CONF4.TXT:    0.69979020
CONF6.TXT:    0.67814051
SUNTZU12.TXT: 0.64950340
PLNSENCA.HTM: 0.56114178
COMRULE.HTM:  0.51658239
TOMCNTND.HTM: 0.50065410
APCTHOM.HTM:  0.48768289
REPORTPL.HTM: 0.47891968
ACTPTNPL.HTM: 0.47778194
BKS.HTM:      0.47725729
SENTANCE.HTM: 0.47653668
REPTPILT.HTM: 0.47355391
```

```
Z:\>new_doc_bool  suntzul.txt
confl.txt OR 0.75

SUNTZU1.TXT:  0.99999999
CONF1.TXT:    0.99999998
CONF2.TXT:    0.92418579
SUNTZU8.TXT:  0.90521829
SUNTZU10.TXT: 0.89864172
CONF3.TXT:    0.88550050
SUNTZU3.TXT:  0.85472377
SUNTZU11.TXT: 0.85381300
SUNTZU13.TXT: 0.85353224
SUNTZU2.TXT:  0.85238124
CONF5.TXT:    0.84852132
CONF8.TXT:    0.83961903
SUNTZU6.TXT:  0.83989037
SUNTZU5.TXT:  0.83654047
SUNTZU9.TXT:  0.83588777
CONF9.TXT:    0.83270307
CONF7.TXT:    0.83205800
SUNTZU4.TXT:  0.82999522
SUNTZU7.TXT:  0.82540432
CONF4.TXT:    0.80410553
CONF6.TXT:    0.78554770
SUNTZU12.TXT: 0.75383431
PLNSENCA.HTM: 0.64710513
COMRULE.HTM:  0.59963388
TOMCNTND.HTM: 0.57831268
APCTHOM.HTM:  0.57252802
REPORTPL.HTM: 0.56209784
ACTPTNPL.HTM: 0.56096201
BKS.HTM:      0.55498588
REPTPILT.HTM: 0.55446255
SENTANCE.HTM: 0.55069749
```

```
Z:\>new_doc_bool  suntzul.txt
confl.txt OR 1

SUNTZU1.TXT:  1.00000000
CONF1.TXT:    1.00000000
SUNTZU10.TXT: 0.96812259
SUNTZU8.TXT:  0.96652910
CONF2.TXT:    0.95785760
CONF3.TXT:    0.94867210
SUNTZU11.TXT: 0.93972055
CONF5.TXT:    0.93911675
SUNTZU3.TXT:  0.93858290
SUNTZU9.TXT:  0.93604917
CONF7.TXT:    0.93428351
SUNTZU5.TXT:  0.93365826
SUNTZU2.TXT:  0.93192063
CONF9.TXT:    0.93101313
SUNTZU6.TXT:  0.93054489
SUNTZU4.TXT:  0.92828905
SUNTZU7.TXT:  0.92593509
SUNTZU13.TXT: 0.91114359
CONF8.TXT:    0.90842086
CONF6.TXT:    0.89295488
SUNTZU12.TXT: 0.85816521
PLNSENCA.HTM: 0.73306848
COMRULE.HTM:  0.68268537
APCTHOM.HTM:  0.65737315
TOMCNTND.HTM: 0.65597126
REPORTPL.HTM: 0.64527600
ACTPTNPL.HTM: 0.64414208
REPTPILT.HTM: 0.63537118
BKS.HTM:      0.63271447
SENTANCE.HTM: 0.62485831
```

6 Discussion

The results presented above show that the Boolean operations proposed perform well and can be used successfully in the meaning vectors construction by using any kind of Boolean expressions. As have been mentioned above, the correct application of the Boolean operations is a key point in the development of the dynamic user profile. The operations can be useful also in the construction of a natural language query system giving the users the opportunity to combine any kind of natural language queries. After the ranked list has been returned the user can provide the system a relevance feedback by pointing out some of the documents as relevant or non-relevant to his or her query. The system will then provide a second ranked list of documents by combining the vector of the user query with the vectors of those documents using the appropriate extended Boolean operations, like this is done at `http://lsi.research.telcordia.com/lsi-bin/lsiQuery`.

7   Conclusion

We think the application of dynamic vector-based user profiles by means of the extended Boolean operations presented above is very promising. We continue our work by experimenting with different kinds of extended Boolean similarity functions and their behavior on different kind of corpuses. A research has been started whose goal is the application of methods for meaning vector creation, different from LSI, because the latter cannot be easily scaled to extremely large quantity of documents. The next stage is the design of a clickstream activity capture and a sophisticated analyzer of the user behavior in order to move further towards the creation of the personalized Web site.

Acknowledgements

Our special thanks go to Jivko Jeliazkov who helped a lot in the experiments and the development of this paper, especially with the Boolean operations.

References

1. Aldenderfer M., Blashfield R.: Cluster Analysis. A SAGE University Paper. Sage Publications (1984)
2. Anick P. and Vaithyanathan S.: Exploiting clustering and phrases for context-based information retrieval. Proceedings of the 20th annual international ACM SIGIR conference on Research and development in information retrieval. (1997) 314–323
3. Bates M.: Subject Access in Online Catalogs: A Design Model. Journal of the American Society for Information Sciences, Number 37. (1986) 357–376
4. Berry M., Do T., O'Brien G., Krishna V., and Sowmini Varadhan: SVDPACKC (Version 1.0) User's Guide. (1993) 190, 195
5. Brin S., Page L.: The Anatomy of Large Scale Search Engine, Stanford University. (1998) 189
6. Caid W., Carleton J.: Visualization of information using graphical representations of context vector based relationships and attributes. United States Patent 6,794,178. Aug. 11, 1998. (1998)
7. Deerwester S., Dumais S., Furnas G., Laundauer, T. and Harshman R.: Indexing by Latent Semantic Analysis. Journal of the American Society for Information Sciences. 41 (1990) 391–47   191

8. Dumais, S. T.: Using LSI for information filtering: TREC-3 experiments. In: D. Harman (Ed.), The Third Text Retrieval Conference (TREC3) National Institute of Standards and Technology Special Publication , in press. (1995)

9. Dumais, S. T. Using LSI for Information Retrieval, Information Filtering, and Other Things. Talk at Cognitive Technology Workshop, (1997).   191

10. Foltz, P. W. and Dumais, S. T.: Personalized information delivery: An analysis of information filtering methods. Communications of the ACM, **35(12)**. Experiment using LSI for information filtering. (1992) 51–60   190

11. Furnas G., Landauer T., Gomez L. and Dumais T.: Statistical semantics: Analysis of the Potential Performance of Keyword Information Systems. Bell Syst.Tech.J., 62, **6**. (1986) 1753–1806   190

12. Harman, D.: An experimental study of the factors important in document ranking. In Association for Computing Machinery Conference on Research and Development in Information Retrieval. Association for Computing Machinery. (1986)

13. Kimball R.: Clicking with your customer. Warehouse Architect, Number 1, Volume 2, January 05. (1999)   190, 191

14. Kimball R.: The Data Webhouse Has No Center. Warehouse Architect, Number 10, Volume 2, July 13. (1999)   190

15. Kimball R.: The Special Dimension of the Clickstream. Data Webhouse, Number 2, Volume 3, January 20. (2000)   190

16. Laudauer T., Foltz P., Laham D.: Introduction to Latent Semantic Analysis. Discourse Processes, **25**. (1998) 259–284   191

17. Marchionini G.: Interfaces for End-User Interfaces Seeking. Journal of the American Society for Information Science, **43(2)**. (1992) 156–163   189

18. Oard, D.: Adaptive Vector Space Text Filtering for Monolingual and Cross-Language Applications, Department of Electrical Engineering, Univ. of Maryland. (1996)

19. Stairmand M. A.: Textual context analysis for information retrieval. Proceedings of the 20th annual international ACM SIGIR conference on Research and development in information retrieval. (1997) 140–147

20. Vlajic N., Card H.: An adaptive Neural Network Approach to Hypertext Clustering. University of Manitoba. (1998)

21. Winter R.: More Than You Hoped For. Scalable Systems. Volume 3, Number 6, April 10. (2000)   190

22. LSA: http://lsa.colorado.edu (1990-99)

23. Religions: http://davidwiley.com/religion.html

24. The Bible: http://www.bible.org/netbible/download.htm

25. The Quran: http://www.usc.edu/dept/MSA/quran/

What Did He Mean by That?

Allan Ramsay and Helen Seville

Dept of Language Engineering, UMIST,
PO Box 88, Manchester M60 1QD, UK
`Allan.Ramsay,Helen.Seville@umist.ac.uk,`
`http://www.ccl.umist.ac.uk/staff/allan`

Abstract. Most tools for supporting language learners concentrate, at best, on the syntactic correctness of the user's productions. There are a number of reasons for this: (i) it's hard enough to develop programs that can perform syntactic analysis, and even harder to develop ones that can construct meaning representations. But for a CALL tool, we need to construct meaning representations *and then see whether they are correct.* (ii) if we do have the computational tools for comparing the user's production with some 'correct' output, we still need some way of obtaining such target analyses for comparison. In situations where the user is allowed to produce open-ended text, it is very hard to see where such target analyses will come from.

The current paper will show how to make sure that what the user says makes sense at all, and then how to compare it with a target utterance. The key to both these activities lies in extensive use of an inference engine which is capable of producing models that give a picture of what someone who utters a given sentence has in mind.

1 The Task

We want to be able to support intermediate language learners by giving them hints about the *content* of what they have said. Clearly, language learners require help with grammar – they need to know that *'I see the man who you were talking to'* is better than *'Me sees the man what you were talking to'* – but intermediate learners also need help with content. They need help with general issues relating to the use of open class words (why do English people get *'on'* buses and *'in'* cars?) and with the semantic effects of tense and aspect markers (why can't you say *'I am knowing her'*, why does *'he is living in Buxton'* seem to report a temporary state of affairs?); and they need help with the meanings of specific terms – they need to be able to explore the consequences of saying *'a bank is an institution that makes a profit for itself by lending out your money and also charges you for the priviledge'*, and to see if this is what someone from the financial services sector would say about banks.

The current paper reports on an attempt to provide this kind of feedback by constructing a sparse representation of the content of what the learner has said, and then reasoning about what else they are likely to have in mind. The way

S. A. Cerri and D. Dochev (Eds.): AIMSA 2000, LNAI 1904, pp. 199–209, 2000.

we construct meaning representations has been described elsewhere [10,11]. It is worth noting here, however, that these representations are constructed strictly compositionally: in other words, the semantic analysis depends critically on a prior syntactic analysis. The grammar we use is entirely constraint based, and permits relaxation of arbitrary constraints, including ones relating to word order, completeness (the requirement that everything which is expected is present) and coherence (the requirement that everything that is present is required) [13,12]. With such a grammar, it is comparatively easy to find and diagnose syntactic errors in what the user writes – we simply specify that certain constraints are 'soft'. Analyses that involve violation of such soft constraints will be considered if no error-free analyses can be found. Thus the system described here will serve the purpose of helping the user improve their understanding of the grammar of the language they are learning: this is not, however, the focus of the current paper - see [14,3] for various applications of this grammar for dealing with syntactically ill-formed texts. More importantly for the present paper, we are able to make a reasonable guess about what the learner was trying to write. This is crucial if we want to construct an interpretation of what they have written: if our meaning representations are to be obtained compositionally [15,7], then we have to have a syntactic analysis to obtain them from. The use of a constraint-based grammar with soft constraints thus serves two purposes for us. It makes it possible to provide the learner with feedback about the grammatical correctness of what they have written, and it enables us to assign a grammatical analysis and thence to obtain a meaning representation.

2   Meanings and Interpretations

In order to see whether what the user has typed makes sense and means what he wants it to mean, we have to construct a representation of its meaning and then reason about it. Our meaning representations are couched in anchored constructive λ-calculus [17], and contain treatments of a range of semantic phenomena. The reasons why we choose this language, and the specific treatments we choose for the phenomena in question, need not concern us here. *Any* computational account of natural language will necessarily involve producing a meaning representation couched in some formal language, and giving some account of these phenomena. The techniques described below will apply to any such approach.

To make this concrete, Fig. 1 shows the logical form that we obtain for

(1)   *A bank lends money.*

This contains much of the information captured in (2), made more explicit (e.g. the fact that the bank is the agent of the lending event) and expressed in a formal language that a computer might be able to do something with. What we want to do with it is to see whether it (a) makes sense and (b) is accurate.

To tell whether something makes sense, we have to have some notion of sensibleness. In other words, we need to have some notion of which ideas can

$$\exists A : \{A \text{ is interval } \& \text{ ends\_after}(ref(\lambda B(speech\_time(B, 1))), A)\}$$
$$\exists C : \{aspect(simple, A, C)\}$$
$$\exists D \forall E : \{memb(E, C)\}$$
$$bank(D)$$
$$\& \theta(E, agent, D)$$
$$\& lend(E)$$
$$\& E \text{ is event}$$
$$\& \forall F : \{\theta(E, object, F)\}money(F)$$

Fig. 1. Logical form for '*A bank lends money*'

go together, of what kinds of things can take parts in what activities. We could capture this by making statements like the following:

MP1: $\forall A \forall B : \{\theta(A, agent, B)\}animate(B)$ Agents are animate
MP2: $\forall A \neg (idea(A) \& animate(A))$ Ideas are not

Then if somebody said

(2)   *An idea slept.*

we would realise that this was not possible, since MP1 says that the agent of the sleeping event has to be animate, but MP2 says that ideas are inanimate.

That's not bad, but if we simply tell our learner that what they have said makes no sense then they won't learn very much. They need to know *why* it makes no sense. Suppose, for instance, they had said

(3)   *Colourless green ideas sleep furiously.*

We would presumably want to tell them that this sentence contains more flaws than (2), since ideas can't be coloured, green things can't be colourless, and sleeping can't be done furiously.

If we want to make much progress with this kind of reasoning about what the learner has said, we need to have access to considerable amounts of background information, and we need to be able to deploy that information. Our background information is expressed as a set of 'meaning postulates' [4] – statements about the relationships between concepts. These meaning postulates are not sets of necessary and sufficient conditions, nor is there is any simple set of primitive concepts to which all others can be reduced. They are, rather, a set of mutual constraints on concepts. We cannot *define* most common terms, but we can explain how they connect to one another, and we can discuss what someone who says one thing must also be committed to (so if a learner says '*A bank lends money to a customer*' they should also be committed to '*A bank has money over which it has control*'; and if they say '*It is raining*' they should also agree that '*Drops of rain are falling from the sky*'. [5] talks of 'semantic traits' – general properties that you would expect an item to have if a particular word is used for describing it).

We currently have about 200 such meaning postulates, ranging from very general statements about sets, linear orders, and similar abstract notions (e.g. MP3) to quite precise observations about specific terms (MP4, which says that if you fire someone then you must have been their employer, and that the firing action terminates the employment relationship).

MP3: $\forall A \forall B : \{B > A\} \forall C : \{A > C\} B > C$
MP4: $\forall A : \{fire2(A)\}$
$\qquad \forall B : \{\theta(A, object, B)\}$
$\qquad\qquad \forall C : \{\theta(A, agent, C)\}$
$\qquad\qquad\qquad \exists D : \{employ(D)\}$
$\qquad\qquad\qquad\qquad \theta(D, object, B) \ \ \& \ \ \theta(D, agent, C)$
$\qquad\qquad\qquad\qquad \& \ termination(A, D)$

Obtaining meaning postulates of this kind is extremely labour-intensive, and even if you have the resources it is very difficult to come up with a consistent framework to work in ([8] report on the difficulties that can arise when you try to do this on a large scale). Nonetheless, you cannot expect to tell a learner much about the content of what they have said unless you have such a set of meaning postulates. If you don't know how the meanings of words are related, how can you possibly tell whether what the learner has said makes sense and conveys his intended meaning?

We will assume, therefore, that our 200 or so meaning postulates could be elaborated to provide reasonable coverage of some specific set of concepts in a restricted domain. If we have such a set, what should we do with it?

We clearly need an inference engine to extract the consequences of what the user has said. An inference engine, in the most general interpretation of the term, is a program which extracts implicit information from a body of explicitly stated facts. There are a range of such programs, from simple database query engines to theorem provers for complex logics. The simpler (= less expressive) the language in which the facts are stated, the easier it is to write an appropriate inference engine. Natural language is an exceptionally expressive means of representing facts and rules, and as a consequence any formal language which is used for representing the meanings of natural language utterances will also have to be extremely expressive. We choose to use a constructive version of [16]'s 'property theory'. [1]

When reasoning with MPs like MP2, we view not(P) as a shorthand for P ==> absurd (this is the standard treatment of negation in constructive logic). With this, we can show that it is absurd to utter (2) if you also believe MP1 and MP2. We usually use this to choose between alternate readings of ambiguous sentences, since if someone says something which has a number of readings then we can easily rule out any which are clearly impossible (see [18] for a similar approach to disambiguation).

---

[1] There are other languages of similar expressive power, e.g. the non-well-founded set theory underlying situation semantics [2,1]. All such languages share a common property: it is very difficult to provide inference engines for them.

Simply showing that what the user has written makes no sense is not, however, all that much use as a support for learners. We want to be able to show them *why* it makes no sense, if this is indeed the case; and we want to be able to show them the discrepancies between what they have said and what we expected them to say.

These are slightly different issues. Our learner may have said something which contradicts general commonsense rules – things like the claim that only physical objects can be coloured, or that mental objects cannot be animate. These rules can be hard-coded in our meaning postulates, as in MP2. They may, on the other hand, have said something which is not self-evidently wrong, but which is nonetheless at odds with what they were expected to say. This will be particularly likely when they are trying to use new vocabulary items – if, for instance, they have been asked to describe some entity that they are only just learning about.

In either case, we need to make the ramifications of what they have said explicit. We need to see what they have said, and what follows from it, and compare this with what we expected. This is a rather non-standard way of using an inference engine. Instead asking the inference engine whether some specific proposition X is provable, we want a picture of *everything* that someone who uttered that proposition might have had in mind. We want a 'model' which makes what the learner has said plus everything else we know true. If we have such a model, we can compare it with a target model, produced for instance on the basis of our own definition of the term in question, to see what discrepancies there are between the two: what is in the user's model but not in the target, what is in the target but not in the user's model?

We produce models by setting our theorem prover the task of proving that what the learner has said is inconsistent with everything else that is embodied in the meaning postulates and the prior discourse. We do not, in fact, want to succeed in this task. If what the learner has said is provably inconsistent then all we can do is report that it makes no sense. If the attempted proof of inconsistency fails, however, then we can use it to construct a model. The theorem prover we use is a version of [9]'s model generation theorem prover, extended to cope with the intensional operators of property theory [6]. Model generation proceeds, as its name suggests, by enumerating partial models. For standard theorem proving, the aim is to show that the negation of the goal has no models: the mechanism can easily be adapted, however, to show that the proposition under consideration does have a model, and to show what that model is like. As an example, Fig. 2 shows the model we obtain after processing (1), where the word *'fired'* has one possible reading where it denotes the act of terminating someone's contract and another related to the discharge of firearms.

(4)   *John fired his secretary.*

The model in Fig. 2 contains a number of entities, and specifies what they are like and how they are related, (including, for instance, the fact that the system was previously unaware that John had a secretary, and hence had to 'accommodate' this fact). If we show this model to the user, they can see some

$$
\begin{array}{ll}
fire(\#121) & ends\_after(\#3(1),\#3(1)) \\
\theta(\#121,object,\#122) & instantaneous(\#3(1)) \\
\theta(\#121,agent,\#92) & start(\#4(\#120),\#120) \\
fire1(\#121) & start(\#4(\#121),\#121) \\
secretary(\#122) & start(\#4(\#3(1)),\#3(1)) \\
of(\#122,\#92) & end(\#5(\#120),\#120) \\
unsexed(\#122) & end(\#5(\#121),\#121) \\
n(\#122) & end(\#5(\#3(1)),\#3(1)) \\
firearm(\#122) & \#5(\#3(1)) \ > \ \#5(\#120) \\
current\_discourse\_state(1) & aspect(simple,\#120,\#121) \\
speech\_time(\#3(1),1) & accommodated(secretary(\#122),of(\#122,\#92)) \\
ends\_before(\#3(1),\#120) &
\end{array}
$$

Fig. 2. Model for (1)

of the consequences of what they have said[2]; and if we compare it with another one, generated on the basis of our own understanding of what has happened, then we can show them some of the differences between what they should have said and what they did say.

3 Gross Errors

For gross errors, we can rely on general knowledge to show that what the learner has said is problematic. MP2', for instance, says that it would be strange to think of an idea as being animate.

MP2': $\forall A : \ \{idea(A) \ \& \ animate(A)\}weird(A)$ Ideas are *normally* inanimate

If we use MP1 and MP2' as the basis for reasoning about (2), we end up with the model in Fig. 3.

This is useful (though opaque: as noted above, we need to provide a better, probably graphical, presentation of the model to the learner if it is to actually be of use to them). It shows the user what the world would be like if what they had said were true, and it marks the idea #1533 as being odd. It doesn't, however, explain *why* it is odd. To get that we need to supplement our meaning postulate with a reason, replacing MP2' by

MP2": $\forall A : \ \{idea(A) \ \& \ animate(A)\}weird(A)$
$$because \ idea(A) \ \& \ animate(A)$$
Remembering why things are weird

(and while we're about it, we'll add

---

[2]   or at least they could if we provided them with a reasonable presentation of the model, for instance by using a graphical interface. Such an interface is currently under development

$$
\begin{array}{ll}
type(\#1531, interval) & ends\_before(\#1428(1), \#1531) \\
sharedloc(\#1531, agent) & start(\#1429(\#1531), \#1531) \\
memb(\#1531, \#1532) & at(\#1429(\#1531), sleep(\#1533)) \\
sharedagentloc(\#1531) & type(\#1429(\#1531), instant) \\
view(\#1531, \#1504(\#1531)) & \#1429(\#1428(1)) > \#1430(\#1531) \\
criterial(\#1531, sleep(\#1533)) & end(\#1430(\#1531), \#1531) \\
static(\#1531) & at(\#1430(\#1531), sleep(\#1533)) \\
sleep(\#1531) & completion(\#1430(\#1531), \#1531) \\
\theta(\#1531, agent, \#1533)\; type(\#1531, event) & type(\#1430(\#1531), instant) \\
animate(\#1533) & type(\#1504(\#1531), concrete) \\
idea(\#1533) & aspect(simple, \#1531, \#1532) \\
type(\#1533, abstract) & weird(\#1533)
\end{array}
$$

Fig. 3. Initial model for *'An idea slept.'*

MP5: $\forall A : \{green(A) \; \& \; \neg(X \text{ is concrete})\} weird(A)$

$$\text{because } green(A)$$
$$\& \; \neg(X \text{ is concrete})$$

Green things must be physical objects)

Then if we try to get an interpretation of

(5)   *A green idea slept.*

we get the model in Fig. 4.

$$
\begin{array}{ll}
type(\#1534, interval) & ends\_before(\#1428(1), \#1534) \\
sharedloc(\#1534, agent) & start(\#1429(\#1534), \#1534) \\
memb(\#1534, \#1535) & at(\#1429(\#1534), sleep(\#1536)) \\
sharedagentloc(\#1534) & type(\#1429(\#1534), instant) \\
view(\#1534, \#1504(\#1534)) & \#1429(\#1428(1)) > \#1430(\#1534) \\
criterial(\#1534, sleep(\#1536)) & end(\#1430(\#1534), \#1534) \\
static(\#1534) & at(\#1430(\#1534), sleep(\#1536)) \\
sleep(\#1534) & completion(\#1430(\#1534), \#1534) \\
\theta(\#1534, agent, \#1536) & type(\#1430(\#1534), instant) \\
type(\#1534, event) & type(\#1504(\#1534), concrete) \\
idea(\#1536) & aspect(simple, \#1534, \#1535) \\
animate(\#1536) & weird(\#1536) \text{ because } idea(\#1536) \\
green(\#1536, \lambda A(idea(A))) & \& \; animate(\#1536) \\
type(\#1536, abstract) & weird(\#1536) \text{ because } green(\#1536) \\
& \& \; \neg(concrete(\#1536))
\end{array}
$$

Fig. 4. Diagnostic model for *'A green idea slept.'*

Further elaboration along these lines will make it possible to show the user a picture corresponding to what they have said, and to pick out things that they have said that conflict with our general knowledge.

4   Fine Errors

We also, however, need to consider whether what the learner has said is what we wanted them to say. The use of meaning postulates that constrain the use of everyday terms will tell us about major misunderstandings, but when we want to know about our learner's comprehension of technical material we have to be a bit more delicate.

The approach we will take is to compare the output of what the learner says with the output of an expert. Suppose, for instance, that the learner has been asked to say what a bank does, and responds by typing

(6)   *A bank lends money to its owner.*

It is not clear what we should say. It all depends on what we think the learner should know by now. Suppose that we think that they should know that a bank borrows money from some of its customers and lends it to others. What we should probably do is to show them a picture of the borrowing and lending activities that a bank takes part in. Suppose we had, as the teacher, input the following sentences:

(7)   *A bank lends money to some customers. It borrows money from others.*

A reasonable response to the user's input might be to highlight the differences between what follows from (4) and (4). To do that, we have to compute those differences and then decide which ones matter. Fig. 5 shows the models that we obtain for these sentences.

These two models contain different entities, introduced by terms such as *'its owner'* and *'some customers'*. We need to find the mapping between entities which minimises the differences between the two models, which we can do as shown in Fig. 6 (where the lending events #114 and #104 have been matched, and the agent #119 of #114 from the first model has consequently been identified with the agent #102 of #104).

And then we need to work out what to do with this mapping – should we tell the learner about all the discrepancies between what he has said and what we wanted him to say, or just about the things that he has said that we were not expecting, or just the ones that he did not say that we were expecting?

5   Conclusions

The techniques outlined above make it possible to investigate the content of what a learner has written, as well as checking their grammar. We can look for gross errors, as in Section 3, by checking whether the user has said anything which leads to an apparent contradiction; and we can check whether we said

A bank lends money to its owner.	A bank lends money to some customers. It borrows money from others.
$lend(\#114)$ $\theta(\#114, to, \#119)$ $\theta(\#114, agent, \#115)$ $bank(\#115)$ $n(\#115)$ $owner(\#119)$ $of(\#119, \#115)$ $f(\#59(\#115))$ $card(\#59(\#115), 1)$ $accommodated(owner(\#119), of(\#119, \#115))$	$customer(\#102)$ $card(\#102, pl)$ $lend(\#104)$ $\theta(\#104, to, \#102)$ $\theta(\#104, agent, \#105)$ $bank(\#105)$ $n(\#105)$ $f(\#59(\#105))$ $card(\#59(\#105), 1)$ $\theta(\#111, agent, \#105)$ $borrow(\#111)$ $from(\#111, \#112)$ $customer(\#112)$ $card(\#112, pl)$

Fig. 5. Two models for comparison

In user model but not in target model: $of(\#102, \#105), owner(\#102),$ $accommodated(owner(\#102),$ $of(\#102, \#105))$	In target model but not in user model: $\theta(\#111, agent, \#105), type(\#111, event),$ $from(\#111, \#112),$ $borrow(\#111), customer(\#112),$ $customer(\#102)]$

Fig. 6. The differences between one model and another (edited)

what they expected, as in Section 4, by comparing the model that results from interpreting what they said with the model that results from what the teacher said.

The methods in Section 3 require us to specify in advance the kinds of error we anticipate. This does not have to be done on a case by case basis. We simply replace statements to the effect that something cannot be the case by ones that say that it should not be the case, so that we replaced a statement that claimed that ideas are not animate by one that said that there is something odd about animate ideas. Statements about what is possible are part of our everyday knowledge, and should be included in our knowledge base anyway. All we have done is to replace them by statements about what is likely, or reasonable, rather than about what is possible. The effects of such facts about the world will emerge when appropriate.

The methods in Section 4 depend on having a model answer, to be compared with the student answer. This is not unreasonable – if a student is trying to acquire a specific set of terms, the teacher is likely to want to provide quite precise tests, and is likely to know what is expected. The task of finding the best match between two sets of propositions, of the kind shown in Fig. 5, is NP-complete. We have some heuristics for pruning the search, but it does take some time to obtain Fig. 6 from Fig. 5.

These techniques, then, provide information about whether the learner has said something sensible, and about whether they have said what we expected. Exactly how such information would be used in an integrated CALL system, and how it should be presented to the user, is an open question. It seems plausible at first sight that some more graphical form of presentation might be suitable, but such presentations do not in fact seem to make it all that much easier to navigate large bodies of information. Both these issues are currently under investigation. The present paper simply reports on the tasks involved in extracting this information about the content of what the learner has said.

References

1. P Aczel and R Lunnon. Universes and parameters. In J Barwise, J M Gawron, G Plotkin, and S Tutiya, editors, *Situation Theory and its Applications II*. CSLI Publications, 1991. 202
2. J Barwise and J Perry. *Situations and Attitudes*. Bradford Books, Cambridge, MA, 1983. 202
3. C P Brocklebank. An experiment in developing a prototype intelligent teaching system from a parser written in Prolog. Technical Report MPhil thesis, UMIST, 1998. 200
4. R Carnap. Testability and meaning. *Philosophy of Science*, 3:401–467, 1936. 201
5. D A Cruse. *Lexical Semantics*. Cambridge University Press, Cambridge, 1986. 201
6. M Cryan and A M Ramsay. A normal form for Property Theory. In *Fourteenth Conference on Automated Deduction*, Townsville, Australia, 1997. 203
7. G Frege. On sense and reference. In D. Davidson and G. Harman, editors, *The Logic of Grammar*, pages 116–128. Dickenson, Encino, CA, 1892. Collection published 1975. 200
8. D B Lenat and R V Guha. *Building large scale knowledge based systems*. Addison Wesley, Raeding, Mass., 1990. 202
9. R Manthey and F Bry. Satchmo: a theorem prover in Prolog. In *Proc. 9th Inter. Conf. on Automated Deduction (CADE-9), LNAI 310*, pages 415–434, 1988. 203
10. A M Ramsay. Dynamic and underspecified semantics without dynamic and underspecified logic. In H Bunt and R Muskens, editors, *Computing Meaning, Volume I*, pages 57–72, Dordrecht, 1999. Kluwer Academic Publishers. 200
11. A M Ramsay. Weak lexical semantics and multiple views. In H C Bunt and E G C Thijsse, editors, *3rd International Workshop on Computational Semantics*, pages 205–218, Tilburg, 1999. 200
12. A M Ramsay. Parsing with discontinuous phrases. *Natural Language Engineering*, in press. 200
13. A M Ramsay and H Seville. Unscrambling English word order. In M Kay, editor, *Proceedings of the 18th International Conference on Computational Linguistics (COLING-2000)*, 2000. 200
14. M Schulze. Textana – text production in a hypertext environment. *CALL*, 10 (1):71–82, 1997. 200
15. R. H. Thomason, editor. *Formal Philosophy: Selected Papers of Richard Montague*. Yale University Press, New Haven, 1974. 200

16. R Turner. A theory of properties. *Journal of Symbolic Logic*, 52(2):455–472, 1987. 202

17. R Turner. *Constructive Foundations for Functional Languages*. McGraw Hill, London, 1991. 200

18. J Wedekind. On inference-based procedures for lexical disambiguation. In *Proceedings of the 16th International Conference on Computational Linguistics (COLING-96)*, pages 980–985, Copenhagen, 1996. 202

Integration of Resources and Components in a Knowledge-Based Web-Environment for Terminology Learning

Svetla Boytcheva[1], Ognian Kalaydjiev[2], Ani Nenkova[2], and Galia Angelova[2]

[1] Department of Information Technologies, FMI, Sofia University,
5 J. Bauchier Blvd., 1164 Sofia, Bulgaria,
svetla@fmi.uni-sofia.bg
[2] Bulgarian Academy of Sciences, Linguistic Modeling Lab,
25A Acad. G. Bonchev Str., 1113 Sofia, Bulgaria,
{ogi,ani,galja}@lml.bas.bg

Abstract. This paper presents the design and currently elaborated components in the knowledge-based learning environment called STyLE. It supports learning of English terminology in the domain of finances with a target user group of non-native English speakers. [1] The components elaborated so far allow for the discussion of the Web-based learning environment, the approach to the building of a learner model, and the adaptive strategies for instructional and content planning depending on the learning situation. The paper emphasises on the specific aspects of learning terminology in a second language and checking the correctness of learner's performance within the application of STyLE.

1 Introduction

Designing tools for learning terminology in a second language is a task deserving special attention. Learning specific vocabulary in a foreign language requires the development of natural language learning environments where learners should be allowed to explore the co-relations between their language capabilities and domain knowledge. Such environments have to provide domain knowledge to be used as a source for diagnosing student's conceptual knowledge and for instructional planning. All these entails that a foreign language terminology learning environment should adopt advanced language analysis methods that focus not only on the form but also on the meaning of the student's input.

Terms constitute a relatively stable and clearly determined kernel of lexical units in any Language for Special Purposes (LSP). It is well-known that many basic terms have stable meaning without ambiguity in the considered domain, with

---

[1] STyLE (Scientific Terminology Learning Environment) is under development in the Copernicus'98 JRP LARFLAST (LeARning Foreign LAnguage Scientific Terminology), November 1999 - October 2001. Partners: CBLU, Leeds, UK; UMIST, Manchester, UK; LIRMM, Montpellier, France; Academy of Sciences, Romania; Simferopol University, Ukraine; Sofia University and Virtech Ltd., Bulgaria.

S. A. Cerri and D. Dochev (Eds.): AIMSA 2000, LNAI 1904, pp. 210–220, 2000.

established typical collocations of usage in that LSP. This linguistic ôstabilityö implies the numerous attempts for acquisition of formal models either as sophisticated terminological lexicons and term banks (see e.g. [1]) or as ontologies of domain knowledge ([2]). Terms and relations between them fix (in a natural way) the choice and granularity of the formal concepts, so the knowledge-based system offers to its user lexical and conceptual units which correspond to the user's intuitive fragmentation of the domain. Projects like [2] show that it is possible to build CALL-oriented domain ontologies in complex domains (law); the "core" ontology encodes the educational content communicated to the learner in order to support understanding and obtaining insight in solving cases in administrative law. Thus, the task of terminology learning exploits a relatively structured (although extremely difficult to acquire) conceptual model. Once acquired, the ontology—in addition to the educational content—might be exploited in two essential ways: *(i)* the correctness of the student's answer can be evaluated within the Knowledge Base (KB) and *(ii)* the planning of moves in the system-user interaction can be guided by this information.

Learning terminology in a foreign language is a stream in second language learning. CALL-applications for other (foreign) LSP address many potential users, by default adults with some professional demands [3]. Hence, sophisticated adaptive systems with learner modelling and proper diagnostics are highly desirable achievements. Language learning presupposes that students type free Natural Language (NL) statements since it is unnatural to acquire a new language by only selecting menu options. CALL systems that provide such learning environments require Natural Language Processing (NLP) techniques to check the correctness of learner's utterances. Due to the very complicated nature of the task, however, it is difficult to find successful examples of intelligent CALL prototypes for second language in general and for terminology in particular. In the state-of-the-art collection of NLP in CALL papers [4], a general conclusion that "so few of these systems have passed the concept demonstration phase" has been made. As application of NLP techniques, the systems described in [4] contain mostly modules for checking students' competence in vocabulary, morphology, and correct syntax usage (parsers); the most sophisticated semantic analysis is embedded in the system BRIDGE/MILD [5], [6], [7] which matches the learner's utterance (a lexical conceptual structure) against the prestored expected lexical conceptual structures. This matching is implemented by an algorithm defining the intuitive notion of a *correct match*; the simple examples for semantic correctness in [7] show that testing semantics is far beyond the foreseen progress expected in near future. To conclude, it seems clear that every project for language learning (including ours) needs to be restricted by a balanced choice of what the system gives to and expects from the learner, what is the main focus, which AI techniques are available to provide reaction in real time etc.

This paper presents results obtained so far in a project where the main focus is improving the understanding/writing competence of the learner (adult, non-native English speaker) in the domain of finances. The implementation, the Web-based tool STyLE, follows some principles and ideas presented in [8].

Section 2 sketches the project as a whole. Section 3 presents in more detail the diagnostic module, the learner model, the design of drills' annotation, the mechanism for checking the correctness of the learner's utterances in free NL, and the pedagogical agent planning local reactions in certain learning situations. Section 4 contains an example. Section 5 concludes the paper by discussing further work.

2 LARFLAST Project Paradigm

The project aims at the development of a Web-based learning environment where the student accomplishes three basic tasks (reading teaching materials, performing test drills and discussing her own learner model with the system). The project is oriented to learners who need to improve their English language competence as well as their expertise in correct usage of English financial terms. Thus in general we attempt at finding some balance in the achievement of the goals: *(i)* to cover enough domain knowledge and relevant English terms; *(ii)* to test students' language and conceptual knowledge, and *(iii)* to find easy ways of student-system communication and discussion of learner misconceptions by diagrammatic representations, which are considered a powerful expressive language (the chosen technique is Open Learner Model (OLM), see e.g. [9]). This ambitiously formulated knowledge-based paradigm implies the necessity:

- to support an intuitive conceptual representation (providing simple graphical visualisation of domain knowledge and learner model facts to the learner),
- to integrate formal techniques for NL understanding, allowing for analysis of the users' answers to drills where the student is given the opportunity to type in free NL text (the system Parasite, developed at UMIST by Allan Ramsay—see e.g. [10]—is already integrated in STyLE).

Knowledge Base. The central knowledge resource in Larflast is a manually acquired Knowledge Base (KB) of conceptual graphs. Domain knowledge in finances is kept in four formats [11]: *(i)* graphical, used by the knowledge engineer during the knowledge-acquisition phase and by OLM for communication of diagrammatic representations to the learner; *(ii)* first order logic, applied when important domain facts are translated as meaning postulates to be used for proving the correctness of learner's utterances by Parasite; *(iii)* CGIF, used for generation of Web-pages explaining the educational content of domain knowledge in immersive context; and *(iv)* Prolog representation used for further KB processing by generalisation, specialisation, natural join, projection etc. Formats *(ii)*, *(iii)* and *(iv)* are automatically generated by the primary representation *(i)*. Specific problems and solutions relevant to acquisition of domain knowledge are considered in [12].

Current Implementation. Fig. 1 shows already elaborated components of STyLE, integrated under a Web-server, and internal software communications.

The system Parasite provides checking of the morphological, syntactic and semantic correctness of the learner's utterances in especially designed drills, while the prover STyLE-Parasite checks the correctness against the available domain knowledge. OLM is developed by the Leeds team [9]. Other STyLE components, which provide learning materials with interface oriented to the student/teacher and which are developed by the other project partners, are not shown in Fig. 1.

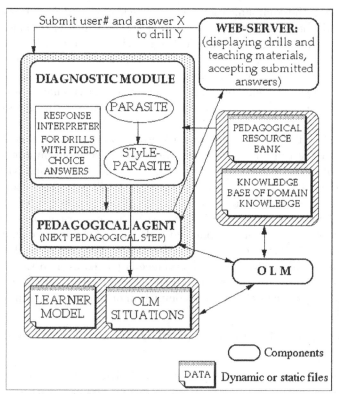

Fig. 1. Architecture of current STyLE components, discussed in this paper

3   Pedagogical Resources and Their Maintenance by STyLE Components

Having the main the responsibility for the integration of the STyLE components, in this paper we focus on the following issues:

- elaboration of the pedagogical resource bank: *(i)* drills and their annotation: predefined drill goals, correct answers, etc.; *(ii)* pedagogical knowledge: weights of domain concepts/relations with respect to teaching, records for possible learners' errors with close-semantic and close-language friends, etc.
- design and maintenance of the learner model;

- development of the prover STyLE-Parasite, which—in drills with free NL input from the learner—takes a logical form from the Parasite's output and proves its domain correctness within the context of the KB facts, by matching the given answer against the expected answer(s);
- design and development of a pedagogical module (pedagogical agent), which plans local reactions in certain learning situations.

At present, the communication between the learner and STyLE is maintained by two main modules—Diagnostic Module (DM), which is responsible for the Learner Model (LM), and Pedagogical Agent (PA). DM assures analysis of the learner's performance and fills in the LM; PA plans what is to be done next and refers, when necessary, to *(i)* OLM, where the learner discusses about her conceptual knowledge, and/or to *(ii)* the generator of dynamic web-pages, where the learner reads relevant texts with immersive context (this generator is not shown in Fig. 1).

Currently STyLE offers test unit, covering about 80 basic English terms in finances. Each test unit consists of an explanatory text about important concepts and a set of drills of both types—with fixed choice answers and with free-text answers (see [13]). After the learner completes a drill with fixed choice answers, the results are submitted to DM where the response interpreter analyses the answer and computes the learner's score. After the learner completes a drill with free text entry, the answer is submitted to Parasite for linguistic analysis and is passed to STyLE-Parasite for proving the domain correctness of the utterance. All information about learner's performance is passed over to the PA, it plans what is to be done next depending on the learning situation and calls OLM if OLM situations have arose after the completion of the previous drill(as in Fig.1).

3.1 Pedagogical Resource Bank of Drills and Pedagogical Knowledge

Following some established practice in web-design of drills (see e.g. the Half-baked educational software [14]), STyLE user is presented with seven types of drills: *Multiple choice, Gap fill, Crossword, Jumbled-sentence, Matching exercise, Ordering exercise* (usually with fixed-choice answers) and *Text-entry* (with free text answers).

An annotation (internal description) is associated with every drill. It

- shows the way the answer is to be checked—how to match the given answer to a preliminary stored set of correct responses. One drill entry can be associated with more than one possible correct answers with different score;
- contains information about how different drills and their items relate to domain concepts, encoded as KB items. A number—weight between 0 and 10—is associated with each concept and it shows the domain importance of this concept in respect to teaching;
- contains explicitly stated goals of drills, showing which facts and relations concerning given concept are being tested. More then one goal can be associated with one and the same drill if it tests different perspectives of relations.

Possible goals are: *test definition of concept X, test relations between X and Y, test similarity between given concepts, test difference between given concepts*. All goals have weighs, which is important for the planning of what is to be shown next.

Fig. 4 shows fragments of drill annotation. The predicate test_aspect/6 records in its 3rd-6th arguments correspondingly the correct answers (strings true/false in this case), the tested relation, the tested KB concept and the concept weight.

3.2 Diagnostic Module

DM checks the correctness of the learner's answer, generates feedback with learner's score to the learner, fills in the LM and organises data for further reflective dialogue with the learner in OLM. As shown in Fig. 1, there are two main modules analysing learner's performance in drills:

Response Interpreter for Drills with Fixed-Choice Answer. It matches the learner's and expected answers and marks all the cases where they coincide and where they differ by asserting the fact that the user knows, respectively does not know the concept and attributes set in the goal of the drill's item. The score is calculated according to the number of correctly answered items in the drill. While matching the answers, the interpreter analyses all the history in the LM facts and if a contradiction arises, it records an "OLM-situation".

STyLE-Parasite Interpreter for Drills with Free-Text Answer. To provide advanced NL understanding in cases when the learner is given the opportunity to type in freely, Larflast integrates the system Parasite.

Parasite either recognises the learner's utterance as a correct one or returns information about linguistic inconsistency of learner's utterances: morphological, syntax and semantic errors (in the later case no logical form can be computed). Answers with correct linguistic semantics are subjects to further considerations of their domain relevance, proved by STyLE-Parasite. At present STyLE-Parasite distinguishes the following cases of wrong conceptualisations: *(i)* over-generalisation, *(ii)* over-specification, *(iii)* usage of concept the definition instead of its name, *(iv)* predicates—i.e. domain facts—included in the answer expectation but missing in the student's answer, *(v)* parts of the student's response that lead to contradictions with the answer expectations. Relevant information about all cases is asserted in the LM.

Domain correctness is proved in several basic steps as follows:

- Preparation of expected answers: preliminary generation and storage as files of the syntax trees and logical forms of all correct expected answers. Human experts choose the "essential minimum" in each answer;

- Preparatory analysis in run-time: application of Parasite to each learner's answer for obtaining the syntax tree and logical form of the learner's utterance;

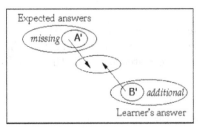

Fig. 2. Space of search in STyLE-Parasite

- Comparison of the inference sets by STyLE-Parasite: the two inference sets (the expected one, A, and the received one, B) are compared as sets of predicates (see Fig. 2). All predicates from $B \backslash A$ are recorded in a file *additional*. Then B is reduced to $B' = B \backslash additional$. All predicates from $A \backslash B'$ are stored as file *missing* and A is reduced to $A' = A \backslash missing$. STyLE-Parasite compares A' and B'. This procedure does not change the number of the occurrences of each of the remaining predicates (with different values as arguments) in each of the resulting sets. If the number of predicates in B' is greater than those in A', then after binding all of the predicates' variables in A', redundant predicates are removed from B' (i.e. those predicates from B' which have some unbound variables) and appended to the file *additional*. If the number of the predicates in A' is greater than the number of those in B', the binding of all variables is impossible and this leads to contradiction.
- Search within the space of possible bindings of the free variables in A' and B'. STyLE-Parasite applies heuristics for binding of the variables in A' and B' predicates: the predicates with more free variables and least binding candidates have priority for binding. Contradiction causes backtracking.

There might be several kinds of mistakes in the received answer, so learner's utterances are to be investigated with respect to all possible error types applying the above-described steps. STyLE-Parasite inference is complete, since it finds all existing ways to bind the variables. But it is not necessary to find all bindings, because the conclusion "correct learner utterances" is indicated after the first correct binding and the proving halts.

3.3   Learner Model

LM keeps track of learner's performance during all sessions. After analysing user's answer to each drill, DM asserts to the user's LM information about her knowledge: e.g.

```
know(UserName, Concept, [List Relations], DrillName, Number).
```

Currently four types of diagnostics about the learner's knowledge are asserted: *know*, *not_know*, *self_not_know* and *know_wrongly*. The Number argument shows for which time the concept is tested. This allows us to keep track of the stability of user's knowledge because we can detect cases of gaps and changing performance.

3.4   Link to Open Learner Model

Analysing learner's answers, DM discovers situations where either the learner or the system need further dialog, providing elaboration of learner's conceptual knowledge. This entails a link to the OLM component. The following situations are diagnosed at present:

- *contradiction*—there are LM-facts *know* and *not_know* about the same concept. This mean that the user's knowledge is not stable or that she does not know some of the more complicated attributes of the concept;
- *confuse close semantic concepts*—LM shows that the learner confuses concepts marked as very closely semantically related (for example money market and financial market). We remind that information about semantic closeness in teaching is explicitly encoded by the domain/teaching expert in the pedagogical resource, to point domain concepts and relations usually confused by novices in the domain;
- *confuse close language concepts*—LM shows that the learner confuses concepts that sound related, because of the words constituting the term. These types of confusion are typical for non-native speakers, who are mislead due to phonological or linguistic similarity [3].

While in the first situation a dialogue in OLM aims at solving the inconsistency in the learner's knowledge, in the next two a further interaction learner-OLM articulates aspects of learner's domain knowledge and assigns possible reasons for the learner's errors. OLM situations are shown at Fig. 6.

3.5   Pedagogical Agent

The main role of PA at present is to plan future learner's moves between lessons and drills. Since considerations concern presentational as well as educational issues, according to the terminology in [15] we would classify our planner as performing some aspects of instructional as well as content planning. There are two main movement strategies—local and global. The local strategy plans moves between drills, testing different characteristics of one and same concept. Its main goal is to create a complete view about learner's knowledge about this concept. This strategy chooses drills with increasing complexity when the learner answers correctly and gives again previously completed drills if the student has performed poorly. The global strategy plans movements between drills, testing different concepts, according to their place in the ontology. PA chooses next learner's movement depending on: *(i)* Predefined drill's goals, *(ii)* KB items, *(iii)* Concept weights and *(iv)* Learner's Score.

If the score is under 50% of the maximal one, PA shows link to readings. If after the learner's answer OLM situation arises, PA shows link to OLM for further discussions. PA always offers the default moves to correct answers and next drill or unit.

4   Example

Figure 3 shows a fixed-choice drill and the corresponding student's answers in the STyLE environment. The internal drill identifier is 'drill_2'

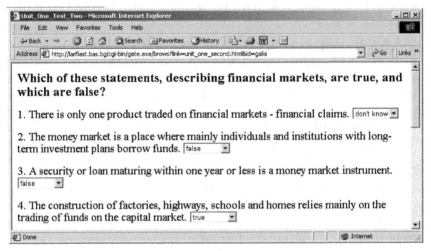

Fig. 3. Student performance in STyLE

Learner's answers are matched with the drill annotation shown in Figure 4. The learner "student007" answers "I don't know" to the first item of the drill, which is recorded as a fact in the LM (see Figure 5). This data is used by PA for selection of suitable study materials.

```
test_aspect(drill_2,item1,[false], [object], financial_market,10).
test_aspect(drill_2,item2,[false], [attribute], money_market, 5).
test_aspect(drill_2,item3,[true], [instrument], money_market, 7).
test_aspect(drill_2,item4,[true], [attribute], capital_market, 5).
```

Fig. 4. Fragments of internal drill annotation

Drill entries two and three are interesting because they test different type of information about the same concept, the learner knows one of them and does not know the other one. Those facts are put in the LM and OLM situation of the first type (contradiction) is registered. As a suggestion for next move PA generates to the learner's web-interface a web-page containing, together with the default hyperlinks, a hyperlink to OLM and another hyperlink to readings, relevant to financial market topics.

```
self_not_know(student007, financial_market, [object], drill_2, 1).
know(student007, money_market, [attribute], drill_2, 1).
not_know(student007, money_market, [instrument], drill_2, 2).
know(student007, capital_market, [attribute], drill_2, 1).
```

Fig. 5. Status of LM obtained after the work of Response interpreter

5   Conclusion and Further Work

This paper considers the present components developed within the ongoing
Larflast project. Current results allow to evaluate important aspects of the final
product: *(i)* we believe that it is possible to achieve a relatively simple but complete ontology of 100-200 terms in the financial domain; *(ii)* on-line integration
of Parasite can be done in a Web-environment by attentive design of appropriate
drills; *(iii)* planning helps essentially in guiding the learner within a rich environment where the learner is offered many choices, including free Web surfing,
and seems to be an obligatory control component.

The future work includes integration of the whole system STyLE and relevant
user study and evaluation.

References

1. Galinski C. and Budin G. (1995) Terminology. In Cole R. A. et al.,
   Eds., Survey of the State of the Art in Human Language Technologies,
   http://www.cse.ogi.edu/CSLU/HLTsurvey/HLTsurvey.html   211
2. Breuker, J., Muntjewerff A. and B. Bredeweg. (1999) Ontollogical Modelling for
   Designing Educational Software. In Proc. AI-ED Workshop on Ontologies for Intelligent Educational Systems, Le Mans, France, July 18–19, France.   211
3. Vitanova, I. Learning Foreign Language Terminology: the User Perspective.
   Larflast report 8.1, August 1999, delivered to the EC.   211, 217
4. Holland, V. M., Kaplan, J. and M. Sams (eds.) Intelligent Language Tutors: Theory
   Shaping Technology. Lawrence Erlbaum Associates, UK, 1995.   211
5. Sams, M. (1995) Advanced Technologies for Language Learning: the BRIDGE
   Project within the ARI Language Tutor Program. In [4], pp. 17–21.   211
6. Weinberg, A., Garman, J., Martin, J. and P. Merlo.(1995) A Principle-Based Parser
   for foreign Language Tutoring in German and Arabic. In [4], pp. 23–44.   211
7. Dorr, B., Hendler, J., Blanksteen, S., and B. Migdaloff. (1995) On Beyond Syntax:
   Use of Lexical Conceptual Structure for Intelligent Tutoring. In [4], pp. 289–310.
   211
8. Alpert, S. R., Singley, M. K. and Fairweather, P. G. (1999). Deploying intelligent
   tutors on the web: an architecture and an example, IJAIED, 10, 183–197.   211
9. Dimitrova, V., J. A. Self and P. Brna. The interactive maintains of Open Learner
   Models. In Lajoie S. P. and Vivet M. (eds.), Proc. 9th Conf. AIED, Frontiers of
   AI and Applications, Vol. 50, IOS Press, pp. 405–412, 1999.   212, 213
10. Ramsay, A. Meaning as Constraints on Information States, in Rupp, Rosner ,
    Johnson (eds.) Constraints, Language and Computation, 1994, Academic Press,
    London: 249–276. Parasite home page at: http://ubatuba.ccl.umist.ac.uk   212

11. Dobrev, P., and Kr. Toutanova. CGWorld - A Web-Based Workbench for Conceptual Graphs Management and Applications. To appear in ICCS-2000, Darmstaht, Germany, August 2000. 212
12. Angelova, G., A. Nenkova, Sv. Boycheva, and T. Nikolov. CGs as a Knowledge Representation Core in a Complex Language Learning Environment. To appear in ICCS-2000, Darmstaht, Germany, August 2000. 212
13. Larflast project site, http://www.larflast.bas.bg/site 214
14. Hot Potatoes at: http://www.halfbakedsoftware.com/licence/ 214
15. Vassileva, J. and B. Wasson. (1996) Instructional Planning Approaches: from Tutoring towards Free Learning. In Proc. EuroAIED'96, Lisbon, Portugal, 1996, pp. 1-8. 217

Maintaining a Jointly Constructed Student Model

Vania Dimitrova, John Self, and Paul Brna

Computer Based Learning Unit, Leeds University, Leeds LS2 9NA, UK
{V.Dimitrova,J.A.Self,P.Brna}@cbl.leeds.ac.uk

Abstract. Allowing the student to have some control over the diagnosis inspecting and changing the model the system has made of him is a feasible approach in student modelling which tracks the dynamics of student behaviour and provides for reflective learning. We present an approach for maintaining the student model in interactive diagnosis where a computer and a student discuss about the student's knowledge. A belief modal operator is adapted to model the knowledge of the learner and to help in maintaining the interaction between the computer system and the learner. A mechanism for finding agreements and conflicts between system and learner's views is described.

1   Introduction

Modelling a learner's cognitive capacity is essential for an intelligent tutoring system to provide individualised instruction and adaptive interaction [1]. Allowing the student to have some control over the diagnosis and to inspect the model the system has made of him is a feasible approach in student modelling [4] which tracks the dynamics of student behaviour [2] and provides for reflective learning [3]. A similar method is applicable to user modelling [5] and building adaptive systems [6]. A constructive interaction guided by the system where both the computer and the learner reflect on the learner's beliefs is the means for involving the user in diagnosis. Designing such an interactive process needs a dialogue management framework [7] and a formal engine to maintain a student model which is jointly constructed by the system and the learner and accumulates their views about the learner's knowledge.

There are few attempts to formalise the process of maintaining the user/learner model when open for inspection and change directly by the user/learner, see [8,9]. In these projects, the notion of the interaction is very constrained and the formalisations they offer do not consider modelling the process of *interactive reflection* which results in a jointly constructed student model. Such a task is addressed in this paper. We present an approach to formalising the process of maintaining a jointly constructed learner model in interactive diagnosis. The kernel of this approach is a mechanism for finding agreed beliefs and conflicts between the computer system and the learner when discussing the learner's knowledge. We have employed an epistemic operator *belief* in a dialogue game interaction model and have adapted formal specifications from [10] into an interactive diagnostic context.

The conception of a jointly constructed student model can be related to the notion of common and distributed knowledge in multi-agent systems where sound and

S. A. Cerri and D. Dochev (Eds.): AIMSA 2000, LNAI 1904, pp. 221-231, 2000.

complete axiomatisations have been provided [11]. However, there is a debatable rationale for adopting strong deductive approaches for inherent problems with computational complexity and natural plausibility in modelling human reasoning [12]. A basic assumption in interactive diagnosis is that the belief set the computer system has about the learner is not complete. Moreover, while the learner is expected to reflect on his knowledge, he may well apply unsound and incomplete reasoning, which the system will seek to correct. Therefore, to model interactive diagnostic situations we have been able to adopt some simplifications.

Several belief models that employ nonmonotonic and limited reasoning have been developed to model agents' beliefs in dialogue simulations (c.f. [12], [13], [14]). Mutual beliefs of the system and the user which these systems consider, particularly mutual beliefs about the user's domain beliefs, are similar to the notion of agreed beliefs in interactive diagnostic dialogue. The agreements play a crucial role in interactive diagnosis presenting the jointly constructed student model. Hence, they have been elaborated in our formalisation, so that not only explicit agreements but also implicit and assumed ones have been modelled. In addition, we define conflicts between the system's and the learner's views about the learner's knowledge which are sources for a negotiative dialogue in interactive diagnosis. This notion of conflicts is different from conflicts between the system's and the user's beliefs which user modelling frameworks use to define the user's erroneous and incomplete knowledge [14]. In our model, the correctness of the learner's beliefs is assessed by comparing the agreements about the student's beliefs with the system's domain knowledge.

Next in the paper, there is a discussion about the process of maintaining the student model in interactive diagnosis and the need for a mechanism for finding agreements and conflicts between the computer and the learner. Such a mechanism will be presented in section 3 and an example of its application will be elaborated in section 4. Finally, further applications of our approach will be discussed.

2   Maintaining the Student Model in Interactive Diagnosis

We use the term *interactive diagnosis* to emphasise the view of diagnosis as an *interactive process* involving two agents, a diagnoser and diagnosee, who discuss and construct together the student model. Open learner modelling environments where the learner is involved in a discussion reflecting upon the model the computer has built of him [4] present interactive diagnostic situations. Other cases are peer diagnosis systems [15] where users reflect on the models they have built about their peers.

2.1   An Example

The example below, which will be further elaborated in section 4, is from a session with STyLE-OLM[1] – an open learner modelling component in a terminology learning

---

[1] STYLE-OLM is an open learner modelling component in the STYLE environment developed within the LARFLAST project: http://www.larflast.bas.bg/. The example here is from a version of STyLE-OLM in a Computer Science domain.

environment [16]. The interaction in STYLE-OLM is grounded on a dialogue maintenance framework [7], the communication language is based on conceptual graphs [17] (for simplicity here we consider propositions stated in a natural language), the domain knowledge base is encoded with conceptual graphs [18].

Initially, the learner model includes learner's beliefs „VISUAL BASIC is an OBJECT-ORIENTED LANGUAGE", „VISUAL C++ is an OBJECT-ORIENTED LANGUAGE", and „OBJECT-ORIENTED LANGUAGE contains OBJECTS". The dialogue strategy of C is to discover a possible misconception behind the learner's erroneous belief that VISUAL BASIC is an OBJECT-ORIENTED LANGUAGE.

(1) C. You think that VISUAL BASIC is an OBJECT-ORIENTED LANGUAGE.
(2) S. I Agree.
(3) C. You think that VISUAL BASIC is a VISUAL LANGUAGE.
(4) S. I Agree.
(5) C. You think VISUAL LANGUAGES are OBJECT-ORIENTED LANGUAGES.
(6) S. I disagree.
(7) C. Do you think that VISUAL C++ is an OBJECT-ORIENTED LANGUAGE.
(8) S. Yes.
(9) C. You think that VISUAL BASIC contains OBJECTS.
(10) S. I agree.
(11) C. Do you think that VISUAL BASIC has a characteristic INHERITANCE?
(12) S. I doubt this.
(13) C. Do you know a relation between OBJECT-ORIENTED LANGUAGE and INHERITANCE?
(14) S. I don't know.
(15) C. You think that VISUAL BASIC is an OBJECT-ORIENTED LANGUAGE BECAUSE it has OBJECTS but OBJECT-ORIENTED LANGUAGES also have a characteristic INHERITANCE which VISUAL BASIC does not have.

The aim of the learner model maintenance is to find out what is to be included in the learner model after the interaction.

2.2   Maintaining the Student Model in Interactive Diagnosis - Main Components

The learner model maintenance process has three main parts (fig.1):
☐ Ascribing participants beliefs from speech acts;
☐ Inferring what has been agreed through the interaction;
☐ Ascribing a level of correctness to learner's beliefs and updating the learner model.

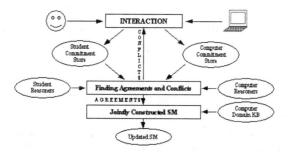

Fig. 1. Maintaining the student model in interactive diagnosis

We have shown elsewhere that a dialogue management framework based on dialogue games [19] can be adapted for maintaining communication in interactive diagnosis [7]. Following a dialogue game model, commitment rules define the effects of moves upon the dialogue participants' commitment stores. These rules ascribe changes in participants' belief stores after a speech act is uttered. The ascribed beliefs are not added directly to the student model but accumulated in temporarily built commitment stores to keep different viewpoints, which is essential in providing the notion of a collaborative dialogue [3]. To maintain the dynamics of the belief stores, a belief revision approach similar to the one described in [8] is employed.

Being responsible for maintaining the student model which is to be used later by other components of the learning environment, an interactive diagnostic module has to have a mechanism for finding what has been *agreed* through the interaction which is the kernel of a *jointly constructed student model*. After an interaction episode finishes, i.e. the participants agree to change the focus of the discussion, an inference mechanism is to be adopted to refine the beliefs of participants and to find out what these agents have agreed about the learner's beliefs. The agreed beliefs are to be attributed a level of correctness by comparison with the expert's knowledge and then used as a source for updating the learner model. The inference mechanism also has to detect which are the *conflict points* in the participants' belief stores. In the following interactions, these points are to be used as the negotia in a negotiative dialogue game. A possible formalisation of finding agreements and conflicts and maintaining a jointly constructed learner model is described in the rest of the paper.

3   Finding Agreements and Conflicts about the Student's Beliefs

3.1   Assumptions

Our starting point of view is that learner's domain knowledge is modelled in terms of *beliefs* that correspond to the conceptual level of the student model. We consider a structure of the learner model $\mathcal{L}$: $\mathcal{L}=\mathcal{B}\cup\mathcal{R}^{mu}\cup\mathcal{R}^{mc}$ where $\mathcal{B}$ is a set of learner's beliefs and consists of correct, erroneous and incomplete beliefs, $\mathcal{R}^{mu}$ is a set of misunderstanding rules that represent patterns of potential conversational failures and $\mathcal{R}^{mc}$ is a set of misconception rules that define possible reasons for learner's erroneous and incomplete beliefs. We consider $\mathcal{R}^{mu}$ and $\mathcal{R}^{mc}$ useful for the diagnoser to plan the interaction and $\mathcal{B}$ *open* for a discussion. Hereafter, we use two agents a *student s* and a *computer c*.

We will use an epistemic operator $B_s(\varphi)$ to denote that the student believes a fact represented by the propositional formula φ. We also use the negation $\neg B_s(\varphi)$ to denote that the student does not believe φ (he may not believe $\neg\varphi$ which is $B_s(\neg\varphi)$).

For the computer, expressions $B_c(\varphi)$ and $\neg B_c(\varphi)$ present its domain expertise and are derived from the system knowledge base. We also consider nested beliefs to represent the beliefs that the computer has about the student. Thus $B_c(B_s(\varphi))$ denotes that c believes that s believes φ. Its negations are: $B_c(B_s(\neg\varphi))$ c believes that s believes

$\neg\varphi$, $B_c(\neg B_s(\varphi))$ c believes it is not the case that s believes φ, $\neg B_c(B_s(\varphi))$ c does not believe that s believes φ. Such expressions build the student model in the traditional diagnosis where the computer has the overall control over the diagnostic process. The computer *opens* these beliefs for a discussion with the learner in interactive diagnosis. Such expressions appear in the computer commitment store throughout the dialogue.

Note that learner's beliefs about system's beliefs have been considered redundant. We assume that in the conversation the learner reflects on his beliefs or challenges those from the system's commitment store, e.g. when the learner agrees with $B_c(B_s(\varphi))$, the corresponding commitment rule will add $B_s(\varphi)$ to the learner belief store and when he challenges $B_c(B_s(\varphi))$, $\neg B_s(\varphi)$ will be ascribed.

Before the interaction, we will consider a base set of computer beliefs I_c, a base set of computer beliefs about student beliefs I_{cs}, and a base set of student beliefs I_s. The beliefs in I_c are encoded by a domain expert and those in I_{cs} and I_s are either stated explicitly or assigned by some initial domain specific inference.

3.2   Reasoning

We consider our agents to have a (not necessarily complete) set of *inference rules* that we will call *reasoners*. We will denote the student reasoners over his beliefs by $\mathcal{R}_s$ and the computer reasoners over its beliefs by $\mathcal{R}_c$. The computer will also have reasoners about the beliefs of the student - $\mathcal{R}_{cs}$.

The rule $\phi_1,...,\phi_n\vdash\phi$ will allow us to infer new beliefs from agents' belief sets. For example, $B_c(\varphi_1),..., B_c(\varphi_n)\vdash_{Rc} B_c(\varphi)$ will allow us to assume that for the computer $B_c(\varphi)$ is *true* if $B_c(\varphi_1),..., B_c(\varphi_n)$ are *true*. The computer might do some inference over its beliefs about the student. For instance, the rule

$$B_c(B_s(\varphi\Rightarrow\psi)), B_c(B_s(\psi)) \vdash_{Rcs} B_c(B_s(\varphi))$$

defines some default reasoning assumptions made by the computer about the learner's reasoning. $\mathcal{R}_s$ is the least determined set presenting learner's reasoning over his beliefs. An example of a possible rule from $\mathcal{R}_s$ is given below.

$$B_s(\varphi\Rightarrow\psi), B_s(\neg\psi) \vdash_{Rs} \neg B_s(\varphi).$$

We will infer new agents' beliefs by applying their reasoners *only once*. As discussed in [10], there is a certain rationale in adopting limitations. Humans tend not to draw all possible conclusions from their beliefs. Also, it might be considered peculiar to assume that an agent believes a proposition which needs a fairly long inference process upon the agent's beliefs in order to be ascribed as true.

We can now define agent's *belief sets* that will be the essence for deriving agents' agreements and conflicts.

$$\mathcal{B}_c=\{\phi|\ \phi\in I_c \text{ or } \exists\ \phi_1,...,\phi_n: (\phi_1,...,\phi_n\vdash_{Rc}\phi)\in\mathcal{R}_c, \phi_i\in I_c, i=1...n\}$$

$$\mathcal{B}_s=\{\phi|\ \phi\in I_s \text{ or } \exists\ \phi_1,...,\phi_n: (\phi_1,...,\phi_n\vdash_{Rs}\phi)\in\mathcal{R}_s, \phi_i\in I_s, i=1...n\}$$

$$\mathcal{B}_{cs}=\{\phi|\ \phi\in I_{cs} \text{ or } \exists\ \phi_1,...,\phi_n: (\phi_1,...,\phi_n\vdash_{Rcs}\phi)\in\mathcal{R}_{cs}, \phi_i\in I_{cs}, i=1...n\}$$

3.3   Agreements

A distinguishing characteristic of an interactive diagnostic dialogue is that agents are talking about the beliefs of one of them. This entails a proper adjustment of the mechanism for searching for what has been agreed throughout the interaction. Following a commonsense view that agents agree with something if they have the same opinion about it, we identify the *agreements* in interactive diagnosis as being those *beliefs of the student* that the computer assumes the student believes and the student himself accepts.

We will consider three groups of agreements. *Explicit agreements* $A_{explicit}$ can be found by simply matching the beliefs in the initial belief stores.

$$A_{explicit} = \{\phi \mid \phi \in I_s \ \& \ B_c(\phi) \in I_{cs}\}$$

In most of the cases, there are few explicit agreements. To define *implicit agreements* $A_{implicit}$ we will consider agents' reasoners and will match the beliefs in $\mathcal{B}_s$ and $\mathcal{B}_{cs}$.

$$A_{implicit} = \{\phi \mid \phi \in \mathcal{B}_s \ \& \ B_c(\phi) \in \mathcal{B}_{cs}\}$$

People tend to agree when they do not contradict one another. Following an autoepistemic notion, we define *assumed agreements*:

$$A_{assumed} = \{\phi \mid ((\phi \in \mathcal{B}_s) \ \& \ (B_c(\phi) \ does \ not \ contradict \ \mathcal{B}_{cs}))$$
$$or \ ((B_c(\phi) \in \mathcal{B}_{cs}) \ \& \ (\phi \ does \ not \ contradict \ \mathcal{B}_s))\}.$$

We will consider that a belief formula ϕ *contradicts* a set of belief formulas Φ if the *negation* of ϕ belongs to Φ.

3.4   Conflicts

Conflicts in interactive diagnosis are sources for negotiation and in most of the cases help in articulating learner's domain beliefs. In accordance to the definitions about agreements, we will define conflicts in computer and student's views about student's beliefs.

Explicit conflicts $C_{explicit}$ will be obtained by matching the beliefs in agents' initial belief sets.

$$C_{explicit} = \{\phi \mid ((\phi \in I_s) \& (B_c(\phi) \ contradicts \ I_{cs})) \ or$$
$$((B_c(\phi) \in I_{cs}) \ \& \ (\phi \ contradicts \ I_s))\}$$

Likewise, we will define *implicit conflicts* $C_{implicit}$ by considering all beliefs derived after agents' reasoners are applied. An ensuing definition of *assumed conflicts* would appear redundant because of its similarity with $C_{implicit}$.

$$C_{implicit} = \{\phi \mid ((\phi \in \mathcal{B}_s) \ \& \ (B_c(\phi) \ contradicts \ \mathcal{B}_{cs}))$$
$$or \ ((B_c(\phi) \in \mathcal{B}_{cs})) \ \& \ (\phi \ contradicts \ \mathcal{B}_s))\}$$

3.5   Jointly Constructed Student Model

The jointly constructed student model $\mathcal{B}$ (we consider only the belief part open for a discussion) consists of all agreements between the computer and the student.

$$\mathcal{B} = A_{\text{explicit}} \cup A_{\text{implicit}} \cup A_{\text{assumed}}$$

3.6   Assigning Degree of Correctness to the Learner's Beliefs

In the previous sections we described how $\mathcal{B}$ - a jointly constructed learner model - will be obtained. The learner's beliefs are assigned categories of correctness. This can be done by comparing the beliefs in $\mathcal{B}$ with the system domain beliefs $\mathcal{B}_c$. We consider the following categories:

φ is a *correct belief iff* $(B_s(\varphi) \in \mathcal{B})$ & $(\varphi \in \mathcal{B}_c)$.

φ is an *erroneous belief iff* $(B_s(\varphi) \in \mathcal{B})$ & $((\neg\varphi \in \mathcal{B}_c)$ or $(\varphi \notin \mathcal{B}_c))$.

φ is an *incomplete belief iff* $(\varphi \in \mathcal{B}_c)$ &
$((B_s(\neg\varphi) \in \mathcal{B})$ or $(\neg B_s(\varphi) \in \mathcal{B})$ or $(B_s(\varphi) \notin \mathcal{B}))$

In this section, adopting an epistemic operator belief and employing agents that do not have a deductive reasoning, we have been able to provide a mechanism for finding agreements and conflicts between a computer and a student when discuss about the student's knowledge. This allows maintaining a jointly constructed learner model. The next section illustrates the use of the mechanism in an interactive diagnostic situation.

4   The Example Analysed

We will now examine the example in section 2 by applying the mechanism described in section 3. The example has been elaborated extensively to show more aspects of the approach. To make the analysis simpler we will denote:

p_1 = VISUAL BASIC is an OBJECT-ORIENTED LANGUAGE.
p_2 = VISUAL C++ is an OBJECT-ORIENTED LANGUAGE.
p_3 = OBJECT-ORIENTED LANGUAGE contains OBJECTS.
p_4 = VISUAL LANGUAGES are OBJECT-ORIENTED LANGUAGES.
p_5 = VISUAL BASIC is a VISUAL LANGUAGE.
p_6 = VISUAL BASIC contains OBJECTS.
p_7 = OBJECT-ORIENTED LANGUAGE has a characteristic INHERITANCE.
p_8 = VISUAL BASIC has a characteristic INHERITANCE.

In STYLE-OLM, computer reasoners $\mathcal{R}_c$ are based on conceptual graphs rules of inference [17]. Some rules from $\mathcal{R}_{cs}$ used in the example are

$$B_c(B_s(\varphi) \Rightarrow B_s(\psi)), B_c(B_s(\varphi)) \vdash_{Rcs1} B_c(B_s(\psi));$$
$$B_c(B_s(\varphi) \Rightarrow B_s(\psi)), B_c(B_s(\psi)) \vdash_{Rcs2} B_c(B_s(\varphi)).$$

I_c are encoded by a domain expert in a conceptual graphs knowledge base. In the example, before the dialogue

$$I_s=\{B_s(p_1),\, B_s(p_2),\, B_s(p_3)\}$$
$$I_{cs}=\{B_c(B_s(p_1)),\, B_c(B_s(p_2)),\, B_c(B_s(p_3))\}.$$

Consulting its knowledge base, STYLE-OLM will discover that $B_c(B_s(p_1))$ is an erroneous belief – an individual has been wrongly assigned to a class. Then the system will search for possible learner's misconceptions to explain this misclassification. There are two potential candidates.

Misclassification_1. The individual has common features with an individual that belongs to the class, i.e. VISUAL BASIC is an OBJECT-ORIENTED LANGUAGE because it is a VISUAL LANGUAGE like VISUAL C++, which is an OBJECT-ORIENTED LANGUAGE.

Here, the system will start with p_2 and by *generalising* it to p_4 will *assume* that $B_c(B_s(p_2)\Rightarrow B_s(p_4))$. Then, it will make a hypothesis that $B_c(B_s(p_4))$ by applying the rule R_{cs1}.

Applying *restriction* over p_4, the system will infer p_5 and will *assume* that $B_c(B_s(p_4)\&B_s(p_5)\Rightarrow B_s(p_1))$. Then, it will make a hypothesis that $B_c(B_s(p_5))$ by applying the default rule R_{cs2}.

Misclassification_2. The individual has features that are part of the class features, i.e. VISUAL BASIC is an OBJECT-ORIENTED LANGUAGE because it contains OBJECTS.

Applying *restriction* over p_3, the system will infer p_6 and will *assume* that $B_c(B_s(p_3)\&B_s(p_6)\Rightarrow B_s(p_1))$. Then, it will make a hypothesis that $B_c(B_s(p_6))$ by applying the default rule R_{cs2}.

Thus, before the interaction the belief sets will be:

$$\mathcal{B}_s=\{B_s(p_1),\, B_s(p_2),\, B_s(p_3)\}$$
$$\mathcal{B}_{cs}=\{B_c(B_s(p_1)),\, B_c(B_s(p_2)),\, B_c(B_s(p_3)),\, B_c(B_s(p_4)),\, B_c(B_s(p_5)),\, B_c(B_s(p_6))\}$$

During the interaction more beliefs will be added as follows.

(4) will add $B_s(p_5)\in I_s$.

(6) will bring $\neg B_s(p_4)\in I_s$ and a challenge to $B_c(B_s(p_2))\in\mathcal{B}_{cs}$ that will imply the explicit question in (7).

(8) will show that $B_c(B_s(p_2))$ will remain in $\mathcal{B}_{cs}$ but $B_c(B_s(p_4))$ will be deleted. *Misclassification_1* will be withdrawn.

(10) will bring $B_s(p_6)\in I_s$.

(11) assuming $\neg B_c(B_s(p_8))\in I_c$, the computer asks about this explicitly.

(12) will show that $\neg B_s(p_8)\in I_s$.

(13) following the answer in (12), the computer will assume $B_c(\neg B_s(p_7))\in I_c$ and will aim at checking it.

(14) will confirm $\neg B_s(p_7)\in I_s$ and *misclassification_2*.

(15) will inform about the discovered misclassification.

Therefore, after the interaction

$$\mathcal{B}_s= I_s = \{B_s(p_1),\, B_s(p_2),\, B_s(p_3),\, \neg B_s(p_4),\, B_s(p_5),\, B_s(p_6),\, \neg B_s(p_7),\, \neg B_s(p_8)\}$$
$$I_{cs}=\{B_c(B_s(p_1)),\, B_c(B_s(p_2)),\, B_c(B_s(p_3)),\, B_c(\neg B_s(p_7)),\, \neg B_c(B_s(p_8))\}$$
$$\mathcal{B}_{cs}=\{B_c(B_s(p_1)),\, B_c(B_s(p_2)),\, B_c(B_s(p_3)),\, B_c(B_s(p_5)),\, B_c(B_s(p_6)),\, B_c(\neg B_s(p_7)),\, \neg B_c(B_s(p_8))\}$$

$$A_{\text{explicit}} = \{B_s(p_1)\ B_s(p_2)\ B_s(p_3),\ \neg B_s(p_7)\}$$
$$A_{\text{implicit}} = \{B_s(p_1)\ B_s(p_2)\ B_s(p_3),\ B_s(p_5),\ B_s(p_6),\ \neg B_s(p_7)\}$$
$$A_{\text{assumed}} = \{\neg B_s(p_4),\ \neg B_s(p_8)\}$$
$$\mathcal{B} = \{B_s(p_1)\ B_s(p_2)\ B_s(p_3),\ B_s(p_5),\ B_s(p_6),\ \neg B_s(p_7),\ \neg B_s(p_4),\ \neg B_s(p_8)\}$$

In addition, during the interaction a misclassification of type 2 was discovered as an explanation of $B_s(p_1)$.

In this example, *explicit conflicts* have not been discovered. An *implicit conflict* about $B_s(p_4)$ was discovered and consequently overcome by deleting $B_c(B_s(p_4))$ from $\mathcal{B}_{cs}$.

Before being added to the learner model, the beliefs from $\mathcal{B}$ will be assigned a level of correctness comparing them with the knowledge in the system domain model. For example, p_1 will be considered as an *erroneous* belief, p_7 will be assigned as *incomplete* and p_6 as a *correct* belief.

The example has illustrated how the mechanism described in section 3 maintains a jointly constructed learner model in an interactive diagnostic situation. Before the interaction, the learner model includes very constrained beliefs about the learner. Throughout the interaction, using its reasoners, the computer system made some hypotheses about learner's beliefs and asked him for verification. At the end of the dialogue, finding system and student's agreements, a more elaborated learner model has been obtained and a learner's misconception has been discovered.

5   Conclusion

In this paper, we have presented an approach for maintaining a jointly constructed student model in interactive diagnosis. We have adapted a belief modal operator to model the knowledge of the learner and to maintain the interaction between the computer system and the learner. The nature of interactive diagnosis where agents' reasoning is not complete and not necessarily sound has allowed us to explore several simplifications and to avoid problems due to computational complexity.

The applicability of the mechanism for maintaining a jointly constructed student model has been demonstrated in STYLE-OLM an interactive diagnosis component in a terminology learning environment.

A substantial insight from formalisation in intelligent systems is that the models developed for one application can easily be employed in another context. The mechanism for maintaining a jointly constructed learner model described above has been adjusted to natural situations of human reasoning. This brings practical advantages of the approach making feasible its extension in peer diagnosis situations where two learners discuss the knowledge of one of them. In this context, the mechanism will provide a computer system with an engine to build models of the peers as well as to mediate the interaction between them. Another potential dimension for future investigations is a possible extension of the mechanism to modelling agreements and conflicts in collaborative dialogues.

References

1. J.A. Self, The defining characteristics of intelligent tutoring systems research: ITSs care, precisely, International Journal of Artificial Intelligence in Education, **10**, 350-364, (1999).
2. J.A. Self, Bypassing the intractable problem of student modelling, in C. Frasson & G. Gauthier eds., Intelligent Tutoring Systems: At the Crossroad of Artificial Intelligence and Education, Ablex, NJ, 1990.
3. S. Bull, Collaborative Student Modelling in Foreign Language Learning, PhD Thesis, University of Edinburgh, 1997.
4. R. Morales, H. Pain, S. Bull & J. Kay, Proceedings of the Workshop on Open, Interactive, and Other Overt Approaches to Learner Modelling, Le Mans, France, July 1999.
5. A. Kobsa, User modelling in dialogue systems: potentials and hazards, AI & Society, **1**, 214-240, (1990).
6. P. Brusilovsky, Methods and Techniques of Adaptive Hypermedia. User Modeling and User-Adapted Interaction, **6** (2/3), 87-129, (1996).
7. V. Dimitrova, J.A. Self & P. Brna, The interactive maintenance of open learner models, in Lajoie S.P. and Vivet M., eds., Proceedings of the 9th conference of AI in Education, Frontiers in AI and Applications, vol. 50, IOS Press, pp. 405-412, 1999.
8. A. Paiva and J.A. Self, TAGUS - a user and learner modelling workbench, User Modeling and User-Adapted Interaction, **4**, 197-226, (1995).
9. J. Kay, The UM toolkit for cooperative user modelling, User Modeling and User-Adapted Interaction, **4**, 149-196, (1995).
10. J.A. Self, Computational Mathetics, http://www.cbl.leeds.ac.uk/~jas/cm.html.
11. R. Fagin, J.Y. Halpern, Y. Moses & M.Y. Vardi, Reasoning about Knowledge, The MIT Press, Cambridge, 1995.
12. J. Taylor, J. Carletta, C. Mellish, Requirements for belief models in cooperative dialogue, User Modelling and User-Adapted Interaction, **6**, 23-68, (1996).
13. A. Ballim and Y. Wilks, Artificial Believers: The Ascription of Belief, Erlbaum, Hillsdale, NJ, 1991.
14. A. Kobsa, and W. Pohl, , The user modeling shell system BGP-MS. User Modeling and User-Adapted Interaction 4(2), 59–106, (1995).
15. S. Bull and P. Brna, Enhancing peer interaction in the Solar system, in Brna P., Baker M. and Stenning K. eds., Roles of communicative interaction in learning to model in Mathematics and Science, Proceedings of the C-LEMMAS conference, April 1999.
16. V.Dimitrova, J.A. Self & P. Brna, STyLE-OLM - an interactive diagnosis tool in a terminology learning environment, in the Proceedings of the Workshop on Open, Interactive, and Other Overt Approaches to Learner Modelling, Le Mans, France, July 1999.
17. J. Sowa, Conceptual graphs: draft proposed American national standard, in Proceedings of ICCS-99 - Conceptual Structures: Standards and Practices, Lecture Notes of Artificial Intelligence 1640, Springer Verlag, Berlin, pp. 1-65, 1999.

18. G. Angelova, A. Nenkova, Sv. Boycheva, and T. Nikolov, CGs as a Knowledge Representation Core in a Complex Language Learning Environment, in the Proceedings of ICCS-2000, Darmstadt, Germany, August 2000, to appear.
19. J. Levin & J. Moore, Dialogue games: meta-communication structures for natural language interaction, Cognitive Science, 1, 395-420, (1977).

Metaphor Processing for Learning Terminology on the Web

Stefan Trausan-Matu [1,2]

[1] "Politehnica" University of Bucharest,
Computer Science Department, Splaiul Independentei, 313, Sector 6, Bucharest 77206
[2] Romanian Academy Research Center for Computational Linguistics, and
Conceptual Modeling, Calea 13 Septembrie, 13, Bucharest, 74311, Romania
trausan@cs.pub.ro
http://sunsite.pub.ro/people/trausan

Abstract. An approach for the usage of metaphors in learning terminology in a foreign language is presented. The approach integrates ideas from the metaphor theory of Lakoff and Johnson [6] with techniques from corpus-based computational linguistics, advanced markup languages on the web (XML and XSL), and knowledge acquisition and processing. Metaphors are identified by semi-automatic methods and are annotated accordingly to domain and metaphor ontologies. The corpus with annotated metaphors, together with the domain and metaphor ontologies are used for dynamically generation of personalized web pages.

Keywords: Metaphors, WWW, XML, Ontology, Knowledge-Based Systems, Corpus Linguistics.

1   Introduction

This paper presents a methodology and an associated knowledge-based framework developed on the web for supporting foreign students to learn non-literal, metaphorical phrases. One of the main ideas is to add a new dimension to the ontology (knowledge)-based systems available now on the web (e.g. [16]). This new dimension is provided by the experientialist theory on metaphors of Lakoff and Johnson [6] in which metaphors are considered to have an essential role in understanding, opposed to traditional ontology-based systems that use subcategorization: "subcategorization and metaphors are two endpoints of a continuum" [6].

The approach was experimented in a system which has been developed for the generation of highly structured World Wide Web pages for learning finance terminology. This system is one of the modules of the Copernicus project LarFLaST [9], which has as main objectives to provide a set of tools, available on the web, for supporting Romanian, Bulgarian and Ukrainian students to learn foreign terminology in finance. A

S. A. Cerri and D. Dochev (Eds.): AIMSA 2000, LNAI 1904, pp. 232–241, 2000.
© Springer-Verlag Berlin Heidelberg

study on learning foreign terminology in finance, performed in LarFLasST [15], has shown that for understanding new concepts in finance, collocations and metaphors play an important role. Metaphors are often used to give insight in what a concept means, like in the following example: "Stocks are very sensitive creatures" [11]. Such insight can not be obtained in knowledge-based approaches centered around taxonomic ontologies. For example, these systems will explain the concept "stock" in terms of its super-concepts like "securities", "capital", "asset" or "possession". Its attributes and relations with other concepts may provide more details. This paper describes an alternative approach, for the identification, annotation and usage of metaphors in corpora as a basis for explanations giving the above mentioned insight.

The approach presented in the paper integrates metaphor processing with ideas from knowledge acquisition and processing (text mining techniques for metaphor identification, knowledge-based web page generation [14]), corpus-based computational linguistics, and advanced markup languages on the web (XML [18] annotation of metaphors and visualization with XSL [18]).

The next section presents the basic ideas of ontologies and their role as a scaffold in intelligent programs for supporting learning. Section 3 introduces some ideas of Lakoff and Johnson's theory on metaphor [6] and discusses the role of metaphors in language understanding. An ontology for metaphors is introduced in section 4. The way metaphors may be processed is analyzed in section 5. A final section is dedicated to some conclusions and to comparisons to other approaches on metaphor processing.

2   Domain Ontology, a Scaffold of a Learning Process

Learning is a knowledge centered activity: One of the main goals of a learning process is the articulation of a body of knowledge for the considered domain. The skeleton of this body is usually a semantic network of the main concepts involved in that domain. These concepts are taxonomically organized, have several attributes and relations connecting them with other concepts. Using other words, the learner must articulate in his mind the ontology of the domain (that he wants to conceptualize):

"An ontology is a specification of a conceptualization....That is, an ontology is a description (like a formal specification of a program) of the concepts and relationships that can exist for an agent or a community of agents".[5].

One common way used in supporting learning by knowledge-based programs is to "build" the domain ontology in the mind of the student. The program is incrementally introducing to the student new concepts from the ontology and tests if he has correctly acquired them. From these tests, a model of what the student has acquired is kept in order to decide what concepts will be considered next. This process is also used in the LarFLasT project [9].

For example, the finance (domain) ontology contains the following fragment of concept taxonomy:

```
Security
  Bond
    Stock
        Common-Stock
        Prefferred-Stock
```

Each concept has attributes. For example, a stock may have the following attributes:

☐ issuing date,
☐ maturity date,
☐ dividends.

Each concept may be related with other concepts. Related terms with share are:

☐ the stockholder,
☐ the issuer.

Ontologies are now available on the web. Ontologies like WordNet [16], EuroWordNet or MikroKosmos [10] provide a lot of useful relations between concepts. For example, WordNet offers hypernyms (super-concepts), hyponyms (sub-concepts) and other related concepts.

WordNet answers to the queries about "stock" are filtered in LarFLasT by the teacher for getting the right sense and in the web page generation phase (see figure 1) the result (which includes important parts of the WordNet answer) will look like in the following example:

stock - is the capital raised by a corporation through the issue of shares entitling holders to partial ownership; "he owns a controlling share of the company's stock"

   is a/an capital, working capital – is assets available for use in the production of further assets

     is a/an asset – is anything of material value or usefulness

     is a/an possession – is anything owned or possessed

stock may be of the following types:

   common stock, common shares, ordinary shares – is stock other than preferred stock

   no-par-value stock, no-par stock – is a stock with no par value specified kin the corporate charter or on the stock certificate

   preferred stock, preferred shares, preference shares – is a stock whose holders are guaranteed priority in the payment of dividends

. . . .

3   The Role of Metaphors in Language Understanding

The information provided by the domain or WordNet ontologies (as depicted in the example that ended the last section) is very useful for understanding the "stock" concept. However, for a deep understanding of what a stock means, classification knowledge is not enough, the experience of other people involved in operation with stocks being also very important. Metaphors are powerful means to cover this gap (e.g. "stocks are very sensitive creatures" [11]). This idea is enforced also by the results of a study in the LarFLaST project on the problems of learning foreign finance terminology:

"... the difficulty of "cracking" metaphors. The language of Economics and Finance is extremely metaphorical and sometimes clusters of metaphors result in rather elaborated images. Very often this is metaphorical elaboration of an everyday word, otherwise completely familiar." [15]

Lakoff and Johnson have developed an influential theory on metaphors [6]. They consider that "subcategorization and metaphors are two endpoints of a continuum", and that metaphors "... form coherent systems in terms of which we conceptualize our experience" [6]. One consequence is that metaphors offer other expressive means than traditional ontology-based systems that use subcategorization. This is related with the idea that the process of understanding something implies an emphatic relation [17], which involves the immersion of the learner in a context:

"emphaty is a phenomenon in which one person can experience states, thoughts and actions of another person, by psychological transposition of the self in an objective human behavior model, allowing the understanding of the way the other interprets the world " [7]

The side effect of trying to understand a metaphor is an emphatic process, a kind of immersion: "The essence of metaphor is understanding and experiencing one kind of thing in terms of another" [6]. For example, the metaphor: "stocks are very sensitive creatures" [11] is giving us very valuable insights in the behavior and characteristics of stocks, we even could understand them by comparing to ourselves, as very sensitive creatures. All the above considerations explain also some other mistakes done by foreigners learning finance terminology in English, in recognizing typical collocations which have often some metaphorical background (e.g., "to sustain a loss"):

"An inability to recognize and co-ordinate typical noun-verb collocations within a given context. Frequently a term is used with a specific verb, which is not a term itself. These collocations are very typical for economics texts in general, e.g. to sustain a loss, to bear the loss, liable for debts, to repay a loan when it is due, etc.".

4   A Metaphor Ontology

Lakoff and Johnson refer to metaphors as a correspondence between two kinds of things, for example: "ARGUMENT IS WAR". The first term ("argument") is the concept being metaphorically described (the target of the metaphor) and the second is the way it is considered ("war", the source of the metaphor).

The usage of metaphors has as side effect the projection of a system of attributes, relations, scenes, scripts etc., from the second concept to the first one. For example, an argument implies usually two sides and follows scripts similar to wars. That implies that a whole system of words and expressions may be used similarly (e.g. "he attacked her with a new fact").

In analyzing the metaphors considered by Lakoff and Johnson, several classes of concepts used as a second part (source) in metaphors may be identified: resources, instruments, physical objects, humans, actions and processes. These may be further grouped according to Lakoff and Johnson as Orientational, Structural and Ontological.

For the purpose of the system presented here, an ontology has been developed for the concepts used as source of metaphors. These concepts are taxonomically organized, as in the following fragment:

Physical_object
    Organism
        Human
    Instrument
    Building
        Pillar

. . .

Metaphors are used for a purpose, they reflect the writer's intentions. We could say, from a speech act theory perspective, that they have strong illocutionary force. For example, saying that something is "a pillar of stability", has an important effect due to the fact that pillars are very important for buildings, and the idea of a reliable building is very important to everyone. Therefore, the reason for which a metaphor is used, the intentionality of the writer behind the metaphor is very important and may give very useful insights for a true understanding of the text where the metaphor has been used.

For capturing the reasons for which a metaphor is used, in our metaphor ontology, for each concept (which can be a source of a metaphor) a set of attributes (transferred to the target concept) is defined. For each attribute, a set of typical values are included. For example, the organism concept is often used in metaphors for expressing a specific state (healthy – "a healthy economy", illness etc.), a sufferance (e.g. pains – "the company experience the growing pains") or a propriety (e.g. sensitivity). All these attributes are specified in the organism concept and may be considered by the metaphor processing system.

The important effect of metaphors may be explained starting from the significance of these attributes for our existence, their resonance with our experience. We could say that these attributes are reflecting the intentionality behind the usage of metaphors. Therefore, these attributes and values are used for explaining specific metaphors in a given context domain (see section 5.3).

5   Metaphor Processing

This section presents a knowledge-based system for the identification, annotation and usage of metaphors in a corpus as a support for learning foreign terminology. The approach has been tested on a collection of documents retrieved from the New York Stock Exchange site [11]. The architecture of the system is presented in figure 1, reflecting the processing done by various modules, the information flow and the interactions. The positions of the professor and of the student are chosen to ilustrate their access to the modules and information in the system.

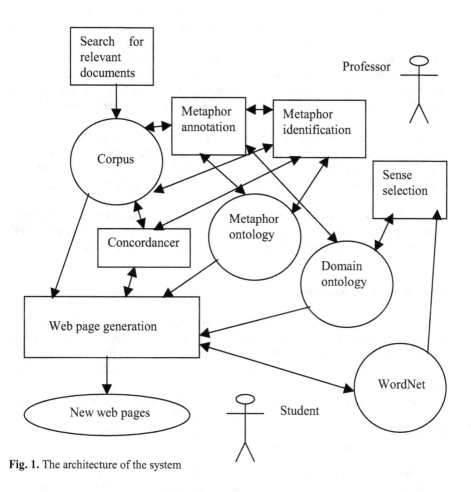

Fig. 1. The architecture of the system

Metaphor processing involves three different activities:

☐ identification (acquisition) of new metaphors,
☐ annotation of the identified metaphors,
☐ usage of the metaphors.

5.1   Metaphor Identification

Metaphor identification may be done manually, with a text editor, or (semi)automatically, with the help of a concordancer. Corpora of texts may be used for the automatic identification of typical collocations. Some of the detected collocations may be candidates for metaphors (e.g. "to sustain a loss"). Metaphor candidates for metaphors may be detected automatically starting from words used often for orientational metaphors (e.g., "high", "in front of" – "high spirit", "high level of expectations", "the future is in front of us", "a challenge is in front of us" etc.), or other metaphorical concepts from the metaphor ontology. For example, all the concordances found for "pillar" in a collection of finance texts from NYSE are metaphors [11]:

ing what is really one of the **pillar**s of our whole system in this country, The N as ever faced. You've been a **pillar** of stability and a great, great leader for or tool and a very important **pillar** of economic education. Going further, thou airman Levitt has been a true **pillar** of strength in bringing the international

Metaphors may be identified also when some semantic constraints are not met after a semantic analysis, like in the example "Stocks are very sensitive creatures" ("stock" is not an animate so it does not meet the constraint imposed by "creature").

5.2   Metaphor Annotation

Text annotation is often used in computational linguistics. The tagged corpora obtained after manual annotation are used for training tagging programs to be used on unannotated texts. In our approach, metaphors are annotated not for training programs but for knowledge-based programs in the aim of providing explanations and perspectives on the metaphors in the corpus.

Metaphors are annotated in the texts in which they occur, according to corpora markup standards. For this, a specific XML (SGML) markup element was defined ("metaph") which may be included in corpora DTD-s (Data Type Definition). The metaphor element has three attributes:

- **What** – the concept that is metaphorically presented (e.g. "stock").
- **How** – the way the concept is presented; the value of this attribute may be one of the types of metaphorical concepts from the metaphor ontology (e.g. "organism").
- **Why** – the reason for which the metaphor was used. This reason may be one of the especially specified attributes of the metaphorical concept in the metaphor ontology. It reflects the intentionality of the writer in choosing to use the metaphor.

An example of a metaphor markup used in LarFLasT is:

```
<metaph what="stock" how="organism" why="reactivity">
Stocks are very sensitive creatures</metaph>
```

5.3   Metaphor Usage

The metaphor annotated corpus may be used in several purposes. In our system, developed for the Larflast project, the corpus is used for explanations in teaching purposes, providing insights for the concepts, which are learned. In this aim, XSL descriptions are used for presenting different (personalized) web pages, starting from the XML corpus encoding. An example of a fragment of a very simple explanation obtained from the corpus and a simple XSL file (referring to the attributes of the "metaph" markup) is given below:

Stocks are seen as:
    object ----> pieces of ownership in the corporation, called stock.
    object ----> stockholders.
    organism ----> Stocks are very sensitive creatures.
    organism ----> They react to all kinds of influences, large and small,
    organism ----> their sensitive reactions register as price changes.
    organism ----> News events can trigger a change in stock prices when they affect
the laws of supply and demand.
    resource ----> a price for its stock.
    ...

Other explanations, obtained with the same corpus but with a different XSL file are:

Some reasons for using these metaphors are:
- -- Stocks are very sensitive creatures -- is reflecting that the stock is a/an organism. Reason --> better reflects the reactivity of stock.
- -- A company faced with growing pains -- is reflecting that the company is a/an organism. Reason --> better reflects the sensitivity of company.

....

The ontology of metaphors may be used in connection with the annotations in the corpus for making inferences about what to include in the explanations. For example, several metaphors may be compared according to the "what", "how", and "why" attributes and, considering also the metaphor ontology inferences may be performed.

Metaphors may be used also in other purposes: linguistic, stylistic, artistic, philosophical or even psychological (metaphors used by a human may reflect his experiences; the best example are the artists) analysis of texts.

The language used in the system was Perl and the object-oriented knowledge representation environment XRL [1], developed in Common Lisp. A translator from the conceptual graphs interchange format CGIF [2] to XRL is under development. Translation to XRL from XML-based ontology markup languages (OML [12], SHOE [13]) will also be considered.

6   Conclusions and Comparison with Other Approaches

Metaphors may be of a real help in teaching activities for providing insights that are fundamental in true understanding of concepts. In fact, every good teacher uses metaphors in his lectures. Moreover, Lakoff [6] considers that they are fundamental for our way of thinking.

Metaphors may be identified in texts semi(automatically), they maybe annotated using SGML (XML), and used in knowledge-based systems. An ontology for metaphors may be developed. The feasibility of this approach has been tested in the frame of the LarFLaST project [9] for explaining metaphors for students learning finance terminology in English.

A similar approach to our metaphor ontology has been proposed by James Martin. His MetaBank [8] includes three kinds of knowledge: about the source, about the target of the metaphor, and about the metaphor itself. The third kind of knowledge comes from the analyses of the Berkley Metaphor Site [3], a web site containing approximately 200 metaphors available textually on web pages indexed by name, source and target domains. Martin also proposed a similar idea of semi-automatical finding of metaphors [8].

Our approach differs from Martin's approach in the usage of corpus annotated with metaphors and in the intentional annotations. Other difference is the main purpose of the usage of the metaphor processing. The systems of Martin [8] and Fass [4] try to find and process metaphors in English text. Our approach combines techniques for metaphor identification and representation in a knowledge-based way with annotation with intentional information. The main purpose of our system is to provide dynamically generated explanations about metaphors in an annotated corpus for foreign students learning English terminology.

References

1. Barbuceanu, M., Trausan-Matu, St., Integrating Declarative Knowledge Programming Styles and Tools in a Structured Object Environment, in J. Mc.Dermott (ed.) Proceedings of 10-th International Joint Conference on Artificial Intelligence IJCAI'87, Italia, Morgan Kaufmann Publishers, Inc., 1987.
2. Conceptual Graphs, http://concept.cs.uah.edu/CG/cg-standard.html
3. Conceptual Metaphor Homepage at Berkeley, http://cogsci.berkeley.edu/
4. Fass, D., Met*, A Method for Discriminating Metonymy and Metaphor by Computer, in Computational Linguistics, vol.17, no.1, pp.49-90.
5. Gruber, T., What is an Ontology, http://www-ksl.stanford.edu/kst/what-is-an-ontology.html

6. Lakoff,G., Johnson, M., Metaphors We Live by, The University of Chicago Press, 1980.
7. Marcus, S., Empatie si personalitate, Ed. Atos, 1997 (in Romanian).
8. Martin, J.H., MetaBank: A Knowledge-Base of Metaphoric Language Conventions, Proceedings of the IJCAI Workshop on Computational Approaches to Non-Literal Language, Sydney, Australia
9. Larflast project, http://www-it.fmi.uni-sofia.bg/larflast/
10. Mikrokosmos, http://crl.nmsu.edu/Research/Projects/mikro/index.html
11. New York Stock Exchange web page, http://www.nyse.com
12. Ontology Markup Language, http://wave.eecs.wsu.edu/CKRMI/OML.html
13. http://www.cs.umd.edu/projects/plus/SHOE/
14. St. Trausan-Matu, Knowledge-Based, Automatic Generation of Educational Web Pages, in Proceedings of Internet as a Vehicle for Teaching Workshop, Ilieni, iun. 1997, pp.141-148.
15. Irena Vitanova, English for Finance. Understanding Money and Markets, http://www-it.fmi.unisofia.bg/larflast/internal/irena.html
16. WordNet, http://www.cogsci.princeton.edu/~wn/
17. von Wright, G.H., Explicatie si întelegere, Humanitas, 1995.
18. Extensible Markup Language (XML), http://www.w3.org/XML/

Development of Lexico-Grammar Resources for Natural Language Generation (Experience from AGILE Project)

Kamenka Staykova and Danail Dochev

Institute of Information Technologies - Bulgarian Academy of Sciences
Acad. Bonchev st., bl 29 A, Sofia 1113, Bulgaria
{staykova, dochev}@iinf.bas.bg

Abstract. The paper discuses some problems of presentation and processing of linguistic knowledge, needed for the development of real-size Bulgarian linguistic resource to be used in a multilingual text generation system, covering software manuals sublanguage. The sublanguage volume is specified by corpus analysis. The text generation is based on the Systemic Functional Linguistics theory. A method for developing lexico-grammar resources by re-using an existing resource for another language is described and illustrated with three examples.

Keywords: Natural language generation, lexico-grammar resources, resource sharing, Systemic Functional Linguistics

1   Introduction

The paper deals with some problems of knowledge presentation and processing for the needs of automatic test generation. The discussion is focused on the presentation and processing of linguistic knowledge, needed for the development of real-size Bulgarian linguistic resource to be used in a multilingual text generation system, created under the international project AGILE [3, 5]. The project aim is to develop a generic set of tools and linguistic resources for generating CAD/CAM software instructional texts in Bulgarian, Czech and Russian. They are developed by an extensive use of the grammar development environment and multilingual sentence generator KPML (Komet-Penman MultiLingual system [2]), which theoretic base is the Systemic Functional Linguistics (SFL, [4]).

2   Corpus Analysis and Sublanguage Specification

Technical manuals within specific domains constitute a sublanguage [8]. An important property of a sublanguage is its lexical and syntactical closure. The lexical closure is

S. A. Cerri and D. Dochev (Eds.): AIMSA 2000, LNAI 1904, pp. 242-251, 2000.

determined by the domain specificity of the sublanguage, as well as by the norms of technical communication, which prefer monosemy to synonymy. The syntactic closure leads to application of small number of rigid syntactical structures.

The sublanguage specification was made on the base of corpus analysis. Because of the sublanguage limitations a small corpus, containing nine procedural texts with 1025 words and 194 coding units, was found to be sufficient for the needs of the project. The corpus processing was used to help in the determination of:

- domain model concepts, i.e. the domain ontology
- text planning processes
- lexical resources
- grammar resources.

The paper will focus further on the determination of lexico-grammar resources.

The corpus analysis, made in terms of the SFL conceptual base, leads to the following conclusions about the sublanguage used in Bulgarian software manuals:

- The great majority of the rank units are clauses and the rest are nominal groups. The prepositional groups do not occur in instructional texts of the corpus.
- The processes are exclusively of the directed-material type. Sometimes relational, mental, and not-material processes are found in the corpus.
- Finite and positive polarities predominate over non-finite and negative polarity features in this particular sublanguage.
- Most of the analysed clauses are non-modal. In the case when modality is expressed in the clause it is of the ability, inclination and obligation type.
- The mood is usually realised by an imperative clause.
- The voice is active, although a few instances of middle were counted. The passive voice was not found in instructional texts at all.
- The user is the most frequent agent, the alternative is program objects appearing as agents.
- Most of the text units are members of a complex clause. The hypotactic relation is realised mainly by a manner or purpose conjunction, although condition and temporal conjunctions occur as well. Paratactic relation is realised by the additive and alternative conjunctions.

3   Approach to Resource Development

The adopted approach for resource development was to re-use an existing large-scale English grammar as a base for the Bulgarian resource due to the following reasons:

1. lack of large-scale Bulgarian computational grammar aimed at automatic text generation;
2. need for fast prototyping;
3. re-usability of the new-build resource, i.e. natural tendency for extension beyond the immediate goal - the coverage of given sublanguage.

This approach has been shown to be effective in several previous developments ([1], [2], [7]) and avoids the necessity of building large-scale grammar from scratch. In [3] the reuse of existing English grammar for typologically different (Slavic) languages is studied across the SFL model. SFL is a functional theory of language, in which the concept of function is reflected in three *metafunctions*: ideational, concerning world representation; interpersonal, reflecting the role relations of speaker and hearer in a discourse; textual, representing the patterns for creation of cohesive and coherent text. The strata distinguished in SFL are lexico-grammar, semantics, and context. Linguistic description, at each stratum, has two aspects, one representing linguistic *systems* (paradigmatic axis), the other the *structural realizations* of these systems (syntagmatic axis). The paradigmatic axis is represented through system network, resembling a type hierarchy supporting multiple inheritance.

According Halliday a system network is a theory of the language as a resource for realising meaning. A system represents a choice between possible semantic, lexico-grammatical or phonological alternatives. Systemic Functional Grammar is an approach to natural language syntax, representing grammar as network of systems. In the process of sentence generation each system, responsible for a given aspect of meaning imposes specific constraints on the form of the sentence. In such a way the generation of a sentence is a satisfaction of a set of constraints, specified by a system network during its tracing. Thus SFG approach describes grammatical structures in terms of co-satisfaction of constraints

The construction of an SFG grammar is led by three organisational principles: *axiality*, *delicacy*, and rank. Axiality expresses the relation between paradigmatic, functionally motivated features and syntagmatic structures realizing them and determines the way systems are formulated: a system has input conditions phrased in terms of grammatical features, and has as output grammatical features, which may be accompanied by realization statements connecting specific constraints on the realization of the surface form to a particular feature. Delicacy is a principle organizing a grammar in a vertical manner, according to levels of specificity. Rank expresses a generalized form of a constituency hypothesis (a sentence can be divided into clauses, clauses into groups, groups or phrases into words, and words into morphemes). . A part of the system network, presenting the highest rank (lowest delicacy) systems for the English SFG Nigel, is shown on Fig.1.

The cross-linguistic analysis in [3] leads to the following observations.

- Languages tend to show more similarities on the more abstract strata of linguistic organisation than on the less abstract ones (i.e., they express similar meanings in different grammatical terms).
- Languages tend to be similar on the paradigmatic axis and less similar in terms of syntagmatic realisation.
- Systems of low delicacy tend to be similar across languages, and systems of higher delicacy tend to be dissimilar.
- There may be different preferences in different languages concerning the grammatical rank at which a particular meaning is expressed.

Different languages may distribute functional responsibilities differently across metafunctions.

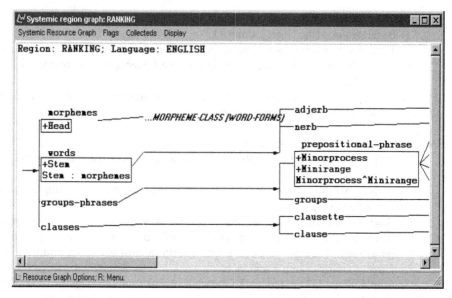

Fig. 1. Part of the system network of the Nigel System Functional Grammar

The cross-linguistic comparison of lexico-grammar features shows that Bulgarian is closer to English than the other Slavic languages with respect to some pragmatically important for the automatic generation syntactical features (lack of cases, explicit articles etc.), so this may facilitate the re-use of English resource for some phenomena. Naturally, Bulgarian differs from English on many other lexico-grammar features as well as on its richer morphology.

The English grammar resource used as basis in the project AGILE is the Nigel grammar, mainly developed by Matthiessen on the SFL foundation [6] and extended by many people afterwards, resulting in a large-scale English computational grammar, that covers broad range of grammatical phenomena. The organization of Nigel separates specifications of syntactic structures from a description of their communicative functions. The analysis in [1] shows that the functional description varies less across languages than the syntactic description and, since the functional component of the description provides the overall organisation of the grammar, the SFL approach to language phenomena can serve as a general guideline for the grammatical description of a wide range of languages without enforcing artificial uniformity. The use and re-use of Nigel is supported by the grammar development environment and multilingual sentence generator KPML, which, like Nigel, is available free of charge.

4   Method of NewResource Development

The approach for developing of a new lexico-grammar resource by re-using an existing resource for another language was implemented by using a Method of NewResource Development, which is sketched below.

Initial information for the method:
1. BaseResource (the Nigel grammar);
2. TargetExamplesSet - set of sentences, representative for the sublanguage revealed during corpus analysis. It covers the lexico-grammar features of the sublanguage.

The method consists of two phases: Phase 1 "Constructing WorkResource" and Phase 2 "Modification of the WorkResource".

Phase 1 "Constructing WorkResource"

Step 1. Tracing of the BaseResource with an example - sentence from the TargetExamplesSet.

Step 2. All the systems from the BaseResource, used in the example tracing are added to the WorkResource.

Step 3. Identification of all places in the system network of inappropriate lexico-grammar choice or gaps in the BaseResource, preventing the example generation. They are added in a GrammarProblemsList with a pointer to the corresponding example sentence.

Step 4. Steps 1-3 are repeated for each sentence from the TargetExamplesSet.

At the end of Phase 1 the following information structures are available:
1. WorkResource – a subset of the BaseResource system network;
2. a list of grammar problems with test examples from the TargetExamplesSet.

Phase 2 "Modification of the WorkResource".

Step 1. Solving a problem from the GrammarProblemsList by modifications in appropriate system networks of the WorkResource. The solution is demonstrated by proper generation of the corresponding example sentence.

Step 2. Adding the example sentence to GeneratedExamplesSet and check of the WorkResource with all the examples of this set.

Step 3. Steps 1-2 are repeated for each problem from the GrammarProblems List.

Step 4. Removal of all system components, representing unused lexico-grammar features from the WorkResource.

It is possible during this phase to process also additional problems with corresponding test examples, inserted in the GrammarProblemsList in order to extend the sublanguage and the NewResource coverage.

The application of the method is illustrated below by three examples (the choices made during tracing the system with the examples are shown in bold italics).

EXAMPLE 1 "Finite in imperative-2person, plural"

The problem: In Bulgarian language the verb form in imperative is finite (in second person, plural for formal, "polite" style), while English imperative form is realised by nonfinite (stem).

Test sentence: "Въведете координатите!" /enter[imperative- 2p, pl] coordinates/

Phase 1: The following system is connected with the problem:

```
MOOD-TYPE (independent-clause-simplex)->
[indicative]  Insert(Subject), Insert(Finite)
[imperative] Insert(Nonfinite),
             Infletify(Nonfinite,stem)
```

Phase 2

Step 1. Necessary modifications – to change the feature Nonfinite in Finite and to fix the verb form in second person plural. Thus the system MOOD-TYPE is modified as follows:

```
MOOD-TYPE (independent-clause-simplex)->
[indicative] Insert(Subject), Insert(Finite)
[imperative] Insert(Finite),
             Infletify(Finite,secondperson-form),
             Inflectify(Finite, plural-form)
```

In Bulgarian language an informal imperative verb form – second person singular is used also. Though it is not covered in the software manuals sublanguage, it may be included in the NewResource by means of additional system and the following modification:

```
MOOD-TYPE (independent-clause-simplex)->
[indicative] Insert(Subject), Insert(Finite)
[imperative] Insert(Finite),
             Inflectify(Finite,secondperson-form)
```

```
IMPERATIVE-TYPE (imperative) ->
[polite-imperative]   Inflectify(Finite, plural-form)
[informal-imperative] Inflectify(Finite, singular-form)
```

If the decision of extending the sublanguage is taken an additional test sentence has to be added: "Въведи координатите!" /enter[imperative- 2p, sing.] coordinates/

```
IMPERATIVE-TYPE (imperative) ->
[polite-imperative]   Inflectify(Finite, plural-form)
[informal-imperative] Inflectify(Finite, singular-form)
```

Step 2. The test examples are added to the GeneratedExamplesSet and all its members are checked for generation against the modified WorkResource.

EXAMPLE 2 Aspect

The problem: Two aspect forms of the verbs are distinguished in Bulgarian language: a/ the imperfective forms emphasise the continuous, incomplete nature of the action; b/ the perfective forms refer to the action as a whole or focus on its completion.

Test examples: "Въведете координатите!" /enter [perfective, imperative- 2p, pl.] /, "Въвеждайте координатите!" /enter [imperfective, imperative- 2p, pl.] /

Phase 1: The BaseResource does not contain an analogue. The new system position is localised by the need to use as input the feature *independent-clause-simplex*.

Phase 2:

Step 1. Inclusion in the WorkResource of the system

```
ASPECT (independent-clause-simplex) ->
[perfective] Classify(Process, perfective-verb)
[imperfective] Classify(Process, imperfective-verb)
```

Step 2. The test examples are added to the GeneratedExamplesSet and all its members are checked for generation against the modified WorkResource. If the GeneratedExamplesSet contains complex sentences with dependent clauses, they will not obtain Aspect variations because of the chosen input of the new system *independent-clause-simplex*. In such case it will be necessary to return to Step 1 and appropriately change the resource until all test examples from the GeneratedExamplesSet are generated correctly.

EXAMPLE 3 Phase

The problem: To generate clauses with complex verb forms, consisting of phase verb and main verb, allowing the presentation of different phases of a process.

Test example: "Започнете да въвеждате координатите!" /begin [imperative- 2p, pl.] to enter[2p, pl.] coordinates/ (See Fig.2)

Phase 1: The following systems are connected with the problem:

```
PHASE (transitivity-unit) ->
[not-phase]
[phase]      Insert(Phase), Classify(Phase, phase-verb),
             Insert(Phasedependent)

PHASEDEPENDENT-TYPE (phase) ->
[phaseinfinitive] Inflectify(Phasedependent, stem),
                  Insert(Tophase), Lexify(Tophase, to),
                  Order(Tophase, Phasedependent)
[ingphase]   Inflectify(Phasedependent, ingparticiple)
```

Phase 2:

Step 1. The following analogy between the English and Bulgarian phase verb exists: the *phaseinfinitive* corresponds to *"da-construction"* in Bulgarian: Begin to enter the coordinates! <-> Започнете да въвеждате координатите!
        /begin [imperative- 2p, pl.] enter[2p, pl.] coordinates/
ingphase or *ingparticiple-form* may be matched with the construction with nominalization in Bulgarian: Begin enterling the coordinates! <-> Започнете въвеждането на координатите!
        /begin [imperative- 2p, pl.] entering [nominalization noun] coordinates/.

In English the Phasedependent verb form in *phaseinfinitive* construction is stem, while in Bulgarian the Phasedependent verb form in *"da-construction"* agrees with the Phase verb on person and number: Begin to **enter** the coordinates! <-> Започнете да въвеждате координатите! /begin [imperative- 2p, pl.] **fill [2p, pl.]** coordinates/

Therefore the following modifications are made:

```
PHASE (transitivity-unit) ->
[not-phase]
[phase]    Insert(Phase), Classify(Phase, phase-verb),
           Insert(Phasedependent)

PHASEDEPENDENT-TYPE (phase)->
[da-phase-construction]
           Insert(Daphase),Lexify(Daphase, da),
           Order(Daphase, Phasedependent),
           Agreement(Phase, Phasedependent, number-form),
           Agreement(Phase, Phasedependent, person-form)
[phase-nominalization]
           Inflectify(Phasedependent,nominalization-noun)
```

A possible sublanguage extension is to add a phase construction with nominalisation (Започнете въвеждането на координатите! /begin [imperative- 2p, pl.] filling [nominalization noun] coordinates/) . For this the corresponding target example has to be included in the TargetExamplesSet and the method is repeated from Phase 1 with the new example, which would need additional systems from the BaseResource and additional problems in the GrammarProblemsList.

Step 2: The test example "Започнете да въвеждате координатите!" is added to the GeneratedExamplesSet and all its members are checked for generation against the modified WorkResource.

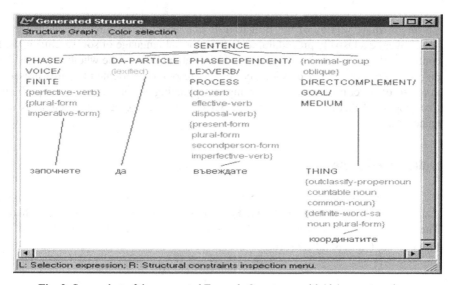

Fig. 2. Screenshot of the generated Example 3 sentence with 'da' - construction

The screenshots on Fig 2. and Fig.3 show the generated sentences from Example 3 (with 'da' - construction' and nominalisation) together with the collected during the system network tracing grammatical features, constraining the generated structure.

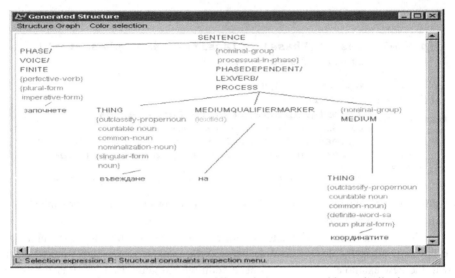

Fig. 3. Screenshot of the generated Example 3 sentence with nominalisation

5   Conclusions

An intermediate version of the Bulgarian lexico-grammar resource, developed up to now, covers exclusively procedural texts from the sublanguage of software manuals. It contains 110 new or modified systems, which is about 20% of the whole resource. The on-going work on further development of this resource is oriented towards presentation also of descriptive texts, concerning text planning and lexico-grammar problems like support of modal clauses, different types of clause aggregation in complex sentences etc.

Acknowledgements

The authors thank all the members of the AGILE team and especially John Bateman, Anthony Hartley, Donia Scott, Ivana Kruijff-Korbayova and Sergey Sharoff. The work reported in this paper has been supported by the EC INCO-COPERNICUS Programme, Grant No. PL961104.

References

1.   Bateman J.A., Matthiessen C.M.I.M., Nanri K, Zeng L. -The re-use of linguistic resources   across languages in multilingual generation components. Proc. of IJCAI'91, Sydney, Australia, Vol. 2, pp. 966—971. Morgan Kaufmann Publishers.

2.   Bateman J.A. - Enabling technology for multilingual natural language genera-
      tion: the KPML development environment. Journal of Natural Language Engi-
      neering, Vol. 3(1997) No1, pp.15--55.
3.   Bateman J, E. Tech, G-J. Kruijff, Iv Kruijff-Korbayova, S, Sharoff, H. Skou-
      malova - Resource for Multilingual Text Generation in Three Slavic Languages.
      Proc. of LREC'2000 (in print).
4.   Halliday M.A.K. - An Introduction to Functional Grammar. Edward Arnold,
      London, 1985.
5.   Kruijff G-J, Iv Kruijff-Korbayova, E. Teich, J. Bateman, H. Skoumalova, S.
      Sharoff, T. Hartley, K. Staykova, J. Hana - Multilinguality in a Text Generation
      System for Three Slavic Languages. Proc. of COLING'2000 (in print).
6.   Mann W,. Matthiessen C.M.I.M.. - A demonstration of the Nigel text generation
      computer program. In Benson J.D, W. S. Greaves, (Eds), Systemic Perspectives
      on Discourse, Vol. 1. Ablex, Norwood, N.J., 1985.
7.   Rayner M., Carter D., Bouillon P. - Adapting the Core Language Engine to
      French and Spanish. In: Proceedings of NLP-IA-96, Moncton, New Brunswick,
      1996.
8.   Sager, J.S. - Language Engineering and Translation: Consequences of Automa-
      tion. Brandstetter Verlag, Wiesbaden, Germany, 1993.

Handling Diphthong and Triphone Symbols: Useful in Automatic English Text Generation from Pitman Shorthand Language Document

P. Nagabhushan and Basavaraj S. Anami

Department of Studies in Computer Science, University of Mysore
Manasgangotri, Mysore-570006, India
pnagabhushan@hotmail.com

Abstract. The paper describes the recognition of diphthong and triphone signs useful in automatic generation of English text from Pitman Shorthand Language (PSL) document. The PSL is used to note down the dictated/spoken text and is widely practiced in all organizations where English is the transaction medium. This has a built-in practical advantage because of which it is universally acknowledged. This recording medium will continue to exist in spite of considerable developments in Speech Processing Systems, which are not universally established yet. Because of wide usage of PSL and the effort in its automation, PSL processing has emerged as a potential problem for research in the areas of Pattern Recognition, Image Processing, Artificial Intelligence and Document Analysis.

There are six long and six short vowels in PSL. These vowels are represented by signs /symbols that over ride a stroke symbol and require recognition for composing English text from phonetic text documented through PSL. The work pertaining to other constructs of PSL is already carried out at word level by the authors [7,8]. But during dictation, it is common that the vowels are joined to form one syllable, called Diphthong. The diphthong appended with a tick-mark is called Triphone and represents any vowel that immediately follows the diphthong in a stroke. The diphthongs are to be cognized and recognized to generate the correct English equivalent text. The present work comprises of the definition of diphthong primitives, creation of knowledge base and the development of an algorithm for their recognition. A suitable shape recognition algorithm is assumed available here. This work is new and this module serves as a prerequisite for the complete recognition of PSL document and generation of an equivalent and correct English text.

Keywords: Diphthong, Triphone, Pitman Shorthand Language, Knowledge Base, English Text.

S. A. Cerri and D. Dochev (Eds.): AIMSA 2000, LNAI 1904, pp. 252-260, 2000.

1   Introduction

The PSL is used to note down the dictated/spoken text based on phonetic composition (PC) of words/sentences. It is widely practiced in all organizations where English is the transaction medium. This has built-in practical advantages, such as compressed mode of recording, phonetic based composition and recording speed that matches dictation, which have made PSL a universally acceptable medium of recording. This recording medium will continue to exist in spite of considerable developments in Speech Processing Systems, which are not universally established yet [4]. The PSL could also find the promising applications in the areas such as private and secret communication, compact storage of documents, speech to text conversion, adaptation of PSL to other languages, etc. These applications can be realized with the developments in both computer and communication technologies. Hence, the problem of automatic generation of complete English text, in the form of printed document, from the spoken/dictated text has emerged as a problem of recent research interest in the areas of Pattern Recognition, Image Processing, Artificial Intelligence and Document Analysis.

Leedham,et.al. [2,3] and Hemanth Kumar & Nagabhushan[1] have addressed the problem of Automatic Recognition of Pitman Shorthand strokes with emphasis to shape recognition. The process of automatic text generation from PSL document is viewed as a 3-phase pattern recognition problem, namely, (i) Shape recognition,(ii) Syntactic specification and analysis and (iii) English text production, as shown in fig(1).

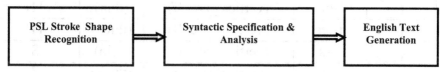

Fig. 1. Three phases in Automatic Text Generation from PSL

The last phase consists of generation of correct and an equivalent English text from PSL document. This is considered a challenging task because of the subtasks such as (i) Converting the phonetic text to English text, (ii) Correct and an equivalent word substitution, (iii) Resolving homophones, (iv) Domain specific context resolution, and (v) Handling of grammalogues, (vi) Grammatical corrections etc. The composition of English text (CET) from phonetic text documented through PSL is attempted as an initial work in this direction and a paper is communicated based on this by the authors [7]. In this paper we present the definitions for PSL stroke primitives, knowledge base representation and creation, the development of an algorithm for recognition of diphthongs and triphones that are encountered during dictation. The remaining issues of automatic text generation from PSL document are still under investigation.

2   Defnition of Primitives

The shape recognition phase gives the primitives that describe the consonant strokes which are the basic characters in PSL. The primitives defined are given in Table(1).

Table 1. PSL Consonants and Primitives

Character	Phonetic Name	Primitives for strokes	Stroke Nature	English Consonant
\	Pee	(120_line)	(thin)	P
\	Bee	(120_line)	(thick)	B
|	Tee	(vertical_line)	(thin)	T
|	Dee	(vertical_line)	(thick)	D
/	Chay	(60_line)	(thin)	CH
/	Jay	(60_line)	(thick)	J
—	Kay	(horizontal_line)	(thin)	K
—	Gay	(horizontal_line)	(thick)	G
(	Ef	(lr_down_arc)	(thin)	F
(	Vee	(lr_down_arc)	(thick)	V
(	Ith	(vertical_arc_lf)	(thin)	TH
(	Thee	(vertical_arc_lf)	(thick)	TH
)	Ess	(vertical_arc_rt)	(thin)	S
)	Zee	(vertical_arc_rt)	(thick)	Z
)	Ish	(lr_up_arc)	(thin)	SH
)	Zhee	(lr_up_arc)	(thick)	ZH
∩	Em	(horizontal_arc_up)	(thin)	M
∪	En	(horizontal_arc_down)	(thin)	N
∪	Ing	(horizontal_arc_down)	(thick)	NG
⌐	El	(up_right_arc)	(thin)	L
/	Ar, ray	(up_left_arc)	(thin)	R
/	ـWay	(bottom_up_hook)	(thin)	W
/	ـYay	Bottom_down_hook)	(thin)	Y
٩	Hay	(bottom_circled_hook	(thin)	H

An algorithm is already devised for the recognition of these basic primitives and is assumed available here [1]. The strokes are written above or on or through the base line based on the sound of first vowel in the word, as shown in fig(2). The vowels are classified into six long vowels, as heard in the words like wah!, ale, each, all, oak, ooz etc and six more short vowels, as heard in the words like at, etch, it, odd, pub, cook etc. The short vowels are represented by light dash (-) and dot (.) symbols and the long vowels are represented by thick dash (-) and dot (.) symbols. There are six vowel positions, three on either sides , on the stroke and are written before and after the stroke depending upon the nature of the vowels. This is depicted in fig(3).

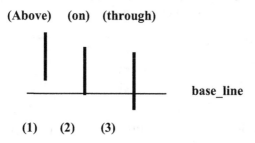

Fig. 2. Three Positions for the Strokes

Before	1		1	**After**
	2		2	
	3		3	

Fig. 3. Vowel positions

3   Diphthongs and Triphones

The diphthongs are the union of two vowel sounds in one syllable, quite commonly used during dictation. There are four diphthongs in PSL, namely , i, ow, oi, and u as heard in the sentence " I now enjoy music". The table(2) gives diphthong signs and the defined primitives.

Table 2. Diphthong signs and primitives

Diphthongs	Contained Vowels	Devised primitive	Sign
I	I+E	(V_sign)	V
OW	O+U	(In_vsign)	∧
OI	O+I	(greater_sign)	>
U	U+E	(In_usign)	∩

The signs for i and oi are written in the first place and the sign for ow and u are written in the third place, as depicted in fig(3). The diphthong signs are conveniently joined to the consonant symbols during recording in PSL. However, in this work it is assumed that the diphthong signs are written separately near the consonant. A novice during writing normally practices this. A small tick-mark appended to the diphthong sign represents any vowel that immediately follows the diphthong in a stroke. These signs are called triphones because they represent three vowels in one sign, refer fig(5). The examples of fig(4) illustrate the usage of diphthongs

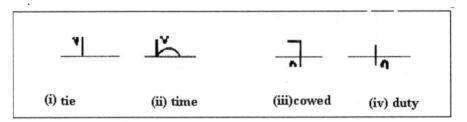

(i) tie   **(ii) time**   **(iii)cowed**   **(iv) duty**

Fig. 4. Examples illustrating usage of diphthongs

The usage of triphones in PSL is illustrated with the examples given in fig (5). The primitives for the triphone-signs are similar to those of diphthongs and their recognition conveys the possible occurrence of any vowel next on the stroke. These signs are small and the separation of the tick-mark from the symbol of a diphthong is a difficult task. Hence, the triphones are are assumed to be independent phonetic units in PSL and the separate primitives defined are given in table(3) . Another sign, right semicircle ($\subset$), is used to mark the initial sound of w in PSL. The frame structure representation is used for storing the knowledge of both Diphthong and Triphone symbols.

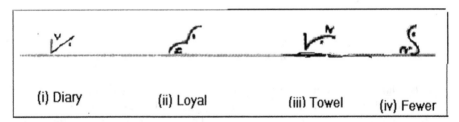

(i) Diary   **(ii) Loyal**   **(iii) Towel**   **(iv) Fewer**

Fig. 5. Examples illustrating usage of Triphones

The format of the knowledge structure is given in fig(6). The hashing technique is employed for the implementation of Knowledge bases namely, Diphthongs' Knowledge Base (DKB) and Triphones' Knowledge Base (TKB) owing to their smaller sizes.

> **(Frame-name(Primitive(Value, value-string))**
> (Eng-equivalent(Value, value-string))

Fig. 6. Frame structure

Rule Base : The following rules are used in handling Diphthongs.

Rule1. If Diphthong is before the stroke then
>   Substitute the phonetic composition before the stroke details
>   And obtain the corresponding English text composition.

Rule2. If Diphthong is after the stroke then
>   Substitute the phonetic composition before the stroke details
>   And obtain the corresponding English text composition.

Rule3. If there is right_semi_circle then
>   The possible occurrences of strokes are kay,gay,em and ar
>   Substitute w before the stroke details and obtain the
>   corresponding English text composition.

Rule4. If w is preceded by a vowel then
>   Substitute the vowel before the stroke   details and obtain
>   phonetic composition and further obtain corresponding English
>   text composition.

Table 3. Triphone Primitives

Triphone Symbols	Primitives
Vᴵ	(ticked_Vsign)
 Λ	(ticked_inVsign)
 ƶ	ticked_greater_sign)
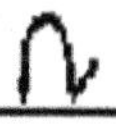 ∩	(ticked Usign)

4   Algorithm Description

The proposed algorithm recognizes the Diphthongs and Triphones and substitutes an equivalent English text based on their phonetic composition. This algorithm should go in conjunction with other algorithms that are already developed and published [7,8]. The length of every phonetic construct is obtained in terms of its primitives during segmentation. It is observed that the length of diphthong is one and the length of triphone is two.

Input: The diphthongs , Triphones and their length .

Output: The English Equivalent text.

Stage 1. Creation of the Diphthongs and Triphones Knowledge bases.
Step1. The Diphthong and Triphone Tables are established.
Step2. The DKB and TKB frames are suitably represented.
Step3. Implement the Knowledge bases using hashing technique.
Stage 2. Recognition of Diphthongs and Triphones.
Step1.Accept the primitives and length information from   word level segmentation.
Step2. Obtain the hash_key for the primitive.
Step3. If (the length of phonetic construct = 1) then
access the DKB and obtain corresponding phonetic composition and go to step 4.
Step4. If (the length of phonetic construct = 2) then
access the TKB and obtain corresponding phonetic composition.
Step5. Generate corresponding English text composition.
Step6. With reference to the rule base substitute the English text in the resulting word.

5   Results and Discussion

The proposed algorithm is tested extensively on all possible Diphthongs and Triphones The following examples illustrate the process given in the algorithm.
Example of Diphthong :

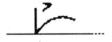

Stroke Details	:	Stroke+Diphthong + Stroke
Phonetic Composition:		Tee + OI + EL
English Equivalent	:	T + O I + L
Probable Word	:	TOIL
Exact Word	:	TOIL

Example of Triphone:

Stroke Details	:	Stroke+Triphone+Stroke+Vowel
Phonetic Composition:		Dee + i + ray + i
English Equivalent	:	D + I + R + I
Probable Word	:	DIRI
Exact Word	:	Diary

The table (4) gives few examples illustrating the usage of diphthongs in PSL.

Table 4. Examples illustrating usage of Diphthongs

Stroke details	Phonetic Composition	English Equivalent	Probable Word	Exact word
	TEE+I	T+I	TI	TIE
	TEE+I+EM	T+I+M	TIM	TIME
	I+TEE+A.+EM	I+T+A+M	ITAM	ITEM
	I+DEE+EL+E	I+D +L+E	IDLE	IDLE

The triphones are also processed by accessing knowledge base (TKB) similar to Diphthongs except that the presence of tick-mark gives information about vowel following the diphthong which acts as a priori knowledge for further processing of primitives. The following table (5) few examples for illustration.

Table 5. Examples illustrating usage of Triphone

	EL+OI +E + EL	L + OI +E +L	LOIEL	LOYAL
	TEE+OW+E+EL	T+OW+E+EL	TOWEL	TOWEL
	Way+Kay+e	W+K+E	WKE	WAKE

6   Conclusion

The work of automatic generation of an equivalent English text from PSL document comprises of different phases. During dictation, the usage of diphthongs is common and hence their recognition becomes important and forms the basis for the further work on the proposed research. The conflicts that arise in substitution of words can be overcome with the domain and the contextual knowledge. The identified subsequent phases require the intelligent dictionary support, conflict resolution technique in case of homophones, techniques for handling PSL dialects, etc. These issues are quite challenging and our present research is in these areas. The total automation requires the definition of dictionaries for making the correct substitution. This work is currently under investigation.

Acknowledgement

The authors wish to acknowledge the support extended by Mr Radhakrishna, Ravi Commercial Institute, Mysore and Dr G. Hemanth Kumar, Reader & Bapu kiranagi, Research Scholar, DOS in Computer Science, University of Mysore, Manasagangotri, Mysore.

References

1. G.Hemanth Kumar: Supervisor P. Nagabhushan, *On Automation of Text Production from Pitman Shorthand Notes*, **PhD Thesis,** University of Mysore, Mysore, 1998.
2. Leedham, *Automatic Recognition and Transcription of Pitman's Hand Written Shorthand,* R Plamondon and C G Leedham Eds, Computer Processing of Handwriting, World Scientific, Singapore 1990.
3. Leedham and A C Downtown, Automatic Recognition and Transcription of Pitman's Hand Written Shorthand - An approach to Shortforms, Pattern Recognition, Vol 20, 1987, pp 341-348.
4. Issac Pitman, *Pitman Shorthand Instructor and Key,* Wheeler Publisher,1976.
5. Dan W. Patterson, Introduction to Artificial Intelligence and Expert Systems , PHI, 1999.
6. Harowitz E and Sahni S , *Fundamentals of Data Structures,* Computer Science Press, 1976.
7. P.Nagabhushan and Basavaraj.S.Anami, **A Knowledge Based Approach For Composing English Text From Phonetic Text Documented Through Pitman Shorthand Language**, Proceedings of International Conference on Cognitive Systems, ICCS-99, New Delhi, India, pp 45.
8. P.Nagabhushan and Basavaraj.S.Anami, A Knowledge Based Approach For Recognition Of Grammalogues And Punctuation Symbols Useful in Automatic English Text Generation from Pitman Shorthand Language Document Proceedings of the National Conference on Recent Trends in Advanced Computing,NCRTAC-2000,Thirunelveli,India, pp 175-183.

Complexity Issues in the Davis and Putnam Scheme

G. Escalada-Imaz and R. Torres Velázquez

Artificial Intelligence Research Institute (IIIA)
Scientific Research Spanish Council (CSIC)
Campus UAB, s/n 08193 Bellaterra, Barcelona (Spain)
gonzalo@iiia.csic.es

Abstract The Davis and Putnam (D&P) scheme has been intensively studied during this last decade. Nowadays, its good empirical performances are well-known. Here, we deal with its theoretical side which has been relatively less studied until now. Thus, we propose a strictely linear D&P algorithm for the most well known tractable classes: Horn-SAT and 2-SAT. Specifically, the strictely linearity of our proposed D&P algorithm improves significantly the previous existing complexities that were quadratic for Horn-SAT and even exponential for 2-SAT. As a consequence, the D&P algorithm designed to deal with the general SAT problem runs as fast (in terms of complexity) as the specialised algorithms designed to work exclusively with a specific tractable SAT subclass.

Keywords: Automated Reasoning, Computational Complexity, Search, Theorem Proving.

1 Introduction

Since the beginning of the current decade [8,1], the widely well known scheme of Davis and Putnam (D&P) [5], whose most appropriate algorithmic description was given in [4], has proved to be faster than many other elaborated schemes.

Throughout this decade, algorithms with the D&P's scheme were empirically compared to other competitive algorithms with success. Thus, this scheme was extensively used for analysing the transition phase phenomenom [3,11] that emerges when solving SAT instances randomly generated. Moreover, during these last years the D&P's mechanism has been essential in the study of heuristics [12,10,2] for propositional theorem proving. Furthermore, finding high performance algorithms for some real-life applications, e.g. [13], has relied on the famous algorithmic scheme as well.

We may also find several proposals [3,17,14,16,15] of different implementations of algorithms stemming from the D&P principle. These implementations based on suitable data structure may enable us to scan fastly the search space.

In this article, we propose a data structure for the D&P's scheme and a new inference rule which allow us to claim that the Davis and Putnam method is strictly linear for the Horn-Sat and 2-SAT sub-classes. Thus, we push beyond the

S. A. Cerri and D. Dochev (Eds.): AIMSA 2000, LNAI 1904, pp. 261–271, 2000.

currently known efficiency of the Davis and Putnam method, since only quadratic and even exponential complexities had been obtained for such subclasses [14,6] until now.

Therefore, our goal in this article is three-fold and it concerns the efficiency of the D&P principle:

1. To propose data structures which may enable to cross rapidly the search space.
2. To introduce a new inference rule, called polarised formula, that prunes large search spaces.
3. To prove indeed, that D&P is even as fast (in terms of complexity) as the specialised algorithms designed to deal only with a specific tractable class (e.g. Horn, 2-Sat) of instances.

The proposed data structures are not complex ones and they are indeed based on classical data structures such as flags, counters, pointers and lists.

The organisation of the article is as follows. The next section presents the classical notions of the SAT problem and those of the D&P scheme. Afterwards, in section 3, an informal description of the proposed algorithm is given. Section 4 specifies the first D&P procedure. After, the changes in the algorithm, in order to select unit clauses first, are described. In section 6, a new inference rule for the D&P method is defined. Finally, it is claimed that the algorithm stemmed from the D&P scheme is linear for several well-known tractable classes.

Due to a lack of space, the proofs of the theorems have been omitted. More details about the contain of this article can be found in [9].

2   Preliminaries

Let us recall the bases and the classical terminology associated with the SAT problem and the D&P algorithmic principle.

Basic Terminology. The number of different propositions is assumed to be n. A positive literal L is a proposition p and a negative literal is a complemented proposition $-p$. The complemented literal of L is noted $-L$. A clause, noted C, is a set of literals which may be empty. A formula, noted Γ, is a set of clauses which may be empty.

Satisfiability. An interpretation I assigns to each literal a value in $\{0,1\}$ and verifies $I(p) = 1 - I(-p)$. An interpretation satisfies a clause iff it assigns 1 to at least one of its literals. An interpretation satisfies a formula iff it satisfies all of its clauses and in this case, the interpretation is called a model. A formula is satisfiable iff there exists at least one interpretation that satisfies it.

Partial interpretation. An interpretation that maps only $0 \leq k < n$ propositions satisfies a certain sub-set of clauses of a formula. If the partial interpretation satisfies all the clauses is called a partial model. All the interpretations covering this partial model are also models. If a partial interpretation unsatisfies all the literals of at least one clause then all the interpretations covering this partial interpretation unsatisfy the formula in question too.

D&P Scheme. Each state of the D&P algorithm is associated with a set of $k \leq n$ literals. A set can include either a literal or its complement but not both. Each set is associated with the Current Partial Interpretation (CPI) that satisfies each literal into the set. A straightforward version of the D&P solver is depicted here below. The procedure *(Inference Γ p)* returns a new formula obtained from the original one by removing from it the clauses containing p and the occurrences of $-p$.

Algorithm 1 Algorithm: D&P scheme. *The function pick.literal selects a literal L from the formula Γ that is not in CPI.*

D&P(Γ, CPI)
1 If $\Gamma = \{\}$ then HALT (sat)
2 If $\{\} \in \Gamma$ then Return(unsat)
3 $L \leftarrow$ pick.literal
4 D&P((Inference Γ p), CPI $\cup$ {p})
5 Return(D&P((Inference Γ $-p$), CPI $\cup$ {-p}))

Theorem 1. D&P *is correct:* D&P$(\Gamma,\{\})$ *returns sat iff Γ is satisfiable.*

Remark. The rules of clause subsumption and pure literal elimination are not considered. Both rules involve a high computational cost and are rarely useful in practice.

D&P algorithm. We will distinguish between a D&P *algorithm* and the D&P *scheme* as follows. The D&P scheme description above omits the data structure employed to represent Γ, CPI and also the specific instructions in pseudo-code. Thus, a D&P scheme where the data structure and its computer instructions are completely specified is called a D&P algorithm.

Remark. The following two statements are equivalent:
(1) The complexity of the D&P scheme is in $O(f(n))$ and,
(2) The best complexity of a D&P algorithm is in $O(f(n))$.
Thus, in the sequel we use statements of type (1).

As mentioned, each state of the search space can be associated with the current partial interpretation CPI. This is formed with the literals which are added incrementally in each recursive call.

The basic data structure consists of:

1. For each literal L: 1) *clauses*(L) is the set of clauses including L and, 2) *new.sat.clauses*(L) is the subset of *clauses*(L) not satisfied by the CPI.
2. For each clause C: *state*(C) = *sat* iff C is satisfied by the CPI.
3. For the formula Γ: counter(Γ) indicates how many clauses are unsatisfied by the CPI.

3   Informal Description of the Algorithm

Bearing in mind both the first general description of the D&P scheme and the described data structure, we can informally describe our specific algorithm as follows:

- *Steps 1, 2 and 3.* They are straightforwardly implemented.
- *Step 4.* The function (Inference Γ p) is accomplished in two steps $4.A$ and $4.B$. These steps are related respectively to the unit-subsumption and to the unit-resolution inferences.
- *Step 4.A: Unit-subsumption.* After a literal L is picked up in step 3, all the clauses C unsatisfied by the CPI but containing L are marked satisfied, namely $state(C) = sat$. The counter of Γ is decremented as many times as new clauses are satisfied. Whenever this counter is set to zero it means that all the clauses are satisfied and thus, the algorithm halts sending "Sat".
- *Step 4.B: Unit-resolution.* When $counter(\Gamma) \neq 0$ the process is continued by decrementing the counters corresponding to clauses having occurrences of $-L$. If no counter is set to zero then, another proposition is selected and the steps $(1) - (4)$ are iterated (this is done calling recursively the main function D&P). If one of them is set to zero the CPI unsatisfies the formula and hence the algorithm stops the search beyond the CPI and backtracks. This implies that the operations done in the last step 4 must be undone. Thus, for each $C \in$ sat.new.clauses, State(C) is set again to *unsat* and counter(Γ) is incremented, and finally *sat.new.clauses* is set to $\emptyset$. These operations are incrementally continued till returning to the last pending recursive call corresponding to a step 5.
- *Step 5.* The process follows the search for models containing $CPI \cup \{-L\}$. The operations in step 5 are equal to those of step 4 as long as L is exchanged by $-L$.

4   A Basic Algorithm Issued from the D&P Scheme

First, we present the four procedures which form the skeleton of our proposed algorithm. **Unit-subsumption** (resp. **Unit-Resolution**) is implemented by the procedure called **Remove-clauses** (resp. **Remove-literals**) and in the backtracking process its steps are undone by the procedure **Restore-clauses** (resp. **Restore-literals**). *This first algorithmic version intends to help the reader to understand the more elaborate and definitive complete algorithm which will be given later.*

Procedure 1 Remove.clauses(L) *It removes from Γ the clauses satisfied by L by decrementing the counter(Γ), once per each clause not satisfied by the current CPI and satisfied by L. If this counter is set to zero, the procedure halts the whole satisfiability test process and it returns "sat".*

```
Remove.clauses(L)                          Restore.clauses(L)
  new.sat.clauses(L) ← ∅                      ∀ C ∈ new.sat.clauses(L) do:
  ∀C ∈ Clauses(L) s.t. state(C)=unsat do:       state(C) ← unsat
    Add C to new.sat.clauses(L)                  Increment counter (Γ)
    state(C) ← sat                             new.sat.clauses(L) ← ∅
    Decrement counter (Γ)                     End
    If counter (Γ)=0 then HALT(sat)
End
```

Procedure 2 Restore.clauses(L). *It undoes the operations carried out by the procedure* Remove.clauses(L).

Procedure 3 Remove.Literals(L). *It removes all the occurrences of L. If at least one clause becomes empty then the CPI unsatisfies all the literals in such clause and thus, the boolean flag UNSAT is set to True. Otherwise, the procedure ends with the flag UNSAT=False.*

Remove.literals(L)
```
   UNSAT ← False
   ∀ C ∈ Clauses(L) do:
     Decrement Counter(C)
     If Counter(C)=0 then UNSAT ← True
End
```

Restore.literals(L)
```
   ∀ C ∈ Clauses(L) do:
     Increment Counter(C)
   End
```

Procedure 4 Restore.literals(L). *It undoes the operations performed in the procedure* Remove.literals(L).

Now using these procedures we can construct our first D&P algorithm.

Algorithm 2 Preliminary D&P algorithm. *Pick.literal selects a literal from the current Γ, namely the formula that results after applying consecutively (Inference Γ L), for each literal L in CPI. In other words, it selects a literal such that CPI(L)=CPI(-L)=Not. Its definition is straightforward and therefore, it will be omitted. Similarly, the initialisation of the data structure is not given here.*

D&P
```
   L ← pick-Literal
   Remove.clauses(L), Remove.literals(-L)
   If UNSAT = False then D&P
   Restore.clauses(L), Restore.literals(-L)
   Remove.clauses(-L), Remove.literals(L)
   If UNSAT=False then D&P
   Restore.clauses(-L), Restore.literals(L)
   Return(unsat)
End
```

Remark. Notice that this algorithm is exactly the same as the previous one: the function (Inference Γ p) is materialised by both procedures Remove.clauses and Remove.literals.

Theorem 2. D&P's correctness. D&P *returns unsat iff Γ is unsatisfiable.*

The proof is straightforward from the definition of the procedures 1 to 4 and theorem 1.

The last version of the D&P procedure can be simplified integrating the operations in Remove-clauses(L) and Remove-literals(-L) in one procedure that we shall call Inference(L) and use from now on. Similarly, Restore-clauses and Restore-literals are merged in Undo-Inference(L). We can modify slightly Remove-literals in a way that it retuns *unsat* instead of using the previous flag UNSAT. Thus, we have:

Remove.literals(L)
```
  UNSAT ← False
  ∀ C ∈ Clauses(L) do:
    Decrement Counter(C)
    If Counter(C)=0 then UNSAT ← True
  If UNSAT return(unsat) Else return(sat)
End
```

D&P
```
       L ← pick-Literal
       If Inference(L)≠unsat do D&P
         Undo-Inference(L)
       If Inference(-L)≠unsat do D&P
         Undo-Inference(-L)
       Return(unsat)
       End
```

5   Selecting Unit Clauses

As it is well known, the rapidity of the D&P scheme increases if one chooses literals from unitary clauses (L) in step 3. The intuitive reason is that the subsequent search with the CPI branch corresponding to the complemented literal $CPI \cup \{-L\}$ is trivially unsatisfiable and therefore it is not executed.

The basic idea is to take a literal from a unit clause and remove all of its complemented occurrences from the formula. These literal removals could give rise to new unit clauses. A direct generalisation of this principle is as follows: Repeat unit clause selection and its subsequent removals of its complemented literals and end when no new unit clauses are generated; if an empty clause is produced indicate unsatisfiability.

Efficient implementations of this strategy, called unit propagation can be found in [7,3]. In [17,16] a somewhat different principle is suggested which is claimed to improve the one proposed in [7,3].

In order to embed properly the Unit-propagation procedure in our D&P, we add two data structures: CPI(L) whose function is $CPI(L) = Yes$ iff $L \in CPI$ and a list called Computed.units, containing the list of emerged literals in unit clauses throughout the Unit.propagation process.

Procedure 5 Unit-propagation *Computed.units is a local variable meanwhile* unit *is a set of literals initialised in the initialisation procedure (once at the begining) and in D&P (in each recursive call of D&P). Inference(L) (resp. Undo-Inference(L)) includes the instruction: CPI(L) ← Yes (resp and CPI(L) ← Not).*

Unit.Propagation
```
  flag ← SAT; Computed.units ← ∅
  While unit ≠ ∅ and flag=SAT do:
    L ← pop(unit); Inference(L); Add L to Computed.units
  If flag ≠ SAT then do:
      ∀L, L ∈ computed.units do: Undo-Inference(L)
    Ret(unsat)
  Else Return(Computed.units)
End
```

Theorem 3. Literal Soundness *If L is pushed into unit then $\Gamma \models L$.*

Theorem 4. Soundness. *If Unit-propagation returns unsat then Γ is unsatisfiable.*

Theorem 5. Literal completeness. *$\Gamma \models L$ iff L is pushed in unit.*

Theorem 6. Completeness. *If Γ is a Horn unsatisfiable instance then Unit-propagation returns Unsat.*

Theorem 7. Correctness. *If Γ is a Horn instance then Unit.propagation returns Unsat iff Γ is unsatisfiable.*

Theorem 8. Linear Complexity. *Unit.propagation ends in $O(\text{size}(\Gamma))$ time.*

Next, we detail the D&P algorithm improved with the unit-propagation strategy.

Algorithm 3 D&P algorithm. *Computed.units is a local variable. The procedure Inference(L) (resp. Undo-Inference) set CPI(L) to Yes, push L into unit and call successively Remove.Clauses(L) and Remove.Literals(-L) (resp. undo all these operations).*

<pre>
Inference(L)   Undo-Inference(L)
   CPI(L) ← Yes   CPI(L) ← Not
   push(unit,L)   Restore-clauses(L)
   Remove-clauses(L)   Restore-literals(-L)
   return(Remove-literals(-L))   End
End
</pre>

D&P
```
   L ← Pick.literal
   If Inference(L) ≠ unsat do:
      Computed.units ← Unit-propagation
      If computed.units ≠ unsat do: D&P
      ∀L' ∈ Computed.units do: Undo-Inference(L')
   Undo-Inferencia(L)
   If Inference(-L) ≠ unsat do:
      Computed.units ← Unit-propagation
      If computed.units ≠ unsat do: D&P
      ∀L' ∈ Computed.units do: Undo-Inference(L')
   Undo-Inferencia(-L)
   Return(unsat)
End
```

It is well known that the integration of Unit.propagation procedure in the D&P scheme is capital to get a good complexity for Horn instances. This will be dealt with in the last section.

Theorem 9. *The D&P algorithm above returns unsat iff Γ is unsatisfiable.*

The proof follows from the theorem 2 (previous D&P correctness), the theorems 3 to 6 (Unit-propagation correctness) and the description of the algorithm above.

6   Detection of Polarised Formulas

In this section, we introduce some notions to speed up the satisfiability test with a new inference rule.

Definition 1. Polarised formulas *We say that a formula has positive (resp. negative) polarity if each clause has at least one positive (negative) literal. Formulas with polarity will be called polarised formulas.*

Corollary 1. Polarised satisfiability. *A polarised formula is trivially satisfiable.*

Indeed, a model is obtained by assigning 0 (resp. 1) to each propositional variable of a negative (resp. positive) polarised formula. Thus, in front of a polarised formula, we can save a large deal of running time by avoiding subsequent splitting rules till non-empty satisfied clauses are obtained. Next, we propose some data structure and algorithmic operations to detect polarised formulas. We prove that this detection is performed in constant time $O(1)$ and hence a significant improvement is achieved in testing the satisfiability of formulas.

The previous counter counter(C) of literals of a clause C is substituted by two counters. Similarly for the formula, counter(Γ) is now separated into two counters. Thus, we have the following data structure:

- For each clause C: pos.counter(C) (resp. neg.counter(C)) indicates the number of positive (resp. negative) literals in C not satisfied by the CPI.
- For the formula Γ: neg.counter(Γ) and pos.counter(Γ) indicate respectively the number of positive and negative clauses unsatisfied by the CPI.

The updated Remove.clauses(L) and Remove.literals(L) are:

Remove.clauses(L)

```
New.sat.clauses ← ∅
∀C ∈ clauses(L) do:
  If state(C)=unsat then do:
    Add C to new.sat.clauses(L)
    state(C) ← sat
    If neg.counter(C)=0 do: decrement pos.counter(Γ)
    If pos.counter(C)=0 do: decrement neg.counter(Γ)
    If pos.counter(Γ)=0 or neg.counter(Γ)=0 then HALT(Sat)
End
```

Remove.literals(L)

```
UNSAT ← False
∀C ∈ clauses(L) do:
  If L=p do: decr. pos.counter(C)
  If L=-p do: decr. neg.counter(C)
  If pos.counter(C)=0 and neg.counter(C)>0 do:
    increment neg.counter(Γ)
```

```
    If pos.counter(C)>0 and neg.counter(C)=0 do:
      increment pos.counter(Γ)
    If pos.counter(C)=0 and neg.counter(C)=0 do: UNSAT ← True
    If pos.counter(C) + neg.counter(C)=1 do:
      Search for L' s.t. CPI(L')=CPI(-L')=Not
      push(L',unit)
  If UNSAT return(unsat) Else return(sat)
End
```

Similarly, the corresponding procedures Restore.Clauses(L) and Restore.Clauses(L) are easily adapted according to the new operations integrated in the two procedures Remove. Together with this, the new data structures, namely neg.counter(C), pos.counter(C), pos.counter(Γ) and neg.counter(Γ), need to be appropriately initialised.

Algorithm 4 *The definitive D&P algorithm is as the previous one defined in section 6, simply substituting the functions in section 4 by those described here above.*

Theorem 10. D&P correctness. *The algorithm 4 returns unsat iff Γ is unsatisfiable.*

7   Some Worst-Case Complexity of the D&P Scheme

Henceforth, we shall write "D&P" instead of "the definitive D&P algorithm 4".
    The polarised rule inference is capital to perform the following complexity behaviours.

Theorem 11. Horn Instances. *D&P is strictly linear for Horn instances.*

Theorem 12. 2-SAT instances. *D&P is strictly linear for the 2-SAT problem.*

Proof sketch. The following facts are at the nucleus of the theorem proof:
(1) When a literal L is selected then Unit.propagation(L) is executed.
(2) Unit.propagation(L) ends when no unit resolution is applicable.
(3) Unit.propagation(L) stops after having removed some binary clauses.
(4) The original formula is satisfiable iff the remaining set of binary clauses is satisfiable.
(5) There is at most one backtracking point corresponding to the branch -L.
(6) The total running time is at most proportional to $2.size(\Gamma)$.

8   Conclusion

In this article, we have studied deeply the D&P scheme in order to design an efficient algorithm for the Satisfiability problem. Our main results have been:
(1) To design an appropriate non-complex data structure to perform efficiently

the inferences; (2) to furnish a new sound inference rule called Polarised Formula; (3) to analyse several worst case behaviours of the proposed algorithm and; (4) to demonstrate that an algorithm stemmed from the D&P scheme can run, on certain tractable instances of high interest in practical applications, as fast as the published algorithms specially designed for dealing with only such tractable classes. Thus, we enhance the theoretical virtues of the D&P method for propositional theorem proving.

Acknowledgements

We thanks R. Lanoligro for his helpful comments on a previous version of this article. This work has been supported by the project TAP 99-1086-C03-02.

References

1. G. Ausiello and G. F. Italiano. Online algorithms for poly normally solvable satisfiability problems. *Journal of Logic Programming,* 10(1), 1991. 261
2. C. M.Li and Anbulagan. Heuristics based on unit propagation for satisfiability problems. In *Proceedings of the 15th IJCAI,* pages 366-371, 1997. 261
3. J. M. Crawford and L. D. Auton. Experimental results on the crossover point in satisfiability problems. In *Proc. of the Eleventh National Conference on Artificial Intelligence, AAAI-93,* pages 21-27, 1993. 261, 266
4. M. Davis, G. Logemann, and D. Loveland. A machine program for theorem proving. *Comunnications of the ACM,* 5:394-397, 1962. 261
5. M. Davis and H. Putnam. A computing procedure for quantification theory. *Journal of the ACM,* 7:394-397, 1960. 261
6. G. Davydov, I. Davydova, and H. K. Buning. An efficient algorithm for the minimal unsatisfiability problem for a classe of cnf. *Annals of Mathematics and Artificial Intelligence,* 23:229-245, 1998. 262
7. R. Dechter and I. Rish. Rirectional resolution: the davis and putnam procedure revisited. In *Proceedings of Knowledge Representattion International Conference, KR-94,* pages 134-145, 1994. 266
8. W. F. Dowling and J. H. Gallier. Linear-time algorithms for testing the satisfiability of horn prepositional formulae. *Journal of Logic Programming,* 3:267-284, 1984. 261
9. D. Dubois, P. Andre, Y. Boufkhad, and J. Carlier. Sat versus unsat. In *Proceedings of the Second DIMACS Challenge,* 1993. 262
10. Z. Galil. On the complexity of Regular Resolution and the Davis-Putnam procedure. *Theoretical Computer Sicence,* 4:23-46, 1977. 261
11. J. N. Hooker and V. Vinay. Branching rules for satisfiability. *Journal of Automated Reasoning,* 15:359-383, 1995. 261
12. J. M. Crawford and L. D. Auton. Experimental Results on the Crossover Point in random 3-SAT. *Artificial Intelligence,* 81:31-57, 1996. 261
13. R. E. Jeroslow and J. Wang. Solving prepositional satisfiability problems. *Annals of Mathematics and Artificial Intelligence,* 1:167-187, 1990. 261
14. H. Kautz and B. Selman. Planing as satisfiability. In *Proceeding of the 10th ECAI,* pages 359-363. European Conference on Artificial Intelligence, 1992. 261, 262

15. A. Rauzy. Polynomial restrictions of sat: What ca be done with an efficient implementation of the davis and putnam's procedure. In U. Mntanari and F. Rossi, editors, *Principles and Practice of Constraint Programming, CP'95,* volume 976 of *Lecture Notes in Computer Science,* pages 515-532. Fisrt International Conference on Principles and Practice of Constraint Programming, Cassis, France, Springer-verlag, 1995. 261

16. T. E. Tarjan. Amortized computational complexity. *SIAM J. Algebraic Discrete Methods,* 6:306-318, 1985. 261, 266

17. H. Zhang. Sato: An efficient prepositional prover. In *proceedings of the 13th Conference on Automated Deduction,* pages 272-275, 1997. 261, 266

18. H. Zhang and M. E. Stickel. An efficient algorithm for unit propagation. In *International Symposium on Artificial Intelligence and Mathematics,* 1996.

19. H Zhang and M. E. Stickel. Implementing the davis-putnam algorithm by tries. Technical report, The University of Iowa, 1994.

Combining Local Search and Constraint Propagation to Find a Minimal Change Solution for a Dynamic CSP

Nico Roos, Yongping Ran, and Jaap van den Herik

Universiteit Maastricht , Institute for Knowledge and Agent Technology,
P.O. Box 616, 6200 MD Maastricht
http://www.cs.unimaas.nl/

Abstract. Many hard practical problems such as Time Tabling and Scheduling can be formulated as Constraint Satisfaction Problems. For these CSPs, powerful problem-solving methods are available. However, in practice, the problem definition may change over time. Each separate change may invoke a new CSP formulation. The resulting sequence of CSPs is denoted as a Dynamic CSP.

A valid solution of one CSP in the sequence need not be a solution of the next CSP. Hence it might be necessary to solve every CSP in the sequence forming a DCSP. Successive solutions of the sequence of CSPs can differ quite considerably. In practical environments large differences between successive solutions are often undesirable. To cope with this hindrance, the paper proposes a *repair-based* algorithm, i.e., a Local Search algorithm that systematically searches the neighborhood of an infringed solution to find a new nearby solution. The algorithm combines *local search* with *constraint propagation* to reduce its time complexity.

1 Introduction

Many hard practical problems such as Time Tabling and Scheduling can successfully be solved by formulating these problems as Constraint Satisfaction Problems. This success can be contributed to three factors: (i) formulating a problem as a CSP does not force us to relax any of the problem requirements; (ii) there are efficient general-purpose solution methods available for CSPs; (iii) known mathematical properties of the problem requirements can be used to speed up the search process by pruning the search space.

Despite of this success, using a CSP formulation in a dynamic environment is not without disadvantages. The main obstacle is that in a dynamic environment, the problem definition may change over time. For instance, machines may break down, employees can become ill and the earliest delivery time of material may change. Hence, a solution of a CSP need no longer be valid after a condition of the problem definition has been changed. To describe these changing CSPs, Dechter and Dechter [2] introduced the notion of Dynamic CSPs (DCSP). A DCSP can be viewed as a sequence of static CSPs, describing different situations over time.

S. A. Cerri and D. Dochev (Eds.): AIMSA 2000, LNAI 1904, pp. 272–282, 2000.
© Springer-Verlag Berlin Heidelberg 2000

In a DCSP, an operational solution may be infringed when a new situation arises. So, we have a problem statement and a complete value assignment to the variables for which some constraints are now violated.

When a previously correct solution is no longer valid, a new solution must be generated. The most simple way to do this is by generating a new solution from scratch. This is however, not always what we want. First, we may have to repeat a large amount of work spent to solve the previous CSP. Several proposals to handle this problem have been made [1, 5, 7, 8]. Second, a meaningful obstacle is that a new solution might be completely different from the previous one. If, for example, the problem at hand is scheduling of people working in a hospital, then such an approach may result in changing all the night shifts, weekend shifts and corresponding compensation days of all employees just because someone became ill. Since people must also be able to plan their private lives, this will definitely result in commotion among the unpleased employees.

Instead of creating a whole new solution, we should try to repair the infringed solution. Here, the goal is to move from a candidate solution that violates some constraints because of an unforeseen incident, to a nearby solution that meets the constraints. What is considered *nearby* may depend on the application domain.

Whether a new solution is nearby the infringed solution is determined by the *cost* of changing to the new solution. In our experiments, the cost of changing to a new solution is determined by the *number* of variables that are assigned a new value. Notice that the presented algorithm is also suited for other ways of assigning costs. For instance, we could use the weighted distances between the new and the old values assigned to each variable, the importance of the variables that must change their value, and so on.

Verfaillie and Schiex [9] have proposed a solution method for DCSPs that explores the neighborhood of a previously correct solution. They start by unassigning one variable for each violated constraint. On the set of unassigned variables, they subsequently apply a *constructive CSP solution method*, such as backtracking search with forward checking. This solution method may make new assignments that are inconsistent with the still assigned variables. When this happens, they repeat the solution method: for each violated constraint one of the still assigned variables will be unassigned. Clearly, this approach may choose the wrong variables to be unassigned, resulting in a sub-optimal solution with respect to the distance to the starting point, the infringed solution.

Local Search is a solution method that moves from one candidate solution to a nearby candidate solution [4]. Unfortunately, there is no guarantee that it will find the most nearby solution. In fact Local Search may also wander off in the wrong direction. Another problem with using Local Search is the speed of the search process. Local Search does not use something like constraint propagation to reduce the size of the search space. The search space is completely determined by the number of variables and the number of values that can be assigned to the variables.

What we wish to have is a solution method that can *systematically* search the neighborhood of the infringed solution, taking advantage of the powerful constraint propagation methods. In this paper we will show that such a repair-based approach is possible. The proposed approach combines Local Search with Constraint Propagation.

The remainder of this paper is organized as follows. Section 2 defines the Constraint Satisfaction Problem. Section 3 presents a repair-based approach for CSPs and Section 4 specifies the algorithm. Section 5 provides some formal results and Section 6 describes the experimental results. Section 7 discusses related work and Section 8 concludes the paper.

2   Preliminaries

We consider a CSP consisting of (1) a set of variables, (2) for each variable a set of domain values that can be assigned to the variable, and (3) a set of constraints over the variables.

Definition 1. *A constraint satisfaction problem is a triple* $\langle \mathcal{V}, \mathcal{D}, \mathcal{C} \rangle$.

- $\mathcal{V} = \{v_1, ... v_n\}$ *is a set of variables.*
- $\mathcal{D} = \{D_{v_1}, ..., D_{v_n}\}$ *is a set of domains.*
- $\mathcal{C}$ *is a set of constraints. A constraint*

$$c_{v_{i_1}, ..., v_{i_k}} : D_{v_{i_1}} \times ... \times D_{v_{i_k}} \rightarrow \{\mathsf{true}, \mathsf{false}\}$$

is a mapping to true or false for an instance of $D_{v_{i_1}} \times ... \times D_{v_{i_k}}$.

We can assign values to the variables of a CSP.

Definition 2. *An assignment* $a : \mathcal{V} \rightarrow \bigcup \mathcal{D}$ *for a CSP* $\langle \mathcal{V}, \mathcal{D}, \mathcal{C} \rangle$ *is a function that assigns values to variables. For each variable* $v \in \mathcal{V}$: $a(v) \in D_v$.

We are of course interested in assignments that are solutions for a CSP.

Definition 3. *Let* $\langle \mathcal{V}, \mathcal{D}, \mathcal{C} \rangle$ *be a CSP and let* $a : \mathcal{V} \rightarrow \bigcup \mathcal{D}$ *be an assignment.* a *is a solution for the CSP if and only if for each* $c_{v_{i_1}, ..., v_{i_k}} \in \mathcal{C}$:

$$c_{v_{i_1}, ..., v_{i_k}}(a(v_{i_1}), ..., a(v_{i_k})) = \mathsf{true}.$$

3   Ideas behind Repair-Based CSP Solving

The problem we have to solve is the following. We have a CSP $\langle \mathcal{V}, \mathcal{D}, \mathcal{C} \rangle$ and an assignment a that assigns values to all variables. The assignment used to satisfy all constraints, but because of an incident some constraints have changed or new constraints have been added. As a result the assignment a no longer satisfies all constraints. Now we have to find a new assignment satisfying the constraints. The cost of changing the infringed solution to the new solution must, however, be minimal. We assume that the cost of changing to a new solution can be expressed as the sum of the costs of changing a single variable. Moreover, we assume that these costs are non-negative. The cost of no change is of course 0.

Since some of the constraints are violated, at least some of the variables involved in these constraints must change their values. To illustrate the idea of repair-based CSP solving, let us assume that a unary constraint has been added and that the value assigned to the variable v is not consistent with this new constraint. Clearly, we must find a new assignment for v. If there exists a value in the domain of v that is consistent with the new constraint and with all other constraints of the CSP, then we can assign this value to v. However as Murphy's law predicts: this will often not be the case. So, what can we do?

The goal is to find the most nearby solution such that all constraints are satisfied. This requires a systematic exploration of the search space. If we fail to find a solution by changing the assignment of one variable, we must look at changing the assignment of two variables. If this also fails, we go to three variables, and so on. Hence, we must search the neighborhood of the variable v using an *iterative deepening* strategy.

Let us return to the general case. Let X be the set of variables involved in the constraints that do not hold.

$$X = \bigcup_{c_{v_{i_1},\dots,v_{i_k}} \in \mathcal{C}, c_{v_{i_1},\dots,v_{i_k}}(a(v_{i_1}),\dots,a(v_{i_k}))=\mathsf{false}} \{v_{i_1},\dots,v_{i_k}\}$$

Obviously, at least one of the variables in X must get a new value. So, we can start investigating whether changing the assignment of one variable in X enables us to satisfy all constraints. If no such variable can be found then there are two possibilities.

- At least one of the other variables in X must also be assigned another value. This is the case if

$$\bigcap_{c_{v_{i_1},\dots,v_{i_k}} \in \mathcal{C}, c_{v_{i_1},\dots,v_{i_k}}(a(v_{i_1}),\dots,a(v_{i_k}))=\mathsf{false}} \{v_{i_1},\dots,v_{i_k}\} = \emptyset.$$

Hence, we must investigate changing the assignment of two variables in X.
- There is an assignment to a variable v in X such that all constraints between the variables of X are satisfied, but for which a constraint $c_{v_{i_1},\dots,v_{i_k}}$ with $v \in \{v_{i_1},\dots,v_{i_k}\}$ and $\{v_{i_1},\dots,v_{i_k}\} \not\subseteq X$, is not satisfied.

In both cases we must try to find a solution by changing the assignment of two variables. In the former case it is sufficient to consider the variables in X for this purpose. In the latter case we must also consider the neighboring variables of X. The reason is that for any assignment satisfying the constraints over X, there is a constraint over variables in X and variables in $\mathcal{V} - X$ that does not hold. We can determine the variables in $\mathcal{V} - X$ after assigning a variable in X a new value, by recalculating X and subsequently removing the variables that have been assigned a new value.

We can conclude that to find a nearby solution, we should assign new values to variables of a set X. The number of variables that should be assigned a new value is increased gradually until we find a solution. Furthermore, the set of variables X that are candidates for change is determined dynamically.

Reducing the time complexity Considering several sets of variables to which we are going to assign a new value is a first source of extra overhead. If we are going to change the values of n variables from a set X containing m candidate variables, we need to consider $\binom{m}{n}$ different subsets of X where each subset is a separate CSP. Since this number can be exponential in m (depending on the ratio between m and n) the number of CSPs we may have to solve is $\mathcal{O}(2^m)$, where each CSP has a worst time complexity that is exponential. This would make it impossible to use a repair-based approach.

There is also a second source of extra overhead in the search process. If we fail to find a solution changing only n variables, we try it for some larger value $n' > n$. Clearly, when changing n' variables we must repeat all the steps of the search process for changing only n variables. This second source of overhead can, however, be neglected in comparison with the first source of overhead.

Constraint propagation can be used to speed up the search process in constructive solution methods by pruning the search space. We will investigate whether it can also be used to avoid solving an exponential number of CSPs. If we could use constraint propagation to determine variables that *must* be assigned a new value, we may avoid solving a substantial amount of CSPs. We could do this by determining the domain values of the variable that are allowed by the constraints, independent of the original assignment. If a variable is assigned a value that is no longer allowed, we know that it must be assigned a new value.

In the same way we can also determine a better lower bound for the number of variables that must change their current value. Thereby we reduce the second source of overhead. The following example gives an illustration of how constraint propagation helps us to reduce both forms of overhead.

Example Let u, v, w be three variables and let $D_u = \{1, 2\}$, $D_v = \{1, 2\}$ and $D_w = \{1, 2\}$ be the corresponding domains. Furthermore, let there be not equal constraints between the variables u and v and between v and w, and let $a(u) = 1$, $a(v) = 2$ and $a(w) = 1$ be an assignment satisfying the constraints.

Now, because of some incident a unary constraint $c_w = (w \neq 1)$ is added. If we enforce arc-consistency on the domains D_u, D_v, D_w using the constraints, we get the following reduced domains $\delta_u = \{2\}$, $\delta_v = \{1\}$ and $\delta_w = \{2\}$. From these reduced domains it immediately follows that all three variables must be assigned a new value. So there is no point in investigating whether we can find a solution by changing one or two variables. Furthermore, we do not have to consider which variables must change their values.

After changing the values of the three variables, there might be constraints that are no longer satisfied. Now, using the new assignments made, we can try, using constraint propagation, to determine the other variables that must also be assigned a new value. The algorithm (called by the procedure 'solve (V, D, C, a)') presented in the next section implements the idea of combining local search (in 'find (F, i, U, X, Y)') and constraint propagation (in 'assign_and_find (v, F, i, Y)').

4   Implementation

Let V be a set of variables, D be an array of containing a domain for each variable, C be a set of constraints and a be an array containing an assignment. Then the procedure 'solve (V, D, C, a)' is used to find a nearby solution.

In the algorithm, all arguments of the procedures are based on *call by value*. The procedure 'constraint_propagation (F)' applies constraint propagation on the future variables F given the new assignments made to the past variables and the current variable v. The function 'cost (v, d, o)' specifies the cost of changing the value o of the variable v to the value d. The minimum cost of changing the values of all the variables in U given their current domains D and current assignments a is given by the function 'set_cost (U, D, a)'. The constant 'max_cost' denotes the maximum cost of changing the infringed solution. The function 'conflict_var (C, a)' determines the variables involved in a constraint violation. The variables m, u, C and D are global variables. Finally, the set of variables Y is used to represent the CSP variables for which new assignments have been tried without success.

```
procedure solve (V, D, C, a)
  solved := false;
  X := conflict_var (C, a);
  constraint_propagation (V);
  U := {v ∈ V | a[v] ∉ D[v]};
  X := X ∪ U;
  m := set_cost (U, D, a);
  u := max_cost;
  while not solved and m ≤ max_cost do
    find (V, 0, U, X, ∅);
    m := u;
    u := max_cost;
  end;
end.


procedure find (F, c, U, X, Y)
  if U ≠ ∅ then
    v := select_variable (U);
    assign_and_find (v, F − {v}, c, Y);
  else
    while not solved and X ≠ ∅ do
      v := select_variable (X);
      X := X − {v};
      assign_and_find (v, F − {v}, c, Y);
      Y := Y ∪ {v};
    end;
  end;
end.
```

```
procedure assign_and_find (v, F, c, Y)
  save_domain (D[v]);
  o := a[v];
  D[v] := D[v] − {o};
  while not solved and D[v] ≠ ∅ do
    d := select_value (D[v]);
    D[v] := D[v] − {d};
    a[v] := d;
    c := c+ cost (v, d, o);
    save_domains_of (F);
    constraint_propagation (F);
    if not an_empty_domain (F) then
      U := {v ∈ F | a[v] ∉ D[v]};
      X := U∪ conflict_var (C, a);
      if X = ∅ then
        solved := true;
        output (a);
      else if c+ set_cost (U, D, a) ≤ m
      and U ∩ Y = ∅ then
        find (F, c, U, (F ∩ X) − Y, Y);
      else if U ∩ Y = ∅ then
        u := min(u, c+set_cost (U, D, a));
      end;
    end;
    restore_domains_of (F);
  end;
  a[v] := o;
  restore_domain (D[v]);
end.
```

$$\text{conflict\_var } (\mathcal{C}, a) := \bigcup_{c_{v_{i_1}},...,v_{i_k} \in \mathcal{C}, c_{v_{i_1}},...,v_{i_k}(a[v_{i_1}],...,a[v_{i_k}])=\text{false}} \{v_{i_1}, ..., v_{i_k}\}$$

$$\text{set\_cost } (U, D, a) := \sum_{v \in U} \min\{\text{cost } (v, d, a[v]) \mid d \in D[v]\}$$

5   Formal Results

The following theorem guarantees that the above algorithm finds the most nearby solution if a solution exists.

Theorem 1. [1] *Let $\langle \mathcal{V}, \mathcal{D}, \mathcal{C} \rangle$ be a CSP and let $a : \mathcal{V} \to \bigcup \mathcal{D}$ be an assignment for the variables.*

The algorithm will find a solution for the CSP by changing the current assignment for the least number of variables in $\mathcal{V}$.

In the example of Section 3, we have illustrated that the algorithm reduces the search overhead by applying constraint propagation. We will now present a result that shows that all overhead can completely be eliminated in case unary constraints are added to a solved instance of a CSP. Since in many practical situations calamities such as the unavailability of resources or the lateness of supplies, can be described by unary constraints, this result is very important.

Proposition 1. [1] *Let $\langle \mathcal{V}, \mathcal{D}, \mathcal{C} \rangle$ be a CSP containing only unary and binary constraints and let the assignment a be a solution.*

If we create a new CSP by adding only unary constraints to the original constraints, then using node-consistency *in the procedure 'solve' and* forward checking *in the procedure 'assign_and_find' avoid considering more than one subset of X.*

The above proposition implies that repairing a solution after adding unary constraints to a CSP will in the worst case have a complexity $\mathcal{O}(T^2)$ where T is the complexity of solving the CSP from scratch. Using constraint propagation such as arc-consistency or better can bring the complexity close to $\mathcal{O}(T)$. If, however, binary constraints are added, the situation changes. If the current solution does not satisfy the added binary constraint, one of the two variables of the constraint must be assigned a new value, and possibly both. Since we do not know which one, both possibilities will be investigated till a new solution is found. This implies that the repair time will double with respect to adding a unary constraint. In general, if T' is the average time needed to repair a solution after adding a unary constraint, then $\binom{2 \cdot m}{m} \cdot T'$ is an upper bound for the average time needed to repair a solution after adding m binary constraints.

6   Experimental Results

The viability of the presented algorithm is best shown by comparing the repair-based approach (RB-AC) with the constructive approach (AC) by the number of

---
[1] Due to space limitations the proofs have been left out.

nodes visited and the number of variables changed. The algorithms used in the comparison both apply *arc-consistency* during constraint propagation.

We have conducted two sets of test, both with randomly generated CSPs. In both tests, the cost of changing the assignment of one variable of the infringed solution is 1. Therefore, the total cost of a new solution is equal to the number of variables that are assigned a new value. To generate the test problems, we used the four-tuple $\langle n, d, p_1, p_2 \rangle$. Here, n denotes the number of variables of the generated CSPs, d the domain size of each variable, p_1 the probability that there is a binary constraint between two variables and p_2 the conditional probability that a pair of values is allowed by a constraint given that there is a constraint between two variables. For several values of n and d, we have generated instances for values of p_1 and p_2 between the values 0 and 1 with step size 0.1. So, we have looked at a 100 different combinations of values for p_1 and p_2 and for each combination 10 instances have been generated randomly.

In the first set of tests, the repair-based algorithm had to find a solution for a CSP nearby a randomly-generated value assignment for the variables. This test presents the worst possible scenario for the repair-based algorithm since in most cases many constraints will be violated by the generated assignment. As we saw in the previous section, if T' is the average time needed to repair a solution after adding a unary constraint, then $\binom{2 \cdot m}{m} \cdot T'$ is an upper bound for the average time needed to repair a solution after adding m binary constraints. For example, the results contained a CSP instance with 10 variables, each having a domain with 10 values, and with $p_1 = 0.6$ and $p_2 = 0.7$, that was solved without backtracking using backtrack search with arc-consistency. The repair-based algorithm with arc-consistency visited 40521 nodes to find a solution.

In the second set of tests, we first solved the generated CSP. Subsequently, we added a unary constraint defined as follows. Choose randomly a variable, delete from the set of domain values half of the number of values, the current value (as in the solution) inclusive. We have conducted the second set of tests for the following values of n and d: $(10, 10)$, $(20, 10)$ and $(50, 20)^2$ The figures below show some typical results. Note that the repair-based algorithm visits more nodes than the constructive algorithm. The overhead is caused by the iterative deepening part of the repair-based algorithm.

7   Related Work

Below we discuss three distinct types of related work. First, as stated above, Verfaillie and Schiex [9] proposed a repair-based method for Dynamic CSPs. Their method starts with unassigning one of the variables of each violated constraint. Subsequently they generate a new solution for the unassigned variables using a constructive search method. The new solution for the variables that were unassigned, might be inconsistent with the remaining variables. To handle this, for

---

[2] In this set of tests, many instances required more than our maximum number of 10,000,000 nodes.

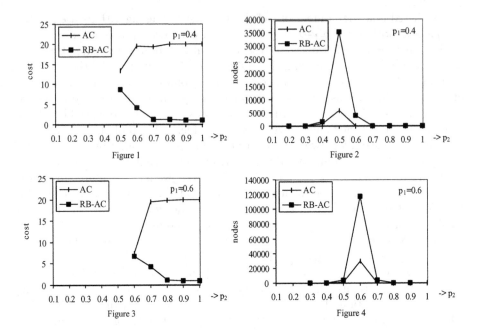

each of these violated constraints one of the remaining variables is unassigned when the constraint violation is encountered.

At first sight, the solution method proposed in this paper might be viewed as an extension of Verfaillie and Schiex's solution method. If only unary constraints are added, the set U used in the solution method proposed in this paper, corresponds in some sense with the set of unassigned variables in Verfaillie and Schiex's solution method. The fact that the variables in U are not unassigned but only change their current assignment, is not really significant.

There are, however, two very important differences. (1) Verfaillie and Schiex apply constraint propagation (forward checking) on the set of unassigned variables while we apply constraint propagation on all the variables. The latter enables an early detection of variables that must change their current assignments. (2) The set of variables that will be assigned a new value by Verfaillie and Schiex's solution method, is rather arbitrary. It depends on choices of new values to be assigned to unassigned variables. There is no way to guarantee that this will result in a nearby solution. This lack of guarantee holds even stronger if non-binary constraints are added.

Second, other approaches that have been proposed for DCSPs try to avoid repetition of work [1, 5, 7, 8]. They keep track of the reason for eliminating values from a variable's domain, possibly using reason maintenance [3], i.e., the search process remembers the position of the search process in the search tree where the previous solution was found. Furthermore, the search process can incorporate changes in the search tree caused by the addition or the removal of constraints. This makes it possible to continue the search process in the new situation without repetition of work.

Approaches for avoiding repetition of work can also be incorporated in the solution method proposed in this paper. Especially, arc-consistency for DCSPs proposed by Bessière [1], and by Neveu and Berlandier [5], can be useful for preprocessing the changed CSP. The solution reuse proposed by Verfaillie and Schiex [7, 8] does not avoid repetition of work when combined with the solution method proposed in this paper. The reason is that the approach proposed in this paper creates a search tree of possible repairs around an invalidated solution. Domain reductions caused by the value assignments to the variables described by the now invalid solution are irrelevant for this search process.

Third, a quite different approach is one that tries to avoid that solutions become invalidated in a DCSP. Wallace and Freuder [10] propose an approach that consists of determining solutions that are relatively stable under successive changes of a CSP. This stability reduces the amount of repair needed. The underlying assumption of the approach is that changes have a certain structure. This is a reasonable assumption in practical problems. The approach can also be combined with the here proposed approach to reduce the amount of repair needed.

Our approach can be viewed as a combination of local search with backtracking search and constraint propagation normally found in constructive solution methods. Schaerf [6], and Zhang & Zhang [11] have also combined local search with a constructive method. Schaerf [6] starts with a backtrack-free constructive method that uses constraint propagation, until a dead-end is reached. After reaching a dead-end local search is applied on the partial solution till a partial solution is reached with which the constructive method can continue. This process is continued till a solution is found. Zhang and Zhang [11] do it just the other way around. They start with generating a valid partial solution for the first k variables. One of the approaches that they consider for this initial phase is hill climbing. Subsequently, they try to complete the partial solution using backtracking search on the remaining variables.

What both these approaches have in common is that they combine constructive and local search technique and that they do not integrate them in one new approach.

8   Conclusion

In this paper we have presented a new algorithm for Dynamic CSPs. The merit of the new algorithm resides in the fact that it is capable to repair efficiently a solution by a minimal number of changes when the circumstances forces us to change the set of constraints. Experimental results point out that repairing a solution is much harder than creating a new solution from scratch if many non-unary constraints are violated by the solution that needs to be repaired. If, however, the original solution is infringed because of addition of a unary constraint, the repair process is not much harder than generating a new solution from scratch. The latter case arises often in practical situations where machines break and goods are delivered too late.

In our future research we intend to extend our algorithm in order to approximate nearby solutions when several k-ary constraints are added. In this way we hope to find near optimal solutions for instances that are infeasible at the moment.

References

[1] C. Bessière, 'Arc-consistency in dynamic constraint satisfaction problems', in *AAAI-91*, pp. 221–226, (1991). 273, 280, 281

[2] R. Dechter and A. Dechter, 'Belief maintenance in dynamic constraint networks', in *AAAI-88*, pp. 37–42, (1988). 272

[3] M. Ginsberg, 'Dynamic backtracking', in *Journal of Artificial Intelligence Research*, volume 1, pp. 25–46, (1993). 280

[4] S. Minton, M. D. Johnston, A. B. Philips, and P. Laird, 'Minimizing conflicts: a heuristic repair method for constraint satisfaction and scheduling problems', *Artificial Intelligence*, **58**, 161–205, (1990). 273

[5] B. Neveu and P. Berlandier, 'Arc-consistency for dynamic constraint problems: an rms-free approach', in *ECAI'94*, (1994). 273, 280, 281

[6] A. Schaerf, 'Combining local search and look-ahead for scheduling and constraint satisfaction problems', in *IJCAI-97*, pp. 1254–1259, (1997). 281

[7] G. Verfaillie and T. Schiex, 'Nogood recording for static and dynamic constraint satisfaction problems', in *Proceedings of the 5th International Conference on Tools with Artificial Intelligence*, pp. 48–55, (1993). 273, 280, 281

[8] G. Verfaillie and T. Schiex, 'Dynamic backtracking for dynamic constraint satisfaction problems', in *Proceedings of the ECAI'94 workshop on Constrint Satisfaction Issues Raised by Practical Applications*, pp. 1–8, (1994). 273, 280, 281

[9] G. Verfaillie and T. Schiex, 'Solution reuse in dynamic constraint satisfaction problems', in *AAAI-94*, pp. 307–312, (1994). 273, 279

[10] R. J. Wallace and E. C. Freuder, *Stable solutions for dynamic constraint satisfaction problems*, volume 1520 of *Lecture Notes in Computer Science*, 447–461, Springer-Verlag, 1998. 281

[11] J. Zhang and H. Zhang, 'Combining local search and backtracking techniques for constraint satisfaction', in *AAAI-96*, pp. 369–374, (1996). 281

Construction of Efficient Rulesets from Fuzzy Data through Simulated Annealing

Francisco Botana

Departamento de Matemática Aplicada, Universidad de Vigo
Campus A Xunqueira, 36005 Pontevedra, Spain
fbotana@uvigo.es

Abstract. This paper proposes a simulated annealing–based approach for obtaining compact efficient classification systems from fuzzy data. Different methods for generating decision rules from fuzzy data share a problem in multidimensional spaces: their high cardinality. In order to solve it, the method of simulated annealing is proposed. This approach is illustrated with two well-known learning sets.

1 Introduction

Rule production systems are, with decision trees, one of the five formalisms used by Quinlan [12] to divide the field of machine learning. In the fuzzy framework, fuzzy–rule–based systems have been applied mainly in control [13], and, to a less extent, in classification. Apart from the obvious way of deriving fuzzy rules from human experts, some methods for automatically generating fuzzy rules from numerical data have been proposed [14,15,7]. Another way of generating rules from fuzzy data consists of going back to the meaning of the implication. From a set–theoretic point of view, the implication $A \to B$ is true if, and only if, $\forall x, x \in A \to x \in B$, that is, $A \subset B$. Fuzzy set theory has a wide class of measures of containment. So, measuring the containment between A and B, we can describe the strength between a set of fuzzy constraints A and a conclusion B.

Independently of the method used to generate the rules, there is a problem common to all of them. The generated set of rules will usually have high cardinality. In order to select a compact and efficient subset of the rules, a method of stochastic search like simulated annealing can be used. This paper addresses this question.

The paper is organized as follows: Section 2 introduces classification systems with fuzzy data, and we describe various approaches to the problem of rule generation. Section 3 summarizes the simulated annealing technique and describes its application to construct compact efficient rulesets from generated rules. In Section 4, simulation results for two well–known problems of classification are shown to illustrate the proposed approach. Finally, Section 5 concludes this paper.

S. A. Cerri and D. Dochev (Eds.): AIMSA 2000, LNAI 1904, pp. 283–291, 2000.

2   Classification Systems

Let X be the universe of objects. Each object is described by a collection of attributes $A = \{A_1, \ldots, A_n\}$. Each attribute A_i measures a feature of an object and has a discrete domain of values $v_{i_1}, \ldots, v_{i_m}$. We assume that an object can have non-zero membership to different values of each attribute. The membership function of the objects in an attribute-value pair $[A_i : v_{i_j}]$ is thus a function

$$\mu_{[A_i : v_{i_j}]} : X \to [0, 1] \ . \tag{1}$$

Each object belongs in some degree to every class of a set $C = \{c_1, \ldots, c_l\}$. So, a known object of the universe, an example, is defined by a fixed–length vector such as

$$(([A_1 : v_{i_1}], \mu_{1 i_1}), \ldots, ([A_1 : v_{i_{m_1}}], \mu_{1 i_{m_1}}), \ldots, (c_1, \mu_{c_1}), \ldots, (c_l, \mu_{c_l})) \ . \tag{2}$$

This vector has a number of components given by the addition of the cardinalities of the attributes and the classes.

2.1   Rule Generation

A classification rule is an if–then statement whose antecedent is a conjunction of attribute-value pairs and the consequent is a class

$$[A_r : v_{r_-}], \ldots, [A_s : v_{s_-}] \to c_p \ . \tag{3}$$

As stated in the Introduction, some methods for automatically generating rules have been reported. For the sake of simplicity, we will assume a two–input one–output system. In [15], the variables x_1, x_2, y are discretized in possibly overlapping categories. Each input–output data pair

$$((x_1^1, x_2^1), y^1) \tag{4}$$

produces a rule

$$[A_1 : C_{x_1^1}], [A_2 : C_{x_2^1}] \to C_{y^1} \ , \tag{5}$$

where $C_{y^1}, C_{x_1^1}, C_{x_2^1}$ are the variable categories for which the membership of the values is the greatest.

A partition of the space of objects by a simple fuzzy grid is used in [7] for generating the rules. Each element of the partition gives rise to a rule. The coordinates of the element are the rule antecedents. Its class can be defined euristically taking the most probable one in this element.

Another way for generating rules from fuzzy data [2] goes back to the meaning of the implication. When dealing with crisp noise–free data an error–free rule such as $p_1, p_2 \to c$ can be inferred if the extension of $p_1 \cap p_2$ is contained in that of c. A direct translation into the fuzzy case, using the containment definition proposed by Zadeh, leads to reject rules where just a case does not fulfill the implication. Fuzzyfying the notion of set–containment [9,3] and discretizing the attribute space, a rule for each possible combination of antecedents can be formed. The rule class is the one which best contains the intersection of the fuzzy antecedents.

2.2   Classification of New Objects

In order to classify an object from a set of rules, we proceed as follows: for each rule, we calculate the membership of the antecedent. The membership of the consequent will be set equal to that one. If there is more than one rule that predicts a class, take the highest membership. So, in general, a ruleset will classify an object in all classes with different membership. An object will be correctly classified if its known class with the highest membership equals the predicted class with the highest membership.

3   The Method of Simulated Annealing

3.1   Introduction of the Algorithm

Simulated annealing is a kind of stochastic search that has its roots in metallurgy. Annealing is a technique used in the fabrication of objects made of metal or glass. When these objects are shaped, small regions of stress develop in response to deformations at the atomic level and cause the object to be prone to fracture. Annealing consists of heating the object till its atoms have sufficient energy to relax any stress, and then, cooling it slowly. If the cooling process is done properly, there will not be regions of stress.

Simulated annealing [8,4] is a method to solve combinatorial optimization problems based in the annealing of solids. The energy of the system is replaced by a cost function, and the temperature by a control parameter. The simulation consists of mimicking the evolution of the system towards its thermodynamic equilibrium, for a given value of its control parameter. The equilibrium state with a small value of the parameter is taken as the solution.

3.2   Application to the Classification Problem

The problem of classification can be stated as follows: Given a set of rules R derived from a data universe U, find the subset G with minimum cardinality such that G is the best classification ruleset for the data U.

This combinatorial optimization problem cannot be solved for optimality, due to the amounts of computation time. The set R can be very large and usually contains many local minima. However, a good local minimum found with the simulated annealing technique may be nearly as good as the global minimum. For a detailed discussion of the convergence of the algorithm see [10].

Let $R = \{r_i : i = 1, \ldots, m\}$. A configuration $conf$ of the system is any subset of R coded as a string of m bits, where a 1 in the i–th position denotes that the rule r_i is present in the configuration, otherwise 0 appears. The cost of a configuration must solve the imprecision in the statement of the problem of classification assigning a weight to each of the mentioned factors, minimum cardinality (w_{card}) or best classification ruleset (w_{clas}):

$$C(conf) = w_{clas} \cdot \#misclassified\_examples + w_{card} \cdot \#present\_rules \ . \quad (6)$$

A transition of the system from a configuration *conf* to another *newconf* is implemented randomly choosing a bit position and complementing its value.

The simulated annealing procedure is then stated in pseudocode as follows

```
begin
    repeat
        repeat
            c <- initial value of the control parameter;
            conf <- random configuration;
            newconf <- transition(conf);
            gain <- C(conf) - C(newconf);
            if gain > 0
                then conf <- newconf;
                else if exp(gain / c) > random[0,1)
                        then conf <- newconf;
        until equilibrium for c is reached;
        c <- reduce(c);
    until global equilibrium is reached
end
```

In order to fully describe the practical implementation of the algorithm there just remains to assign values to the parameter c and check whether the conditions are met. This description is referred to as a cooling schedule. The proposed schedule is:

- initial value of the control parameter.
  With the aim that almost all transitions from any starting configuration will be accepted, we begin with a usually large value for c, and perform a number of transitions. If the ratio between accepted and proposed transitions is less than 0.8, double the value of c. When this ratio exceeds 0.8, take this value of c as the initial one.
- decrement of the control parameter: $reduce(c) = 0.9c$
- reaching the equilibrium for a value of c.
  For any value of c the system is in equilibrium if at least 50 transitions are accepted.
- stop the algorithm.
  The algorithm will be halted after 25 decrements of the control parameter.

4   Experimental Results

4.1   Symbolic Data

The classification problem proposed in [11] and reformulated in [17] will be used to test our approach with non–numeric data. The classification task consists of deciding which sport to play on a Saturday morning knowing a bit of information about the weather. There are three classes {*swimming, volleyball, weight_lifting*} and mornings are characterized by four attributes with values *outlook*={*sunny, cloudy, rain*}, *temperature*={*cool, mild, hot*}, *humidity*={*high, normal*} and *wind*={*true, false*}. The fuzzy membership of each attribute-value pair and each class for 16 examples is shown in Table 1.

Table 1. The learning set used in the experiment

Ex.	Attributes										Class		
	Outlook			Temperature			Humidity		Wind				
	Sunny	Cloudy	Rain	Hot	Mild	Cool	High	Normal	True	False	Voll	Swim	Wlif
1	0.9	0.1	0.0	1.0	0.0	0.0	0.8	0.2	0.4	0.6	0.0	0.8	0.2
2	0.8	0.2	0.0	0.6	0.4	0.0	0.0	1.0	0.0	1.0	1.0	0.7	0.0
3	0.0	0.7	0.3	0.8	0.2	0.0	0.1	0.9	0.2	0.8	0.3	0.6	0.1
4	0.2	0.7	0.1	0.3	0.7	0.0	0.2	0.8	0.3	0.7	0.9	0.1	0.0
5	0.0	0.1	0.9	0.7	0.3	0.0	0.5	0.5	0.5	0.5	0.0	0.0	1.0
6	0.0	0.7	0.3	0.0	0.3	0.7	0.7	0.3	0.4	0.6	0.2	0.0	0.8
7	0.0	0.3	0.7	0.0	0.0	1.0	0.0	1.0	0.1	0.9	0.0	0.0	1.0
8	0.0	1.0	0.0	0.0	0.2	0.8	0.2	0.8	0.0	1.0	0.7	0.0	0.3
9	1.0	0.0	0.0	1.0	0.0	0.0	0.6	0.4	0.7	0.3	0.2	0.8	0.0
10	0.9	0.1	0.0	0.0	0.3	0.7	0.0	1.0	0.9	0.1	0.0	0.3	0.7
11	0.7	0.3	0.0	1.0	0.0	0.0	1.0	0.0	0.2	0.8	0.4	0.7	0.0
12	0.2	0.6	0.2	0.0	1.0	0.0	0.3	0.7	0.3	0.7	0.7	0.2	0.1
13	0.9	0.1	0.0	0.2	0.8	0.0	0.1	0.9	1.0	0.0	0.0	0.0	1.0
14	0.0	0.9	0.1	0.0	0.9	0.1	0.1	0.9	0.7	0.3	0.0	0.0	1.0
15	0.0	0.0	1.0	0.0	0.0	1.0	1.0	0.0	0.8	0.2	0.0	0.0	1.0
16	1.0	0.0	0.0	0.5	0.5	0.0	0.0	1.0	0.0	1.0	0.8	0.6	0.0

For each class there are $(3 + 3 + 2 + 2) + (3 \cdot 3 + 3 \cdot 2 + 3 \cdot 2 + 3 \cdot 2 + 2 \cdot 2) + (3 \cdot 3 \cdot 2 + 3 \cdot 2 \cdot 2 + 3 \cdot 3 \cdot 2) + 3 \cdot 3 \cdot 2 \cdot 2 = 131$ possible rules. Using a well–known fuzzy subsethood measure [9] to decide their classification, a set of 131 rules is obtained. The cost function is defined to favor the number of correctly classified examples versus the cardinality of the ruleset. So, taking into account the average number of rules in a random configuration and the size of the learning set, the selected weights are $w_{clas} = 100, w_{card} = 1$.

The results of five trials of the simulated annealing algorithm are shown in Table 2. The best result returned five rules with 13 terms that correctly classify all the learning examples:

- temperature=mild, wind=false → volleyball.
- outlook=cloudy, temperature=hot, wind=false → swimming.
- outlook=sunny, temperature=hot, humidity=high, wind=true → swimming.
- temperature=cool, wind=true → weight_lifting.
- humidity=normal, wind=true → weight_lifting.

The classification results for this set of five rules are shown in Table 3.

Table 2. Simulation results for the Sports learning set

Trial no.	Rewriting accuracy	No. of rules	No. of terms
1	15/16	6	11
2	16/16	6	17
3	15/16	5	8
4	16/16	5	13
5	16/16	8	24

These results outperform those obtained in [17] with a fuzzy ID3 strategy and in [16] with an information gain based method for deriving rules. Both approaches report a rewriting accuracy of 13/16 with 6 rules, and 11 and 9 terms, respectively.

Table 3. The Sports learning set results (best trial)

Ex.	Classification known in training data			Classification with learned rules		
	Volleyball	Swimming	Weight_lifting	Volleyball	Swimming	Weight_lifting
1	0.0	0.8	0.2	0.0	0.4	0.2
2	1.0	0.7	0.0	0.4	0.2	0.0
3	0.3	0.6	0.1	0.2	0.7	0.2
4	0.9	0.1	0.0	0.7	0.3	0.3
5	0.0	0.0	1.0	0.3	0.1	0.5
6	0.2	0.0	0.8	0.3	0.0	0.4
7	0.0	0.0	1.0	0.0	0.0	0.1
8	0.7	0.0	0.3	0.2	0.0	0.0
9	0.2	0.8	0.0	0.0	0.6	0.4
10	0.0	0.3	0.7	0.1	0.0	0.9
11	0.4	0.7	0.0	0.0	0.3	0.0
12	0.7	0.2	0.1	0.7	0.0	0.3
13	0.0	0.0	1.0	0.0	0.1	0.9
14	0.0	0.0	1.0	0.3	0.0	0.7
15	0.0	0.0	1.0	0.0	0.0	0.8
16	0.8	0.6	0.0	0.5	0.0	0.0

4.2   Iris Data

The Iris database [1] is a well–known test bench in the pattern recognition and machine learning communities. The data set contains 3 crisp classes of 50 examples each, where each class refers to a type of iris plant (*Setosa, Versicolor* and *Virginica*). There are four attributes (the length and width of plant's petal and sepal in centimeters). In Figure 1 the domains for the problem are given. Each attribute has 3 linguistic values: short/narrow, medium and long/wide.

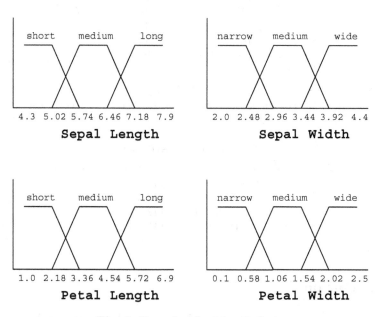

Fig. 1. Domains for iris attributes

The results of the simulated annealing technique for the Iris dataset are shown in Table 3. The number of rules is 155 and $w_{clas} = 100, w_{card} = 1$. In all trials the obtained rulesets misclassify 4 examples. The best results, regarding the number of terms, were returned in two trials:

- petal width=narrow → Setosa.
- petal length=medium, petal width=medium → Versicolor.
- petal length=long → Virginica.
- sepal length=medium, petal width=wide → Virginica.

- petal length=short → Setosa.
- petal length=medium, petal width=medium → Versicolor.
- petal width=wide → Virginica.
- sepal length=medium, petal length=long → Virginica.

The results of other algorithms on the Iris dataset are shown in Table 4 for comparison.

Table 4. Simulation results for the Iris dataset

Trial no.	Rewriting accuracy	No. of rules	No. of terms
1	146/150	4	6
2	146/150	8	17
3	146/150	4	6
4	146/150	4	7
5	146/150	6	14

Table 5. Accuracies of other algorithms on the Iris dataset

Algorithm	Accuracy
GA approach [7]	149/150
FIL [16]	144/150
GVS [6]	142/150
IVSM [5]	141/150

5   Conclusion

In this paper, we proposed a simulated–annealing–based approach to the construction of compact fuzzy classification systems with if–then rules. This approach is conceptually and computationally simple. Experimental results show that this method produce efficient rulesets, with an accuracy better than or similar to other learning systems.

References

1. Blake, C., Keogh, E., Merz, C. J. UCI Repository of machine learning databases [http://www.ics.uci.edu/~mlearn/MLRepository.html]. Irvine, CA: University of California 288
2. Botana, F.: Learning rules from fuzzy datasets. Proc. 5th Europ. Congress on Intel. Techniques and Soft Comp., Aachen, Germany (1997) 1109–1113 284
3. Botana, F.: Deriving fuzzy subsethood measures from violations of the implication between elements. Lec. Notes Artif. Intel. 1415 (1998) 234–243 284
4. Černy, V.: Thermodynamical Approach to the Traveling Salesman Problem: An Efficient Simulation Algorithm. J. Optim. Theory Appl. **45** (1985) 41–51 285
5. Hirsh, H.: Generalizing version spaces. Mach. Learning **17** (1994) 5–46 290
6. Hong, T. P., Tseng, S. S.: A generalized version space learning algorithm for noisy and uncertain data. IEEE Trans. Knowledge Data Eng **9** (1997) 336–340 290

7. Ishibuchi, H., Nozaki, K., Yamamoto, N., Tanaka, H.: Construction of fuzzy classification systems with rectangular fuzzy rules using genetic algorithms. Fuzzy Sets Syst. **65** (1994) 237–253 283, 284, 290

8. Kirpatrick,S., Gelatt, C. D., Vecchi, M. P.: Optimization by Simulated Annealing. Science **220** (1983) 671–680 285

9. Kosko, B.: Neural networks and fuzzy systems. Prentice Hall, Englewood Cliffs (1992) 284, 287

10. Laarhoven, P., Aarts, E.: Simulated Annealing: Theory and Applications. Reidel, Dordrecht (1987) 285

11. Quinlan, J. R.: Induction of decision trees. Mach. Learning **1**(1) (1986) 81–106 286

12. Quinlan, J. R.: C4.5: Programs for Machine Learning. Morgan Kaufmann, San Mateo (1993) 283

13. Sugeno, M.: An Introductory Survey of Fuzzy Control. Inf. Sci. **36** (1985) 59–83 283

14. Takagi, T., Sugeno, M.: Fuzzy Identification of Systems and its Applications to Modeling and Control. IEEE Trans. Systems Man Cybernet. **15** (1985) 116–132 283

15. Wang, L. X., Mendel, J. M.: Generating fuzzy rules by learning from examples. IEEE Trans. Systems Man Cybernet. **22** 6 (1992) 1414–1427 283, 284

16. Wang, C. H., Liu, J. F. et al.: A fuzzy inductive learning strategy for modular rules. Fuzzy Sets Syst. **103** (1999) 91–105 288, 290

17. Yuan, Y., Shaw, M. J.: Induction of fuzzy decision trees. Fuzzy Sets Syst. **69** (1995) 125–139 286, 288

Fuzzy-Neural Models for Real-Time Identification and Control of a Mechanical System

Ieroham S. Baruch[1], J. Martín Flores[1], J. Carlos Martínez[1], and Boyka Nenkova[2]

[1] CINVESTAV-IPN
Av.IPN No 2508, A.P. 14470 México D.F., C.P. 07360 México.
[2] IIT-BAS, Sofia, Bulgaria
baruch@ctrl.cinvestav.mx

Abstract. A two-layer Recurrent Neural Network Model (RNNM) and an improved Backpropagation-through-time method of its learning are described. For a complex nonlinear plants identification, a fuzzy-neural multi-model, is proposed. The proposed fuzzy-neural model, containing two RNNMs is applied for real-time identification of nonlinear mechanical system. The simulation and experimental results confirm the RNNM applicability.

1 Introduction

Recent developments in science and technology provide a wide scope of applications of high performance electric motor drives in various industrial processes. In high-performance motor drive applications involving mechatronics, such as robotics, rolling mills, machine tools, etc., an accurate speed or position control is of critical importance and there **DC**-motors are still widely used to accomplish this task. There is an increasing number of applications in high precision motion control systems in manufacturing, i.e., ultra precision machining, assembly of small components and micro drives It is very difficult to assure high positioning accuracy due to many factors affecting the precision of motion, such as friction, backlash and stiffness in the drive system, [13,11]. Friction is a natural resistance to relative motion between two contacting bodies. The friction model has been widely studied by numerous researchers. Extensive work can be found in [1,4,7] and [8]. It is commonly modelled as a linear combination of Coulomb friction, stiction, viscous friction, and Stribeck effect. The presence of nonlinear friction forces is unavoidable in high performance motion control system. In servo systems, if the controller is designed without consideration of the friction, the closed-loop system may show steady-state tracking error and/or oscillations. In addition, the friction characteristics may change easily due to the environment's changes like load variations, temperature and humidity changes, and some dynamic effects could be observed . So the standard **PID** type servo

S. A. Cerri and D. Dochev (Eds.): AIMSA 2000, LNAI 1904, pp. 292–300, 2000.

control algorithm is not capable of delivering the desire precision under the influence of friction. The friction compensation is not an easy problem as the friction function is highly nonlinear non-monotonic function. Some early works proposed to use an additive high frequency signal at near to zero velocity control for nonlinear friction effects linearization. Other researchers proposed to compensate the friction effects by means of adaptive schemes. In [9], adaptive control was explored for the positioning of table with friction. A nonlinear compensation technique which has a nonlinear proportional feedback control force for the regulation of one degree of freedom mechanical system was proposed by [8]. Adaptive friction compensation for **DC**-motor drives and robot control systems are given by [13] and [11]. Some advanced works also are done on Neural Networks (**NN**) application for adaptive friction compensation. The cited in [7], works applied **CAMAC** based **NN** for robust control of systems with friction. [7], applied a reinforcement adaptive learning, based on Radial Basis Function (**RBF**) **NN** for friction compensation of high speed precise mechanical system. [13] and [11] applied a Feedforward **NN**s for identification and control of **DC**-motor drives. As it can be seen, the proposed schemes in the literature of **NN** learning control systems possesses higher complexity and higher dimensionality, which makes them hardly applicable. To avoid this complexity, it is appropriate to use the multi-model **NN** approach, as it is done for **NN** identification of hysteresis and backlash model, [5] and [12]. Some works in this field, allowing to identify complex nonlinear dynamic objects by means of multi-model neural network, has been done by [2] and [3]. So, the purpose of this paper is to apply the fuzzy neural multi-model approach, [2,3], to identify in real-time an unknown mechanical system with friction.

2   Recurrent Neural Model. Fuzzy-Neural Multi-Model. Control Algorithm

In [2] and [3] a discrete-time model of Recurrent Trainable Neural Network (**RTNN**), and the dynamic Backpropagation (**BP**) weight updating rule, are given. The **RTNN** model is described by the following equations:

$$
\begin{aligned}
X(k+1) &= JX(k) + BU(k) \\
Z(k) &= S[X(k)] \\
Y(k) &= S[CZ(k)]
\end{aligned}
\tag{1}
$$

where $x(\cdot)$ is a n - state vector of the system; $u(\cdot)$ is a m-input vector; $y(\cdot)$ is a l- output vector; $z(\cdot)$ is an auxiliary vector variable with dimension l , $S(\cdot)$ is a vector-valued sigmoid function with appropriate dimension; J is a weight-state block-diagonal matrix with (1×1) and (2×2) blocks; B and C are weight input and output matrices with appropriate dimensions and block structure, corresponding to the block structure of J. As it can be seen from equations (1), the given **RTNN** model is a two-layer hybrid one, with one feedforward output layer and one recurrent hidden layer. It is also completely parallel parametric one, so it is useful for identification and control purposes. This **RTNN** model is nonlinear in large and linear in small, so the linearization of the sigmoid functions allows to study its dynamic properties, such as stability, observability and controllability. To preserve the **RTNN** stability during the learning, the model poles (the diagonal elements of the matrix J) must be restricted to remain inside the unit circle. The general **BP** learning algorithm is given in the form:

$$W_{ij}(k+1) = W_{ij}(k) + \eta \Delta W_{ij}(k) + \alpha \eta \Delta W_{ij}(k-1) \qquad (2)$$

where $W_{ij}(C, J, B)$ is the ij-th weight element of each weight matrix (given in parenthesis) of the **RTNN** model to be updated; ΔW_{ij} is the weight correction of W_{ij}; η, a are learning rate parameters. The updates ΔC_{ij} , ΔJ_{ij}, ΔB_{ij} of model weights C_{ij} , J_{ij}, B_{ij} are given by:

$$\Delta C_{ij}(k) = [T_j(k) - Y_j(k)]Y_j(k)[1 - Y_j(k)]Z_i(k) \qquad (3)$$

$$\Delta J_{ij}(k) = RX_i(k-1) \qquad (4)$$

$$R = C_i(k)[T(k) - Y(k)]Z_j(k)[1 - Z_j(k)] \qquad (5)$$

$$\Delta B_{ij}(k) = RU_i(k) \qquad (6)$$

where T is a target vector with dimension l and $[T-Y]$ is an output error vector, also with the same dimension; R is an auxiliary variable.

For some nonlinear plant models with smooth nonlinearities, the given **BP** learning algorithm has demonstrated a fast convergence and a small mean square error in the final epoch of learning [2]. But in the case of nonlinear plants with non invertible or asymmetric nonlinearities, the learning was going bad, with large mean square error or it was impossible to perform. In these cases, some other approximation technics, like the fuzzy linguistic or relational models, could be applied. The classical fuzzy rule based approximation technics suffer of the disadvantage that it needs to apply defuzzification to obtain the fuzzy model output. The Takagi-Sugeno model is mix linguistic and mathematical regression model which does not need defuzzification because the consequent rule are crisp mathematical functions of the model inputs. The function used, in the consequent part of the rule, could be static or dynamic (state-space) model, which validation is determined by the membership function. To extend the validation limits of the membership functions which depends on the approximation error, the authors of [2] and [3], proposed as a consequent crisp function to use a **RTNN** function model, so to form a fuzzy-neural multi-model. The fuzzy rule of this model is given by the following statement:

$$R_i : \text{IF x is THEN } y_i(k+1) = N_i[x(k), u(k), \quad i = 1, 2, \ldots, p] \qquad (7)$$

where: $N_i(\cdot)$ denotes the **RTNN** function, given by eq. (1); i is the model number; p is the total number of **RTNN** models, corresponding to fuzzy rules R_i.

The aim of this paper is to propose an adequate control law, corresponding to this fuzzy-neural multi-**RTNN** model and to apply it for a real-time identification and control of nonlinear mechanical system with friction. It is expected that the application of a learning adaptive model like the fuzzy-neural multi-**RTNN** model will be well suited for identification and control of such nonlinear process with unknown variable parameters, asymmetric nonlinearity and unknown dynamic effects. First a trajectory tracking control law, corresponding to the linearized **RTNN** model could be defined.

Following [10] and [6], the next adaptive tracking control law could be written:

$$U(k) = [CB]^{-1}\{CJX(k) + Y^d(k+1) + \gamma[Y^d(k) - Y(k)]\} \qquad (8)$$

where γ is a constant with values between -0.999 and 0.999; C, B are J are real matrices of dimensions corresponding to the **RTNN** model, given by (1) and $Y^d(k)$ is the reference signal. If the **RTNN** is controllable and observable, then the matrix product of the **RTNN** parameters (1) must be $CB \neq 0$. In the multi- model case, the corresponding fuzzy coordination rule is given by the statement:

$$R_i : \text{If } x \text{ is } A_i \text{ Then } u_i(k) = F_i[X(k), Y^d(k), Y(k)], \quad i = 1, 2, \dots, p \qquad (9)$$

where $u_i(k) = F_i[X(k), Y^d(k), Y(k)])]$, denotes the corresponding control function (8), i is the model number; p is the total number of **RTNN** models, corresponding to fuzzy rules R_i, given by (7).

The following part of the paper gives a brief description of this process and shows its general equations and parameters.

3 Friction Model

The general equation of an **1-DOF** mass system with friction is given in the form, [1,4,7] and [8]:

$$m\ddot{q}(t) + fr(\dot{q}, t) + d(t) = k_o u(t) \qquad (10)$$

where m is the mass, $q(t)$ is the relative displacement, $v(t) = \dot{q}(t)$ is the velocity, $fr(v, t)$ is the friction force, $u(t)$ is the control force, k_o is the system gain, and $d(t)$ is a bounded external disturbances due to measurement noises or other load forces. It is assumed that the external disturbance is bounded by an unknown upper bound d :

$$|d(t)| \leq d; \, t > 0 \qquad (11)$$

The stick-slip friction force $fr(v, t)$ is assumed to be modeled as follows, [7,8]:

$$fr(v, \, t) = F_{\text{slip}}(v)a(v) + F_{\text{stick}}(u)[1 - a(v)] \qquad (12)$$

$$a(v) = \begin{cases} 1, v(t) > \alpha \\ 0, v(t) \leq \alpha \end{cases}; \alpha > 0 \qquad (13)$$

The sticking friction provides the value of the friction forces at zero velocity. The term is used to describe whether the mass will stick or break free from the static friction forces. The positive and negative limits on the static friction forces are given by F_s^+ and F_s^-, respectively. Generally, they are not equal in magnitude, and the model should consider these asymmetry. The sticking friction is modeled as follows:

$$F_{\text{stick}} = \begin{cases} f_s^+, & u(k) \geq F_s^+ \\ u(k), & F_s^- < u(k) < F_s^+ \\ 0, & u(k) \leq F_s^- \end{cases} \tag{14}$$

The mass cannot move until the applied force is greater in magnitude than the respective static friction force. The slipping function $F_{\text{slip}}(v)$ provides values of the friction at non-zero velocity and is given by:

$$F_{\text{slip}}(v) = F_d^+ b(v) + F_d^- b(-v) \tag{15}$$

$$b(v) = \begin{cases} 1, & v(t) > 0 \\ 0, & v(t) \leq 0 \end{cases} \tag{16}$$

$$F_d^+(v) = F_s^+ - \Delta F^+ [1 - e^{(-v/v_{cr}^+)} + \beta^+ v] \tag{17}$$

$$F_d^-(v) = F_s^- - \Delta F^- [1 - e^{(-v/v_{cr}^-)} + \beta^- v] \tag{18}$$

where ΔF^+ and ΔF^- are the respective drops from the static to the kinetic force level; v_{cr}^+ and v_{cr}^- are the critical Stribeck velocities, and β^+ and β^- are the viscous friction coefficients. The friction force is modeled as a summation of the Coulomb friction, viscous friction, and the Stribeck effect. The Stribeck effect models the fact that friction force is decreasing with increasing fluid lubrication. Some models, [1], consider dynamic lag effect of the friction force with respect to the velocity, which effect can be neglected. For sake of simplicity, some slip friction parameters for both velocity directions could be considered as equal (e.g. $v_{cr}^+ = v_{cr}^- = v_{cr}$; $\beta^+ = \beta^- = \beta$).

4   Simulation Results

Let us consider a **DC**-motor - driven nonlinear mechanical system, to have the following friction parameters: $\alpha = 0.001 m/s$; $F_s^+ = 4.2N$; $F_s^- = -4.0N$; $\Delta F^+ = 1.8N$; $\Delta F^- = -1.7 N$; $v_{cr} = 0.1 m/s$; $\beta = 0.5 Ns/m$. Let us also consider that position and velocity measurements are taken with period of discretization $T_0 = 0.1 s$, the system gain $k_o = 8$, the mass $m = 1 kg$, and the load disturbance depends on the position and the velocity $(d(t) = d_1 q(t) + d_2 v(t); d_1 = 0.25; d_2 = -0.7)$. So the discrete-time model of the **1-DOF** mass mechanical system with friction, is obtained in the form:

$$x_1(k+1) = x_2(k)$$
$$x_2(k+1) = -0.025 x_1(k) - 0.3 x_2(k) + 0.8 u(k) - 0.1 fr(k) \tag{19}$$

$$v(k) = x_2(k) - x_1(k) \tag{20}$$

$$y(k) = 0.1 x_1(k) \tag{21}$$

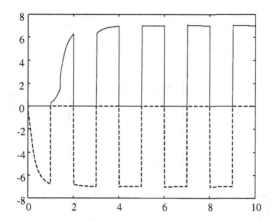

Fig. 1. On line system identification. Continuous line, positive **RTNN-1** output; dashed line, negative **RTNN-2** output. Parameters of learning $\beta = 0.01$, $\alpha = 0.01$

where: $x_1(k)$, $x_2(k)$ are system states; $v(k)$ is system velocity and $y(k)$ is system position; k is a discrete time variable and the friction force $fr(k)$ is governed by the equations (12) to (18) with given values of friction parameters.

Simulation results of on-line identification and control of mechanical system with friction, are given on Fig. 1, 2, 3, 4 and 5. The Fig. 1 shows the 10-th seconds result of on-line system identification by means of two **RTNN** models (positive and negative). Both **RTNN** have the same architecture with one input, one output and two hidden nodes. The parameters of learning used are $\beta = 0.01$, $\alpha = 0.01$. The state and parameter information, obtained by **RTNN** 1, 2 is used for system control. The reference input signal is a pulse train with frequency 0.5 and amplitude 7. The Fig. 2 shows the reference signal tracking by the Fuzzy-neural system, applying the control law (8) and the fuzzy rule (9). The Fig.3 shows the control signal. The instantaneous and the **MSE** tracking errors are given on Fig. 4 and Fig. 5 respectively. The on-line simulation results show that an overshoot of the control due to improper identification occur in the beginning, but after few seconds this error decrease in normal values.

5   Conclusions

A comparative study of various mechanical systems with friction compensation, is done. The paper propose to use two **RTNN** models for mechanical system identification and control, and gives its configuration as a fuzzy-neural indirect adaptive control structure. The proposed recurrent fuzzy-neural multi-model approximates the complete nonlinear system dynamics including all nonlinear static and dynamic friction effects. As this model is dynamic in nature, so it

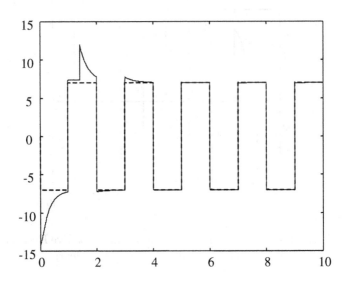

Fig. 2. Reference signal tracking. Continuous line, system output; dashed line, reference signal. The reference signal is a pulse train with frequency 0.5 and amplitude 7.0

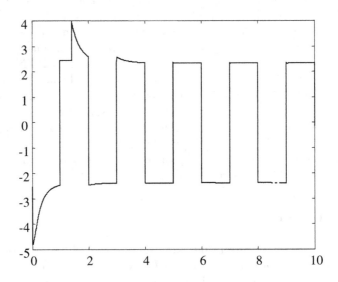

Fig. 3. Control signal, generated by the fuzzy-neural system. The parameter $\gamma = 0.9$

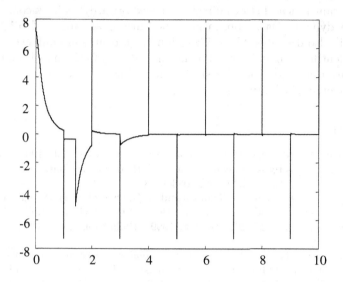

Fig. 4. Instantaneous error

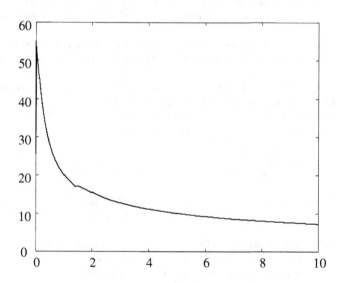

Fig. 5. MSE of reference signal tracking

is well suited for unknown dynamic effects (as elasticity) approximation too. The **RTNN** model have a Jordan canonical system structure which permits to use its parameters and states directly for feedforward/feedback control systems design. A dynamic Backpropagation-type learning algorithm of **RTNN** model training is also described. The simulation given results of nonlinear mechanical system identification and control by means of two **RTNN** models and two fuzzy identification and control rules show a good convergence and confirm **RTNN** multi-model applicability.

References

1. B. Amstrong-Helouvry, P. Dupont and C. Canudas De Wit (1994). A survey of models, analysis tools and compensation methods for the control of machines with friction. Automatica Vol.30 , pp. 1083-1138 292, 295, 296
2. I. Baruch,.E. Gortcheva, F. Thomas and R. Garrido (1999a). A neuro-fuzzy model for nonlinear plants identification. In: Proc. of the IASTED Int. Conf. "Modelling and Simulation", (MS'99), May 5-8, 1999 , Philadelphia, PA, USA, pp. 291-021, 1-6. 293, 294
3. I. Baruch, R. Garrido, A. Mitev and B. Nenkova (1999b). A neural network approach for stick-slip friction model identification. In: Proc. of the 5-th Int. Conf. On Engineering Applications of NNs (EANN'99), Sept. 13-15, 1999 , Warsaw, Poland. 293, 294
4. C. Canudas De Wit, P. Noel, A. Aubin, and B. Brogliato (1991). Adaptive friction compensation in robot manipulators: Low velocities. The Int. J. of Robotics Research, Vol. 10, pp. 189-199 292, 295
5. D. Cincotti, and I. Daneri (1997). Neural network identification of a nonlinear circuit model of hysteresis. Electronic Letters, Vol. 33, pp. 1154-1156. 293
6. A. Isidori (1995). Nonlinear, Control systems, third edition, Springer-Verlag, London. 295
7. Y. H. Kim, and F. L. Lewis (1998). High-level feedback control with neural networks, chap.8, World Scientific Publ. Co, Singapore, New Jersey, Hong Kong. 292, 293, 295
8. S. W. Lee and J. H .Kim (1995).Robust adaptive stick-slip friction compensation. IEEE Thans. on Ind. Elect., Vol. 42 , pp. 474-479. 292, 293, 295
9. W. Li and X. Cheng (1994). Adaptive high precision control of positioning tables - theory and experiments. IEEE Trans. on Control Systems Technology, Vol. 2, pp. 265-270. 293
10. K. S. Narendra, and K. Parthasarathy (1990). Identification and Control of Dynamic Systems using Neural Networks, IEEE Transactions on NNs, Vol. 1, No1, pp. 4-27. 295
11. M. A. Rahman and A. Hoque (1997). On-line self-tuning ANN-based speed control of a PM **DC**-motor. IEEE/ASME Trans. on Mechatronics, Vol. 2, No 3, pp.169-178. 292, 293
12. D. R. Seidl, S. L. Lam, J. A. Putman and R. D. Lorenz (1995). Neural network compensation of gear backlash hysteresis in position-controlled mechanisms. IEEE Trans on Industry Applications, Vol. 31, No 6, pp. 1475-1483. 293
13. S. Weerasooriya and M. A. El-Sharkawi (1991). Identification and control of a **DC**-motor using back-propagation neural networks. IEEE Trans. on Energy Conversion, Vol. 6, No 4, pp. 663-669. 292, 293

A Neural Network Tool to Organize Large Document Sets

R. Rizzo and E. G. Munna

C.N.R. I.T.D.F. via Ugo La Malfa 153, 90146 Palermo, Italy
rizzo @mail.itdf.pa.cnr.it

Abstract. Document clustering based on semantics is a fundamental method of helping users to search and browse in large cllections of documents. Recently a number of papers have reported the applications of self-organizing artificial neural networks in document clustering based on semantics. In particular Growing Neural Gas is a growing neural network that allows the user to reproduce the topological distribution of the inputs, but the structure obtained often has the same complexity as the input data structure; if the input space has more than three dimensions it is impossible to visualize or represent the GNG network as well as the input data structure. In this paper the authors propose a LBG modified network, called LBG-m, that can simplify the GNG structure in order to visualize and summarize it. The two algorithms constitute a tool for browsing large document sets and generating a set of semantic links between clusters of similar documents.

1   Introduction

Direct browsing into a document set is the usual way of searching for information if the topic is not familiar and it is not possible to formulate a satisfactory query. Browsing into a document set of hundreds or thousands of documents is certainly an imposing task but it can be made easier if the user is guided within the document space. To do this the document space must be ordered in some way; document clustering or taxonomies are the easiest and the most direct way of doing this. Artificial intelligence can provide useful and effective algorithms for organizing or arranging data into clusters as the artificial neural network (ANN) models. These models are inspired by our present understanding of the biological nervous system and are made up of a dense interconnection of simple non-linear computational elements corresponding to the biological neurons. Each connection is characterized by a variable weight that is adjusted, together with other parameters of the net, during the so-called "learning stage".

The self organizing networks, and in particular the Self Organizing Feature Map (SOM) [3], are ANNs that try to build a representation of some feature of the input vector used as "learning input set" during the learning stage. Recently this network

S. A. Cerri and D. Dochev (Eds.): AIMSA 2000, LNAI 1904, pp. 301-309, 2000.

has been used to classify information and documents in "document maps". These are two-dimensional graphical representations in which all the documents in a document set are depicted. The documents are grouped into clusters which all concern the same topic, and clusters related to similar topics are near each other on the map.

The Growing Neural Gas [7] is a self-organizing neural network that has no pre-defined lattice, like the two-dimensional SOM grid, but is able to generate a set of interconnected clusters in the input space. The GNG network is capable of following the input distribution even when it is complicated or has different dimensions [5]. The topology of the GNG structure reflects the properties and complexity of the input vector distribution so that the visualization is only possible for two or three dimensional input spaces [1], but the absence of topological constraints makes it attractive and particularly suitable for the reproduction of the original structure of a hypertext. A GNG network was used in [9] to organize the nodes of a hypertext and the original structure of the hypertext was compared to the structure generated by the neural network. The GNG network generates 2356 links between documents of which 146 are in the original hypertext, 40.1 % of the total number of links, but the structure generated is difficult to manage. In fact the absence of a simple geometric structure makes it difficult to have an overall idea of the set of documents, something which it is possible to have in a SOM map (a two dimensional map which is easy to visualize, understand and remember).

Consequently on one hand we have the SOM network that is a good visualization tool [10], [11]; but on the other by using the GNG network it is possible to organize the documents in an hypertext fashion, even though the two dimensional visualization is lost. A possible solution to this problem is to use another neural network to create an overall representation of the GNG network if this network is trained in high dimensional input space. The network used is a sort of modified LBG network [2], called LBG-m network, that is trained by using the GNG network as input. After the learning stage of the LBG-m network, the links between the neurons are taken into account and a link set is created between the LBG-m units in order to reproduce the configuration of the input GNG network. The two networks, the LBG-m and the GNG constitute a tool for navigating large document sets: the GNG network is used to obtain the document clusters connected by a links structure and the LBG-m algorithm is used to obtain an upper level structure that gives an idea of the structure of the cluster distribution in the input space.

2   The LBG Algorithm

The LBG algorithm allows the user to build a set of code vectors by moving them to the center of their Voronoi sets. The algorithm converges through a finite number of adaptation steps in a local minimum of the distortion error function. The initial values of the network units determine the local minimum, so that different initial values can give very different results. Another drawback of the algorithm is the presence of "dead units": units that have an empty Voronoi set (i.e. without input vectors); this problem can be avoided using a subset of the input vectors as initial values.

Assuming that the LBG network has a set of N_L units :

$$L = \{l_1, l_2, ..., l_{N_L}\}$$

and each of them has a reference vector $\mathbf{w}_{li}$

$$\mathbf{W}_{li} = \{w_1, w_2, ..., w_n\}$$

the learning algorithm of the LBG network follows:

1. Initialize the set of code vectors W_L using a subset of the input data D

$$D = \{d_1, d_2, ..., d_{N_L}\}$$

2. For each unit i of LBG find its Voronoi set

$$V_i = \{d \in D \mid \|d - w_i\| \le \|d - w_{l_j}\| \, \forall l_j \in L\}$$

3. Move each unit to the mean of its Voronoi set

$$\mathbf{w}_{li} = \frac{1}{|V_i|} \sum_{d \in V_i} d$$

4. If during step 3 a unit changes place then go back to step 2, otherwise go to step 5.

5. Return the current set of vector LBG

Recently the LBG-U algorithm has been proposed [6]: this algorithm can reduce the number of codebook vectors and determine a better approximation of the input data distribution.

3 The Proposed LBG-m Algorithm

The aim of the LBG-m algorithm is to build a new structure that can give an overall picture of the distribution and of the "shape" of a trained GNG network, using the smallest possible number of neurons. Moreover the LBG-m can link the units in such a way as to "reproduce" the "shape" of the GNG network in the input space. The LBG-m is based on the LBG algorithm; it has to be trained using a GNG network as input. During the learning stage of the LBG-m algorithm the GNG network is divided into parts, one for each Voronoi set of the LBG-m units, and a new LBG-m unit is added for each unit that has an unconnected GNG graph inside its Voronoi region.

In fig.1 the LBG-m units A and B are shown, the gray areas represent the input distribution; the LBG-m unit A has an unconnected GNG graph in its Voronoi region, so that the new LBG-m unit will be added in the area A.

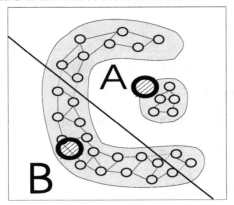

Fig. 1. An example of the unit adding method

The LBG-m learning stage is repeated each time a new unit is added or the maximum number of units is reached. At the end the LBG-m units are linked together if the corresponding GNG subgraphs are linked together.

Assume that the Growing Neural Gas network consists of a set of N_G units

$$G = \{g_1, g_2, ..., g_{N_G}\}$$

where each unit has a reference vector

$$W_{gi} = \{w_1, w_2, ..., w_{n_G}\}$$

and assume there is a set of connections C between the GNG units:

$$C \subset G x G$$

If N_{LMAX} is the maximum number of LBG-m units allowed, the LBG-m algorithm follows:

1. Initialize an LBG network with two units

2. While *end* == **false**

    2.1. Update the position of the LBG-m units according to the LBG algorithm, and use the W_G set as input (the reference vectors of the GNG network);

    2.2. For each unit l_i of the LBG-m network
        2.2.1. Take the set of GNG units in the Voronoi region corresponding to l_i and the connection set C_{li}

$$V_{l_i} = \{g_i \in G \mid \|l_i - g_i\| \le \|l_i - g_h\| \forall g_h \in G\}$$
$$C_{l_i} = \{(g_1, g_2) \in A \mid g_i, g_j \in V_{l_i}\}$$

2.2.2. If the graph defined by C_{li} is not connected and $N_L < N_{LMAX}$ then add a new unit to the LBG-m network.

2.3. If no neuron was added then *end* = **true**

3. Update the position of LBG-m units.

4. Create the link between the LBG-m neural units that have, in their V_{li} regions, connections that extend beyond their Voronoi regions.

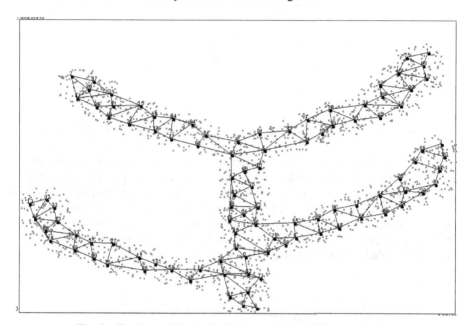

Fig. 2a. The "cactus" input distribution and the GNG approximation

Adding a new unit to the LBG-m network modifies the error function, so different strategies for adding a new unit to the LBG-m structure have been tried; obviously this can affect the topology of the network obtained. Some of the criteria used to initialize a new unit are the following:

−   random values; this criteria gives some dead units;
−   using the centroid of one of the section of the graph; this gives poor results;
−   random values inside the hypercube obtained by using the max component of the vectors in the Voronoi region; this criteria has given the best results

To depict the LBG-m algorithm the classical "cactus" image was chosen. In fig. 2a it is possible to see the GNG approximation of the input distribution, the network obtained using the LBG-m algorithm is shown in fig.2b. This picture also shows the section of the GNG graph that belongs to each LBG-m unit.

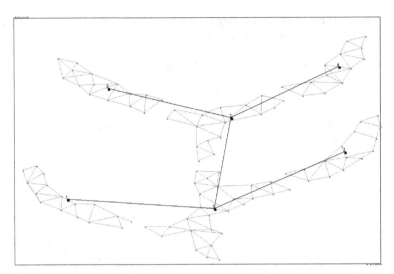

Fig. 2b. The LBG-m approximation and the graph that belong to each LBG-m unit

In fig. 3 the GNG approximation of another input distribution is shown with the resulting LBG-m network in bold print. In this picture it is also possible to see that the network seems to approximate the GNG network using an error minimization criteria (not the constant entropy criteria). In fact in the rectangle to the right, where the input vectors are denser, there are many GNG units but only one LBG-m unit, so that no information is provided on the distribution of the inputs. The reason for this is that a new unit is added by using topology considerations.

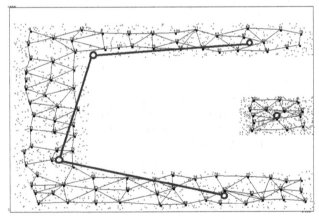

Fig. 3. The LBG-m approximation of another GNG structure

It has to be said that the LBG-m gives the worst results if the input distribution is not very complex or widely scattered in the input space, as shown in fig. 4. In this case only two LBG units, A and B, are obtained because each of them has a connected graph in its Voronoi region and the algorithm does not add any new unit.

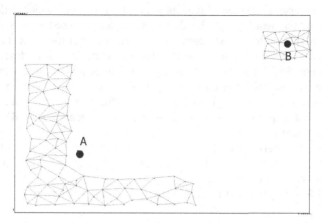

Fig. 4. An example of wrong classification

Finally the LBG-m algorithm is compared to another GNG network which is trained using the results of the first one: the results obtained show that the LBG-m algorithm works better. This is not surprising: the GNG network works better if the number of neurons is high enough. In fig.5 the results obtained by training a 10 unit GNG is shown, as it is possible to see the GNG network requires more units to approximate the input "shape".

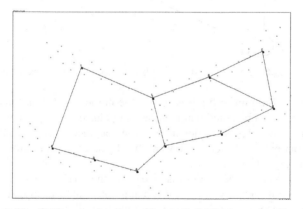

Fig. 5. The GNG approximation of "cactus" distribution using 10 units

4   An Application of LBG-m Algorithm for Document Classification

The proposed algorithm is applied to a set of inputs from a high dimensional space: the vectors that represent a set of documents. Assuming a dictionary vector D, each document can be represented as a vector V where the element v_i is the weight of the word d_i for that document. The word weight can be calculated using the Term

Frequency * Inverse Document Frequency (TFIDF) scheme which calculates the interest value of the word [12]. The document collection used to test the LBG-m algorithm is an HTML hypertext course on hypermedia and hypertext (available on the Internet at http:// wwwis.win.tue.nl/2L670/course.zip). This hypertext is made up of 162 nodes and 357 links. The vocabulary consists of 6568 words; however only 536 words are used to build the document representation vector for each node; these words have been obtained by neglecting stopwords (like articles) and rare words. The training set is made up of 162 vectors of 536 real components obtained by using the TFIDF transformation.

Using the GNG a network composed of 43 linked clusters has been obtained, with a mean of 4 documents for each unit. This structure is in a space of 536 dimensions so it is difficult to inspect or to visualize.

Using the LBG-m network it is possible to obtain the graph in fig. 6.

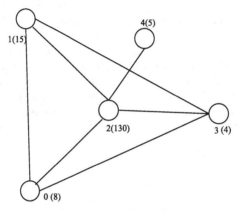

Fig.6: The LBG-m structure obtained form the hypertext data

Near each LBG-m unit in fig. 6 is shown the number of GNG units that are in the Voronoi region. It can be noted that there is a big cluster of documents near the LBG-m unit 2, and 4 small clusters of documents: the documents near the LBG-m unit 1 are about the hypertext model called tower, the documents near unit 3 are about the browsing strategies of hypertexts.

The structure built by the LBG-m is visualized in an HTML table, and can be used to browse the set of documents; users can handle the 5 units easily, and they may also find the labels assigned to each LBG-m unit to be helpful. Users can access the GNG network when they want to look at the information structure in more details or when they want to read a document.

5   Conclusions

Browsing into a document space of hundreds of documents is really a imposing task, but it can be made easier if a hypertext-like structure is created in the document space. The GNG network can create this structure by sorting the documents into clusters and linking these clusters together. Generally speaking the GNG algorithm approximate an input distribution in a flexible way, by adding new neurons when it is necessary to reduce the approximation error, but, if the input space has more than 3 dimensions, the visualization of the GNG network structure is very difficult. Neither is it possible to build another GNG structure using the first one as input, because the GNG network works well only if the number of neurons is quite high. The proposed LBG-m algorithm can approximate the structure of a GNG network using a low number of units and can reproduce the "shape" of the GNG structure. The results obtained also show that the network tries to minimize the quantization error so a small number of units is also used to approximate a dense input region.

References

1. Fritzke B., "Growing Self-Organizing Networks - Why?", ESANN'96: European Symposium on Artificial Neural Networks, Brussels 1995, p. 61-72
2. Linde Y., Buzo A., Gray R. M., "An Algorithm for Vector Quantizer Design", IEEE Transactions on Communication, COM-28:84-95, 1980.
3. Kohonen T., "Self Organizing Maps", Springer Verlag
5. Tesauro G., Touretzky D. S., Leen T. K. (eds.) "A growing Neural Gas Network Learns Topologies", *Advances in Neural Information Processing Systems 7*, MIT Press, Cambridge MA, 1995, p. 625-632.
6. Fritzke B., "The LBG-U method for vector quantization - an improvement over LBG inspired from neural networks". *Neural Processing Letters*, 5 (1), 1997.
7. Fritzke B., "A growing neural gas network learns topologies", NIPS 1994, Denver.
8. Balabanovic M., Shoham Y., "Learning Information Retrieval Agents: Experiments with Automated Web Browsing", *Proceedings of the AAAI Spring Symposium on Information Gathering from Heterogenous, Distributed Resources,* Stanford, CA, March 1995.
9. Rizzo R. "Self Organizing Networks to Map Information Space in Hypertext Development", *Proceedings of the International ICSC/IFAC Symposium on Neural Computation NC'98,* September 23-25, 1998, Vienna, Austria.
10. Rizzo R., Allegra M., Fulantelli G., Hypertext-like Structures through a SOM Network, in Proc. of ACM Hypertext '99, (Darmstadt, Germany, Feb. 21-25, 1999).
11. Rizzo R., Allegra M., Fulantelli G., Hy.Doc: a System to Support the Study of Large Document Collections, in Proc. of ICL99 workshop, (Villach, Austria, Oct. 7-8,1999). ISBN 3-7068-0755-6.
12. Salton G., Allan j., Buckel C., Automatic Structuring and Retrieval of Large Text Files, Communications of ACM, 37, 2, 1994, pp.97-108

User Authentication via Neural Network

Abd Manan Ahmad and Nik Nailah Abdullah

Software Engineering Department, Faculty of Computer Science and Information
Technology, Universiti Teknologi Malaysia, Skudai 81310 Johor, Malaysia
e-mail: manan@fsksm.utm.my

Abstract. The major problem in the computer system is that users are
now able to access data from remote places and perform transaction on-
line. This paper reports on the experiment and performance of using
keystroke dynamics as a user authentication method. The work is
designed such that it is possible for the computer system to identify
authorized and unauthorized user. This is desired to control access to a
system that will assign the authorized user upon entering the system.
The technique used to discriminate the data is Neural Network. This
paper describes the application of neural networks to the problem of
identifying specific users through the typing characteristics exhibited
when typing their own name. The test carried out uses two kinds of
neural network model, i.e. ADALINE and Backpropagation Network.
A comparison of these two techniques are presented.

1   Introduction

Identifying a person seems straightforward. People do it all the time. But modern
society has complicated things, a hacker accesses sensitive database and a
counterfeiter makes copies of banks cards. At all levels, a sure-fire means of
identification has never been in more demand. Today the average businessperson may
use more than a dozen computer passwords-personal identification numbers (PINs)
for automated teller machines, licenses and telephone calling, membership, and credit
cards. Yet finding satisfactory methods of identifying user can be difficult. Some
techniques are easy to fool and others are felt to be too intrusive.

One area where technology is enhancing, and often simplifying, our ability to
identify people is biometrics. Biometrics systems are automated system of verifying
or recognizing the identity of a living person on the basis of some physiological
characteristics, like a fingerprint or iris pattern, or some aspect of behavior, like
handwriting or keystroke patterns. Verification requires the person being identified to
lay claim to an identity, so that system has a binary choice of either accepting or
rejecting the person's claim. Biometrics is also catching up on automated teller
machines (ATMs). Still, it is a steady technology. Although there are number of other
automated biometrics system such as iris recognition and voice recognition, the tools
needed to capture is costly.

S. A. Cerri and D. Dochev (Eds.): AIMSA 2000, LNAI 1904, pp. 310-320, 2000.

Fingerprints vary with emotional state. Voice too, is cheap to capture, relying on low-cost microphones or existing telephones, but varies when emotions and states of health change, and has a large template size. Keystrokes dynamics also known as typing rhythms, is one of the most eagerly awaited of all biometrics technologies in the computer security arena. This method analyzes the way a user types at a terminal by monitoring the keyboard of inputs 1000 times per second. The analogy is made to the days of telegraphy when operators would identify each other by recognizing the "fist of the sender". The modern system has some similarities, most notably that the user does not realize he is being identified unless told. Also, the better the user is at typing, the easier it is to make identification. Both the National Science Foundation, Washington, D.C, and the National Institute of Standards and Technology, Gaithersburg, MD have conducted studies establishing that typing patterns are unique to the typist.

The advantages of keystroke dynamics in the computer environment are obvious. Neither the enrolment nor the verification disturbs the regular flow because the user would be tapping the keys anyway. Since the input device is the existing keyboard, the technology costs less. Despite the increased activity, published reports of the basic data and/or methodology are noticeably missing. Thus, this case study was carried out in hope to find the best technique to solve the problem of classifying and filtering the data collected from the users. The limitation of the work was to capture user's typing data. The experiment carried out was based on the previous data collected from the inventor of system, Joey Rogers.

2   Keystroke Dynamics

The system is based upon the concept that the coordination of a person's fingers is neurophysiologically determined and unique for a given genotype. A user typing or keystroke characteristics can be measured by examining the timing of the keystrokes or the pressure of the keystrokes. Vectors is used to represent the data. The vector was constructed using interleaved hold times and digraph latency times.

The hold time of a key time is obtained by subtracting the press time of the key from the release time of the key. A digraph is a two keystroke combination. The digraph latency is obtained by subtracting a first key's release time from a second key's press time. The ordering elements of the vector is not important but the vectors should be constructed such that the samples relating to a user are constructed in the same manner so that they can be properly compared. The components of the vectors are physical characteristics of a person's keystroke characteristics.

These physical characteristics are used to construct vectors which are processed, transmitted and stored within the system as signals. The vector can be made up of data pertaining to the key press time, key release times, digraph latency times, key hold times, keystroke pressure, keystroke accelaration or deceleration, or any features relating to the user's keystroke characteristics. Once the data is collected and placed in vector format, the vetors can be analyzed to determine if the user is authorized or an imposter. The data was normalized using the transformation linear method which is shown below;

$$xi' = 1/N \sum_{n=1}^{N} xi^{n}$$

$$\sigma^2 i = 1/N{-}1 \sum_{n=1}^{N} (x^n i - xi')^2$$

where n=1,...,N for number of patterns.

Next, we need to find a set of variable definition that is scaled, given by;

$$x^n i' = \frac{x^n i - xi'^2}{\sigma i}$$

Below, is the data of the authorized user, Joey Rogers whom is the sole inventor of this system.

Table 2.0(a) The raw data of authorized user, Joey Rogers

PRESS	RELEASE	TIME
SHIFT		0
J		87
	SHIFT	177
	J	186
O		220
E		339
	O	347
Y		409
	E	462
BACKSPACE		535
	Y	571
SHIFT		659
R		769
	SHIFT	821
	R	859
O		894
G		974
	O	1012
	G	1054
E		1076
R		1179
	E	1243
S		1285
	R	1400
	S	1433
ENTER		1478
	ENTER	1572

Table 2.0(b) Data of hold time

KEY	"HOLD"
SHIFT	177
J	99
O	127
E	123
Y	162
BACKSPACE	133
SHIFT	162
R	90
O	118
G	80
E	167
R	221
S	148
ENTER	94

Table 2.0(c) Digraph Latency Time

DIGRAPH	LATENCY
SHIFT;J	-90
J;O	34
O;E	-8
E;Y	-53
Y	-36
SHIFT	-9
SHIFT;R	-52
R;O	35
O;G	-38
G;E	22
E;R	-64
R;S	-115
S;ENTER	45

The data gathered from the user need to be normalized before feeding it into the neural network.

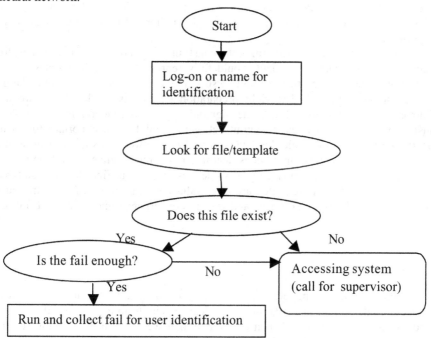

Fig. 2.0(d) Algorithm for keystroke dynamics method

3   Neural Networks Method

The main concern of this research was to find the best method to discriminate/purify the data collected. In this study, two kinds of neural network model and architecture was used to perform as the basic data or methadology. This paper describes the application of neural networks to the problem of identifying specific users through the typing characteristics exhibited when typing their own names.

The network was chosen based on the problem to be solved. First of all, the previous study was done to compare two kind of methods to discriminate the data which are geometric distance and Euclidean distance. The system under investigation was then tested using two kind of neural network architecture and model. There are ADALINE and Backpropagation network. The network was chosen based on network model, architecture, data and the type of problem.The choice of network model depends heavily on the type of problems you would like to solve. The nature of the problem usually restricts the choice of network to one or two model. Sometimes the choice of network comes down to personal preference or familiarity.in this case, the problem to be solved is a pattern classifier problem since it needs to determine which pattern belongs to the authorised or non-authorised user. The input layer consists of 27 nodes, which is equivalent to the number of the input elements. Whereas for the middle layer, it is a single middle layer with 24 nodes, which is 90% of the input nodes. There will be two output nodes, 1 for the authorised user and 0 for the non-authorised user.

The availability and integrity of data constitute the most important factor for training neural networks. The data should fully represent all possible states of the problem being tackled and there should be sufficient data to allow test and validation data sets to be extracted. The right preparation of data is needed to ensure the accurateness of the output. Since the sigmoid activation function is used as the transfer function, it generates its output between 0 and 1. It is important for us to perform normalisation to scale the data so it will fall between this range. During the experiment, the number of input nodes, learning rate value, number of hidden nodes, momentum value and performance goal value was changed to find the most suitable parameter values. The appropriate parameter values are chosen based from trial and error performed during experiment and on the convergence and goal performance result.

3.1   ADALINE

ADALINE is a processing element developed to take multiple input values and produce a single output. The Adaline's significance is in its ability to learn the correct outputs from a set of inputs. When new inputs that were not in the training set are presented to the ADALINE, the outputs produced will be based on its training experience. It uses the LMS algorithm for its operation. It consists of linear combination, hard limiter and a mechanism to change the weights. The summation of input $x1, x2, \ldots\ldots.xn$ will be used to determine the value of $+1$ or -1.

The control mechanism of the LMS depends heavily on the error signal e that is measured by the difference between the desired output d and the linear combination u before quantifying. The weights given by w1,w2,....wp and the threshold value will change accordingly to the LMS algorithm. ADALINE is usually used in application where the main concern is solving a linear problem and to distinguish noises in a signal processing. The LMS algorithm is an adaptive signal processing. The formula for this algorithm originated from spatial filtering. This method is usually used to solve problems like temporal filtering. Filter uses tapped delay filter as a signal-flow graph. The input vectors are defined as tap to the filter, which is shown below as;

$$\mathbf{x}(n) = [x(n),x(n-1),\ldots\ldots,x(n-p+1)]' \quad [5]$$

where p is the number of tap. The function of LMS algorithm is to change the weights of tap to enable the output filter y(n) to produce the desired output in least mean square. LMS operation consists of two processes that makes up of the feedback loop.

3.2   Backpropagation Network

Backpropagation network that was used in this case study is a simple 3-layer architecture Backpropagation network. It consists of processing elements that can produce complex output. It is capable of learning complex pattern, such as the pattern of human typing. Nonetheless, a Backpropagation network can recognise pattern that has gone through changes. The structure is almost the same as a Multi-Layer Perceptron , where the perceptron uses the Backpropagation as the learning algorithm . Backpropagation is a type of feedforward paradigm that consists of 1 input layer, 1 or more of hidden layer and I output layer. The value of input is in a binary form. The activation function that is used is the sigmoid hard limiter activation function. Backpropagation is a supervised learning. The Backpropagation paradigm is used for the operation of complex logic, classification of pattern and speech analyses .There is a training set that consists of input and output vector that is desired. The output that is desired is in a vector form, not in value.

$$Ik = \chi 0,\chi 1,\chi 2,\ldots\ldots\ldots\ldots\chi n => \text{'Desired\_Ok'} = Z0,Z1,Z2,\ldots\ldots\ldots.Z \quad [4]$$

Output from the backpropagation neural network will be calculated using the procedure known as forward pass and feedback pass.

i. The input layer will propagate to the component of the input vector to each node of the middle layer

ii. The middle layer node will be calculated as the output value which will in return serve as the input value for the node in the output layer.

$M_1 = f (\Sigma I_{kc} W_{ik})$
M = Middle layer
W_i = connection of weights between the input and middle layer.
C = input node
I = middle layer node
F = activation function

The output node will calculate the network output for the input vector ;

$o_j = f (\Sigma M_1 W_{2ji})$

o = output layer

J = output node

W_2 = weight connection between the middle layer and output layer

The activation function used in the forward pass will squash the dot product of input vector and weights vector that is equivalent to a value that is easy to manage. The function must have certain characterisitics in order to facilitate the learning process, it must be non-linear, everywhere defined,and differentiable. The transfer function used is shown below;

$$f(\chi) = \frac{1.0}{1.0 + e^{-x}}$$

The forward pass produces and output vector for a given vector based on the current state of the network weights. Since the network weights are initialized to random values, it is unlikely that reasonable outputs will result. The weight are adjusted to reduce the error by propagating the output error backwards through the network. This process is where the backpropagation neural network gets its name and is known as the backward pass.

i. Compute the error values for each node in the output layer:

$f'(\chi) = \chi(1-\chi)$

$E_j = f'(O_j)(Desired\_O_{kj} - O_j)$

E_j = error for each output node

where Ej is the error for each output node. The error for each node can be computed because the desired output for each node is known. The difference is multiplied by the derivative of the transfer function in preparation for the next step.

ii. Compute the error for the middle layer nodes:

$E_{1j} = f'(M_i) \Sigma W_{2ij} Ej$

E_{1j} = error for the middle layer

where Ej is the error for the middle layer terms. This method of computing error terms for the middle layer nodes, is responsible for making the backpropagation neural network .

iii. Adjust the weigh values to improve the network performance using the Delta rule

$W_{1k} = \beta E_{1i} \Delta I_{kc} + \alpha Previous(\Delta W_{1k})$

$W_{2j} = \beta E_j M_i + \alpha Previous(\Delta W_{2ji})$

$W_i = W_i + \Delta W_i$

iv. Compute overall error to test network performance :

The training set is repeatedly presented to the network and the weight values are adjusted until the overall error is below a predetermined tolerance.

4   Results of User Authentication via Neural Network Experiment

The objective of the latest research was to study the effectiveness of identifying authenticate user via neural network. Matlab neural network toolbox ver 5.2 was used to carry out the experiment. The experiment used two authentication methods to gather comparative performance data, the ADALINE and backpropagation neural network. Each model was tested by using the above data and impostor data was randomly generated by the computer. Below are the result of the experiment.

4.1   ADALINE Network

There will be two sets of samples to train the network, which consists of the training samples and test samples. The error rate will be plotted against a graph and these error will distinguish between the authentic user and non-authentic user. The ADALINE network does not suffer from the local minima problems. However, it is a tedious task to classify the data since ADALINE network is not capable of classifying patterns. The data of the authentic user will be trained for 100 times before the data of the impostor is trained. Delays is used to enable the network to process one element of data at a time. For each training, a graph will be plotted againts the authentic user and the impostor. The experiment conducted used 20-30 impostor data to perform the training. Each impostor data was compared to the authenticate user. Typically, an acceptable range of modification of each feature must be defined if there is an occurance of difference in features value. In this experiment , the difference between the desired output and output is calculated and taken into consideration for the purpose of allowing an acceptable range. The sufficient value for determing the acceptable range is 0.35. The user's data captured is in milisecond and was normalised. Thus, the value of 0.35 is after normalisation of data.

Each impostor user was trained against the authentic user. Thus, the graph plotted below is to show the training of ADALINE network for each user. The graph which will be represented is for one user, each graph symbolises the steps taken for each training for each impostor and authentic user.

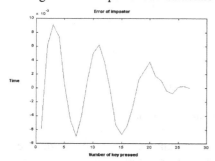

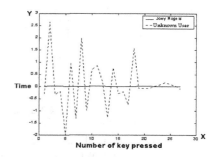

Fig. 4.1(a) Error for the first impostor user

Fig. 4.1(b) Comparison between Impostor and user

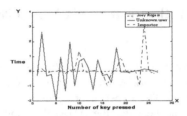

Fig. 4.1(c) The result for the ADALINE network

Above is the final result obtained after training 20 sets of data. The result above is to distinguish between the unknown user, impostor and authentic user. The authentic user line is a straight line, because the error rate is so small that it almost seems like a straight line.

4.2   Backpropagation

There will be two sets of samples, training samples and test samples. The technique done was similar to ADALINE network. The parameters chosen are sum-squared error performance function. It is a network performance function. It measures performance according to the sum squared of errors. This network function usually uses log sigmoid transfer function. The output generated is between 0 and 1. The data of each user was normalised and simulated, both authorised and unauthorised normalised data will then be kept in matrices. Later during training, this value will be compared and calculation will be performed upon these values. The experiment conducted involved 30 users. However, the most obvious difference was that the network was able to classify the patterns of samples. The value 1 will classify the pattern as an authentic user whereas the value 0 will classify the pattern as unathorized user.

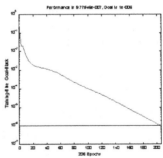

Fig. 4.2(a) Backpropagation performance

The curve line is to show the performance of the training. As for the straight line, it is to show the target. Which is 1e-6 of sum-squared error performance. As it hits the target, a user interface says that if the user is Joey Rogers or an impostor.
Below is the result of the training of backpropagation network.

TRAINGDX, Epoch 0/5000, SSE 0.418556/1e-006, Gradient 0.729983/1e-006
TRAINGDX, Epoch 20/5000, SSE 0.00186359/1e-006, Gradient 0.00512648/1e-006
TRAINGDX, Epoch 40/5000, SSE 0.00115658/1e-006, Gradient 0.00406104/1e-006
TRAINGDX, Epoch 60/5000, SSE 0.000572851/1e-006, Gradient 0.00200267/1e-006
TRAINGDX, Epoch 80/5000, SSE 0.000220868/1e-006, Gradient 0.00066173/1e-006
TRAINGDX, Epoch 100/5000, SSE 9.88475e-005/1e-006, Gradient 0.000254151/1e-006
TRAINGDX, Epoch 120/5000, SSE 4.67756e-005/1e-006, Gradient 0.000118904/1e-006
TRAINGDX, Epoch 140/5000, SSE 1.9626e-005/1e-006, Gradient 4.76147e-005/1e-006
TRAINGDX, Epoch 160/5000, SSE 7.84937e-006/1e-006, Gradient 1.81029e-005/1e-006
TRAINGDX, Epoch 180/5000, SSE 3.15447e-006/1e-006, Gradient 6.96721e-006/1e-006
TRAINGDX, Epoch 200/5000, SSE 1.28054e-006/1e-006, Gradient 2.72398e-006/1e-006
TRAINGDX, Epoch 206/5000, SSE 9.77546e-007/1e-006, Gradient 2.06044e-006/1e-006
TRAINGDX, Performance goal met.

    a1=sim(net,P)
    a2=sim(net,Pjr)
    a3=sim(net,Pimp)

The result obtained was;

    a1 = 0.99928   0.00067355
    a2 = 0.99928
    a3 = 0.00067355

    HI I am Joey Rogers!

a1 is the value of authentic and impostor user after testing the network. It is calculated by subtracting the output from the desired output. The command above is the output during testing of the user data. TRAINDGX is a network function that updates weights and bias according to gradient descent with momentum and adaptive learning rate backpropagation. The epoch is the complete cycle of training. SSE is a network performance function. It measures performance according to the sum of squared errors. When the performance goal hits the target, the training will halt and stop.

5   Summary and Discussion

The neural network was able to recognize the authorized user pattern. However, certain tehcniques is more sensitive towards some set of identifiable traits in an individual typings pattern which another technique is missing, while the sensitiveness are reversed for a different individual.

   Further research should be carried out to refine the techniques used to discriminate data collected. Although keystroke dynamics seems like the best method to solve problems in identification of user identity, much research work should be done. This is because the degree of familiarity, emotional influence and environment plays an important role in pattern typing. However, the difference is not so obvious.

The Backpropagation network seems much more suitable for pattern classifier because it can solve a non-linear problem and for its ability to classify pattern. The backpropagation network wins over ADALINE because it is better in generalization.

In the past papers, one of the approach to refine the methadology used along with keystroke dynamics is to include some representations of the Euclidean distance as an additonal inputs to the neural network. The Euclidean distance is a vector, which compares the distance of certain cluster to find the shortest distance to the center of the part/point. It is hoped that this will add the additional sensitivity and the keystroke dynamics should be able to breath new ideas into identification problems.

References

1. Garcia, John D. (1986). "Personal Identification Apparatus" (U.S Patent 4,621,334).
2. Young, James R. (1989). "Method and apparatus for verifying an individual's identity" (U.S Patent 4,805,222).
3. John Legget, Glen Williams. (1988). "Verifying identity via keystroke characteristics". International Journal of Man-Machine Studies.**28**,67-76.
4. Simon Haykin . (1994). "Neural Networks, A Comprehensive Foundation". 1st.ed.Macmillan College Publishing Company: Macmillan.134-135.
5. Karla Yale (1997). " Preparing the right data diet for training neural networks" IEEE Spectrum. 64-66.
6. Benjamin Miller (1994). "Vital Signs of Identity". IEEE Spectrum. 22-30.
7. Kuperstein, Micheal. (1991). " Self organizing neural network method and system for general classification of patterns". (U.S Patent 5,048,100).
8. Weiss,Kenneth P. (1991). " Method and apparatus for personal verification utilizing nonpredictable codes and biocharacteristics". (U.S Patent 4,998,279).
4. John Legget, Glen Williams dan Mark Usnick.(1991). "Dynamic identity verification via keystroke characteristics".International Journal of Man-Machine Studies.**35**, 859-870.
9. Christopher Bishop.(1995). "Neural Networks for Pattern Recognition".2nd.ed. Bookcraft Ltd,Great Britian: Oxford University Press.295-299.
10. Jacek M.Zurada.(1992)."Introduction to Artificial Neural System". 2nd.ed. Access and Distribution, Singapore: West Publishing.165-167, 206-217.
11. Mark Beale.(1998)."Neural Network Toolbox, For Use with Matlab".5th.ed..The Mathworks Inc,MA: The Mathworks Inc.4-16 – 4-27, 5-3 – 5-17.
12. Carson, William C. (1983). "Keystroke queueing system". (U.S Patent 4,410,957).
13. Wolf, Chris L.(1990). " System for selectively modifying codes generated by touch type keyboard upon detecting of predetermined sequence of makes codes and break codes".(U.S Patent 4,937,778).

Applying Preference Biases to Conjunctive and Disjunctive Version Spaces

E. N. Smirnov and H. J. van den Herik

IKAT, Department of Computer Science, Maastricht University,
P.O.BOX 616, 6200 MD Maastricht, The Netherlands
{smirnov,herik}@cs.unimaas.nl

Abstract. The paper considers conjunctive and disjunctive version space learning as an incomplete search in complete hypotheses spaces. The incomplete search is guided by preference biases which are implemented by procedures based on the instance-based boundary sets representation of version spaces. The conditions for tractability of this representation are defined. As a result we propose to use instance-based boundary sets as a basis for the computationally feasible application of preference biases to version spaces.

1 Introduction

Concept learning is a basic task in machine learning. It is defined under the assumption that any concept is a set of the instances in a domain of discourse. The instances are expressed in an instance language Li and their descriptions in Li form the extensional representation of the concept. Since the extensional representation can be infinite we study the concept in a language Lc of concepts. The concept language Lc is a set of descriptions that represent concepts intensionally, i.e., they recognise all extensional representations of the concepts in the instance language Li. To make this possible we define a predicate M between Li and Lc s.t. a description c in Lc corresponds to a description i in Li, if and only if the instance, represented by i, is a member of the concept, represented by c.

The concept learning task is a quadruple $\langle Li, Lc, M, \langle I^+, I^- \rangle \rangle$: given languages Li and Lc, and the predicate M, the task is to find version space VS of a target concept specified by sets I^+ and I^- of positive and negative training instances. The version space VS is defined as a set of all the descriptions in Lc consistent with training sets [4]. Learning the version space VS is a complete search in the concept language Lc: when new training instances are given VS is updated s.t. descriptions that incorrectly classify the instances are removed.

Classifying with version spaces is based on restriction bias [4]. A restriction bias means that the concept language Lc is not *complete. The language Lc is (not) complete if it is (not) true that every concept, extensionally defined in the instance language Li, has an intensional description in Lc.* The restriction bias has led to three main version-space shortcomings:
(S1) the inability to learn concepts not present in concept languages;

S. A. Cerri and D. Dochev (Eds.): AIMSA 2000, LNAI 1904, pp. 321–331, 2000.

(S2) the inability to handle noisy training instances.

Additionally to (S1) and (S2) Haussler has shown in [1] that:

(S3) the basic-version space representation and algorithm are intractable [4].

This paper avoids the shortcomings (S1) to (S3) by applying preference biases in version-space learning. (A bias is preferential if there exists a strong preference for certain concepts description over others.) Applying a preference bias requires:

(R1) a complete concept language; and

(R2) a computationally feasible procedure that implements the bias.

We fulfil requirement (R1) and overcome shortcoming (S1) by introducing conjunctive and disjunctive extensions of two well-defined concept languages: union and intersection preserving languages. We define conditions when the extensions are complete concept languages, and thus we introduce conjunctive and disjunctive version spaces as classical version spaces defined in these languages.

We overcome shortcoming (S3) by representing conjunctive and disjunctive version spaces with instance-based boundary sets [6] that are tractable for union and intersection preserving languages. We show that the instance-based boundary sets can be used for building computationally feasible procedures that implement different preference biases. Thus, we fulfil requirement (R2) and overcome shortcoming (S2). The latter is empirically justified by experiments.

2   Terminology and Definitions

Instance and concept languages Li and Lc are sets of descriptions. To search in Lc we structure Lc. The structure is based on the relation "more general" ($\geq$).

Definition 1. $(\forall c_1, c_2 \in Lc)((c_1 \geq c_2) \leftrightarrow (\forall i \in Li)(M(c_1, i) \leftarrow M(c_2, i)))$.

The relation is a partial ordering [4]. Hence, Lc is a poset that we restrict s.t. every subset $C \subseteq Lc$ has minimal and maximal elements.

Definition 2. $MIN(C) = \{c \in C | (\forall c' \in C) \neg (c' < c)\}$
$MAX(C) = \{c \in C | (\forall c' \in C) \neg (c' > c)\}$.

To determine when a concept description c is consistent, we define the consistency predicate.

Definition 3. *A concept description c is consistent w.r.t. to sets I^+ and I^- iff:*

$$cons(c, \langle I^+, I^- \rangle) \leftrightarrow ((\forall i \in I^+)M(c, i) \wedge (\forall i \in I^-) \neg M(c, i)).$$

We use the *cons* predicate to define version spaces formally.

Definition 4. *A version space VS w.r.t. a task $\langle Li, Lc, M, \langle I^+, I^- \rangle \rangle$ is:*

$$VS = \{c \in Lc \mid cons(c, \langle I^+, I^- \rangle)\}.$$

Version spaces VS can be represented by minimal and maximal boundary sets S and G specified in definition 5 [4].

Definition 5. $S = MIN(VS)$
$G = MAX(VS)$.

3   UPL Languages and Their Conjunctive Extensions

Union preserving languages (UPL) are specified in definition 6 [6].

Definition 6. *A concept language Lc is a union preserving language (UPL) iff Lc is a complete upper semi-lattice s.t. for every nonempty subset $C \subseteq Lc$:*

(1) the least upper bound of C is in Lc; i.e., $lub(C) \in Lc$; and
(2) $(\forall i \in Li)((\exists c \in C)M(c,i) \leftrightarrow M(lub(C),i))$.

Conjunctive extensions of UPL languages are specified below.

Definition 7. *The language CLc is the conjunctive extension of a UPL concept language Lc if and only if:*

$$CLc = \{C|C = c_1 \wedge ... \wedge c_n, n \geq 1, c_1, ..., c_n \in Lc\}.$$

To relate languages CLc and Li we define the predicate M_C.

Definition 8. *Consider a UPL concept language Lc and a language CLc that is a conjunctive extension of Lc. If $C \in CLc$ then:*

$$(\forall i \in Li)(M_C(C,i) \leftrightarrow (\forall c \in C)M(c,i)).$$

To determine when a conjunction $C \in CLc$ is consistent, the consistency predicate $cons_C$ on CLc is defined analogously to definition 3. The predicate is used in theorem 9 to determine when a conjunctive extension CLc is complete.

Theorem 9. *If CLc is the conjunctive extension of a UPL language Lc then:*

$$(\forall i \in Li)(\exists c \in Lc)cons(c, \langle Li{-}\{i\}, \{i\} \rangle) \leftrightarrow (\forall I \subseteq Li)(\exists C \in CLc)cons_C(C, \langle I, Li{-}I \rangle).$$

Theorem 9 states that a conjunctive extension CLc of a UPL language Lc is a complete language iff for every instance $i \in Li$ there exists a description $c \in Lc$ that does not cover only this instance.

4   Conjunctive Version Spaces

Conjunctive version spaces are defined in conjunctive extensions.

Definition 10. *(Conjunctive Version Space (CVS)) Consider a task $\langle Li, Lc, M, \langle I^+, I^- \rangle \rangle$. If Lc is a UPL language and CLc is the conjunctive extension of Lc then the conjunctive version space CVS of the task is defined as follows:*

$$CVS = \{C \in CLc \,|\, cons_C(C, \langle I^+, I^- \rangle)\}.$$

Since conjunctive extensions are defined in UPL languages we project conjunctive version spaces into UPL languages. Therefore, we define conjunctive version spaces in pure UPL languages (see theorem 1) by means of version spaces with respect to negative instances (see notations 11 and 12).

Notation 11. If i_n is the n-th instance of the set I^- then the version space $\{c \in Lc | cons(c, \langle I^+, i_n \rangle)\}$ is denoted by VS_n. A version space $\{c \in Lc | (\forall i \in I^+) M(c, i)\}$ is denoted by VS_0.

Notation 12. P is the number of positive instances; N is the number of negative instances; p is an index of positive instances; n is an index of negative instances.

Theorem 13. *Consider a task* $\langle Li, Lc, M, \langle I^+, I^- \rangle \rangle$. *Then* [1]:

$$CVS = \bigwedge_{n=0}^{N} VS_n.$$

By theorem 1 we learn conjunctive version spaces CVS by learning version spaces VS_n w.r.t. negative instances.

5   Instance-Based Boundary Sets

The version space boundary sets can grow exponentially in the number of training instances [1]. This holds for the version spaces VS_n: the minimal boundary sets S_n can grow exponentially in the number of positive instances. To overcome this problem we use instance-based boundary sets for representing the version spaces VS_n. We start introducing instance-based boundary sets by lemma 14 [6].

Lemma 14. *Consider a task* $\langle Li, Lc, M, \langle I^+, I^- \rangle \rangle$ *and its conjunctive version space* $CVS = \bigwedge_{n=0}^{N} VS_n$. *Then:*

$$(\forall n \in 0..N)(VS_n = \bigcap_{p=1}^{P} VS_{n,p})$$

where $VS_{n,p} = \{c \in Lc | cons(c, \langle \{i_p\}, \{i_n\} \rangle)\}$.

Lemma 14 states that each version space VS_n is the intersection of simple version spaces $VS_{n,p}$ w.r.t. positive instances. $VS_{n,p}$ allow to define instance-based boundary sets of the version spaces VS_n.

Definition 15. *(The instance-based boundary sets (IBBS))* If Lc is UPL then a version space VS_n is represented by an ordered pair $\langle \langle S_{n,1}, ..., S_{n,P} \rangle, G_n \rangle$ where:

$S_{n,p} = MIN(VS_{n,p})$ for all $p \in 1..P$;
$G_n = MAX(VS_n)$.

IBBS are "instance-based" since they express the minimal boundary sets S_n of the version spaces VS_n with the minimal boundary sets $S_{n,p}$ of simple version spaces $VS_{n,p}$ associated with particular positive instances. It has been shown in [6] that the IBBS correctly represent the version spaces VS_n.

---

[1] $\bigwedge_{i=1}^{N} S_i = \{C | (\forall i \in 1..N)(S_i \cap C \neq \emptyset) \wedge (C \subseteq \cup_{i=1}^{N} S_i)\}$

$$\boxed{\begin{array}{l}
\textbf{FOR}\ \ \text{each training instance } i\ \textbf{DO} \\
\quad \textbf{IF}\ \ i \text{ is a positive instance } i_{P+1}\ \textbf{THEN} \\
\quad\quad \textbf{FOR}\ \ n = 0\ \text{TO } N\ \textbf{DO} \\
\quad\quad\quad S'_{n,P+1} = MIN(\{c \in Lc \,|\, cons(c, \langle\{i_{P+1}\}, \{i_n\}\rangle)\}) \\
\quad \textbf{IF}\ \ i \text{ is a negative instance } i_{N+1}\ \textbf{THEN} \\
\quad\quad \textbf{FOR}\ \ p = 1\ \text{TO } P\ \textbf{DO} \\
\quad\quad\quad S'_{N+1,p} = \{s \in S_{0,p} \,|\, \neg M(s, i_{N+1})\} \\
\quad\quad\quad G'_{N+1} = MAX(\{c \in Lc \,|\, cons(c, \langle I^+, \{i_{N+1}\}\rangle)\})
\end{array}}$$

Fig. 1. The CVS Learning Algorithm

6 The CVS Learning Algorithm

Our learning algorithm updates conjunctive version spaces w.r.t. new training instances. Since conjunctive version spaces are given by the version spaces VS_n, their updating is reduced to updating the spaces VS_n. Updating the version spaces VS_n represented by IBBS is based on theorems 16 and 17 [6].

Theorem 16. *Consider a task* $\langle Li, Lc, M, \langle I^+, i_n\rangle\rangle$ *with version space* VS_n *given by IBBS:*$\langle\langle S_{n,1}, ..., S_{n,P}\rangle, G_n\rangle$, *and a task* $\langle Li, Lc, M, \langle I^+ \cup \{i_{P+1}\}, i_n\rangle\rangle$ *with version space* VS'_n *given by IBBS:*$\langle\langle S'_{n,1}, ..., S'_{n,P+1}\rangle, G_n\rangle$. *If Lc is UPL then:*

$$S'_{n,p} = S_{n,p} \text{ for all } p \in 1..P;$$
$$S'_{n,P+1} = MIN(\{c \in Lc \,|\, cons(c, \langle\{i_{P+1}\}, \{i_n\}\rangle)\}).$$

Theorem 17. *Consider a task* $\langle Li, Lc, M, \langle I^+, \emptyset\rangle\rangle$ *with version space* VS_0 *given by IBBS:*$\langle\langle S_{0,1}, ..., S_{0,P}\rangle, G_0\rangle$ *and a second task* $\langle Li, Lc, M, \langle I^+, \{i_n\}\rangle\rangle$ *with version space* VS_n *given by IBBS:*$\langle\langle S'_{n,1}, ..., S'_{n,P}\rangle, G'_n\rangle$. *If Lc is UPL then:*

$$S'_{n,p} = \{s \in S_{0,p} \,|\, \neg M(s, i_n)\} \text{ for all } p \in 1..P;$$
$$G'_n = MAX(\{c \in Lc \,|\, cons(c, \langle I^+, \{i_n\}\rangle)\}).$$

The learning algorithm is based on theorems 16 and 17, and is given in figure 1. If a new positive instance i_{P+1} is given then the algorithm updates every version spaces VS_n for $n \in 0..N$ as follows:
(1) the maximal boundary set G_n is not changed.
(2) the minimal boundary sets $S_{n,p}$ are not changed for $p \in 1..P$.
(3) the minimal boundary set $S'_{n,P+1}$ is generated as a set of minimal descriptions in Lc that cover i_{P+1} and do not cover the corresponding negative instance i_n.

¿From steps (1) to (3) above, it follows that the IBBS representations of S_n and G_n of VS_n are generalised to cover the instance i_{P+1}. Therefore, the conjunctions in CVS that do not cover i_{P+1} are removed.

If a new negative instance i_{N+1} is given then the algorithm generates only the IBBS representation of the new version space VS'_{N+1}:
(4) the S'_{N+1} part of the IBBS is generated from the minimal boundary sets $S_{0,p}$ (for all $p \in 1..P$) by removing the elements covering the instance i_{N+1}.

(5) the set G'_{N+1} of the IBBS is generated from the maximal elements in Lc that cover the set I^+ and do not cover the instance i_{N+1}.

From steps (4) and (5) it follows that the conjunctions in CVS that cover i_{N+1} are removed by adding to CVS the version space VS'_{N+1}.

7   Classification Based on Restriction Biases

If theorem 9 does not hold then the conjunctive extensions CLc are incomplete. Hence, we have restriction bias and we can apply the unanimous vote classification rule [4]: if all descriptions in a conjunctive version space CVS agree on a classification of an instance then the instance gets the classification. Since CVS is given with the version spaces VS_n and $(\forall n \in [0, N])(VS_0 \supseteq VS_n)$ (see notation 11) then the unanimous vote rule works by theorem 1 as follows: (1) if the version space VS_0 agrees on the positive classification of an instance then the instance is classified as positive; (2) if at least one version space VS_n agrees on the negative classification of an instance then the instance is classified as negative; (3) if the cases (1) and (2) have failed then the instance is unclassified.

8   Classification Based on Preference Biases

If theorem 9 holds then conjunctive extensions CLc are complete. Hence, preference biases can be applied. Classification based on preference biases is computationally feasible when IBBS can be used for building procedures that implement these biases. IBBS facilitate implementing preference biases since:

(1) removing any minimal boundary set $S_{n,p}$ for given n and p means that the corresponding VS_n is not consistent anymore with the positive instance i_p;

(2) removing the IBBS of a version space VS_n for a given n means that the conjunctive version space CVS is not consistent anymore with the negative instance i_n (a corollary of theorem 1);

(3) each minimal boundary set $S_{0,p}$ is the union of the minimal boundary sets $S_{n,p}$, i.e., $S_{0,p} = \bigcup_{n=0}^{N} S_{n,p}$ for all $p \in 1..P$ (a corollary of theorem 17).

We use properties (1) to (3) and propose two types of approaches for implementing preference biases.

8.1   Separate-and-Conquer Approach

The separate-and-conquer approach is based on the IBBS of the minimal boundary set S_0 which is a rich structure containing complete information about positive training data. Hence, it can use this structure to build a large spectrum of separate-and-conquer algorithms. In this light we give two simple separate-and-conquer algorithms that demonstrate the vitality of the approach.

$C = \emptyset$
while $\neg \ StoppingCriterion(C, I^+, I^-)$ **do**
$\quad c = \emptyset$
$\quad$ **for** $p = 1$ to P **do**
$\qquad maxPerf = Perf(c, I^+, I^-)$
$\qquad maxS = \emptyset$
$\qquad$ **for** each $s \in S_{0,p}$ **do**
$\qquad\quad$ **if** $(Perf(c \lor s, I^+, I^-) > MaxPerf)$ **then**
$\qquad\qquad maxS = s$
$\qquad\qquad maxPerf = Perf(c \lor s, I^+, I^-)$
$\qquad\qquad c = c \lor maxS$
$\quad C = C \land c$
$\quad$ Remove from I^- all instances that are not covered by c

Fig. 2. The CLc-Separate-Conquer Algorithm

CLc-Separate-and-Conquer Algorithm. The algorithm (CLc-SCA) learns conjunctions of target concepts in conjunctive extensions CLc (see figure 2). It starts with an empty conjunction C. Then it "greedily" builds every conjunct c of C from these elements of the sets $S_{0,p}$ ($p \in 1..P$) that maximise a user supplied function $Perf$ in a disjunction. Hence, every conjunct c is a disjunction of so-chosen elements of the set $S_{0,p}$. The process of generating conjuncts c stops when the $StoppingCriterion$ fires.

Note that the **for** loops, that learns conjuncts c, search in UPL concept languages Lc. The outer loop **while** learns conjunctions C in conjunctive extensions CLc. That is why the algorithm is labeled with CLc.

DNF-Separate-and-Conquer Algorithm. The main problem with the CLc-sequential-covering algorithm is that the size of the conjunctions C can be exponential in the number of positive instances [1]. To avoid this problem we propose a DNF-separate-and-conquer algorithm (DNF-SCA) given in figure 3.

The DNF-separate-and-conquer algorithm learns disjunctions of target concepts; the disjuncts belong to conjunctive extensions CLc (see figure 3). It starts with an empty disjunction D. Each disjunct C_p of D is initialised equal to the conjunction of all elements of the corresponding set $S_{0,p}$. The conjuncts s of C_p are "greedily" removed s.t. the disjunct C_p maximises a user supplied function $Perf$. Revising a disjunct C_p stops when $StoppingCriterion$ fires. The disjunction D is formed when all minimal boundary sets $S_{0,p}$ are visited.

Note that the **for** loop, learning disjuncts C_p, searches in subspaces of conjunctive extensions CLc. The disjunction D is learned in a disjunction of these subspaces. Hence, D is formed in DNF extensions of UPL concept languages. That is why the algorithm is labeled with DNF.

In both separate-and-conquer algorithms the user supplied function $Perf$ can be any metric used in bottom-up induction. In our experiments we use the m-etsimate with $m = 3$ [2]. The $StoppingCriterion$ is a predicate that becomes

$$D = \emptyset$$
for $p = 1$ to P **do**
$\quad C_p =$ conjunction of all elements of the set $S_{0,p}$
$\quad maxPerf = Perf(C_p, I^+, I^-)$
$\quad$ **while** $\neg$ $StoppingCriterion(C_p, I^+, I^-)$ **do**
$\quad\quad maxS = \emptyset$
$\quad\quad$ **for each** $s \in S_{0,p}$ **do**
$\quad\quad\quad$ **if** $(Perf(C_p - \{s\}, I^+, I^-) > MaxPerf)$ **then**
$\quad\quad\quad\quad maxS = s$
$\quad\quad\quad\quad maxPerf = Perf(C_p - \{s\}, I^+, I^-)$
$\quad\quad\quad\quad C_p = C_p - \{maxS\}$
$\quad D = D \vee C_p$

Fig. 3. The DNF-Separate-Conquer Algorithm

true when 3 percent of the negative instances remain uncovered. The resulting predictive accuracies for the Monks tasks [3] is given in figure 4.

8.2   Voting Classification Approach

The voting classification approach is based on an approach given in [5]. If a new instance has to be classified then its classification is determined by an $\mathcal{N}$-vote of version spaces VS_n for $n \in 1..N$. The $\mathcal{N}$-vote means that $\mathcal{N}$ numbers of version spaces VS_n have to classify the instance as positive in order to obtain the positive classification. The procedure for classification with one version space VS_n is based on two parameters $\mathcal{S}$ and $\mathcal{P}$. The parameter $\mathcal{S}$ determines how many descriptions for particular $S_{n,p}$ have to cover an instance in order to classify it as positive. Analogously, the parameter $\mathcal{P}$ determines how many minimal boundary sets $S_{n,p}$ classifying the instance as positive are needed s.t. the instance is classified as positive by the corresponding version space VS_n.

The parameters $\mathcal{N}$, $\mathcal{S}$ and $\mathcal{P}$ can be adjusted globally for all VS_n by a process of trials and errors proposed in [5]. The training set is divided into two training sets . The first one (70%) is used for inducing the conjunctive version space CVS given with the version spaces VS_n represented by IBBS. The second training set (30%) is used for adjusting the parameters $\mathcal{N}$, $\mathcal{S}$ and $\mathcal{P}$. The measured predictive accuracies for the Monks tasks are given in figure 4.

Algorithm	M1	M2	M3
CLc-SCA	100%	64%	95.55%
DNF-SCA	100%	64%	95.55%
$\mathcal{N}$-vote	94%	69%	92%

Fig. 4. The Predictive Accuracy on the Monks Tasks

9   Analytical Complexity Analysis

The analysis is made in terms of P and N (see notation 12); and Σ and Γ - the largest sizes of the minimal and maximal boundary sets of version spaces $VS_{n,p}$.

The space complexity of a conjunctive version space with $N + 1$ number of spaces VS_n is $O(N(P\Sigma+\Gamma))$ since the complexity of IBBS of one VS_n is $O(P\Sigma + \Gamma)$. The space complexity of the resulting conjunctions C and disjunctions D of CLc-SCA and DNF-SCA algorithms is $O(P\Sigma)$ since in the worst case it is equal to the space complexity $O(P\Sigma)$ of IBBS of the set S_0.

The time complexity of the CVS learning algorithm is equal to the complexity $O(N(G(S'_{n,P+1})))$ for handling positive instances plus the complexity $O(P\Sigma + G(G'_{N+1}))$ for handling negative instances, where $G(S'_{n,P+1})$ and $G(G'_{N+1})$ are generation complexities of the sets $S'_{n,P+1}$ and G'_{N+1}.

The time complexity of the unanimous positive classification is $O(P\Sigma)$ since it is based on the S-part of IBBS of the version space VS_0. The same complexity in the case of negative classification is $O(N\Gamma)$ since it is based on the G-part of IBBS of the version spaces VS_n.

¿From the complexity analysis follows that IBBS representations of conjunctive version spaces, conjunctions C and disjunctions D are tractable iff Σ and Γ are polynomial in relevant properties of UPL languages. This holds for the CVS algorithms based on restriction biases. They are tractable iff Σ, Γ, $G(S'_{n,P+1})$, $G(G'_{N+1})$ are polynomial in relevant properties of UPL languages.

10   Experimental Complexity Analysis

The analysis is based on the experiments of our CVS systems implemented in JAVA2 on a Pentium-II computer. The results reported were observed during experiments with the Monks tasks.

The size of IBBS of conjunctive version spaces grows linearly with the number of the training instances. This is due to our current implementation based on a single representation trick, i.e., $Li \subseteq Lc$. Thus, the IBBS of conjunctive version spaces are represented with the positive instances.

The resulting conjuncts C of the CLc-SCA algorithm contain in average 5 to 6 conjuncts. Each conjunct has 3 to 4 descriptions of Lc. The resulting disjunctions D of the DNF-SCA algorithm contain P numbers of disjuncts. Each disjunct has 3 to 4 descriptions of Lc. To reduce the number of disjuncts we remove their repeated exemplars. Thus, the average number of disjuncts is 5 to 6.

The running time per training instance of the CVS learning algorithm grows linearly between 6 to 9 millisec. The running times per training instance of CLc-SCA and DNF-SCA algorithms are comparable. They grow quadratically between 4 and 1200 millisec. The running time for adjusting parameters $\mathcal{N}$, $\mathcal{S}$ and $\mathcal{P}$ for the $\mathcal{N}$-vote classification is problematic since we use a brute-force algorithm. The time varies between 460 000 and 670 000 millisec.

11   The Dual Part of the Paper

Intersection preserving languages, their disjunctive extensions and version spaces can be derived by duality from the previous eight sections. Unfortunately, the space considerations preclude presenting details.

12   Comparison with Relevant Work

We can compare our work solely with [5] since this is the only work in applied version spaces. The paper [5] introduces the voting classification in the context of disjunctive version spaces. Its approach faces the same problem as the $\mathcal{N}$-vote : the number of compound version spaces in disjunctive and conjunctive version spaces can be exponential in the number of training instances. Moreover, we discovered an analogous problem with the CLc-SCA algorithm : the size of the conjuncts C can be exponential. That is why we proposed the DNF-SCA algorithm that successfully solves this problem.

13   Conclusion

This paper proposes to avoid the main shortcomings (S1) to (S3) of version spaces (see section 1) via applying preference biases. Shortcoming (S1) is overcome by introducing conjunctive and disjunctive extensions of union and intersection preserving languages. The condition for the extensions to be complete concept languages is shown, and in this context conjunctive and disjunctive version spaces are defined. Shortcoming (S3) is resolved by representing conjunctive and disjunctive version spaces with instance-based boundary sets of which the conditions for tractability are analysed. It is shown that the instance-based boundary sets can be used for building computationally feasible procedures implementing preference biases. Thus, the most serious shortcoming (S2) is also overcome: we can handle noisy training data with version spaces (see the predictive accuracy for the M3 task with 5% noise in figure 4).

Coverage-Based Semi-distance between Horn Clauses

Zdravko Markov[1] and Ivo Marinchev[2]

[1] Department of Computer Science, Central Connecticut State University
1615 Stanley Street, New Britain, CT 06050, U.S.A.
markovz@ccsu.edu
[2] Faculty of Mathematics and Informatics, University of Sofia
5 James Bouchier Str., 1164 Sofia, Bulgaria
ivo@fmi.uni-sofia.bg

Abstract. In the present paper we use the approach of *height functions* to defining a semi-distance measure between Horn clauses. This appraoch is already discussed elsewhere in the framework of propositional and simple first order languages (atoms). Hereafter we prove its applicability for Horn clauses. We use some basic results from lattice theory and introduce a family of language independent coverage-based height functions. Then we show how these results apply to Horn clauses. We also show an example of conceptual clustering of first order atoms, where the hypotheses are Horn clauses.

1 Introduction

Almost all approaches to inductive learning are based on generalization and/or specialization hierarchies. These hierarchies represent the hypothesis space which in most cases is a partially ordered set under some generality ordering. The properties of partially ordered sets are well studied in lattice theory. One concept from this theory is mostly used in inductive learning – this is the *least general generalization (lgg)* which given two hypotheses builds their most specific common generalization. The existence of an *lgg* in a hypothesis space directly implies that this space is a semi-lattice (the lgg plays the role of infimum). Thus the lgg-based approaches are theoretically well founded, simple and elegant.

Lgg's exist for most of the languages commonly used in machine learning. However all practically applicable (i.e. computable) lgg's are based on *syntactical* ordering relations. A relation over hypotheses is syntactical if it does not account for the background knowledge and for the coverage of positive/negative examples. For example, dropping condition for nominal attributes, instance relation for atomic formulae and θ-subsumption for clauses are all syntactical relations. On the other hand the evaluation of the hypotheses built by an lgg operator is based on their coverage of positive/negative examples with respect to the background knowledge, i.e. it is based on *semantic relations* (in the sense of the inductive task). This discrepancy is a source of many problems, where overgeneralization is the most serious one.

S. A. Cerri and D. Dochev (Eds.): AIMSA 2000, LNAI 1904, pp. 331–339, 2000.

The idea behind the lgg is to make "cautious" (minimal) generalization. However this property of the lgg greatly depends on how similar are the hypotheses/examples used to build the lgg. For example there exist elements in the hypothesis space whose lgg is the top element (empty hypothesis). This is another source of overgeneralization.

An obvious solution of the latter problem is to use a distance (metric) over the hypothesis/examle space in order to evaluate the similarity between the hypotheses/examples. The basic idea is when building an lgg to choose the pair of hypotheses/examples with the minimal distance between them. Thus the lgg will be the minimal generalization over the whole set of hypotheses/examples. Various distance measures can be used for this purpose. The best choice however is a distance which corresponds to the lgg used, that is the pair of the *closest hypotheses* must produce the *minimal lgg*. To ensure this, the distance and the lgg must be well coupled. Ideally such a distance exists in semi-lattices, however it is based on syntactical relations and as we mentioned above the best way to evaluate the similarity between hypotheses is to use semantic relations. This is a typical problem in Inductive Logic Programming ([4]), where the hypotheses are usually Horn clauses which are generated by syntactical operators (e.g. θ-subsumption lgg) and evaluated by coverage-based functions.

In the present paper we use the approach of *height functions* to defining a semi-distance on a join semi-lattice. This appraoch was already discussed for propositional and simple first order languages (atoms) in [3]. Hereafter we prove its applicability for Horn clauses. For this purpose we repeat some of the basic results and further elaborate the notions introduced in [3].

The paper is organized as follows. The next section introduces some basic notions from lattice theory used throughout the paper. Section 3 describes the height-based approach to defining a semi-distance on a join semi-lattice. Section 4 proves the applicability of this appraoch to Horn clauses and Section 5 shows an example of this. Finally Section 6 concludes with a discussion of related approaches and directions for future work.

2 Preliminaries

The discussion in this section follows [3] with some modifications and elaborations (the proofs of the theorems are also skipped).

Definition 1 (Semi-distance, Quasi-metric). A *semi-distance (quasi-metric)* is a mapping $d : O \times O \to \Re$ on a set of objects O with the following properties $(a, b, c \in O)$:

1. $d(a, a) = 0$ and $d(a, b) \geq 0$.
2. $d(a, b) = d(b, a)$ (symmetry).
3. $d(a, b) \leq d(a, c) + d(c, b)$ (triangle inequality).

Definition 2 (Order preserving semi-distance). A semi-distance $d : O \times O \to \Re$ on a partially ordered set $(O, \preceq)$ is *order preserving* iff for all $a, b, c \in O$, such that $a \preceq b \preceq c$ it follows that $d(a, b) \leq d(a, c)$ and $d(b, c) \leq d(a, c)$

Definition 3 (Join/Meet semi-lattice). A *join/meet semi-lattice* is a partially ordered set $(A, \preceq)$ in which every two elements $a, b \in A$ have an infimum/supremum.

Definition 4 (Diamond inequality). Let $(A, \preceq)$ be a join semi-lattice. A semi-distance $d : A \times A \to \Re$ satisfies the *diamond inequality* iff the existence of $sup\{a, b\}$ implies the following inequality: $d(inf\{a, b\}, a) + d(inf\{a, b\}, b) \leq d(a, sup\{a, b\}) + d(b, sup\{a, b\})$.

Definition 5 (Size function). Let $(A, \preceq)$ be a join semi-lattice. A mapping $s : A \times A \to \Re$ is called a *size function* if it satisfies the following properties:

S1. $s(a, b) \geq 0, \forall a, b \in A$ and $a \preceq b$.
S2. $s(a, a) = 0, \forall a \in A$.
S3. $\forall a, b, c \in A$, such that $a \preceq c$ and $c \preceq b$ it follows that $s(a, b) \leq s(a, c) + s(c, b)$ and $s(c, b) \leq s(a, b)$.
S4. Let $c = inf\{a, b\}$, where $a, b \in A$. For any $d \in A$, such that $a \preceq d$ and $b \preceq d$ it follows that $s(c, a) + s(c, b) \leq s(a, d) + s(b, d)$.

Consider for example the partially ordered set of first order atoms under θ-subsumption. A size function $s(a, b)$ on this set can be defined as the number of different functional symbols (a constant is considered a functional symbol of arity zero) occurring in the substitution θ mapping a onto b ($a\theta = b$). A family of similar size functions is introduced in [1], where they are called a *size of substitution*. Although well defined these functions do not account properly for the variables in the atoms and consequently cannot be used with non-ground atoms.

Theorem 1. Let $(A, \preceq)$ be a join semi-lattice and s – a size function. Let also $d(a, b) = s(inf\{a, b\}, a) + s(inf\{a, b\}, b)$. Then d is a *semi-distance* on $(A, \preceq)$.

A widely used approach to define a semi-distance is based on an order preserving size function and the diamond inequality instead of property $S4$. The use of property $S4$ however is more general because otherwise we must assume that (1) all intervals in the lattice are finite and (2) if two elements have an upper bound they must have a least upper bound (supremum) too. An illustration of this problem is shown in Figure 1, where a_3 is an upper bound of b_1 and b_2 and $e = sup\{b1, b2\}$. Generally the interval $[e, a_3]$ may be infinite or e may not exists. This however does not affect our definition of semi-distance.

Further, a size function can be defined by using the so called *height functions*. The approach of height functions have the advantage that it is based on estimating the object itself rather than its relations to other objects.

Definition 6 (Height function). A function h is called *height* of the elements of a partially ordered set $(A, \preceq)$ if it satisfies the following two properties:

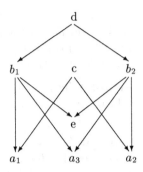

Fig. 1. A semi-lattice structure

H1. For every $a, b \in A$ if $a \preceq b$ then $h(a) \leq h(b)$ (isotone).
H2. For every $a, b \in A$ if $c = inf\{a, b\}$ and $d \in A$ such that $a \preceq d$ and $b \preceq d$
then $h(a) + h(b) \leq h(c) + h(d)$.

Theorem 2. Let $(A, \preceq)$ be a join semi-lattice and h be a height function. Let
$s(a, b) = h(b) - h(a), \forall a \preceq b \in A$. Then s is a *size function* on $(A, \preceq)$.

Corollary 1. Let $(A, \preceq)$ be a join semi-lattice and h be a height function. Then
the function $d(a, b) = h(a) + h(b) - 2h(inf\{a, b\}), \forall a, b \in A$ is a *semi-distance*
on $(A, \preceq)$.

3   Semantic Semi-distance on Join Semi-lattices

In this section we briefly outline the approach to defining a semantic semi-
distance on join semi-lattices originally introduced in [3].

Let A be a set of objects and let $\preceq_1$ and $\preceq_2$ be two binary relations on A.
Let also $\preceq_1$ be a partial ordering and $(A, \preceq_1)$ – a join semi-lattice.

Definition 7 (Ground elements of a join semi-lattice (GA)). GA is the
set of all maximal elements of A w.r.t. $\preceq_1$, i.e. $GA = \{a | a \in A \text{ and } \neg \exists b \in A :$
$a \preceq_1 b\}$.

Definition 8 (Ground coverage). For every $a \in A$ the *ground coverage* of a
w.r.t $\preceq_2$ is $S_a = \{b | b \in GA \text{ and } a \preceq_2 b\}$.

The ground coverage S_a can be considered as a definition of the semantics
of a. Therefore we call $\preceq_2$ a *semantic relation* by analogy to the Herbrand interpretation in first order logic used to define the semantics of a given term. The
other relation involved, $\preceq_1$ is called *constructive (or syntactic) relation* because
it is used to build the lattice from a given set of ground elements GA.

The basic idea of our approach is to use these two relations, $\preceq_1$ and $\preceq_2$ to
define the semi-distance. According to Corollary 1 we use the syntactic relation $\preceq_1$ to find the infimum and the semantic relation $\preceq_2$ to define the height

function h. The advantage of this approach is that in many cases there exists a proper semantic relation however it is intractable, computationally expensive or even not a partial order, which makes impossible to use it as a constructive relation too (an example of such a relation is logical implication). Then we can use another, simpler relation as a constructive one (to find the infimum) and still make use of the semantic relation (in the height function).

Not any two relations however can be used for this purpose. The following teorem states the necessary conditions for two relations to form a correct height function.

Theorem 3. Let A be a set of objects and let $\preceq_2$ and $\preceq_1$ be two binary relations in A such that:

1. $\preceq_1$ is a partial order and $(A, \preceq_1)$ is a join semi-lattice.
2. For every $a, b \in A$ if $a \preceq_1 b$ then $|S_a| \geq |S_b|$[1].
3. For every $a, b \in A$ and $c = \inf\{a, b\}$ such that there exists $d = \sup\{a, b\}$ one of the following must hold:
   C1. $|S_d| < |S_a|$ and $|S_d| < |S_b|$
   C2. $|S_d| = |S_a|$ and $|S_c| = |S_b|$
   C3. $|S_d| = |S_b|$ and $|S_c| = |S_a|$

Then there exists a family of *height functions* $h(a) = x^{-|S_a|}$, where $a \in A$, $x \in \Re$ and $x \geq 2$.

Proof.

1. Let $a, b \in A$, $a \preceq_1 b$. Then by the assumptions $|S_a| \geq |S_b|$ and hence $h(a) \leq h(b)$.
2. Let $a, b \in A$, $c = \inf\{a, b\}$ and $d = \sup\{a, b\}$.
   (a) Assume that C1 is true. Then $|S_d| < |S_a|$ and $|S_d| < |S_b| \Rightarrow |S_a| \geq |S_d| + 1$ and $|S_b| \geq |S_d| + 1 \Rightarrow -|S_a| \leq -|S_d| - 1$ and $-|S_b| \leq -|S_d| - 1$. Hence $h(a) + h(b) = x^{-|S_a|} + x^{-|S_b|} \leq x^{-|S_d|-1} + x^{-|S_d|-1} = 2x^{-|S_d|-1} \leq x \cdot x^{-|S_d|-1} = x^{-|S_d|} = h(d) \leq h(c) + h(d)$.
   (b) Assume that C2 is true. Then $|S_d| = |S_a|$ and $|S_c| = |S_b|$. Hence $h(a) + h(b) = h(c) + h(d)$.
   (c) Assume that C3 is true. Then $|S_d| = |S_b|$ and $|S_c| = |S_a|$. Hence $h(a) + h(b) = h(c) + h(d)$.

4 Coverage-Based Semi-distance between Horn Clauses

Within the language of Horn clauses we use θ-*subsumption* for the constructive relation $\preceq_1$ and *logical implication* (semantic entailment) for the semantic relation $\preceq_2$.

Definition 9 (θ-subsumption). Let a and b be Horn clauses. Then a θ-subsumes b denoted $a \preceq_\theta b$, iff there exist a substitution θ, such that $a\theta \subseteq b$ (the clauses are considered as sets of literals).

---

[1] Generally an isotone property is required here. However we skip the other case, $|S_a| \leq |S_b|$ since it is analogous.

Under θ-subsumption a set of Horn clauses with same predicates at their heads (same functors and arity) forms a join semi-lattice, where the join operator is the θ-subsumption-based least general generalization (lgg_θ). Further, we will show that θ-subsumption and logical implication can be used to define a correct height function on this semi-latice which in turn implies the existence of a coverage-based semi-distance between Horn clauses.

Definition 10 (Model). A set of ground literals which does not contain a complementary pair is called a *model*. Let M be a model, c – a clause, and C – the set of all ground clauses obtained by replacing the variables in c by ground terms. M is a model of c iff each clause in C contains at least one literal from M.

Definition 11 (Semantic entailment). Let f_1 and f_2 be well-formed formulae. f_1 *semantically entails* f_2, denoted $f_1 \models f_2$ (or $f_1 \preceq_{\models} f_2$) iff every model of f_1 is a model of f_2.

Corollary 2. Let a and b be clauses such that $a \preceq_\theta b$. Then $S_a \supseteq S_b$ and $|S_a| \geq |S_b|$.

Proof. Let a and b be clauses and let a θ-subsumes b. According to Definitions 9 and 10 a semantically entails b, i.e. $a \preceq_{\models} b$. Then according to Definition 8 $S_a \supseteq S_b$ and $|S_a| \geq |S_b|$.

Now we will show that the two assumptions of Theorem 3 hold:

1. Let a and b be clauses and let $a \preceq_1 b$. Then by Corollary 2 $|S_a| \geq |S_b|$.
2. Let $d = sup\{a, b\}$ w.r.t. $\preceq_\theta$. Then $a \preceq_\theta d$, $b \preceq_\theta d$, and by Corollary 2 $|S_d| \leq |S_a|$ and $|S_d| \leq |S_b|$. Further, we will show that actually $|S_d| < |S_a|$ and $|S_d| < |S_b|$. First, we assume that for any two clauses c_1 and c_2 if $S_{c_1} \equiv S_{c_2}$ then $c_1 \equiv c_2$. Thus, in fact instead of clauses we use *equivalence classes* of clauses w.r.t. $\preceq_{\models}$. Let $x \in S_a \triangle S_b$ (symmetric difference). Assume now that $x \in S_d$. Then by Corollary 2 $S_d \subseteq S_a$ and $S_d \subseteq S_b$, that is $x \in S_a \cap S_b$ which is a contradiction. Hence $x \notin S_d$, i.e. $S_d \subset S_a$ and $S_d \subset S_b$, i.e. $|S_d| < |S_a|$ and $|S_d| < |S_b|$.

Then according to Corollary 1 the following function is a semi-distance

$$d(a, b) = x^{-|S_a|} + x^{-|S_b|} - 2x^{-|S_{lgg_\theta(a,b)}|},$$

where a and b are Horn clauses and S_a, S_b and $S_{lgg_\theta(a,b)}$ are models of a, b and $lgg_\theta(a, b)$.

5   Example

To illustrate the semi-distance between Horn clauses we use the inductive algorithm described in [3,2]. The algorithm starts with a given set of examples (ground atoms) GA and builds a hierarchy of Horn clauses covering this examples (i.e. a partial lattice, where GA is the set of maximal elements of the lattice). The algorithgm is as follows:

1. Initialization: $G = GA$, $C = GA$;
2. If $|C| = 1$ then exit;
3. $T = \{h|h = lgg_\theta(a, b), (a, b) = argmin_{a,b \in C}d(a, b)\}$;
4. $DC = \{h|h \in C \text{ and } \exists h_{min} \in T : h_{min} \preceq_2 h\}$;
5. $C = C \setminus DC$;
6. $G = G \cup T$, $C = C \cup T$, go to step 2.

We use 10 instances of the **member** predicate and supply them as a GA set to our algorithm. Figure 2 shows the lattice structure built upon this set of examples. The two successors of the top element form the well known definition of *member* (the recursive clause contains a redundant literal). The generated tree structure can be seen as an example of *conceptual clustering of first order atoms*, where the hypotheses are Horn clauses.

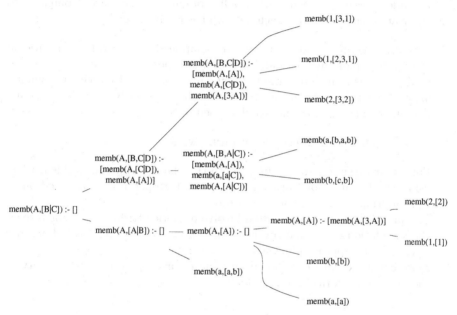

Fig. 2. Hypothesis space for the instances of the **member** predicate

A major problem in applying our algorithm is the *clause reduction*. This is because although finite the length of the lgg_θ of n clauses can grow exponentially with n. Some well-known techniques of avoiding this problem are discussed in [4]. By placing certain restrictions on the hypothesis language the number of literals in the lgg_θ clause can be limited by a polynomial function independent on n. Currently we use *ij-determined* clauses in our experiments (actually 22-determinated).

6   Conclusion

Distance measures are widely used in machine learning, pattern recognition, statistics and other related areas. Most of the distances in these areas are based on attribute-value (or feature-value) languages and further elaborate well known distances in feature spaces (e.g. Euclidean distance, Hamming distance etc.). Recently a lot of attention has been paid to studying distance measures in first order languages. The basic idea is to apply the highly successful instance based algorithms to relational data described in the much more expressive language of first order logic. Various approaches have been proposed in this area. Some of the most recent ones are [1,5,6,7]. These approaches as well as most of the others define a simple metric on atoms and then extend it to sets of atoms (clauses or models) using the Hausdorff metric or other similarity functions. Because of the complexity of the functions involved and problems with the computability of the models these approaches are usually computationally hard. Compared to the other approaches our approach has two basic advantages:

- It is language independent, i.e. it can be applied both within propositional (attribute-value) languages and within first order languages.
- It allows consistent integration of generalization operators with a semantic distance measure. This makes the approach particularly suitable for inductive algorithms, such as the one discussed in Section 5.

We see the following directions for future work:

- Particular attention should be paid to the clause reduction problem when using the language of Horn clauses. Other lgg operators, not based on θ-subsumption should be considered too.
- The practical learning data often involve numeric attributes. In this respect proper relations, lgg's and covering functions should be investigated in order to extend the approach for handling numeric data.
- More experimental work should be done to investigate the applicability of the proposed algorithm in real domains.

References

1. A. Hutchinson Metrics on terms and clauses. In M. van Someren and G. Widmer, editors, *Machine Learning: EC ML-97,* volume 1224 of *Lecture Notes in Artificial Intelligence,* pages 138-145. Springer-Verlag, 1997. 333, 338
2. Z. Markov. An algebraic approach to inductive learning. In *Proceedings of 13th International FLAIRS Conference,* page in print, Orlando, Florida, May 22-25, 2000. AAAI Press. 336
3. Z. Markov and I. Marinchev. Metric-based inductive learning using semantic height functions. In R. L. de Mantaras and E. Plaza, editors, *Machine Learning: ECML 2000,* volume 1810 of *Lecture Notes in Artificial Intelligence,* page in print. Springer, 2000. 332, 334, 336

4. S. Muggleton. Inductive logic programming. In S. Muggleton, editor, *Inductive Logic Programming,* pages 3-28. Academic Press, 1992. 332, 337
5. S.-H. Nienhuys-Cheng. Distance between herbrand interpretations: a measure for approximations to a target concept. Technical Report EUR-FEW-CS-97-05, Erasmus University, 1997. 338
6. J. Ramon, M. Bruynooghe, and W. V. Laer. Distance measure between atoms. Technical Report CW 264, Katholieke Universiteit Leuven, 1998. 338
7. J. Ramon, M. Bruynooghe, and W. V. Laer. A framework for defining a distance between first-order logic objects. Technical Report CW 263, Katholieke Universiteit Leuven, 1998. 338

Supervised Classification for the Triple Parity Strings

Tony Y. T. Chan

The University of Aizu
Aizu-Wakamatsu Shi, Fukushima Ken, 965-8580 Japan
t-chan@u-aizu.ac.jp

Abstract. A method is proposed for supervised learning to classify bit strings for three classes. The learner was modeled by two formal concepts: transformation system and stability optimization. Even though a small set of short examples were used in the training stage, all bit strings of any length were classified correctly in the online recognition stage. The learner successfully learned to devise a way by means of metric calculations to classify bit strings according to 3-parity-ness while the learner was never told the concept of 3-parity-ness.

Keywords: supervised learning, unifying metric approach, stability quotient, stability optimization, transformation systems

1   Introduction

In [3], a general model was proposed for inductive learning in two classes. It solved the unsupervised parity problem of unbounded length beautifully with 100% accuracy. No other general learning algorithm, including neural networks, has been able to achieve that result because they all assume a fixed normed vector space throughout the learning process. This paper extends the supervised part of [3] for learning in three classes. This line of the metric approach to learning has been applied to the benchmark parity problem [3], supervised classification of chromosomes [6], unsupervised classification of chromosomes [1], classifications of Irises and Pima Indians Diabetes, etc. [2]. Wong, Shen, and Wong [7] used it for texture classification and did experiments on hundreds of training objects at a time. Liang and Clarson used it on brainwaves [4]. The approach is related to Fisher's discriminant [5, p. 115], which maximizes the distance between class centers while at the same time minimizing the within-class scatters.

A pattern language describes a set P of objects. The object set is divided into exactly three mutually-exclusive subsets, $Q_1, Q_2, Q_3 \subset P$. Presumably, each of these subsets is a class of objects. The teacher supplies three finite *training groups* of objects to the learning agent. The union of the training groups $\check{Q}_1 \cup \check{Q}_2 \cup \check{Q}_3$ is called the *training set*. The agent then autonomously devises a way to distinguish the three sets $Q_1, Q_2,$ and Q_3 by means of metric calculations. Hence, the next time an unknown object $p \in P$ is presented to the agent, it will be able to classify it as belonging to $Q_1, Q_2,$ or Q_3. The learner accomplishes this by deriving a

S. A. Cerri and D. Dochev (Eds.): AIMSA 2000, LNAI 1904, pp. 340–347, 2000.

stable metric space to separate the training groups. A stable metric space is one containing well-separated, compact clusters.

2   The Model

Let $T = (P, S)$ be a transformation system, where P is an underlying set of structural objects described by a pattern language.

Let $s = x \leftrightarrow y$ be a substitution operation where x and y are subobjects. An object X can be transformed to the object Y via rule s by matching a subobject x from X and replacing it with y. Substitution rules are bidirectional in that the substitution of subobject x by subobject y implies that the substitution of y by x is also possible. When $x = \theta$ is empty, the operation is called insertion. When y is empty, the operation is called deletion. $S = (s_1, s_2, \ldots, s_m)$ is a list of m bidirectional substitution operations.

Now we introduce weights to the substitution rules. With each substitution s_i, we associate a weight w_i, $w_i \geq 0$, so that it costs w_i to operate s_i. Let $W = (w_1, w_2, \ldots, w_m)$ and $\triangle_W(p_1, p_2) = $ the smallest total cost to transform p_1 into p_2. When all the weights are 1, $\triangle$ simply counts the minimum number of operations required to transform one object into another.

Definition 1. *The* average intra-group distance *for a training group k is*

$$\rho_k(\triangle_W) = \frac{2}{n(n-1)} \sum_{i=2}^{n} \sum_{j=1}^{i-1} \triangle_W(\breve{q}_i, \breve{q}_j)$$

where $\breve{q}_i, \breve{q}_j \in \breve{Q}_k$ and the size of $\breve{Q}_k$ is n.

Given a specific training group and a specific distance function, ρ returns the average distance within a group of training objects. Note that for this formula to work, there must be at least two training objects. When n is equal to 1, we trivially define $\rho = 0$. We may drop the subscript or the input argument for ρ when it is clear from the context which subscript or argument is meant.

Definition 2. *The* average inter-group distance *between groups k and h is*

$$\upsilon_{k,h}(\triangle_W) = \frac{1}{nn'} \sum_{i=1}^{n} \sum_{j=1}^{n'} \triangle_W(\breve{q}_i, \breve{r}_j)$$

where $\breve{r}_j \in \breve{Q}_h$ and the size of $\breve{Q}_h$ is n'.

Here n' can equal 1. In essence, these two rather standard definitions capture the idea of the average distance of a distance table where distances are listed between pairs of objects.

Definition 3. *The* stability quotient *for three groups, 1, 2, and 3, is*

$$Z_{1,2,3}(\triangle_W) = \frac{\rho_1 + \rho_2 + \rho_3}{\upsilon_{1,2}\,\upsilon_{1,3}\,\upsilon_{2,3}}.$$

The learning algorithm or strategy is extremely simple. The stability quotient serves as the objective function of an optimization procedure so that we can simultaneously minimize the within group distances and maximize the between group distances. Obviously, we would like to configure the topology in such a way that, within a group, objects are close to each other, while at the same time they are far from objects of other groups. The goal is to try to keep all intra-group distances equal to zero and none of the inter-group distances equal to zero.

Definition 4. *The stability optimization is to minimize*

$$Z(\triangle_W)$$

subject to the constraint that $\sum_{i=1}^{n} w_i = 1$.

In other words, we want Z to get as close to zero as possible since negative costs are not allowed.

Now, we are ready to consider the evolving nature of this system. We begin with the given P, an underlying set of structural objects; S_0, the initial given set of substitution operations; and $\mathcal{G}$, a generator. The generator systematically generates new substitution operations from previous substitution operations. These new substitutions are called macros. At each macros generation step $t > 0$, we have $S_t = S_{t-1} \cup \mathcal{G}(S_{t-1})$ so that $S_0 \subset S_1 \subset S_2, \ldots$. At each step $t \geq 0$, we associate with the current transformation system (P, S_t) its own stability optimization having its own Z_t. There is a simple way to test whether or not the current Z_t is satisfactory after arriving at a certain step t. We suspend the optimization loop at that step and try out the current optimum solution on the training set as well as on the test set. If the resulting classifications are satisfactory, we go to the on-line recognition stage. If not, we continue further until another stable step is suspected. Then we repeat the cycle of testing. In this way, convergence can, to some extend, be verified experimentally.

Throughout the adaptation process, P and $\mathcal{G}$ are fixed. From an implementational time-complexity point of view, we have, in effect, added another loop on top of the optimization loop (Figure 1). The optimization loop tries out different cost vectors while the macro generation loop tries out larger and larger sets of macro substitution operations. Each stability optimization corresponds to a family of metric spaces. The number of times through the macros generation loop corresponds to the number of families being examined by the agent. The stopping criterion has always been the same: loop until it finds a stable metric space. Given enough time, the system can always discover some stable classes even though they may not be the ones that the human designer had in mind. Alternatively, the human designer can preset a time limit, after which the training process will be halted and new training objects can be introduced into the training set and/or some old training objects can be taken out of it. In the ideal case, stable means $Z = 0$. Otherwise, stable means that the groups in the metric space form well-defined clusters/blobs to the satisfaction of the learning agent, judging by, for example, the mis-classification rate in the test run. Then,

the entire learning process stops and the agent is ready to go on-line to deal with
any of the objects in the specified environment.

Loop on set of substitution operations (t-loop).
  Optimization on weight vector until the metric space is stable.
    Distance calculation of two objects, $\triangle_W(p_1, p_2)$

$\vdots$

End loops

Fig. 1. Control structure of the supervised inductive learning model

After the training phase is over, one can prepare for the recognition stage.
We store the shortest object from each training group as the representative of
the group. Also, we store the most stable substitution cost vector W^* at the end
of the training process. When an unknown object is presented to the system, its
distances to the representatives will be calculated using the weights W^*. It can
then be classified according to the nearest neighbor rule.

3   Application

Now we apply the model to the triple parity problem on bit strings. The idea
of triple parity is a generalization of the usual parity problem. The usual parity
problem is to classify strings as either even parity or odd parity. In the triple
parity case, we first count the number of 1's in a bit string. Then we divide
the count by 3 and get the remainder. If the remainder is 0, then the string
belongs to group 1; if 1, then group 2; if 2, then group 3. The underlying set of
structural objects P is the set of all finite strings of **0**'s and **1**'s. The initial set
of substitution operations is

$$S_0 = \{\mathbf{0} \leftrightarrow \theta, \mathbf{1} \leftrightarrow \theta\},$$

where θ is the null string; i.e., we have two rules: insertion (or deletion) of a **0**
and insertion (or deletion) of a **1**. The generator is

$$\mathcal{G}(S) = \{ab \leftrightarrow \theta \mid a \in \{\mathbf{0},\mathbf{1}\}, b \leftrightarrow \theta \in S\}.$$

Consider the training set in Fig. 2. There are three training groups for three
classes of objects. Each class is represented by only two or three relatively short
examples. The size of P is infinite and the longest example from P is also infinite.
We shall see how the learner proceeds step by step to discover the idea of triple
parity.

At step $t = 0$, the learner can find no satisfactory weight vector for classification. Given the three training groups and given the two insertion operations,

	Group 1
1	**00**
2	**10101**

	Group 2
1	**01111**
2	**1011001**

	Group 3
1	**11**
2	**11011001**
3	**001010111111**

Fig. 2. Training groups

no matter what W we tried, Z is a relatively large value. There are too many mis-classifications in the training set itself. If we had specified a test set, there would be many mis-classifications in the test set as well.

The system begins to evolve to the next step $t = 1$ by generating more operations. Applying $\mathcal{G}$ to S_0, we obtain 4 more substitution operations as follows:

$$S_1 = \left\{ \begin{array}{l} \mathbf{0} \leftrightarrow \theta \\ \mathbf{1} \leftrightarrow \theta \\ \mathbf{00} \leftrightarrow \theta \\ \mathbf{01} \leftrightarrow \theta \\ \mathbf{10} \leftrightarrow \theta \\ \mathbf{11} \leftrightarrow \theta \end{array} \right\}.$$

Applying stability optimization under the transformation system (P, S_1), we again find no good separation of classes. Even with six rules, no matter how we spread out the weights, no clear clusters are formed. The training objects still intermingle with one another in these metric spaces.

However, when $t = 2$, we have

$$S_2 = \left\{ \begin{array}{l} \mathbf{0} \leftrightarrow \theta \\ \mathbf{1} \leftrightarrow \theta \\ \mathbf{00} \leftrightarrow \theta \\ \mathbf{01} \leftrightarrow \theta \\ \mathbf{10} \leftrightarrow \theta \\ \mathbf{11} \leftrightarrow \theta \\ \mathbf{000} \leftrightarrow \theta \\ \mathbf{001} \leftrightarrow \theta \\ \mathbf{010} \leftrightarrow \theta \\ \mathbf{011} \leftrightarrow \theta \\ \mathbf{100} \leftrightarrow \theta \\ \mathbf{101} \leftrightarrow \theta \\ \mathbf{110} \leftrightarrow \theta \\ \mathbf{111} \leftrightarrow \theta \end{array} \right\}.$$

Here, we achieve ideal stability $Z = 0$. Specifically, all average intra-group distances are zero, i.e., $\rho_1 = \rho_2 = \rho_3 = 0$; and all average inter-group distances are $\frac{1}{10}$, i.e., $v_{1,2} = v_{1,3} = v_{2,3} = \frac{1}{10}$. Fig. 3 shows the ideal weight vector as $(0, \frac{1}{10}, 0, \frac{1}{10}, \frac{1}{10}, \frac{1}{10}, 0, \frac{1}{10}, \frac{1}{10}, \frac{1}{10}, \frac{1}{10}, \frac{1}{10}, \frac{1}{10}, 0)$. Choosing the shortest object from each group to represent the group, we have **00** from group 1, **01111** from group 2 and **11** from group 3 as representatives. The stable metric space contains three point-clusters because we have ideal stability. Each cluster is represented by its chosen prototype. The distance between any two clusters or prototypes is exactly $\frac{1}{10}$.

Index	Substitution	Weight
1	**0**↔ θ	0
2	**1**↔ θ	$\frac{1}{10}$
3	**00**↔ θ	0
4	**01**↔ θ	$\frac{1}{10}$
5	**10**↔ θ	$\frac{1}{10}$
6	**11**↔ θ	$\frac{1}{10}$
7	**000**↔ θ	0
8	**001**↔ θ	$\frac{1}{10}$
9	**010**↔ θ	$\frac{1}{10}$
10	**011**↔ θ	$\frac{1}{10}$
11	**100**↔ θ	$\frac{1}{10}$
12	**101**↔ θ	$\frac{1}{10}$
13	**110**↔ θ	$\frac{1}{10}$
14	**111**↔ θ	0

Fig. 3. Ideal weights

When an unknown object from P such as **1010010111** is presented to the agent to be classified, we calculate its distance from each of the three prototypes using the ideal weight vector. If the distance between prototype i and the unknown is zero, then the unknown belongs to class i. In this way, all strings from the underlying infinite environment P are classified correctly in the on-line recognition stage even though only a small-sized training set is used and only one object is chosen from each class for comparison.

4   Conclusion

Concept generalization, induction, and indeed, learning itself, are seen here as the process of deriving a stable metric space to separate the training groups. A stable metric space is one containing well-separated, compact clusters. We have extended the model in [3] for supervised inductive learning in three classes. All bit strings were classified correctly in the on-line recognition. The agent has successfully learned to devise a way to classify bit strings according to 3-parity-ness, even though the agent was never told the concept of 3-parity-ness.

References

1. Tony Y. T. Chan. Unifying metric approach to chromosome classification. In *Proceedings of the World Multiconference on Systemics, Cybernetics and Informatics*, volume 3, pages 296–303. International Institute of Informatics and Systemics, 1997. 340

2. Tony Y. T. Chan. A fast metric approach to feature subset selection. In *Proceedings of the Workshop on Computational Intelligence of the 24th Euromicro Conference*, volume 2, pages 733–736. IEEE Computer Society, 1998. 340

3. Tony Y. T. Chan. Inductive pattern learning. *IEEE Transactions on Systems, Man, and Cybernetics—Part A: Systems and Humans*, 29(6):667–674, November 1999. 340, 345

4. Virginia Clarson and Joseph J. Liang. Mathematical classification of evoked potential waveforms. *IEEE Transactions on Systems, Man, and Cybernetics*, 19(1):68–73, 1989. 340

5. Richard O. Duda and Peter E. Hart. *Pattern Classification and Scene Analysis*. John Wiley & Sons, New York, 1973. 340

6. Lev Goldfarb and Tony Y. T. Chan. An application of a new approach to pictorial pattern recognition. In *Proceedings of the 4th IASTED International Symposium on Robotics and Automation*, pages 70–73, Zurich, 1984. Acta Press. 340

7. Andrew K. C. Wong, Helen C. Shen, and Puiwing Wong. Search-effective multi-class texture classification. *International Journal of Pattern Recognition and Artificial Intelligence*, 4(4):527–552, 1990. 340

Appendix: Metric Definition

Given a set S, a real-valued scalar function δ of two arguments,

$$\delta : S \times S \to \Re$$

is called a *metric function* on S if for any $x, y, z \in S$ the following conditions are satisfied:

non-negative $\delta(x, y) \geq 0$,
semi-reflexive $x = y \implies \delta(x, y) = 0$,
symmetric $\delta(x, y) = \delta(y, x)$,
triangle inequality $\delta(x, y) + \delta(y, z) \geq \delta(x, z)$.

The pair (S, δ) is called a *metric space* or *unifying metric space*.

Note that the semi-reflexive condition means that the distance between itself must be 0 and the distance between two different members from the set S could possibly be 0 as well.

In order to see the relationship between this definition of the metric space and the usual definition, let us define *standard metric space* by the inclusion of the following additional axiom:

definiteness $x = y \impliedby \delta(x, y) = 0$.

Now, induce an equivalent relation on the set S by saying that $x \sim y$ if $\delta(x, y) = 0$ and define a function

$$\tilde{\delta} : \tilde{S} \times \tilde{S} \to \Re$$

with the set restricted to the set of equivalent classes $\tilde{S} = S/\!\!\sim$ so that $\tilde{\delta}(\tilde{x}, \tilde{y}) = \delta(x, y)$ where $x \in \tilde{x}$ (i.e., $\tilde{x}$ is the equivalent class of x) and $y \in \tilde{y}$.

The pair $(\tilde{S}, \tilde{\delta})$ is a standard metric space.

Proof by contradiction. Assume $(\tilde{S}, \tilde{\delta})$ is not a standard metric space. Then there exists $\tilde{x}$ and $\tilde{y}$ such that $\tilde{x} \neq \tilde{y}$ and $\tilde{\delta}(\tilde{x}, \tilde{y}) = 0$. But

$$\tilde{\delta}(\tilde{x}, \tilde{y}) = 0 \Rightarrow \delta(x, y) = 0$$
$$\Rightarrow x \sim y$$
$$\Rightarrow x, y \in \tilde{x} \text{ and } x, y \in \tilde{y}$$
$$\Rightarrow \tilde{x} = \tilde{y}.$$

In this way, we can always induce the standard metric space from a given (unifying) metric space. Hence, in this regard, we are justified in our usage of the term *metric space*.

Effective Iris Recognition System by Optimized Feature Vectors and Classifier

Shinyoung Lim[1], Kwanyong Lee[1], Okhwan Byeon[2] , and Taiyun Kim[3]

[1]Electronic Commerce Team, Electronics and Telecommunications Research Institute, Gajong-dong, Yusong-gu, Taejon, 305-600, Korea
{sylim, kylee}@econos.etri.re.kr
[2]KORDIC, # 1, Uheun-dong, Yusong-gu, Taejon, 305-333, Korea
ohbyeon@garam.kreonet.re.kr
[3]Department of Computer Science, Korea University, Seoul, Korea
tykim@netlab.korea.ac.kr

Abstract. This paper presents an effective system for recognizing the identity of a living person on the basis of iris patterns that is one of the physiological and biological features with high reliability. To represent the iris pattern efficiently, a new method for optimizing the dimension of feature vectors using wavelet transform is proposed. In order to increase the recognition accuracy of competitive learning algorithm, an efficient initialization of the weight vectors and a new method to determine the winner are also proposed. With all of these novel mechanisms, the experimental results showed that the proposed system could be used for personal identification in an efficient and effective manner.

1 Introduction

Controlling the access to secure areas or information systems, reliable personal identification infrastructure is required. Conventional methods of recognizing the identity of person by using a password or cards are not altogether reliable. The reason is they can be forgotten or stolen. Biometric technology, which is based on biological and physiological features of human such as face, fingerprints, signature and eyes, has now been considered as an alternative to extant systems in a great deal of application domains such as the alternative of passwords or ID cards, user authentication of Internet electronic commerce, and entrance management for specific areas.

Iris patterns have been focused for the last few decades in biometric technology in that human features should be stable and distinctive in order to be a good feature for personal identification. That is because every iris has a fine and unique pattern and does not change over time since 2 or 3 years after the birth, so it might be called as a kind of optical finger print[1][2].

S. A. Cerri and D. Dochev (Eds.): AIMSA 2000, LNAI 1904, pp. 348-357, 2000.
© Springer-Verlag Berlin Heidelberg

In this paper, we propose some optimized and robust methods for improving the performance from the practical viewpoint. To achieve the optimization of the proposed system, we conduct the related works: the analysis of the popular feature extraction methods - Gabor transform and Haar wavelet transform - to select a good method suitable for iris patterns, the optimization of the dimension of feature vectors by using the selected feature extraction method, and the performance improvement of a competitive learning neural network by revised novel mechanisms for the initialization of weight vector and winner selection. The contents of this paper are related works in chapter 2, analysis and recognition of iris image in chapter 3, experimental results in chapter 4, and finally the conclusions in chapter 5.

2   Related Works

Most of works on personal identification and verification by iris patterns have been done in the 1990s [4-8]. Some works have limited capabilities in recognizing the identity of person accurately and efficiently, so there is much room for improvement of some technologies affecting performance in a practical light.

Recent noticeable studies in personal identification based on the patterns and colors of the iris are those of Daugman[4], Boles *et al.*[6], and Wildes *et al.*[8].

Daugman implemented the system with 2-D Gabor wavelet filter for localization of iris, Gaussian transform for feature extraction, and 256-byte iris code for computation. The major contribution of Daugman is to provide statistical theories for degree of iris code agreement.

Boles *et al.* implemented the system operating the set of 1-D signals and obtaining the zero-crossing representations of these signals. The main idea of the Boles *et al.* is to represent the features of the iris by fine-to-coarse approximations at different resolution levels based on the wavelet transform zero-crossing representation. The prototype also have the advantage of processing 1-D iris signatures rather than 2-D images used in both [4] and [8].

Wildes *et al.* iris-recognition system consists of an image acquisition rig(low light video camera, lens, framegrabber, diffuse polarized illuminator, and reticle for operator positioning) interface to a Sun SPARCstation20. Most of the Wildes *et al.* work is concentrated on the grabbing the images of iris and making routine procedures of iris recognition system efficient by applying Laplacian pyramid and hierarchical gradient-based image registration algorithm in pattern matching.

In this paper, the proposed iris recognition system is optimized by the 2-D wavelet transform for feature extraction, a novel initialization method and multi-dimensional winner selection for recognition. The previous systems in the size of feature vectors use more than 256-byte iris code for represent the feature sensible for iris patterns[4][8] but in this paper, only 87-bit size of feature vector is exploited to reduce space and time. And the proposed system is evaluated under the 4000 experimental iris data from 200 persons to show that 87 bit feature vector is better enough to represent iris patterns effectively and efficiently.

3   Analysis and Recognition of Iris Image

The overall structure of the proposed system is illustrated in Fig. 1, and its processing flow is as follows. At first, an image surrounding human eye region is obtained at a distance from a CCD camera without any physical contact to the device. In the preprocessing phase, the following steps are taken. First, we detect eyelids and exclude them if they intrude, and eliminate the reflected light caused by the environmental illumination. Second, we should localize an iris, the portion of the image to be processed actually. Last, the normal coordination system of the image is converted into the polar coordination system so as to facilitate the feature extraction process. In the feature extraction phase, 2-D wavelet transform is used to extract a feature vector from the iris image. In the final phase, the identification and verification phase, a revised competitive learning method is exploited to classify the feature vectors and recognize the identity of person. In order to improve the efficiency of the system, some improved methods are applied to the feature extraction phase and the identification phase.

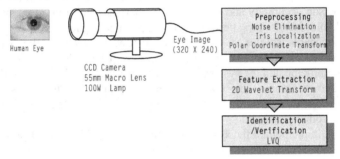

Fig. 1. The proposed iris recognition system

3.1   Preprocessing Phase

We should first check whether eyelids intrude the image, and then exclude them if they are. The reflected light resulted from the environmental illumination is eliminated by blurring and enhancing the image with a threshold.(see Fig. 2) After eliminating noises, we determine an iris part of the image by localizing the portion of the image derived from inside the limbus (outer boundary) and outside the pupil (inner boundary). To localize an iris, it is required to find the center of the pupil and it is also used to convert the iris into polar coordination system. When the center of the pupil is found, we find the inner boundary and the outer boundary by extending the radius of a circle from the center of pupil and checking the intensity of the background. Fig. 3 shows the two boundaries for the image of Fig. 2.

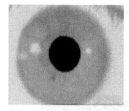

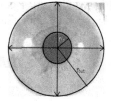

Fig. 2. Blurred and enhanced iris image

Fig. 3. Process of finding the inner and outer boundaries from the center of the pupil

The localized iris part of the image is transformed into polar coordination system to extract features in an efficient way. The portion of the pupil is excluded from the conversion process because it has no biological characteristics at all. Fig. 4 shows the process of converting the orthogonal coordination system into the polar coordination system for the iris image. By increasing the angle θ by $0.8°$ for an arbitrary radius r, we obtain 450 values. We can get a 450×60 iris image for the plane (θ, r) by repeating this process until the radius is increased to 60.

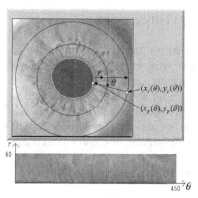

Fig. 4. Representation of iris image by polar coordination system

3.2   Feature Extraction Phase

Gabor transform and wavelet transform are typically used for extracting feature vector from human iris patterns[4][9][10][11]. In this paper, wavelet transform is used to extract features vector from human iris image. Among the mother wavelets, we use Harr wavelet as a basis function.

After finishing the preprocessing, we apply Haar wavelet transform to the image represented by the polar coordination system to obtain a feature vectors. For the iris image with the size of 450×60 obtained from the preprocessing, we apply wavelet transform four times in order to get a 28×3 subimage with the same properties of the original iris image. This means we apply a multiple-level decomposition four times to the iris image signal. Finally, we organize the feature vector by combining 84 features of the highpass filter of the fourth transform(the least black box in Fig 5) and each representative value for the three other high pass filter areas(the three other black boxes in Fig 5). The dimension of the resulting feature vector is 87. Fig. 5 shows the conceptual process of obtaining the feature vector with the optimized dimension.

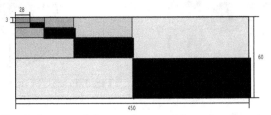

Fig. 5. Conceptual diagram for organizing a feature vector

Each value of 87 dimensions has a real value between –1.0 and 1.0. To reduce space and computational time, we quantify each real value into one of two integer values by simply converting the positive value into 1 and the negative value into 0. Therefore, we can express iris image with only 87 bits.

3.3   Identification and Verification Phase

In general, the competitive learning neural network like LVQ has the faster learning mechanism than error back-propagation algorithm but its performance is easily affected by initial weight vectors[12][13].

To solve such a problem for at least iris patterns, a new method for initializing the initial weight vectors in an effective manner is proposed. This method generates the initial vectors that can be located around the boundary of each class. In the learning process, the usual learning process for LVQ is accomplished after initializing the weight vectors by the proposed method. In the recognition process, we set the acceptance level and use it to determine whether the final result is accepted or rejected[15][16].

The process of the proposed initialization algorithm, what we called the uniform distribution of initial weight vectors is as follows.

Step 1 Set initial weight vectors with the vector of the first training data of each class and other weight vectors to be zero.

$$W_1^k = X_1^k \quad for \ k = 1,2,...M \tag{1}$$

, where

X_1^k : the vector of the first input data of the k - th class.

W_1^k : the first weight vector of the k - th class

M : the number of class.

Step 2 Select another data of each class as a new training data

Step 3 Calculate the Eucledian distance d_j between the training data and the weight vector by the following equation.

$$d_j^2 = \sum_{i=0}^{N-1}(X_{ip}^k - W_{ij}^k)^2 \tag{2}$$

, where

X_{ip}^k : the i - th component of the p - th learning data of k - th class

W_{ij}^k : the i - th component of the j - th weight vector of k - th class

N   : the dimension of a training data

Step 4 Determine whether the class of the weight vector with the minimum distance among all d_j is equal to the class of the training data. If the class of the weight vector is not equal to the class of the training data, then add the vector of the training data as a new weight vector.

Step 5 Goto step 2 until all of the training data are used in the learning process.

The winner selection method based on Euclidean distance that is generally used in competitive learning neural networks has no problem in determining the minimum distance of each class. However, if the dimension of feature vectors is increased, it has high possibility of selecting a wrong winner because of the failure of obtaining the information on each dimension. To solve such a problem, a new algorithm of winner selection called multidimensional winner selection method is proposed. The proposed algorithm is to determine the winner of each dimension, count the frequency of becoming the winner according to each class, and then select a class with the largest value as the final winner.

4   Experimental Results

To evaluate the performance of the proposed human iris recognition system, we collected 4000 data acquired from 200 people for 3 months with the help of volunteers of universities. All of them are Asians. The environment of image data grabbing is composed of a CCD camera with 55-mm positive meniscus lens, two 60Watt halogen lamps, and about 400 infrared LED illuminators. The distances between the camera and target ranged from 32 cm to 20 cm. A half of data is used as the training data for LVQ and the remaining half as the test data. The parameters used in LVQ such as the learning rate and the iteration number are shown in Table 1.

Table 1. Parameters for LVQ

Initial learning rate	0.1
Update of learning rate	$\alpha(t) = \alpha(0)(1 - \dfrac{t}{\text{total number of iteration}})$
Total iteration	300

Under the experimental environments above, the following subsections describe the results on each phase or the proposed methods.

4.1   Feature Extraction Method

Table 2 shows the recognition rate on two different feature extraction methods, Gabor transform and Haar wavelet transform, under the same classifier. The recognition rate on the training data is almost same each other, but in case of the test data, the recognition rate of wavelet transform is better than that of Gabor transform by 2.1%. Therefore, we used Harr wavelet transform as the basis feature extraction method in the following experiments.

Table 2. Comparison of two feature extraction methods

	Gabor Transform	Wavelet Transform
Training data	95.8 %	96.2 %
Test data	92.3 %	94.4 %

4.2   Weight Vector Initialization Method

Table 3 shows the results of the accuracy comparison of two initialization methods under the same experimental environments. In the case of the proposed method called the uniform distribution of initial weight vectors, the experimental results on both the training data and the test data showed better performance than those of the initialization with random values which is regarded as a basic initialization method.

Table 3. Comparison of weight vector initialization methods

	Initialization with random values	Proposed method
Training data	96.2 %	96.8 %
Test data	94.4 %	97.0 %

4.3   Winner Selection Method

Table 4 shows the experimental results on two winner selection methods when we use Haar wavelet transform for feature extraction and LVQ with the proposed initialization method. You can see that the proposed method, the multidimensional method showed a good result for human iris features.

Table 4. Comparison of winner selection methods

	Euclidian distance method	Multi-dimensional method
Training Data	96.8 %	98.1 %
Test Data	97.0 %	97.6 %

4.4   Size of Feature Vector

From the three experimental results of 4.1, 4.2, and 4.3, we selected each method with high accuracy to configure a good system for personal identification based on iris patterns. The selected methods for each phase are as follows; Haar wavelet transform for feature extraction, uniform distribution method for initializing weight vectors, and multidimensional method for winner selection.

With the iris recognition system composed of these methods, we try to minimize or optimize the dimension of feature vector without any influence to the recognition accuracy. We proposed a new feature extraction process. This method can efficiently represent a feature vector with 87 dimensions and it requires only one bit per dimension. Regardless of the successive transform of an image four times, we can separate an input space according to the degree of matching as shown in Fig.6. In the Fig.6, the black ball points mean success of match and the white ball points mean failure of match. And x-axis means group of iris data and y-axis means degree of match. It is possible to verify the identification of a human by 65% of degree of match by 87 dimensions for a feature vector from his/her iris data calculating the Eucledian distance between input vector and reference vector. But if we run five times of transform of the image, we can not keep a threshold of recognition even though we might obtain much less size of feature vector as shown in Fig.7. Table 5 shows the performance evaluation according to the size of a feature vector.

For efficient comparison with the proposed scheme for organizing feature vector, we used 256 dimensions(1 byte per dimension) for each vector which is introduced in [4]. All of the experimental results on the proposed methods are summarized in Table 6. As the difference of size of feature vectors by 20 times compared with the 256 dimensions(1 byte per dimension), the improvement of performance in the process of recognition and verification is expected.

Table 5. Performance evaluation according to the size of feature vectors

	256 dimension (1 byte/dimension)	87 dimension (1 bit/dimension)
Training Data	98.1 %	98.1 %
Test Data	97.6 %	97.7 %

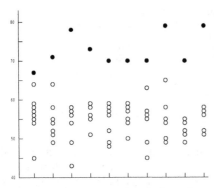
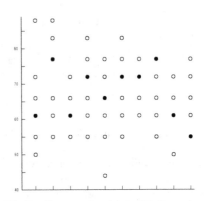

Fig.6. Degree of match by 87 dimensions for a feature vector

Fig.7. Degree of match by 18 dimensions for a feature vector

5   Conclusions

In this paper, an effective method for personal identification and verification by means of human iris patterns is presented. To process the iris patterns in an efficient

Table 6. Performance evaluation on the propsed methods

	Feature Extraction	Gabor transform	*Wavelet transform*		
Comparison Factors	Recognition	Initializaiton with random values	*Uniform distribution of initial weight*		
		Eucledian distance-based winner selection		*Multi-dimensional Winner Selection*	
	Size of Feature Vector	93 dimension (4 bytes/dimension : 2976 bits)			*87 dimension (1 bit/dimension) 87 bits*
Performance	Success Ratio of Training Data	95.8 %	96.2 %	96.8 %	98.1 %	98.1 %
	Success Ratio of Test Data	92.3 %	94.4 %	97.0 %	97.6 %	97.7 %

and effective way against existing methods, the following works are conducted; First, two methods - Gabor transform and Haar wavelet transform which are widely used for extracting features - were analyzed. From this analysis, Haar wavelet transform had better performance than that of Gabor transform. Second, Harr wavelet transform was used for optimizing the dimension of feature vectors in order to reduce processing time and space. With only 87 bits, we could represent an iris pattern without any influence to the system performance. Last, we improved the accuracy of a classifier, a competitive learning neural network, by proposing an initialization method of the weight vectors and a new winner selection method designed for iris recognition. Thanks to these methods, we could increase the recognition performance to 97.7% for the test data. From the experimental results, we convinced that the proposed system is optimized enough to be applied to various applications.

References

1. Adler F. H., *Physiology of the Eye: Clinical Application*, The C. V. Mosby Company, 1965.
2. Hallinan P. W., "Recognizing Human Eyes", *SPIE Proc. Geometric Methods in Computer Vision*, 1570, pp. 214-226, 1991.
3. Flom L. and Safir A., "Iris recognition system," U.S. Patent 4 641 349, 1987.
4. John G. Daugman, "High Confidence Visual Recognition of Persons by a Test of Statistical Independence", *IEEE Trans. on Pattern Analysis and Machine Intelligence*, 15(11), pp. 1148-1161, 1993.
5. Wildes, R.P., "Iris Recognition: An Emerging Biometric Technology", *Proc. of the IEEE*, 85(9), pp.1348-1363, 1997
6. Boles, W.W.; Boashash, B., "A Human Identification Technique Using Images of the Iris and Wavelet Transform", *IEEE Trans. on Signal Processing*, 46(4), pp.1185-1188, 1998
7. Williams, G.O., "Iris Recognition Technology", *IEEE Aerospace and Electronics Systems Magazine*, 12(4), pp.23-29, 1997
8. Wildes, R.P., Asmuth, J.C., et.al, "A System for Automated Iris Recognition", *Proc. of the Second IEEE Workshop on Applications of Computer Vision*, pp.121-128, 1994
9. Randy K. Young, *Wavelet Theory and Its Application*, Kluwer Academic Publisher, 1992.
10. Rioul O. and Vetterli M., "Wavelet and Signal Processing", *IEEE Signal Processing Magazine*, pp. 14-38, October 1981.
11. Gilbert Strang, Truong Nguyen, *Wavelets and Filter Banks*, Wellesley-Cambridge Press, 1996.
12. Fausset L., *Fundamentals of Neural Networks*, Prentice Hall, 1994.
13. Kohonen T., The Self-organization and Associate Memory, Springer-Verlag, 1985
14. Ilgu Yun, *et al.*, "Extraction of Passive Device Model Parameters Using Genetic Algorithms", ETRI J., Vol. 22, No.1, pp.38-46, 2000.
15. Sang-Mi Lee, Hee-Jung Bae, Sung-Hwan Jung, "Efficient Content-based Image Retrieval Methods using Color and Texture", ETRI J., Vol.20, No.3, pp.272-283, 1998.
16. Young-Sum Kim, *et al.*, "Development of Content-based Trademark Retrieval System on the World Wide Web", ETRI J., Vol.21, No.1, pp.40-53, 1999.

Enabling Knowledge Creation, Sharing and Reuse on the World-Wide-Web (Extended Abstract)

Enrico Motta

Knowledge Media Institute
The Open University
Walton Hall, MK7 6AA
Milton Keynes, UK
e.motta@open.ac.uk
http://kmi.open.ac.uk/people/motta

1 Towards a Knowledge Web

The World-Wide-Web has traditionally been viewed as a large hypertextual structure. However, recent developments in mark-up languages [16, 19], interoperability protocols [2] and web-based knowledge representation languages [8, 10, 12] have introduced new perspectives on the web. For instance, XML can be used to realise a *database perspective* on the web, supporting data integration across multiple applications. The work on RDF and RDFS provides the initial building blocks to go beyond simple integration based on structure towards semantic integration. Web-based knowledge representation languages such as OIL [8], Shoe [10] and XOL [12] move closer to this objective, providing advanced knowledge representation functionalities to support semantic interoperability and intelligent search. These approaches can be seen as informed by a distinct perspective on the web, which is often called *the semantic web*. The defining aspect of this perspective is the desire to move away from uni-dimensional hypertext, or simple data integration to achieve semantic integration between agents, based on shared conceptualizations. These shared conceptualization are normally called *ontologies* [9].

Of course, all of these perspectives are important in their own right and adopting one or another largely depends on the specific scenario in hand. For example, let's consider a search scenario. If one takes a semantic web perspective, then search can be supported by intelligent engines able to disambiguate a query and home in on the 'right' resource. This approach affords important advantages in terms of efficiency and precision. However, there may be cases in which such efficient behavior is undesirable. For instance, in those scenarios where the pedagogical gains afforded by browsing through a web of resources are more important than the efficiency of homing in quickly on the 'right' resource.

In addition to three perspectives mentioned above, there is another perspective which can be imposed on the World-Wide-Web, which we call *the knowledge web* [7]. This perspective characterizes the web as the locus in which knowledge is

S. A. Cerri and D. Dochev (Eds.): AIMSA 2000, LNAI 1904, pp. 358-361, 2000.
© Springer-Verlag Berlin Heidelberg

created, shared and reused. A number of web-based technologies, developed at the Knowledge Media Institute of The Open University in UK, support these processes of knowledge creation, sharing and reuse over the web. These technologies include tools supporting document-centred discussion and debate [14, 18], tools for collaborative ontology development [4], modelling languages [13], high-level interfaces supporting semantic queries [14], publishing tools [5, 6] and online reasoning services [11]. These technologies have been used in over a dozen projects in domains such as guideline-centred healthcare [15], digital libraries [1], electronic publishing [5] and to support creation and sharing of best-practice repositories in industrial organizations. While of course each scenario presents distinct challenges, a number of research questions cut across all our work:

- How can we use knowledge technologies to facilitate discussion and debate on the web, beyond what provided by structured discussion spaces?
- What are the appropriate frameworks and modelling languages which allow reuse of knowledge components over the web?
- How can knowledge and HCI technologies can be harnessed to allow non-experts to collaboratively develop domain models, which can then be exploited by reasoning agents?
- What are the required characteristics, which make a domain suitable for an approach like ours, which uses ontologies to support collaborative model building by non-experts?

Detailed (although necessarily partial) answers to these questions can be found in the given references to our work. In a nutshell, the web provides a powerful infrastructure, accessible from anywhere, where tools can be seamlessly integrated and different services can be delivered in a variety of media. Within this context, the integration of knowledge and HCI technologies appears to be a promising approach to support knowledge creation, sharing and reuse both within specific organizations and within generic communities of practice. However, subtle issues apply here and a holistic approach is needed in order to provide effective solutions, which takes into account the various user-related, organization-related and technology-related issues. Technologies have to be seamlessly integrated with existing work-practices and the knowledge sharing activities should ideally occur as by-products of normal work activities. Much research points out that "formality can be harmful" [17] and therefore it is important that modelling solutions only impose the minimal degree of structure needed to support the envisaged services. A related, crucial issue is that the underlying ontologies have to be shared and (ideally) 'owned' by all potential users, to ensure the feasibility of collaborative model construction. Finally, as it is well known from the knowledge management literature [3], no matter how sophisticated the technology, knowledge sharing and reuse can only take place if the appropriate organizational culture and motivation apply. There is more to knowledge sharing and reuse than any particular technology.

References

1. Buckingham Shum, S., Motta. E. and Domingue, J. B. (2000). ScholOnto:An Ontology-Based Digital Library Server for Research Documents and Discourse. International. Journal on Digital Libraries, 3(3) (August/Sept., 2000), Springer-Verlag.
2. Chaudhri, V. K., Farquhar, A., Fikes, R., Karp, P. D. and Rice, J. P. (1998). OKBC: A Programmatic Foundation for Knowledge Base Interoperability, Proceedings of the National Conference on Artificial Intelligence, AAAI-98, Madison, WI.
3. Davenport, T. H. and Prusak, L. (1999). Working Knowledge. Harvard Business Press.
4. Domingue, J. (1998). Tadzebao and WebOnto: Discussing, Browsing, and Editing Ontologies on the Web. In B. Gaines and M. Musen (editors), Proceedings of the 11th Knowledge Acquisition for Knowledge-Based Systems Workshop, April 18th-23th, Banff, Canada.
5. Domingue, J. & Motta, E. (2000). Planet-Onto: From News Publishing to Integrated Knowledge Management Support. IEEE Intelligent Systems, 15(3), May/June 2000.
6. Domingue, J. and Scott, P. (1998). KMi Planet: Putting the Knowledge Back into Media. In M. Eisenstadt, and T. Vincent, (editors), The Knowledge Web: Learning and Collaborating on the Net, Kogan Press, pp. 173-184.
7. Eisenstadt, M. and Vincent, T. (editors), The Knowledge Web: Learning and Collaborating on the Net. Kogan Press.
8. Fensel, D., Horrocks, I., Van Harmelen, F., Decker, S., Erdmann, M. and Klein. M. (2000). OIL in a Nutshell. Knowledge Acquisition, Modeling, and Management, Proceedings of the European Knowledge Acquisition Conference (EKAW-2000), R. Dieng et al. (eds.), Lecture Notes in Artificial Intelligence, LNAI, Springer-Verlag, October 2000.
9. Gruber, T. R. (1993). A Translation Approach to Portable Ontology Specifications. Knowledge Acquisition, 5(2).
10. Heflin, J., Hendler, J. and Luke, S. (1998). Reading Between the Lines: Using SHOE to Discover Implicit Knowledge from the Web. AAAI-98 Workshop on AI and Information Integration. Available online at http://www.cs.umd.edu/projects/plus/SHOE/shoe-aaai98.ps.
11. IRS (1998). Internet Reasoning Service. http://kmi.open.ac.uk/projects/irs/
12. Karp, P. D., Chaudhri, V. K. and Thomere, J. F. (1999). XOL: An XML-Based Ontology Exchange Language. Technical Note 559, AI Center, SRI International, 333 Ravenswood Ave., Menlo Park, CA 94025.
13. Motta E. (1999). Reusable Components for Knowledge Models. IOS Press, Amsterdam.
14. Motta E., Buckingham-Shum, S. and Domingue, J. (2000). Ontology-Driven Document Enrichment: Principles, Tools and Applications. International Journal of Human-Computer Studies, 52(6), pp. 1071-1109.
15. Motta, E., Domingue, J., Hatala, M., Buckingham Shum, S. and Quaglini, S. (1999). Ontology-Driven Management of Medical Guidelines. PatMan Project Deliverable D6, Knowledge Media Institute, The Open University, UK.

16. RDF (1999). http://www.w3.org/RDF/.
17. Shipman, F. M. & Marshall, C. C. (1999). Formality Considered Harmful: Experiences, Emerging Themes, and Directions on the Use of Formal Representations in Interactive Systems. Computer Supported Cooperative Work, 8, 4, pp. 333-352.
18. Sumner, T., and Buckingham Shum, S. (1998). From Documents to Discourse: Shifting Conceptions of Scholarly Publishing. Proc. CHI 98: Human Factors in Computing Systems, (Los Angeles, CA), 95-102. ACM Press: NY. Available at: http://kmi.open.ac.uk/techreports/papers/kmi-tr-50.pdf.
19. XML (1999). http://www.w3.org/XML/.

Continuations and Conversations

Christian Queinnec

UPMC – LIP6
Christian.Queinnec@lip6.fr

Networking forces us to adopt more and more a protocol-centric view of programming that is, to stop developing monolithic applications but, rather, glue components exchanging messages together. One of the key problem then is to design how components interact. Interaction design is not limited to the conception of an API (Application Programmer's Interface) stating the functionalities and the nature of exchanged data but includes how to make these components behave appropriately along all their lifetime.

A *conversation* with a component is often viewed as a single-threaded process. A component is a server that keeps a state for each user and evolves that state as messages come in. The classical way to program servers is to adopt an event-driven style with a single event loop that dispatches messages according to the user's state. Unfortunately, this model is inappropriate with regards to the current use of the web.

The use of browsers to surf over Internet has developed new conversation styles. It is rather common to fill a form, to submit it and to analyze the obtained results. If these results are unsatisfactory then the user may come back to the previous form, adjust the answer and re-submit it. This is the "what if" style favored by the Back and Forward buttons offered by browsers. This use of backtrack does not fit well with the event-driven style as the server is required to detect the regression of the user and to fetch some past user's state.

But this situation is even more complex since browsers also allow to clone windows and, for example, to fill the same form in two different windows with different information and to submit them concurrently. Clearly, the server has now to process, concurrently and for the same user, two different independent requests. The event-driven style cannot cope simply with these new demands: such conversations are too difficult to sustain.

Fortunately, there exists a powerful concept named *continuation* that perfectly fits these new requirements. The sole programming language, widely taught as well as formally defined, that offers continuations is Scheme. At any given point in a program under evaluation, the continuation of an expression represents what to do next with the value of that expression. Thus a continuation naturally appears as a unary function that expects a value in order to be resumed.

Continuations come from the work of Strachey and Wadsworth [7,6] and were first used to denote control features such as goto i.e., unconditional jump. Continuations were shown to be the basic feature supporting all sequential control operators such as escapes, exceptions handling, coroutines [8] or engines [2].

S. A. Cerri and D. Dochev (Eds.): AIMSA 2000, LNAI 1904, pp. 362–363, 2000.

If a conversation is represented by a program in a server, every interaction point (displaying a page to the user, asking a question, etc.) can be associated to a continuation; the user may resume any of these continuations. A continuation automatically packs everything needed to resume a conversation (in implementational terms: registers and call stack). Continuations remove the need for a single, big, complex, event loop surrounded by a number of modules implementing transitions (pages, servlets, etc.)

Continuations allow to concentrate a whole conversation in a single program written in the so-called direct style. A program transformation exists, named CPS (standing for Continuation-Passing Style), that converts a program using continuation operators into a somewhat bigger, more opaque program where these operators are eliminated in favor of explicit continuations reified as regular unary functions. It is possible to directly write programs in CPS style and this is indeed the case with the event-loop style. Direct style is of course easier to read, write and maintain [1].

Continuations simplify work-flow programming; they also offer the possibility to have richer conversation where one may jump back to some older question and answer it again or even to answer twice concurrently to the same question. These new possibilities open exciting new forms of conversations.

The talk will present continuations [3, chapter3] and their use within conversations. It will be based on two recent papers [4] (in French) presents an overview of an educational cdrom using continuations and [5] that analyzes some problems raised by continuations and browsers.

References

1. Matthew Fuchs. *Dreme: for Life in the Net*. PhD thesis, New York University, September 1995. 363
2. Christopher T. Haynes and Daniel P. Friedman. Engines build process abstractions. In *Conference Record of the 1984 ACM Symposium on Lisp and Functional Programming*, pages 18–24, Austin, TX., 1984. 362
3. Christian Queinnec. *Lisp in Small Pieces*. Cambridge University Press, 1996. 363
4. Christian Queinnec. Enseignement du langage C à l'aide d'un cédérom et d'un site – Architecture logicielle. In *Colloque international – Technologie de l'Information et de la Communication dans les Enseignements d'ingénieurs et dans l'industrie*, Troyes (France), October 2000. 363
5. Christian Queinnec. The influence of browsers on evaluators or, continuations to program web servers. In *ICFP '2000 – International Conference on Functional Programming*, Montreal (Canada), September 2000. 363
6. J C Reynolds. The discoveries of continuations. *International journal on Lisp and Symbolic Computation*, 6(3/4):233–247, 1993. 362
7. C Strachey and C P Wadsworth. Continuations: A mathematical semantics for handling full jumps. Technical Monography PRG-11, Oxford University, Computing Laboratory, Oxford University, England, 1974. 362
8. Mitchell Wand. Continuation-based program transformation strategies. *Journal of the ACM*, 27(1):164–180, 1980. 362

Author Index

Lecture Notes in Artificial Intelligence (LNAI)

Lecture Notes in Computer Science